PRACTICAL

METHODS

IN SPEECH

Second Edition

PRACTICAL

METHODS

IN SPEECH

SECOND EDITION

Harold Barrett

CALIFORNIA STATE COLLEGE

AT HAYWARD

Holt, Rinehart and Winston, Inc.

New York / Chicago / Atlanta
Dallas / San Francisco
Toronto / Montreal / London

To Jake and Lee—joy twofold

PREFACE

In this second edition the underlying purpose of *Practical Methods in Speech* remains the same: to make past and present scholarship available for current use and appreciation. Hopefully the treatment of content not only honors our heritage and discipline but also communicates the substance and spirit to readers of differing abilities and backgrounds.

In pursuit of this end, the author has sought to make the style relaxed and readable, and to introduce an abundance of aids—including sample outlines, numerous and varied exercises, model speeches (some by students, some with the elements of speechmaking sidenoted), extensive illustrative material and a variety of additional features.

In the second edition speech is stressed as a choice-making and social act. Emphasis is placed on the adjustment of the speaker to the speech situation for effective functioning and the need for speakers to find bases of understanding with audiences—common ground. This edition stresses participation of the listener in the act of oral communication. Sections covered briefly in the first edition are now expanded; however the basic structure and philosophy remain the same.

Part I, Rudimentary Methods, deals with fundamental modes that are covered in most beginning courses: choosing a subject, wording a purpose, organizing ideas, using various aids and materials to strengthen and support ideas, using the extemporaneous style, and so forth.

Part II, Complementary Methods, includes chapters on language, delivery, and listening. This is a resource section from which the teacher can draw at any point in the course—whenever he decides that basic methods should be complemented with instruction in language, delivery, or listening.

Part III, Supplementary Methods, can serve as the core of a second-quarter or second-semester course; however, some instructors may wish to utilize its chapters in a one-term course.

Although the second edition retains the built-in potential for instructors' sequencing student experience in their classes (that is, following a step-by-step progression in introducing elements of theory), instructors may assign chapters as their inclinations or class needs dictate. Many instructors will choose to follow Chapters One to Six in order, while augmenting instruction with other chapters at points along the line. Some may wish to begin a course with the chapter on listening or the chapter on group discussion, and so forth. The structure of the book allows for accommodation of various plans.

The preface of the first edition noted, "For inspiration and academic training, I shall always be indebted to many people who have helped to lay key steppingstones which have led directly or indirectly to the publication of this book." The author reaffirms that statement and salutes, for a second time, those persons whom he acknowledged in 1959.

In the nine-year interim between publication of the first and second editions many persons have served positively to influence the new publication. Chief among them have been Professor Bower Aly, exemplar of scholarship and art in rhetoric and public address; Professor Robert D. Clark (now a college president), master of the basic course as well as the graduate seminar; Professor Robert C. Martin, department chairman with great and praiseworthy capacity to indulge and encourage individual projects of his staff members; and all members of the speech departments at the University of Oregon, Southern Oregon College, and California State College at Hayward.

A special word must go to Mr. John M. Fanucchi and Mr. Peter Altpeter (and their colleagues at San Joaquin Delta College and Ventura College), old friends who gave aid and counsel to me for the first edition and who now have lent their many years of successful experience to help shape the second.

I also wish to acknowledge the invaluable help of two wonderful colleagues, Brenda Robinson Hancock and Joseph Caesar.

For secretarial assistance, I should like to thank Carol Ramsey, Shirley Vernick, Vivian Perez, and Anita Castellano.

And to my wife, Carol, I have looked for the prime source of happy spirits for carrying out this and all endeavors.

Hayward   H. B.
JANUARY 1968

CONTENTS

Preface   vii

PART I   RUDIMENTARY METHODS   1

ONE / APPROACHING THE STUDY OF SPEECH   3

TWO / GETTING STARTED   18

THREE / ORGANIZING YOUR THOUGHTS   35

FOUR / STRENGTHENING YOUR THOUGHTS   63

FIVE / DEVELOPING YOUR THOUGHTS   85

      WITH PHYSICAL MATERIALS

SIX / DEVELOPING YOUR THOUGHTS   105

      WITH VERBAL MATERIALS

PART II   COMPLEMENTARY METHODS   133

SEVEN / USING EFFECTIVE LANGUAGE   135

EIGHT / REFINING SPEECH DELIVERY   154

NINE / IMPROVING LISTENING SKILLS   177

PART III SUPPLEMENTARY METHODS   187

TEN / PARTICIPATING IN GROUP DISCUSSION   189

ELEVEN / APPLYING PARLIAMENTARY LAW   218

TWELVE / FINDING BASES OF PERSUASION   232

THIRTEEN / PREPARING FOR VARIOUS OCCASIONS   264

FOURTEEN / READING ALOUD   276

PART IV APPENDIXES   305

A. PRACTICAL METHODS APPLIED: MODEL SPEECHES   307

B. READINGS IN SPEECH   329

Index   345

PART I

RUDIMENTARY
METHODS

CHAPTER ONE

Approaching the Study of Speech

Whoever you are, wherever you go to school, whatever you hope to do with your life, you now find yourself enrolled in a speech class. You may have made an independent decision to study speech or an adviser may have recommended it. Friends who have had the course might have advocated your enrollment, or speech may be required in your program. Whatever the reasons, either you or someone who has an interest in you recognized the wisdom of a remark made by a perceptive author, Robert Louis Stevenson, who said, "The first duty of a man is to speak; that is his chief business in this world." Speaking has for many years been central in your life; moreover, you will find its significance increasing as you move toward achievement of your personal and occupational objectives. The decision to take the course is a commendable first step toward greater proficiency in the art and skill that is your "chief business in the world."

SPEECH AS A SOCIAL ACT

Man is a gregarious creature, that is, he habitually associates with others in groups. For purposes of survival and in pursuit of a good life, he follows his communal sense and participates with others as a member of organized society. In relating to others, he acts upon them in various ways. A father shaking a warning finger at a child, a boy kissing a girl, a driver dimming his headlights, a politician deciding to run for office are all examples of people commiting social acts—a few of the infinite number possible to mankind. Speaking, too, is a social act; one of the most common and significant. People use speech for various reasons: to do things with people and sometimes to people. An employer may use it to "pat" a deserving worker on the back; a parent, through speech, may "spank" a naughty child; a legislator may "spur on" a senate to vote for a tax bill. One can list hundreds of examples to prove that oral action does affect others. The proud statement of a threatened child, "Sticks and stones will break my bones, but words will never hurt me," probably reflects bravado more than real assurance of safety, for words *can* hurt. Consider the unhappy wife's plaint to her erring husband, "Nothing that you say, only what you do, will bring us together." She is not wholly accurate, for "saying" *is* "doing"—whether as a caressing word for a wounded wife or as a verbal blow of one child against another.

Meeting of Minds

In affecting others through oral social action (speech) we seek ways to *reach* them, to *meet* them, to *get together* and *share* with them. Indeed, the dictionary defines "to communicate"—the purpose of speech—as "to cause another or others to partake of or share in." To study speech (your concern in this class) is to discover means to influence others to "share in" one's thinking and message. Though the messages vary from situation to situation, the basic process remains the same. For example, a student's attempt to explain a difficult concept of mathematics at a pre-examination study session in the coffee shop is fundamentally akin in nature to an instructor's lecture. Both speakers wish to inform and to seek ways to *relate* thoughts to others, to influence others with a message.

Henry Clay before the United States Senate in 1850 spoke to convince his colleagues that his compromise proposals should be adopted for the good of the *entire* nation. He was successful; he found ways to cause a majority to share in his ideas, to be aware of the probable *common* good to result. Similarly, a group of student leaders recently discovered the means for showing the administration and faculty of their college that registration time could be shortened. The students' success came from their ability to demonstrate benefits available to the entire college, a goal desired by all.

The foregoing are examples of useful speech, employed well to accomplish a purpose. They reveal the sine qua non of communication: mutual concern of speaker and listener, a common ground for thinking and acting. A speaker who is in idea or attitude apart or separated from his listener and is at a loss to find ways to bridge the gap cannot hope to achieve communication. His problem is the lack of a basis for a meeting of minds. This phenomenon partly explains the difficulty in communication sometimes experienced by people of different generations, of persons in different cultures, of a boy and girl who have "drifted apart," of you and someone you might name with whom you cannot seem to "make contact" or "occupy the same wave length." You see, speaker and listener shape thought together. As the French author, Joseph Joubert once implied, you cannot talk about poetry with someone unless he brings a little poetry with him. The fundamental question is simple but difficult: On what bases can the speaker and listener communicate? This course is planned to offer you theory, methods, and experience in answer to that question.

THE SPEECH CLASS

People who have never been in a speech class find the experience quite different from those of most other classes.

First of all, the greatest part of your work will be oral. This fact is surely no revelation to you. Although you will learn much about speaking and speech preparation without actually talking, you will not receive the full benefits of your investment of time and thought until you give speeches. In this sense, *we learn to speak well by speaking*.

Secondly, the speech class (hopefully) will be a small class. In this fast-moving age with the necessity for indexing people by number, we are sometimes treated rather impersonally, even in school. Perhaps your campus is free of this twentieth-century malady. In any event, you will have ample opportunity in the speech class for personal treatment. The process of learning in speech is not mechanical. The instruction in the process is, in the best meaning of the term, subjective; that is, concerned with *you* and *your speech*.

A third distinguishing feature of the speech class is that it is necessarily a social situation—one in which you will have relationships with others. You speak to the class; you get feedback of one sort or another from the class and perhaps direct suggestions; you, in turn, may give suggestions to class members. In short, speaking involves an immediate exchange with others. A social unit, the class, will provide you with the reason and justification for speaking and will act in different ways as a responding agent in communication to answer your vital question, "How am I doing?"

A fourth feature—related to the third and very important—is that speaking is not "performing" as some people mistakenly believe. It is not a tour de force or display of virtuosity. As put by the authors of one book, it is "a transaction carried on with other minds." [1] Its use is in communication.

Speech is different from other classes in at least one other way. One speech student summed it up well when he said, "In this course you really learn more than how to be a better speaker. You have a chance

[1] Carroll C. Arnold and others, *The Speaker's Resource Book*, rev. ed. (Chicago, 1966), p. 297.

to learn about people and their thoughts and experiences. By hearing them discuss their ideas, you seem to develop a greater respect and appreciation for them." Speech improvement can help you to make your life better and more useful in various ways, four of which follow.

Enhancing General Education

In this instance general education refers to strengthening the processes of reasoning, developing intellectual and critical powers, accepting the rigors of handling ideas, and so forth. Methods learned in the discipline of speech have applicability in other domains of daily functioning. For example, speech teachers, time and again, hear students report that problem-solving methods learned in the speech class were useful outside of class or how the pattern of organizing ideas for speeches worked so well in organizing essays. Also, how methods of weighing evidence—the process of selecting and rejecting materials—proved invaluable in writing a history paper. Admittedly, speaking—especially preparation—is hard work, but the dividends are great, not only those gained immediately as consequents of a speech but also those coming later when at another time and place the person trained in speech applies his acquired mental powers.

Additionally, elements of general education available in the speech class are the knowledge and appreciation of the heritage of speech. The teaching and theories of speechmaking go back to ancient Greece and beyond. Although many men over the centuries contributed to the body of thought about speechmaking that we possess today, a few of the giants stand out. Hopefully, you will find the opportunity to investigate some of the theorists and their ideas, for they promise to add to your general education. For example:

Corax and Tisias (fifth century, B.C.)—Greeks who developed a system of persuasion, with special attention given to a plan for arranging ideas effectively and the theory of probability as it relates to speaking.

Aristotle (384–322, B.C.)—Wrote the *Rhetoric,* the major work of all time on speaking, with decided significance and influence in our own day.

Cicero (106–43, B.C.)—Adapted and clarified theories in his several books to meet demands of his time; was Rome's greatest orator.

Quintilian (c. 35–95, A.D.)—Roman who wrote the most exhaustive work on speaking, the twelve-volume *Institutes of Oratory,* which prescribes the training for speakers from infancy to old age.

George Campbell (1719–1796)—His *Philosophy of Rhetoric* established new insights in speaking theory, for example, audience psychology and analysis.

Hugh Blair (1718–1800) —Was a Scotsman (like Campbell) whose *Lectures on Rhetoric and Belles Lettres* was the most popular book for students of speech in nineteenth-century America.

Richard Whately (1787–1863)—British author of *Elements of Rhetoric,* popular text in America, stressed logical proof and sound argument; continues to influence debating and general speaking practice today.

James A. Winans (1872–1956)—An American who followed concepts of psychologist William James, emphasizing the gaining and holding of attention in effective speechmaking.

Kenneth Burke (1897–   )—An American whose writings have introduced rich dimensions and offered new perspectives regarding the use people make of language in carrying out their purposes.

Improving the Personal Life

People get along better with themselves if they like themselves, if they respect themselves.

It follows that if you improve yourself you will have more reason for self-respect. This is certainly true in speech improvement. Speech characteristics are a central and vital part of personality; when the part is strengthened, the whole is strengthened. When you grow in your ability to communicate orally, your total personality grows and develops.

You can expect, then, to work for personality enhancement in this course.

Another dimension of increasing one's self-respect involves the handling of fear. Now, most people experience fear in speaking—even those in your class who may appear to have full confidence in themselves. People may feel threatened and insecure, afraid of damage to the ego or exposure of an inner self or behavior contradicting the self-concept. They are worried about making mistakes that deflate the ego and thus cause embarrassment in the presence of others. Said another way, they become fearful because they know they are being observed. They cannot "pull down the shade" or isolate themselves in a room or talk to a tree on some distant hill. In the speaking situation, there is always an audience, always at least one observer. Once again, the situation is necessarily social.

A speaker may respond to the observers in different ways. For example, he may feel inspired by his audience and give a successful speech because of them, or he may be so affected by their presence that he fails to use his capabilities well. In other words, fear is both constructive and destructive, and which result dominates depends upon how the speaker looks at himself in the speaking environment. Part of the task of speech instruction is to help the student to feel reasonably confident, secure, and thankful for the opportunity to speak. Also, it is to allay feelings of being out of place, of embarrassment, of inferiority, of shame—being destined to err. Most persons so plagued come to discover the absence of foundation for their doubts and fears. They learn to take themselves less seriously and come to know that freely taking a chance before the audience is not such an ego-threatening situation after all.

Speech instructors know well, and can document with cases, how fearful students have learned to handle themselves with real self-assurance. Though each person's case is different and degrees of insecurity vary, part of the solution lies in adequate preparation, part lies in personal resolve to master the situation, part in assessment of oneself—asking and attempting to answer the big question, "Why?" —"Why, on this occasion, with this speech, before this audience, am I afraid?" Students who have done soul-searching with this question report considerable success. But a solution may take time in coming, perhaps months or longer. Start the search now; be earnest, yet of good cheer—and be patient.

Remember that it is impossible to eradicate fear totally; besides, a modicum of fear is a good thing. As Harry Emerson Fosdick, speaker of reknown, said, "Any man who isn't tense before he speaks can't speak. Fear is not something to be feared, but something to be sublimated."[2] Dr. Fosdick means one should convert to good use whatever fear exists; let it work for you as a private, hidden force—a source of power in communication.

Incidentally, fear *is* largely hidden in the great majority of incidences. People do not reveal a fraction of the fear to which they attest. It does not show all *that* much.

Speech instruction, then, helps the student to feel worthy, to realize that he can be successful, that he does have a right—in fact, an obligation—to share his ideas with others. He will take a major step toward improving his personal life when he comes to know that a residue of fear can spur him on while blind, unattended fear can hold him back. He will examine the blind fear which retards and causes loss of effectiveness, allowing the remaining fear to act as a stimulus for doing well.

Bettering the Social Life

Now, it is impossible to separate personal life from social life—at least when considering most persons' conditions. Very few hermits

---

[2] Stated in an interview with Roy C. McCall; reported in "Harry Emerson Fosdick, A Study in Sources of Effectiveness," *American Public Address*, Loren Reid, ed. (Columbia, Missouri, 1961), pp. 59–71.

exist these days, and as one person remarked, "There is no place to hide anyway." We are communal creatures. To function satisfactorily and to strive for the good life, we put ourselves into a society, into a variety of societies. We belong to family social units, clubs, interest groups, religious organizations, and, of course, we find ourselves in an infinite number of less intimate, ever-varying social locales. Belonging is significant in our lives.

When we accept John Donne's thought that no man is an island, that the lives of people are connected by the causeways of spirit, if not always of direct affiliation, we then begin to seek means of acquiring more social effectiveness. How can we relate usefully in this world full of people? How can we understand others and be understood by them? How else than by communication? Communication can topple the walls that separate people and, where hatred and distrust exist, prepare the way for understanding and mutual respect. Perhaps the most urgent need today is for better communication among people.

In speech, you will study communication: how to be understood and how to understand. When that study is extended and applied outside of the speech classroom, you can expect to become a socially more effective person.

Increasing Vocational Strength

Can you think of an occupation or profession which does not involve speaking? It is true that some fields seem to call for more than others. We immediately think of law, sales, politics, radio and television, teaching, the ministry, personnel work, and public relations as careers which emphasize the need for skillful speaking; however, we should not overlook the value of the spoken word to accountants, physicians, commercial artists, librarians, social workers, foresters, technicians, and engineers. Increasingly, industry and government are relying on their employees to speak for them in the community, to tell the consumers and taxpayers about products, services, problems of operation, and so forth. Often the people who can fill this role are the ones who rise in the organization. The fundamentals of speech that you will learn and apply in your class are applicable to the speaking activities in which you will engage in your vocational life.

We once made a study of the speaking methods of twenty-seven leading business and professional people in a medium-size American community. The purpose was to determine the extent to which these citizens used speaking methods similar to those taught in the classroom. We asked them such questions as: "Do you limit your speaking subject?" "Do you consider it necessary to analyze the audience and the occasion?" "Do you outline your speeches?" "What do you plan to accomplish in your introduction?" Over 85 percent of those interviewed indicated on most of the questions that their most effective methods were the same ones taught in speech classrooms.

Where did the twenty-seven interviewees learn their speech methods? Doubtless, their speaking experiences since leaving school helped them to refine and perfect their methods, but it is interesting to note that twenty-six of the twenty-seven had had a speech course of one kind or another.

Your conscientious study and practice of the time-tested principles of speaking will assist you toward whatever vocational end you may pursue.

GOALS OF THE CLASS

To make gains possible in the four areas of potential improvement discussed above, we suggest your careful consideration and adoption of the following goals:

1. *Develop ease in the speaking environment.* This is, necessarily, the first and continuing order of business. Effective participation is based upon one's response to the environment in which he is to operate. One cannot be free to function to the limits of his capabilities until he feels at home, until he adjusts himself to his surroundings. For example, one member of a speech class, before feeling free in giving speeches, had to be convinced (more accurately, had to convince himself) that he really did belong in the "role of speaker," that speaking before others was not an alien act for him. He discovered that he was indeed a social being, and his speaking improved.

2. *Master the time-tested methods of speech composition.* As we noted earlier, most of the basic principles to be covered in this course are by no means new. They were developed and taught by great minds hundreds of years ago—by Aristotle, Quintilian, and Cicero. We of the twentieth century have merely added to them in certain instances and revised them for modern usage. Though largely ancient in origin and few in number, they form the cornerstone of practical oral communication. Remember that speech is a discipline concerned with finding means for acting with others to achieve some end in a given situation. You will observe as you read the book and listen to speeches (in class and out) that the fruitful means to accomplish an end are those revealing common interests or shared concerns among members of the communicative exchange. They are the means which unify in idea or attitude and lead to understanding and consensus between listener and speaker.

3. *Develop greater skill in the use of language.* The vocabularies of

most people can be improved for more effective speaking. Attention-compelling practices in pronunciation can be discovered and altered. One can learn to change usage habits that interfere with communication. Looking broadly at the matter of using language, we shall encourage use of elements which help make the idea clear and cogent, and we shall discourage those which detract from the idea and which put attention where it should not be—for example, on grammar or word choice, and so forth.

4. *Discover and refine a fitting individual mode for presenting ideas orally.* Some otherwise mature people continue to experiment with their physical and vocal bearing in speaking, just as some people sample different types of handwriting or means of serving a tennis ball. They do not seem to have found an optimum and comfortable mode of appearance (mode of social acting) before an audience. If you are in this category, your diligence and sincere desire to improve can help you to discover your individual manner for presenting your thoughts. Accomplishing that end, you can, along with mastering the other speaking principles, devote the balance of the term to strengthening and vitalizing your delivery. In any event, you will want to find what is *your* oral style, *your* best means of expression.

5. *Become a more effective listener.* Probably the majority of people consider themselves good listeners—when they want to be. While it is true that the desire to listen helps one to listen, it is also true that most untrained listeners are rather inefficient. Good listening—as essential to avoid being bilked by an unscrupulous salesman of counterfeit uranium stock certificates as it is in understanding a lecture in sociology—can be learned. We shall strive toward this end.

ACHIEVING THOSE GOALS

The five goals discussed above are demanding. They ask for a personal investment of thought and work—your best in self-reliance and self-discipline. But from commitment can come satisfaction, a notable reward in itself.

Now let us discuss, specifically, important aspects of daily functioning in the speech class. The following advice, termed responsibilities, results from experience with hundreds of speech students and from the thinking of many speech teachers. It is offered to help you make the most of your efforts.

Responsibilities to Yourself

1. *Be yourself.* Allow the most creditable personal assets you possess to come forth. For some people, these are frozen assets, now lying dormant and not allowed to circulate. Persons so held back often have

greater potential for expansion than they realize but have lacked only the courage or willingness to release themselves, to respond to the fullest.

Will you take the chance? The best thing you can do for yourself is to resolve at the outset that you will make a determined attempt to free the worthwhile thoughts and feelings which you may have been reluctant to express heretofore. This is not to recommend your assuming the character of someone whose patterns of expression and behavior you admire. Not at all. Be an individual; be free; and be your true self.

2. *Take advantage of this opportunity.* Make the most of your time by assuming the responsibility of having assignments ready on time, being regular in attendance, and being prompt.

Know that the successful application of nearly any principle is based on a knowledge of that principle. This assumption is especially relevant to speech training. Conscientious study of subject matter leads to commendable application. The question, "Which ought to be emphasized, theory or practice?", is not often debated among scholars of public address. We stress both, for both are essential in meeting the desired ends of learning. They are interdependent. Your instructor will set up the speaking assignments—the practical situations; only you can do the other work—assimilate the theory.

In sum, a vital part of readying yourself for speaking is study of the book, notetaking on lectures and discussions, and attentive listening to other speeches.

3. *Develop an attitude for accepting helpful criticism.* No aspect of your program for acquiring greater speaking proficiency is more vital than the part devoted to criticism. Your work will be criticized; and perhaps at some time during the course, you will be expected to offer criticism.

Now what is criticism? First of all, like a coin, it has two sides. Criticism may refer to strengths of the speaking effort or to points needing improvement. Too often we think of criticism as only negative, whereas good criticism (though it may be a comment on a problem condition) is both positive and constructive.

You can expect to be criticized in several ways, either by the instructor's direct comments in class or by his written suggestions. When the instructor analyzes your speech orally, it may be to help him teach the entire class, to draw attention to a feature of your speech from which others can learn. Again, he may be referring indirectly to you, and others, when he discusses the work of the whole class. When he is talking about another student's speech, some of the items covered may pertain to your own speaking. Finally, you may have an opportunity to be criticized by your class members. On all of these occasions you will have a chance to learn something about speechmaking.

Comments on your speaking are intended to be positive, designed to further your speech development. Perhaps it is only natural for a person to resent criticism of his work, especially when he has wholeheartedly invested himself in the creation of it. But every human production can be improved, and constructive reactions make improvement possible.

In receiving criticism, you, too, should have a positive point of view, a willingness to help yourself by accepting the considered observations of others.

Specifically:

a. Listen to and read the criticisms offered.
b. Ask for clarification of any remark that you do not understand.
c. Remember that criticism is not complete rejection; the very time taken in criticism indicates recognition of actual or potential merit.
d. Be objective; take criticism maturely.
e. Follow the considered suggestions made to you.

Responsibilities to Your Class

A speech class is a collection of persons that exhibits a limited degree of cohesiveness on the first day together. As you observe cohesiveness grow with the passage of time, you might ponder reasons for this phenomenon. The instructor plays a central role, certainly, but beyond that are the operations of all individuals who meet at this time and place. Arbitrarily thrown together at the beginning, they begin to take on a unity of spirit and purpose. They become a group. This eventuality involves you.

1. *Accept the need for your active participation.* A group is not shaped by people going in opposite directions, nor is it formed without some flexibility on the part of the members. People must give something occasionally—something of themselves. Become a part of the class. Listen thoughtfully and courteously to the other speakers. Enter actively into general class discussions, and be able to offer reasoned observations when called upon. You will find the returns ample and rewarding.

2. *Observe the time limit set for each speaking assignment.* The instructor has a number of assignments he would like to accomplish, and perhaps he wishes that he could allow you to speak as long as you desire on any given subject. Realistically, for your benefit and for welfare of the class in general, he will have to limit your speaking time. So, in observing the time limits established, you will show consideration for others and for yourself.

Actually, the discipline of planning to conform to the dictates of a "tyrant time clock" is a very beneficial part of speech education. "Would that more people had formed this habit before coming to us to speak," stated a weary member of a civic club in the Midwest. Furthermore, it might help to bear in mind the words spoken by humorist Will Rogers after a lengthy speech: "Gentlemen, you have just been listening to that Chinese sage, On Too Long."

Responsibilities to Society

By society, we mean all the people with whom you will be speaking throughout your entire life.

1. *Recognize the power of the spoken word.* Speaking moves people. Much of what we buy, how we vote, what we do and think can be traced back to the influence other people have had on us; and to gain such an influence they have relied to a considerable extent on speech.

Does it not follow that *you* are an influencer, that you, too, change people's lives? Does it not follow that with increased speaking proficiency you will strengthen your power to influence? Certainly. People speak for recognized or unrecognized purposes of affecting others. Usually, those with more ability are more effective than those with less. As the course unfolds, notice the effect that you and your fellow speakers have on the class. Notice audience reactions, for example—evidence of the power of the spoken word.

3. *Be aware of the choices before you.* As the speaker goes about his job of choosing and rejecting ideas, lines of reasoning, methods, and so forth, he is guided by the pragmatic question, "What will work to achieve my end on this occasion with this audience?" But happily, this is not the only concern of most speakers. Besides striving for effect, most people, on this quest, grant status and respectability to those with whom they speak. Except for a few who cannot make their personal interests consonant with the interests of their fellowmen, people operate with a sense of society. Though many rebel and challenge the established order, few reject social order entirely. That is to say, most people recognize the values in relating humanely to others and in adopting codes to enhance relationships.

In the final analysis, pragmatic ends—ends for effectiveness—and ethics are usually intertwined, for effective speech is "social" speech. As we noted earlier in the chapter, speaking is based on finding and establishing points of contact between speaker and listener. Good listeners mentally "ask" about a speaker's sincerity and intent. They may sense antisocial behavior; they often know when a speaker is not concerned with their welfare.

So we see, the speaker makes a twofold choice: not only about how to be effective but also about how he will treat his audience. A speaker who is pondering whether to use a half-truth or whether to include emotionally charged statements of prejudice faces a problem. His choice-making has to do with ethics. Will he in his excitement for his cause think only of possible immediate gain? Or will he rationally remember that any person's "program" is not of ten-minute's duration —the length of this one social act—but of three score and ten years or more?

Nearly all important decisions in life are those that affect others, for good or ill. The speechmaker's decisions are no exception.

LET US SUMMARIZE AND LOOK AHEAD

Up to this point we have discussed the usefulness of speech, values and goals of speech training, the social aspects of oral communication, and finally, ways of making the most of the opportunity for improvement.

Guided by your instructor whose field of professional specialization is speech, this course is designed to take you in step-by-step movements toward speaking proficiency. The recommended plan of assignments calls for starting with a basic principle and for proceeding by introducing one or two new principles into each successive assignment. You might call it the one-thing-at-a-time or stone-upon-stone approach. After practicing one element of speechmaking, you will add to it another element and then another. This building process goes on until all of the basic ingredients of speaking have been successfully integrated into your oral efforts. Now your instructor may choose to follow a different scheme, using chapters of the book in another order. In any event, the design is to work steadily toward the goal.

For some, the development will be more rapid than for others. Whatever is your lot, be patient. Remember that the rate of development does not always indicate the quality of development. Work hard; take first things first; and keep in mind the words of that eminent Roman teacher of speech, Quintilian:

> Nature has herself appointed that nothing great is to be accomplished quickly, and has ordained that difficulty should precede every work of excellence.

Let us start.

BASIC ASSIGNMENT

Prepare to give a very brief and informal "This I Believe" talk on one of the topics listed below. Express your personal views frankly and freely.

Speech as a Social Act
Uses of Speech
Getting Accustomed to the Speaking Environment
Individual Style
Use of Language
Effective Listening
Ethics and Speech

Suggested Exercise A

A veteran speech teacher recommended this exercise utilizing repetition and association, as a proven means for class members to learn each other's names, to become acquainted and foster a sense of relatedness, and to break the ice through participation in an informal and valuable speaking experience.

The instructor asks a student in the back row to "sign in" by writing his name in large letters on the blackboard. Then, after focusing on the name and possible associations for it, he briefly interviews him: "Why are you taking this course?" "What do you expect from it?" "What are your major interests?" "What are your vocational plans?" and so forth. After a few questions, the instructor retires to the side of the room and another student comes up, signs in, and the first student becomes the interviewer along with students from the class who ask questions. On returning to his seat, the student repeats the names of all students who have preceded him. If it is kept moving, the chain interview exercise should allow for participation of all students during a class hour.

Suggested Exercise B

To give your instructor information about your speech experiences and needs, answer the following questions carefully and completely.
1. Have you ever had a course in speech? When and where?
2. Have you ever participated in debate, discussion, extemporaneous speaking, student congress, radio, dramatics, oratory, or other such oral activities? When and where?
3. Have you ever had a speaking or hearing defect? If so, explain.
4. Are you nervous when you talk to people? When and with whom?
5. Are you dissatisfied with any of your present speaking habits or characteristics? Which ones?
6. What types of speaking are demanded by your chosen occupation?
7. If you were prepared, are there several topics on which you could speak briefly? List a few.
8. If you had a choice, are there several topics on which you would like to hear other class members speak? List a few.

Suggested Exercise C

Prepare a brief statement on one of the following topics designated by your instructor.

How I Expect Speech to Play a Part in My Life
Values of Good Speech
How I Have Learned to Accept Criticism
What Do Instructors Have a Right to Expect of Us as Students?
How I Have Learned to Handle Fear
A Topic Based on a Provocative Idea Implied in One of the Questions from Suggested Exercise B

Your instructor may wish to ask you to put these ideas down in the form of a simple outline for later presentation in a speech or group discussion.

CHAPTER TWO

Getting Started

The first, and sometimes most difficult, phase of speech preparation is finding a subject. "What shall I talk about?" is probably the question speech students most frequently ask.

From the other side of the desk, the answer instructors most frequently give to the query, and indeed the only answer, is "The choice is *yours*; talk about what you would like to talk about." In the final analysis, the choice *is* yours. After all, who knows your thinking better than you? Who has to direct the planning, the practicing, and the presentation? Who is responsible for its final outcome? Speechmaking is inextricably associated with choice-making. You make the decisions from beginning to end; however, it is the first decision which can be especially taxing. Three factors should guide you in deciding on a subject: yourself, your audience, and the occasion.

CONSIDER YOURSELF

What do you want to talk about? What are your interests? What are your favorite subjects of conversation? When you have an informal discussion among friends, what subjects seem to stimulate you and draw your response? In your opinion, what subjects of interest deserve your attention? What ideas have the highest priority in your thinking at this juncture of your life?

The answers to such questions will remind you of where to start your thinking in this business of finding an idea for a speech. Talk about what you like to talk about. For instance, a person interested in music has many possibilities:

Record Collections
Appreciation of Jazz
Listening to Music
Instruments of the Orchestra

group from England, several speech students gave talks on the entertainers' vocal and physical characteristics, their charm—or lack of it—and their probable effect on our culture. The subject was appropriate; for the audience was interested and judged the speakers' ideas significant.

"What subjects, even though presently *not* appealing to my audience's interests, might I feel personally obliged to discuss with them?" This is a rather dangerous question to put forth, but it seems appropriate as we conclude this section on analysis of the audience. If your moral or social convictions compel you to consider preparing a speech on an unpopular subject, along a line counter to the thinking of most audience members, perhaps no one should restrain you. It is said that the greatest challenge to a statesman is speaking out against a popular war. A good example is the courage of John Bright in his speaking campaign against the popular Crimean War. His action, counter to majority sentiment in England, cost him his seat in Parliament. Perhaps you have "wars" to speak out against—or for. Then speak out. But do not forget your audience. Do not forget that your purpose is communication, not mere self-expression. You will be successful only to the extent that you cast your thought in accordance with the make-up of your audience. History may ultimately support your position, but you address people in the here and now. The present opportunity to communicate may be the only one.

CONSIDER THE OCCASION

What subject is fitting for the occasion? In the speech class the occasion probably remains about the same unless your instructor chooses to vary it. Ordinarily, you meet in the same room, at the same time, and for the same purpose. Therefore, the greatest demand is the same as that imposed by any social situation. Choose an idea that will be appropriate for the "society" in which you are speaking. Use good taste and avoid embarrassing yourself or your audience. You have freedom, true; however, a certain amount of discretion is called for when dealing with people. A former Chief Justice of the Supreme Court, Charles Evans Hughes, expressed a similar thought: "Freedom of expression gives the essential democratic opportunity, but self-restraint is the essential civic discipline."

On future occasions you may be restricted by the purpose of the gathering, the season of the year, or the time of day. For suggestions on meeting special demands, see Chapter Thirteen, "Preparing for Various Occasions."

One suggestion from Chapter One bears repeating here. Make the classroom occasion an opportunity to communicate with people; talk with them; work to cause them to understand your idea or to be moved by your line of reasoning. Recognize the occasion as a time and place for realistic experiences in communication, not as a situation for mechanical or indifferent completion of assigned tasks. This positive attitude and way of approaching your work will produce the best results, be assured; start right—with a fitting subject.

NARROW YOUR SUBJECT TO A TOPIC

Would you be astonished at all if a speaker announced to his audience, "Today I shall discuss the history of Oregon"? You ought to be. Is it possible in a single speech to cover the history of Oregon, or even the history of Ashland, Oregon? Of course not. The areas are too broad. Writers have written scores of books and articles on Oregon, and motion pictures and television programs have treated the subject. No one yet has exhausted the subject. Even the director of the Ashland Chamber of Commerce would be hard put to tell you all about the city in one sitting—his knowledge and enthusiasm, notwithstanding.

Obviously—and experience will tell you if the need is not readily apparent—subjects must be limited, cut down to size to comply with the demands of time and purpose. You must narrow your *subject* (a general area of interest) to a *topic,* a much more specific subarea. The topic delimits the scope and clearly implies the boundaries by its wording. Furthermore, the topic may reflect the speaker's attitude or relationship to the idea, that is, give a hint as to the speaker's position on the matter.

One wishing to prepare a speech on Ashland has to discover a part or aspect of his subject and give his attention to that part only. As he goes about solving this problem, he may arrive at "Recreation in Ashland," but that is still a broad subject. What kind of recreation? "Outdoor Recreation," perhaps. But will it be "Hunting"? "Fishing"? "Hiking"? "Insect-collecting"? "Attending the Shakespearean Festival"? Let us say that he selects Shakespeare as the subject, and finally, reducing it one more step, arrives at the "Excitement of Watching *Macbeth* at the Shakespearean Festival in Ashland." Standing back, we can visualize the trail of the speaker's planning, in a general-to-specific order of deliberation:

From Recreation in Ashland, he went to
    Outdoor Recreation, to
        Hunting, Fishing, Attending the Shakespearean Festival, and so forth, to
            Attending the Shakespearean Festival, to
                The Excitement of Watching *Macbeth* at the Shakespearean Festival . . .

Is the idea as finally evolved a topic, a sufficiently limited thought? If not, the breakdown process must go on until the speaker finds a portion to which he can do justice in the time allowed—without hurrying or touching only the high points.

Let us look at some other examples:

1. The subject as first conceived: Dogs
    First limiting: Training Dogs
        Second limiting: Training a Collie
            Third limiting: Steps in Training a Collie to Heel
2. The subject as first conceived: Unemployment
    First limiting: Unemployment in the Cities
        Second limiting: Some Causes of Unemployment in the Cities
3. The subject as first conceived: Drug Addiction
    First limiting: The National Problem of Drug Addiction
        Second limiting: The Local Problem of Drug Addiction
            Third limiting: The Incidence of Local Drug Addiction
4. The subject as first conceived: Philosophy
    First limiting: Philosophy of Life
        Second limiting: The Need for a Philosophy of Life
            Third limiting: Arriving at a Philosophy of Life
                Fourth limiting: Arriving at a Philosophy of Life through Experience

The last limiting of each subject in the series above might prove to be an adequate topic for a speech. But do not be satisfied too soon. As you go through the process, seriously ask yourself these questions:

1. Can I cover the topic in the allotted time?

But since mere coverage is not communication, you must ask:

2. Can I cover it adequately, without having to neglect any important points?

In selecting and refining the initial idea, then, satisfy yourself first; that is, consider your reservoir of knowledge and experience and your desires. Such careful consideration will go a long way toward satisfying the audience and meeting the requirements of the occasion. Words of Byron, quaint but apt in this context, provide the right tone for concluding this section of the chapter.

> Suit your topics to your strength,
> And ponder well your subject, and its length;

Nor lift your load, before you're quite aware
What weight your shoulder will, or will not bear.

TO WHAT END?

Perhaps you have been raising mental questions about the possible purposes of speeches during the discussion of choosing subjects and arriving at topics. For example, "In what direction could a speaker lead his audience with a speech on 'Steps in Training a Collie to Heel'?" or "What would be the probable object in a treatment of 'Arriving at a Philosophy of Life through Experience'?" A general answer to both questions comes easily: you propose to lead your audience to respond by sharing in your ideas on the topics. This broadly stated end may be the object of most speeches, but it does not acknowledge the varying emphases of speeches. In other words, though the fundamental end of any speech as a social act is to affect others, the speaker may plan for a *particular* result. Theorists usually classify speeches this way.

As George Campbell put it in the eighteenth century, "In speaking, there is always some end proposed, or some effect which the speaker intends to produce in the hearer." Writing later in the century, his fellow Scot, Hugh Blair, wrote, "Whenever a man speaks or writes, he is supposed as a rational being, to have some end in view: either to inform or to amuse or to persuade, or, in some way or other, to act upon his fellow creatures." How do you wish to act upon your "fellow creatures"? In preparing a speech, determine the desired response and plan toward that end. Decide if your objective is to inform, to convince, to persuade, or to entertain.

Though adhering to one dominant end in your speech, you will doubtless find that one or another of the remaining three objectives will, at times, be central. To illustrate: a speech designed to convince people of a motion picture's merits may, at points, be primarily informative. In presenting steps in the training of a collie to heel, a speaker may include entertaining commentary in places. In telling *how* one arrives at a philosophy of life through experience, a speaker is likely to tell or suggest *what* to do. If he does, he is at that moment in the area of persuasion.

As you see, the strands that we call the ends of speech are typically intertwined; nonetheless, let us examine each individually.

To Inform

Doubtless, many speakers in your class will prepare speeches designed to give information. Talks with this end foremost in mind are, of course, common. When informing, the speaker's purpose is to enlighten the audience, to tell the listeners how to do something, to explain the characteristics of some person, place or thing, to describe or make clear. The following ends are essentially informational:

To define applied psychology
To describe the eruption of Old Faithful
To clarify the purposes of a modern artist
To explain the styles of high jumping
To differentiate between stalagmites and stalactites
To give a character sketch of a fascinating next-door neighbor

To Persuade

Technically speaking, we could separate conviction from persuasion in this section and say that the goal, or end, to which conviction refers is use of primarily *logical* means to affect a person's *beliefs,* while persuasion refers to the use of *all available means* to affect a person's *behavior.* Some theorists recognize such a distinction. On the other hand, it may be reasonable to group the two ends, for they very often become indistinguishable. For our purposes, we shall take them as one, as a unified and single function of communication, and call the union persuasion.

To persuade is to affect beliefs—to establish new ones in listeners' minds, to reinforce those held, or to cause abandonment of those held. (These are the goals of conviction when it is discussed separately.) Furthermore, to persuade is to influence behavior—to influence one to do something, to stop doing something, or to do something another way, and so forth. In a word, in persuasion, you appeal to people to believe something or to take some action. Now not all of the audience may be moved to believe immediately, nor may any action be immediate; nevertheless, the speaker's goal is to convince or to secure action at once or for some future time. These ends are persuasive:

To show why either a conservative or a liberal should be elected President of the United States
To develop an appreciation for the customs of Nigeria
To advocate the taking of a course in logic
To relate values of military experience
To explain why everyone should contribute to the United Fund
To stress the significance of World War II in our history
To encourage student attendance at the basketball games

To Entertain

Any speech, regardless of its end, may have elements of entertainment and humor. There are speeches, however, that are planned solely for entertainment. These are not as common in the speech classroom

as are informative and persuasive speeches. Talks to entertain are difficult, and it takes a special flair to sustain humor and carry it off well.
Then, too, many teachers of speech believe that speech training will be
more profitable if the oral assignments are completed with more serious
goals in mind. Nonetheless, you may find an opportunity to give an
entertaining speech, either at some time during the course or in another situation. The following might represent such an aim:

To ridicule the do-it-yourself craze
To show how to get rid of friends in three easy lessons
To characterize the typical freshman at the end of his first day
    of classes
To discuss the antics of a three-year-old
To describe hair styles of the future
To poke fun at vulnerable human characteristics

As you choose a subject and narrow it to a topic you should be con-
templating the end of your planned discourse; and remember to hold
your focus on your dominant objective.

WORD YOUR PROPOSITION

With your topic in mind, your next task will be to write your specific
purpose. The specific purpose or *proposition,* as we shall call it, is a
part of the speech. In a sentence, it is your statement to your audience
employed to indicate what you desire to discuss. It makes known your
intent, the ground you will cover, where you are going. To prevent
misunderstanding and vagueness, the proposition must be a complete
sentence and include only one idea. Moreover, it should be stated
briefly and designed for audience acceptance. It is to be purposive.

Let us digress momentarily in order to put the all-important proposition in its place as a member of a "four-man speech team." As we will
explain in Chapter Three, a speech is made up of an introduction, a
proposition (specific purpose), a body, and a conclusion. Each has a
vital function. The introduction leads up to the objective of the talk;
the proposition states the objective; the body works to attain that
objective; and the conclusion clinches the attainment of the objective.
Is it not evident that the specific objective—the proposition—is the
heart of the speech? It is the theme or central idea.

It is little wonder, then, that the proposition requires so much care
in phrasing. A fault here can cause the entire effort to go awry. Note
the weaknesses of these propositions:

1. Men's fashions of the 1920s.
2. May I acquaint you with a crystal radio set and tell you how to
   test television tubes?

3. It is my purpose to explain the various functions of an internal combustion engine that is designed to offer maximum efficiency when the spark plugs have been either thoroughly cleaned or replaced with the best on the market today.
4. Let me tell you about (or of) the Democratic party.
5. Sensible people, those who matter in the first place, do not buy houses in developments.

Do you observe the faults of these propositions? No. 1 is incomplete. It is an undirected topic, not a proposition. We might ask, "What about men's fashions of the 1920s?" Is it the speaker's aim to evaluate the fashions? To describe them? To show that they are coming back into style? We just do not know, and the wise speaker will prevent such a problem from occurring by telling the audience his goal in a complete sentence. He might say:

My object is to discuss some features of men's fashions of the 1920s that would appeal to men of today.

or

Consider with me the widely applauded decline and fall of men's fashions of the 1920s.

Proposition 2 is a full sentence but too confusing. What is the purpose? Actually the proposition is two-headed; it indicates two purposes. A speaker employing this purpose sentence would be ambitious, indeed, if he were to suppose that he could accomplish both aims. It is enough of a task to realize *one* objective. Listening is sufficiently difficult, without adding complications. Be the good guide; take the listener in but one direction. When confronted with a two-headed proposition, discard one of the ideas, or save it for another speaking occasion. An improved proposition would be:

May I acquaint you with a crystal radio set?

or

These are the functioning parts of a crystal radio set.

or

In testing television tubes, follow four easy steps.

Proposition 3 is ambiguous because of its extreme length and involvement. It should stop after "engine." Explanations and necessary ramifications can come at a later point in the speech. The job at this point is to state the purpose, briefly and simply.

In addition to discarding half the wording, another refinement seems indicated for a short speech. Limit the extent of your "contract" with the audience by use of qualifiers, for example:

It is my purpose to explain *two* functions of an internal combustion engine.

or

My purpose is to explain the function of the carburetor of an internal combustion engine.

No. 4 is another ambiguous proposition. Again, what *about* the Democratic party? What *of* the Democratic party? What is the speaker's intent? Will he discuss history? Leaders? Policies? Future prospects? Take it as a sign of danger whenever your proposition includes the phrasing "talk *about*" this or that, or "talk *on*" or "tell *of*." Prepositions like "about," "on," and "of," so placed, tend to generalize and flatten out statements of purpose. They work against requirements of specificity and interest. These statements show improvement:

I'd like to relate to you the position of the Democratic party on balancing the budget, a document affecting all in this room.

or

Let us take note of just three of Thomas Jefferson's many contributions to the Democratic party's basic philosophy.

Proposition 5 will alienate the audience most likely. The speaker may have some good reasons for not liking tract houses, but he needs listeners before he can do any convincing. His proposition should be rhetorical, shaped for listeners' reception. The lives of people in the audience may be associated in some way with housing developments (as are the lives of most Americans). If that is the case, he might do better to employ a less direct proposition. He can still make his point, but tactfully. He might say:

Here are some points to weigh in buying a house in a development.

or

Shop carefully before investing in a future home.

A well-phrased proposition, we see, gets the speaker off to a good start by definitely specifying his objective. Remember:

It must be a complete sentence.
It must include a single idea.
It must be uninvolved and reasonably brief.
It must be designed for audience acceptance.
It must be purposive.

USE THE EXTEMPORANEOUS MODE

Speakers in past decades relied more on memory in delivering speeches than do their counterparts today. Reportedly, some would recall large passages or even entire speeches. Historians of public address relate that some of the most effective and praiseworthy speakers were often those with the best memories. But they had trained themselves and had accepted the discipline as part of the preparation for speaking. This part of the art has lost its place in our culture. Times have changed ("fortunately," say those with poor or uneducable memories), and today we hear heavily memorized speeches infrequently. There are good reasons for the change. Few people can deliver a speech which is committed to memory without having it show. Too often such a talk is stilted, stiff, and held at a distance from the audience. There is also the ever-present fear of forgetting, and this causes the speaker to be on his guard and in dread of missing one word, one word which may throw the whole effort off.

As William Norwood Brigance, one of America's most highly respected scholars in speech cautioned, "a memorized speech *sounds* memorized. It sounds 'canned' like the music of a hurdy-gurdy. The speaker, like the monkey, shuffles through his performance—then waits at the end for the applause. People applaud both in much the same spirit. It was pretty good for a monkey." [1]

Another method of presenting ideas is manuscript style, or reading. This system is used considerably by politicians, government officials, some business executives, and some clergymen. When done well, it can be effective; when done poorly, communication does not take place. Too often the speaker never gets his speech off the page and out to his audience. Too often there is no meeting of the eyes and, it may follow, no meeting of the minds. Eugene Smith expresses the thought cleverly: [2]

> I always dislike using a manuscript in making a speech. It's like courting a girl through a picket fence. Everything that is said can be heard, but there isn't much contact.

Because of the possible hazards inherent in memorization and manuscript reading, we shall emphasize the *extemporaneous mode*. Do not confuse this use of the term with the "extemporaneous" speaking contest which allows a participant forty-five minutes or an hour for preparation.

When you use the extemporaneous method, you prepare, certainly, but you do not memorize your speech nor do you write it out word for word. You will benefit from the experiences of thousands like yourself, if you follow five key steps:

1. Select familiar and interesting ideas, ideas you have a *desire* to communicate and *want* your listeners to hear.
2. Use an outline, either mental or written. Avoid cluttering it with

[1] *Speech, Its Techniques and Disciplines in a Free Society*, 2d ed. (New York, 1961), p. 274.
[2] *Quote*, XXXIII (May 19, 1957), p. 8.

so much detail that it becomes a verbatim representation of your speech. Include the skeleton of your talk and key details, just enough to help you carry the thought along.

3. Let your speeches take shape gradually. Start preparing well ahead of your speaking date, and allow the ideas to sift through your mind. Some thoughts you will discard, others you will keep, and you will add new ones as they occur to you. The retained ideas will become a part of you, and there will be no cause to want to memorize or read the speech.

4. Practice! Practice aloud in seclusion. Practice before family or friends, and try out ideas in dinner-table conversation. Practice to get that confident feeling that comes from assimilation of the thought, from knowing what you are saying and where the thought is going. Practice purposefully—with your goal in mind. Practice as often as necessary to get yourself ready to communicate your ideas.

5. Speak naturally and conversationally with your audience. *Talk* with them. They are human, you are human, and both of you are engaging in a human activity, a sharing. Keep it that way—an unmechanical, human exchange of thought.

The wisdom of a fine poet might be germane here. Robert Frost once explained the seeming paradox of his following definite conventions and forms of poetry, while finding, nonetheless, an ease and genuine freedom of expression. He accounted for his freedom by saying that he had learned to "work easy in harness." This can well be your goal with the extemporaneous method. Accept the form—the "harness" or an outline—and come to "work easy," through sound preparation, attention to necessary revision, and useful practice.

LET US SUMMARIZE

In getting started, then, put forth your best and:
1. Choose an appropriate subject.
2. Narrow the subject to a topic.
3. Determine the end.
4. Word your proposition carefully.
5. Use the extemporaneous and conversational mode.
6. Practice! Practice! Practice!

Put forth the best that you have to offer, and remember that the single most effective element in speaking often is the personal element —*you* and how the audience is disposed toward *you*. Show your interest in the well-being of the audience and your desire to communicate something worthwhile to them. People will be prepared to listen to a speaker who is sincere, of good character, and well prepared.

James Albert Winans, a theorist and teacher of speech mentioned in Chapter One, was perhaps more influential than anyone else in leading speech instruction away from emphases on "performing" and the excesses of artificial methods of elocution. That he should have the final word of this chapter is fitting. He advised that "true speech is a dialogue; better even than talking *to* us is talking *with* us. It is conversation with an audience." [3]

BASIC ASSIGNMENT

Prepare a short speech. You need not include an introduction or conclusion. Merely state a carefully prepared proposition, and develop it. In other words, stand before your audience, announce your goal, and speak toward that end.

Reminders

1. Choose a subject that is interesting and familiar to you.
2. Narrow the subject to a topic.
3. Do not memorize or read your speech.
4. Plan carefully in order to achieve your goal in the allotted time.

Suggested Exercise A

Write five propositions which are sound in every way, and label each with the general end it suggests.

Suggested Exercise B

Listen to two speeches (lectures, sermons, political addresses, and so forth). Summarize each in a paragraph. State the general end and specific purpose of each.

Suggested Exercise C

Select a topic (one which could be covered in a four-minute speech) for each of the following broad areas:

Aviation	Philosophy
Politics	Medicine
Customs	Language
Science	Music
Dancing	Economics

Suggested Exercise D

Students frequently say that the most difficult aspect of speech preparation is choosing a subject. Is this true for you? If so, have you really thought about it objectively? Do you *really* believe that you have nothing worthwhile to say? Are you one who believes that everyone else in the class knows more about any subject than you do?

[3] *Public Speaking* (New York, 1917), p. 38.

Let us try the positive approach. List two subjects of interest to you, and explain why you are well qualified to speak on at least one aspect of each.

Suggested Exercise E

From your personal observations, make a list of characteristic habits, attitudes, and preferences of people in the eighteen-to-twenty age bracket. What guidelines for communicating with people in this age group can you draw?

Suggested Exercise F

Can you think of any subject that could be inappropriate for presentation to this class? Your answer may be useful in a class discussion on choosing subjects.

Suggested Exercise G

Each of the following propositions has at least one weakness. Determine the weak point of each, and revise the statement.

No. 1 When camping out, what to do in case of rain.

No. 2 Theodore Roosevelt was a strong advocate of conservation of natural resources.

Suggested Exercise H

Read two of the following three speeches appearing in *Appendix A* of the book:

Ann Blasdell, "The Waste of War"

Howard W. Runkel, "Making Lincoln Live"

Nellie Williams, "Habits and Customs of People"

What are the speakers' propositions? What is the end of each? To persuade? Inform? Entertain?

CHAPTER THREE

Organizing Your Thoughts

Imagine yourself turning the pages of the daily newspaper. Start with page one, and notice the headline, DISORGANIZED TROOPS ROUTED, and down the page a bit, FIRE CAUSES PANIC. Turn to the sports page, and read a heading CONFUSED TIGERS LOSE TO TECH. In the second section you find an article titled HOW NOT TO BE THE MUDDLED HOSTESS, and finally you see on the financial page UNSYSTEMATIC SPENDING HARMFUL TO BUSINESS.

ORDER VERSUS CHAOS

What is the key thought suggested in all these newspaper headings? Worded positively, the key thought is that in most human endeavors organization is necessary for success. In other words, the elements having to do with purposeful action must be handled systematically, and when we think of a *system,* we think of order, planning, arrangement, and method. Down through the centuries, men have expressed the need for order in many ways. For example:

> Order means light and peace, inward liberty and free command over one's self; order is power.
>
> *—Amiel*
>
> A place for everything, everything in its place.
> *—Benjamin Franklin*
> Set all things in their own peculiar place,
> And know that order is the greatest grace.
>
> *—Dryden*

Whether it is in flower-arranging or in electioneering, order cannot be neglected. The human activity of speechmaking is no exception. To speak well is to do more than stand and talk; to speak well is to stand and talk purposefully, using a plan which will help you to accomplish your purpose. You have chosen your subject, trimmed it down to size, and worded your specific purpose. It now becomes necessary to plan the course for achieving your purpose.

BENEFITS OF ORGANIZATION

A river can be directed into channels to provide the greatest good for all people, or it can be allowed to run at will. So it is with speech. Ideas can be channeled for ease in reception, or they can be allowed to ramble aimlessly, unmanaged and wasted—for listeners have expectations of and hopes for order. Wise speakers know that, and to accommodate their thinking to their listeners' yearnings, they structure their thoughts, thus providing one more basis for a meeting of minds. The patterning of ideas, the orderly setting up of ideas to fit listeners' mental frames, answers their anticipation and fundamental need of order. Order acknowledges a human requirement; it satisfies by dispelling the frustration of disorientation.

Let us put it in more practical terms. Listeners want guidance and direction; they find structure and arrangement helpful and disarrangement baffling. Literally, a speaker must "parcel out" the thoughts to his audience. Knowing of the ever-present possibilities for misunderstanding and confusion, the speaker sets up a plan of distribution and addresses his audience accordingly. Good organization leads to good listening, for the exchange is methodical, first things first and part by part. And, of course, good organization helps the speaker to accomplish the purpose of his speech. In preparation, a plan guides him in his own thinking on the subject matter. Furthermore, his knowing how he will progress in delivering the content adds to his confidence. In sum, good organization leads to communication.

OUTLINING

The basic representation of a speech plan is the outline. It is the framework of the entire speech that shows the principal points to be covered, the order in which they will be covered, their relationship to one another, and often their relative weight or importance.

For most speech assignments your instructor will probably ask for an outline, before you speak. A soundly prepared outline, frequently the result of rigorous effort, has no substitute in speech planning. It is your master plan for speaking, a physical representation of your proposed course of thought. From this full outline, you can abstract your speaking notes: a brief listing of the main points of your outline. The notes can be mental or written, depending on you or on your instructor's prescription. At the end of the chapter you will find a set of speaking notes taken from a full outline.

The outline also will be useful to your instructor in ascertaining the progress of your class work and your needs. It will tell him what you set out to do in a given speech and your plan for proceeding.

Class requirements will dictate the type of outline, either topical or in sentence form. Model outlines at the end of the chapter illustrate both forms.

Headings and Indentations

The mechanics of outlining call for care in choosing symbols for headings and in indenting. Use numbers and letters alternately to indicate points and divisions of points. Indent each subdivision of a point to show graphically its relationship to the point. In typewriting terms, indentations are usually either three or five spaces, depending on your choice or possibly on the features of the typewriter. Spacing distance for handwritten work is comparable—perhaps somewhat greater.

Head the first point with a Roman numeral. Then, to head a division of the first point, indent and use a capital letter. To head a division of *that* point, indent and use an arabic numeral. If it is necessary to break down the latest point, you indent and use a small letter; then, if necessary, you use an alternation of an arabic numeral in parentheses with a small letter in parentheses. The system does provide for further division, but those details are of no real value to us—or to the great majority of outline users. Rarely will any point in a practical speech outline be broken down beyond the small-letter stage, the fourth level. The partial outline form below, obviously an incomplete outline, is included to exemplify use of symbols for headings and typical indentations. The first six items illustrate our current discussion. Observe the value of indentation to show progressive "funneling" of thought from the general to the more specific.

I• Western Hemisphere
    A.   North America
        1. United States
            a. Northeastern United States
                (1) Massachusetts
                    (a) Boston
                    (b) Springfield
                (2) Maine
            b. Southeastern United States
        2. Canada
    B.   South America

Coordinate Points

Outlines consist of coordinate points and subordinate points. The coordinate heads in an outline are those of equal weight, those of the same approximate value or nature. Symbols for their headings are also of the same class. North America and South America, above, are coordinate points. The contents of the headings are equal in substance, and the symbols reflect the equality, both being large letters. Note that four additional points in the outline have paralleling points. To illustrate further, the following means of transportation are set up as coordinate headings:

I• Aircraft
II• Automobiles
III• Trains

And these headings, as complete sentences this time:

I• Organized crime may be centered in a single city.
II• Organized crime may be national in scope.
III• Organized crime may be international in scope.

Subordinate Points

Divisions of larger points are called subordinate points. They are secondary to and parts of the larger ones and either explain the larger heading or enumerate the contents of it. A leg (subordinate) is part of a man (larger points). *Room* is subordinate to *house*. In our geographical outline above, North America and South America are subordinate to Western Hemisphere. The United States and Canada are directly subordinate to North America. Observe other subordinate relationships in the outline. Subordinate headings under the previously mentioned modes of transportation could be the following:

I• Aircraft
   A. Propeller-driven
   B. Jet-propelled
   C. Rocket
II• Automobiles
   A. Four-cylinder
   B. Six-cylinder
   C. Eight-cylinder
III• Trains
   A. Steam
   B. Diesel
   C. Electric
   D. Diesel-electric

In organizing ideas, we find that every point *can* have a subordinate point, and every subordinate point can have a point immediately subordinate to it. This is illustrated by the children's song, "And the Green Grass Grew All Around." Do you remember it? In part, it goes:

> In the woods there grew a tree; on this tree there was a limb; on this limb there was a branch; on this branch there was a bough; on this bough there was a twig; on this twig there was a nest; in the nest there was a bird. . . .

Each succeeding part is subordinate to the preceding one, and we observe a movement from the general to the specific. That is outlining. We have general headings and specific subheadings under them. Over-extended though it appears, here is an outline of the "Green Grass" excerpt.

I• Woods
   A. Tree
      1. Limb
         a. Branch
            (1) Bough
               (a) Twig
                  1. Nest
                     a. Bird

THE SPEECH OUTLINE

In the fourth century B.C., Plato has Socrates say in the dialogue, *Phaedrus,* about the speech outline:

> . . . every speech ought to be put together like a living creature, with a body of its own, so as to be neither without head, nor without feet, but to have both a middle and extremities, described proportionately to each other and to the whole.

Today, in the twentieth century, we still accept this ancient "figure of speech." The main section of a speech is the body. Attached to it are the head (introduction) and the feet (conclusion). Agreeing with Plato's pupil, Aristotle, we insert a statement—the specific purpose which, as you recall from Chapter Two, we call the proposition.

Let us analyze the functions of each part of the speech outline.

The Introduction

This is the beginning of your speech, and you will use this introductory phase to accomplish two important goals.

1. *Establish a base for meeting your audience.* To capture attention and develop interest, many speakers will reveal an area of common interest or common concern in their opening remarks. Often they include such thought without consciously realizing its full value as

ground upon which to build a relationship for communication. To seek mutuality of experience, of interest, or of sentiment—whether in formal speaking or in casual conversation—seems to be a basic motive of people in our culture. Though not advised for speeches, questions like "What do you think of the weather?" or "Is it hot enough for you today?" point up efforts of us humans in social interplay to discover references to topics of general concern. We look for the common ground. This is social strategy, the way we function with one another.

Applying this social lesson in the speech class, you might begin a speech by referring to an incident (or person or thing or belief, and so forth) which promises to be meaningful to the audience. Perhaps there was a campus event that can be tied in with your topic and thus serve as an example for launching your talk. As a case in point, let us say that you plan to discuss "Ways to Use the Library" and that everyone knows about the recent invasion of the library by three dogs. Use your imagination here. You might start with, "Everybody—and thing— uses the library."

You can start your speech by making a reference to a classmate's speech, an event experienced in common. Use that base, already set down, to assist you in getting started. If on Wednesday Bob showed the advantages derived from a college education and on some future day you plan to talk on "Improving Listening," you might open your speech by saying, "On Wednesday, Bob told us why we need a college education, and today I would like to analyze one of the means for achieving this education."

Sometimes a startling statement, question, or statistic will touch on a topic of general interest and thus get response. If your purpose is to encourage the listeners to be careful of their hearts, you can start by announcing, "More people die from heart ailments than from any other single cause." Your topic might be traffic safety, and you might begin with statistics. "Did you know that last year 40,000 people lost their lives on America's streets and highways?" A word of caution should be offered about using startling statements. Use discretion, and avoid a shock which might mean the loss of attention. In one campus speech contest an enthusiastic speaker, desiring to get attention at the outset of his speech, pulled out a track pistol and fired it. Needless to say, it produced a shock, so much of a shock that no one was able to listen for the balance of the program.

A short speech to offer hints on outdoor barbecuing might be started with quoted material, like this hypothetical introduction:

> Owen Meredith, English statesman and poet, once said,
>> We may live without poetry, music and art;
>> We may live without conscience and live without heart;

> We may live without friends, we may live without books,
> But civilized man cannot live without cooks.
> Now, possibly you don't agree that we may live without heart or friends, but certainly you appreciate his main sentiment—his respect for cooks. And for my purposes today, may I add *outdoor* cooks. I refer to the artist, male or female, who is at home with grill, pit, or *hibachi*. Acquiring competence before the burning briquets is not as difficult as you might think. [The proposition then follows]

The more the speaker and listener are separated in custom, nature, or belief, the more attention the speaker should give to making aspects of their basic kinship known. For communication, he strives to show some fundamental bond with his listeners. The opening words of a speech by Winston Churchill, retired Prime Minister of England, illustrate one speaker's attempt to stress similarities and mutual sympathies of peoples. Now you may never find yourself in a similar speaking situation, but observe that the *principles* of audience adaptation demonstrated in the speech might be followed by any speaker.

Sir Winston delivered the speech at Westminster College in Fulton, Missouri, in 1946. The "Westminster" to which he refers is that part of London in which the English Parliament is located. Incidentally, it was in this speech that Churchill first uttered the ominous statement, ". . . an iron curtain has descended across the continent."

> I am glad to come to Westminster College this afternoon and am complimented that you should give me a degree. The name Westminster is somehow familiar to me. I seem to have heard it before. Indeed it was at Westminster that I received a very large part of my education in politics, dialectic, rhetoric, and one or two other things.

2. *Guide the audience to the proposition.* After you establish rapport, lead your audience to the proposition. You must prepare them for the announcement of your purpose. Avoid stating the proposition before you have unfolded preliminary background or explanatory material. After all, you want your listeners to accept the proposition, and you need to justify its worth or importance by building up to it. If your purpose is to discuss the need to increase property taxes, it may be necessary in the introduction to work at dispelling negative feelings that people may have about taxes. If you are advocating a compulsory class in biology, a careful build-up before presenting your purpose will be needed. Almost all topics, but especially controversial ones, require some kind of preparatory setting of the scene.

The following introduction was used successfully before a speech class to introduce a short speech. Relying primarily on definition, the speaker in just thirty seconds or so caught the listeners' interest and laid out a pathway to the door of his proposition.

Most people know what initials like MPH, FDR, and RSVP stand for, but the other day when one of my instructors mentioned the initials GNP, I noticed that a lot of people in class looked puzzled. Do you know the initials? Though they affect the lives of every American, too few can explain them. Webster says, the GNP—gross national product—is the "total market value of a nation's goods and services, before any deductions or allowances are made." GNP is what the country is worth, economically. "Yes," you say, "but what does GNP mean to me?" That's just the question I hope to answer today. [The proposition then follows]

Here is another introduction—a short one, but long enough to ready listeners for the proposition. The speaker is Francis H. Horn, president of the University of Rhode Island, who spoke at a convocation at Ricker College. His mentioning "events that could have ended our civilization" are in reference to America's bold demands to the USSR to remove missile bases from Cuba. His speech proposes to show that despite crises, man will move on to the greatest future he has ever known.

Several weeks ago I received a letter from the Ford Foundation's Fund for the Republic which said: "The world has just witnessed historic events that could have ended our civilization had not reason prevailed. Mankind was saved. But can we count on such good fortune at the next confrontation of naked power and overstrained nerves? This is the overwhelming concern of every thinking person in our society today."

I wish to direct your attention to this problem of the prospect for civilization. Let me emphasize that I am not an expert on the subject. I am not a historian or a political scientist. I come to you as a "thinking person," to whom, as the Fund's letter states, this matter of survival and the kind of a world tomorrow will bring is the "overwhelming concern." [1]

Of the four parts of a speech, we have discussed the introduction first because, of course, it is the first part that you deliver to the audience. But it should not be the first part that you prepare. Actually, the best time to plan the introduction is *after* you have prepared the balance of your speech, for you cannot give a final shaping to opening remarks until you have determined what it is you are to introduce. Does the method seem logical? Practical experience with the method—one perhaps unfamiliar to you now—is the best means for discovering its merits. Try it.

The Proposition

In delivery, the proposition follows naturally from the introduction. It embodies what you have been working toward and leading up to in the introduction. After a good introduction, the proposition will fall in place and take a position of central importance.

Recall (from Chapter Two) that your proposition is a complete sen-

[1] "The Prospect for Civilization," *Representative American Speeches: 1962–1963*, Lester Thonssen, ed. (New York, 1963) pp. 82–96.

tence and, being purposive, states your objective clearly. Furthermore, it must include only one idea, be short, and be designed for audience acceptance. Here are three samples:

Allow me to point out the advantage of going away to college.

My purpose today is to discuss four features of the republican form of government.

These are my reasons for saying that everyone should be a radio and television critic.

The Body

The body is a discussion of the proposition and is composed of the main ideas to be presented. In this section you develop your purpose, that is, you tell your audience what you told them you would tell them.

But how do you tell them? First of all, you tell them in an orderly manner. It is folly in speaking to stand and cast ideas in all directions with the hope that by some mysterious means your listeners will pick up your thoughts. Speech is too important to be treated so haphazardly. You must be more purposeful and scientific about it and proceed step by step.

1. *Analyze your proposition; determine its contents.* What are the proposition's inherent parts? What sections or divisions of thought does it contain? It is made up of pieces of thought. What are they? These divisions of the proposition will be the chief points in the body of your speech. We call them *main heads.* Let us look at some sample propositions and main heads.

Proposition: It is my purpose to discuss the extent of our basic national defense planning.

Body
A. We are ready to meet land attacks.
B. We are ready to meet air attacks.
C. We are ready to meet sea attacks.

Proposition: Allow me to plan one day's menu of nutritious and wholesome food for you.

Body
A. Start the day with a hearty breakfast.
B. Do not neglect an ample lunch.
C. Complete your daily eating with a delicious dinner.

The main heads are parts of the proposition. The proposition is like a pie and the body is made up of pieces of the pie. In the first example, the three pieces (or subareas) of national defense plans deal with land, air, and sea defense. The second case shows that breakfast, lunch, and dinner are the logical points from which to consider the planning of a day's menu.

What does such analysis do for the speaker? First of all, it helps him to get his thinking straight. By planning and studying, he determines what his chief ideas will be, what main points he wants to present to the audience.

Secondly, a careful analysis of the propositions makes for audience understanding. How much communication would take place if the speaker threw the whole "pie" at the audience without giving thought to arrangement and purposeful distribution? Actually, very little. On the other hand, when the speaker announces what the whole pie will be, and then proceeds to distribute it piece by piece, there is an absence of confusion. The process is an orderly one because the speaker presents ideas one at a time, part by part. It is easier for a listener to handle thought when it is given to him in bits. He can understand and assimilate smaller pieces of information better and is able to see how each relates to the whole.

2. *Choose only two, three, or four main heads.* Divide your proposition into at least two parts. In fact, there are many propositions which lend themselves to just two main heads. You have heard speeches, for example, that have dealt with the "pros and the cons," the "advantages and the disadvantages," the "right and the wrong," the "east and the west," "before and after," and so forth.

Only in rare cases should you have more than four main parts. Among the many experienced speakers who recommend limiting the number of main heads, is Harry Emerson Fosdick. Professor Roy C. McCall paraphrased Fosdick's advice: "Audiences cannot grasp more than three at one sitting; four, perhaps, if the speaker exercises special care in keeping the outline constantly before them." In recalling his experience in once giving a speech with six main heads, Fosdick said, "It came out like a broom, in a multitude of small straws." [2] We must be realistic and recognize that listeners can manage only a few thoughts at one time. A point of diminishing returns can be reached in speaking, a point at which the listener can absorb no more new ideas. In a metaphor contrasting with but supporting Fosdick's metaphor, we might say that it is like shoveling gravel onto the flat bed of a truck. You reach a point at which it is useless to continue. The added gravel merely rolls down from the high pile as fast as you shovel it on.

Finding yourself in possession of more than four main heads may signal a topic of too much breadth. In that case, you obviously must limit your scope. Another explanation of main heads in excessive abundance may be your failure to recognize fewer but broader divisions of the proposition. Your solution in this second instance is to

[2] Roy C. McCall, "Harry Emerson Fosdick, A Study in Sources of Effectiveness," in *American Public Address,* Loren Reid, ed. (Columbia, Missouri, 1961), p. 66.

combine certain main heads or to reclassify them. For example, assume that in planning a speech to discuss the usefulness of the parts of a book, you set up these main heads:

A. Title Page
B. Preface
C. Introduction
D. Text
E. Appendix
F. Bibliography
G. Index

Anticipating your listeners' problems in grappling with seven separate thoughts, you seek a better way to handle the ideas. Rightly, you decide upon a regrouping into three main heads:

A. Preliminary Pages
    (with Title Page, Preface, and Introduction as subheads)
B. The Text
C. Auxiliary Material
    (with Appendix, Bibliography, and Index as subheads)

Remember your audience and purpose; choose only two, three, or four main heads.

3. *Check your main heads for balance.* After analyzing your proposition, test the chosen main heads. Determine if they are coordinate.

You will remember in discussing outlining earlier in the chapter that we defined coordinate points as those equal in weight or nature. Now since main heads are the primary parts of the proposition, they must be coordinate. Each one must be parallel to the other. Notice the balance and parallel structure in the following set of main heads.

A. One way to learn is to read.
B. One way to learn is to listen.
C. One way to learn is to experiment.

Here is an upsetting of the balance, an upsetting of coordinate relationships:

A. One way to learn is to read.
B. One way to learn is to listen.
C. To learn is difficult.

Do you see what happened? *A* and *B* refer to specific means for learning while *C* comments upon the difficulty of the process. *C* does not belong because it is of a different nature. In handling such a problem, the speaker must make a choice as to what unifying characteristic he wants his main heads to have, and then make certain that each one assumes that characteristic.

4. *Check your main heads to eliminate any overlapping.* Each unit of the proposition should be mutually exclusive of each other unit; that is, it should be concerned with a single and separate point of its own. Each main head is to represent a limited domain of thought, distinct from that of each other main head. Overlapping indicates that one main head is part of another, and the outline should be arranged with that part shown to be subordinate. In the following example, *C* does not deserve main head status, for it is part of *B*.

A. A good salesman believes in himself.
B. A good salesman believes in his product.
C. A good salesman chooses a product in which he can believe.

A better arrangement would be:

A. A good salesman believes in himself.
B. A good salesman believes in his product.
    1. He should choose a worthy product to sell, first of all.

Here is another example of overlapping.

A. Psychology is a study of human behavior.
B. Psychology is a study of human experience.
C. Psychology is a study of human reaction.

What is the difficulty here? *A* and *C* are very closely related, and since *reaction* is a type of *behavior, C* should be subordinate to *A,* and placed as a subhead to *A.*

Be wary of overlapping. It can intrude quite easily if you are not alert.

5. *Maintain unity of form in casting main heads.* If your main heads are unified, they will conform to a single form—either time order, space order, reason order, topic order, problem-solution order, or some other structural order.

When ordered according to *time,* the main ideas of the body suggest something to do with the clock, the calendar, or periods, eras, seasons, decades, and so forth. You will choose this frame of reference if you consider elements of time as the key thoughts to emphasize. For example:

Proposition: I'd like to contrast the two periods of last week's championship basketball game.

Body
    A. During the first half, we saw skillful defensive play.
    B. In the second half, the offenses sparkled.

Proposition: It is my desire to show briefly at what points our specific social abilities develop.

Body
A. In childhood we begin our development.
B. In adolescence we experiment.
C. In adulthood we refine our social skills.

To unify your main heads in terms of *space* means that you wish to focus on areas, regions, districts, zones, or locations. Space may refer to an area either microscopic in size, or conceivably to the whole universe.

Proposition: May I recommend four popular American vacation states to you?

Body
A. Go to California's beaches for a sun tan.
B. See the historic sights of Massachusetts.
C. Relax at a dude ranch in Arizona.
D. Fill your creel in Michigan's lakes.

Proposition: Let me relate the main floor plan features that I shall include when I build my ideal house.

Body
A. The kitchen will be spacious.
B. The bedrooms will be convenient to bathrooms.
C. The living room will be out of traffic paths.
D. The den will be isolated.

You may use *reason* order to arrange your main heads when you plan a speech designed to uphold a point of view. You word your proposition to state your point of view, and word each main head as a reason for your stand. Each main head, each argument for your case, when properly worded, could start with "because" or "for."

Proposition: I believe that everyone should join some worthwhile social organization.

Body
A. (Because) Everyone needs to belong to something.
B. (Because) Everyone should learn to work with others.

Proposition: Allow me to tell you why I believe that each person should develop his strong individual characteristics.

Body
   A.   (For) He will like himself better personally.
   B.   (For) He will be more capable socially.
   C.   (For) He will be advanced further vocationally.

When you divide your proposition *topically,* you select the mere "neutral" parts of the proposition, parts not tinged with a time, space, or reason character. Topic order is probably the most common, and we might define it best by saying that it is what other patterns are not.

Proposition: Every good teacher has three major strong points.

Body
   A.   He knows his subject.
   B.   He knows teaching techniques.
   C.   He knows people.

Proposition: It is my purpose to describe the functions of several common office machines.

Body
   A.   First, let us consider calculating machines.
   B.   Next, there are recording machines.
   C.   Finally, we should discuss duplicating machines.

A fifth pattern which your main heads might assume is *problem-solution* order. If this form suits the potential development of your proposition, you will have only two main heads. The first main head discusses a problem, and the second presents one or more solutions. Of course, you would use the problem-solution order only if your purpose were to present a problem and solve it.

Proposition: The matter of marriage failure should concern all of us.

Body
   A.   The problem is serious.
   B.   There are solutions.

Proposition: Control of your weight is important to your health.

Body
   A.   Let us examine the nature of the problem.
   B.   Let us analyze possible solutions.

Among the many special forms for framing main heads (some merely adaptations of those discussed above) are the following:

Cause and Effect (or Effect, then Cause)
Climactic (ordering from least significant to most significant)
Biographical (a topical form used when a person is discussed;
    ordered with headings like Early Life, Goals, and
    Accomplishments)
Need-Plan-Benefits (used extensively in argumentation, especially
    debate)
Past-Present-Future
Series of Questions (for example: Where are we? How did we
    get there? Where do we go from here?)

In summary, divide the proposition into two, three, or four parts. Also, it is necessary to check the relationships of your main heads to be sure that they are balanced and coordinate. Develop your proposition with a time, space, reason, topic, problem-solution, or alternate emphasis, but be consistent. If you start with *time,* stay with it, and word all of your main heads in terms of *time.* Avoid mixing elements and you will do much toward avoiding audience confusion.

The Conclusion

The conclusion, of course, is the final phase of the speech. This is your last opportunity to accomplish your purpose—to make the audience favorably disposed in their reaction to your proposition. Neglect of the conclusion is a common failing of inexperienced speakers, as speech teachers will tell you. A speech on a good subject, that is clear in purpose and well conceived in other ways, deserves a carefully planned conclusion; moreover, and from a more important perspective, communication may depend on your handling of the closing remarks.

1. *Summarize your main heads.* Remind the audience of the main points you have covered. People forget more readily than many of us realize, and it is a wise speaker who does not take it for granted that his listeners have retained all he has said.

In addition, remember another human characteristic—semantic confusion. Words have different meanings for different people. You can express a thought in one way and get very little response, while your expression of the same thought in different terms may cause a noticeable reaction. When you summarize the main heads, choose new wording. If only one listener has been enlightened as a result, you can consider it worth the effort.

As the course progresses, employ various summary techniques. Some student speakers have been successful with example summaries. For instance, one speaker, after discussing three baseball skills, summarized by citing Mickey Mantle of the Yankees as an example of an outstanding player who possessed all three skills. You might employ an effective quotation to remind the audience of what you have covered. If you have "Freedom in a democracy" and "Control in a democracy" as your two main heads, this quotation of George Sutherland might provide a meaningful summary: "Liberty and order are the most precious possessions of man, and the essence of the problem of government is reconciliation of the two."

2. *After you have summarized and, in so doing, re-emphasized your main thoughts, make an appropriate ending.* Round out your speech to give a feeling of completeness. Avoid both abrupt and drawn out endings, and never make apologies. Above all, finish on a note which is consistent with your purpose. Your purpose may indicate that you should make an appeal at the end, or possibly you should leave the audience with a challenge or with a provocative thought.

Once again it may be appropriate to end with a fitting story or example or with the well-chosen words of an authority in the field. Remember that your job is to adapt your ideas to the lives of your listeners, to end with your audience mindful of your proposition. This fact should dictate your choice of closing content.

Let us assume that one of your fellow classmates plans to speak next week on the topic, "Gaining Respect for Redwood Trees." He will develop his proposition, "I want to remind you today of three uses of redwood trees," with these main heads:

A.   We use them for lumber.
B.   We use them for recreation.
C.   We use them as objects of aesthetic enjoyment.

After preparing the body of his speech, he begins to plan the conclusion. Of the many possible ways to complete his speech, which should he choose? Perhaps after his summary he could work in a quotation from Joyce Kilmer's "Trees," for instance. He decides that Kilmer's poem is overused, too trite. He could include statistics about the number of board feet of lumber produced annually or how many dog houses could be built from one tree. But, no, he reasons, cold figures would not convey to the audience his prime idea. He wants to end with an emphasis on the trees' grandeur. In addition, he would like to lighten the conclusion with some humor, if it would not detract from the main thought. After much thinking, he arrived at a conclusion. These are the words of the conclusion as he rehearsed it:

I have asked you today to give your attention to just three valuable benefits available from the two types of redwoods—*Sequoia sempervirens* and *Sequoia gigantea* [proposition restated]. We build with them, picnic beneath them, and gain inspiration from their beauty [summary]. You know, I once heard a story that brings out another benefit. It has to do with a man named Green who claimed to be a descendant of Sequoyah, the famous American Indian after whom the trees are named. Now Green wanted added family status. And so, inspired by the coastal redwoods, he chose as his family motto the Latin phrase used by botanists, *Sequoia sempervirens*—Sequoia ever*green*.

Whatever are our various uses of these noble creations, let us protect them and make sure that generations to come will also enjoy their magnificence.

One additional illustration of a conclusion to a speech may be helpful. Francis H. Horn, whose introduction to a speech you read earlier in the chapter, ended that speech to the students and faculty of Ricker College by relying on several typical methods for concluding. He used an authoritative quotation, challenged his audience, expressed faith in his audience, and throughout the conclusion, appealed to their idealism. At the same time, he consistently kept his thesis before the audience. He stressed that man, even in the face of great problems, will prevail in the making of a better world.

Given men and women of reason, moral earnestness, and a drive for a better world, a better world is possible. Man is responsible in this day of the bomb, just as surely as he was in the day of the bow and arrow, for the directions of his own life, of the society of which he is a part, and of the course of history. Karl Jaspers in his volume *The Future of Mankind* writes: "No single person can control history, but each is responsible for trying to influence it creatively. This is true in spite of all the demonic forces in personal and social life which tend constantly to pervert or destroy man's freedom and reason."

I urge you students to believe that there is no cause to feel insignificant or helpless; it is wrong to be indifferent or apathetic because the world seems too vast, its problems too complex, for one individual to do anything important about them. The world of tomorrow will be what individuals today want it to be. It is we who make it—you and I and other individuals like us.

The prospect for civilization, therefore, is good if each of us develops our intellectual powers to the maximum and then uses reason based upon knowledge in tackling problems. In college, you must do your best to learn not just facts, but those habits of thought and approaches to problems that mark the rational man.

But, again, intellectial capacity is not enough. You must commit yourself to high values. Your conduct must be governed by moral and spiritual considerations. Especially in these days, you must put concern for mankind over self-interest. If you and all of us do not, if we bow before the gods of materialistic self-interest, civilization is doomed just as surely as if someone pressed the button and released the missile or bomb that means nuclear war and ultimate destruction.

I have faith, particularly in young people, with whom I've worked as teacher and administrator for over thirty years. There is evidence on every hand that youth recognizes their responsibility for a better world; that they are accepting the challenge for service to society above self-interest. I believe that as new generations come along, dedicated to their own intellectual and moral best, the holocaust of war will be avoided and that slowly but surely mankind will move toward the longed-for world of true peace and universal brotherhood. The prospect for civilization, I am convinced, is a hopeful one.[3]

LET US SUMMARIZE

1. Recognize the need for and benefits of organization.
2. Continue to improve your outlining skill.
3. In the introduction, establish rapport with the listeners and guide them to the proposition.
4. State your proposition clearly and precisely.
5. Select for the body two, three, or four coordinate main heads which do not overlap.
6. In the conclusion, summarize, keep the proposition before the audience, and make appropriate final remarks.

SPEECH IDEAS

Your reservoir of knowledge and experience constitutes your best source of speech ideas; however, the following subjects may be consulted during the course—at least to stimulate your thinking.

The problem of juvenile delinquency
Liberal education or specialized education?
Armed service experiences
The values of an education
Rearing children
Student life and student government
Arts, crafts, hobbies, pets
People: Habits and characteristics
Hunting and fishing
Cooking and eating
Speaking and listening
Manufacturing and construction
Travel and places
Writing, literature, drama

Photography
Boating and water skiing
Religions of the world
A sense of humor
Salesmanship
Study methods
Ambitions and ideals
Astronomy
Fads and fashions
Police science, ballistics, fingerprinting
Choosing a major
Skin diving and spear fishing
Skiing and tobogganing
Words and meanings
Family life
Agriculture

3 "The Prospect for Civilization," pp. 95–96.

History	Alcohol and narcotics problems
Communities: Agencies and problems	Student-teacher relationships
Personal adventures and experiences	Customs and mores of other peoples
World affairs	Dancing
The guitar	Mining
Archaeology	The United Nations
Man's predicaments	Hypnotism
	Unidentified flying objects

MODEL SPEECH OUTLINE 1

(In sentence form and with introduction and conclusion written out)

Help Awaits

I• *Introduction*

You would be surprised at how many students go through a whole school year in need of instructors' extra help in their courses but who never take steps to get the help. Some may be afraid for one reason or another, like one girl who lived in fear of revealing her lack of knowledge of a subject. She thought that a visit to the instructor would certainly result in a low grade for the course.

Many of the reluctant ones might be encouraged to take advantage of the teacher's assistance if they could see how easy it is to go about it. That is what I want to talk about.

II• *Proposition:*   Follow these simple procedures for consulting with an instructor.

III• *Body*

A.   Arrange to see him during an office hour.
   1.   Choose a time when both of you are free.
   2.   Knock before entering.
   3.   Express clearly the purpose of your visit.
   4.   Listen carefully to his comments.
   5.   Do not take more than your share of time.
      a.   Remember, as one student unfortunately did not, that other students may be waiting. (*Example*)
      b.   Respond to clues that "tell" when time is up.
B.   Arrange to see him just before class.
   1.   Arrive a few minutes earlier than usual.
   2.   Meet him at the front of the room.
   3.   Once again, be clear and precise in stating your purpose.

        4. Avoid holding him beyond the class's starting time, as did the person who went on for twenty minutes while the class waited. (*Example*)

   C. Arrange for a special appointment

        1. Telephone or see him personally to make arrangements, as I did just this week. (*Example*)

        2. Follow suggestions for office hour consultation.

           a. Show courtesy by knocking.

           b. Be clear and purposeful.

           c. Listen carefully.

           d. Leave when your time is up.

IV• *Conclusion*

You see, it is not difficult. Dozens of people use these standard procedures every day. The next time that you have a problem, try one of them. Determine the instructor's office hours and knock on the door; or catch him before class (or right after class); or if these are not convenient, arrange for an appointment.

And do not be afraid. Instructors know that they cannot possibly distribute all of their vast store of collected wisdom of the ages in a class period. They expect to have people come by. They expect to see *you.*

John Steinbeck has some words in *The Grapes of Wrath* which I hope he will not mind my using for a purpose different from his. He said, or rather, one of his characters said, "I'm learnin' one thing good. Learnin' it all a time, ever' day. If you're in trouble, or hurt or need—go to the poor people. They're the only ones that'll help—the only ones." [4]

Maybe not *all* teachers are impoverished, but you can be sure that they will help when you approach them as I have explained.

MODEL SPEECH OUTLINE 2

(In topic form with introduction and conclusion fully outlined)

Lingual Logic

I• *Introduction*

   A. An American strength: Good government

        1. Democratic

        2. Functional

   B. An American weakness: Scant knowledge of languages

        1. Cannot communicate with foreign visitors

---

[4] From *The Grapes of Wrath* by John Steinbeck. Copyright 1939, © 1967 by John Steinbeck. Reprinted by permission of The Viking Press, Inc.

      2. Cannot communicate abroad
        a. An American mayor's trouble in Brussels (*Example*)
        b. An Olympics athlete and a Finnish girl (*Example*)

II• *Proposition:* Consider with me reasons why everyone should be able to speak at least one additional language.

III• *Body*
  A. Increased foreign travel
    1. Social embarrassment
    2. Shopping problems (*Example*)
  B. Expanded international business
    1. Loss of goodwill
    2. Loss of immediate business
      a. Experience of one sales representative (*Example*)
      b. Estimated over-all loss (*Statistics*)
  C. Greater need for diplomacy
    1. The diplomatic corps
    2. The private citizen as a diplomat
      a. Loss of prestige in Copenhagen (*Example*)
      b. The case of a traveler in Madrid (*Example*)
    3. Servicemen as diplomats
    4. Peace Corps

IV• *Conclusion*
  A. The shrinking world
    1. Travel
    2. Business
    3. Foreign affairs
  B. Must understand others and their culture
  C. Army language school proves practicability (*Example*)

ALTERNATE OUTLINE FORM

Some instructors prefer that their students center the names of the four parts of a speech and not attach a number or letter to them, as this revision of the first model illustrates in partial reconstruction.

Introduction
You would be surprised at how many students go through a whole school year in need of instructor's help. . . .

Proposition
Follow these simple procedures for consulting an instructor.

Body
I• Arrange to see him during an office hour.

A.   Choose a time . . .
B.   Knock . . .
>>>>>>>>>>>>>>>>>>>>>>and so forth.

II•   Arrange to see him just before class.
>>>>>>>>>>>>>>>>>>>>>>and so forth.

III•   Arrange for a special appointment.
>>>>>>>>>>>>>>>>>>>>>>and so forth.

Conclusion

You see, it is not difficult. Dozens of people use these standard procedures. . . .

MODEL SPEAKING NOTES

In giving the speech represented by the first model outline, your speaking notes, if you were to use any, might include the following points (see page 57), placed on a 3x5 card.

Using the Notes

1. Write the notes in large letters, and avoid cluttering them with nonessential data.

2. Write just enough of a heading to allow for recall of its meaning.

3. Upon going up to speak, place your notes on the speakers' stand or hold them in your hand, whichever is more comfortable and less distracting.

4. Use them openly. Avoid trying to conceal your notes in the palm of one hand, and do not cast desperate and furtive glances into your hand in attempts to keep your audience from knowing that you are using them. Such behavior is unnecessary and distracting. You cannot fool most people. Why should you want to anyway?

5. Refer to your notes as infrequently as possible—only when you need to be reminded of the next thought to cover. Calmly look down, pick up the thought quickly, and speak along as far as possible before having to look down again. Remember, overuse can cause separation of speaker and audience, the antithesis of communication.

6. You probably should read long quotations and complicated or specific data—statistics, for example. But this gives no excuse for neglecting eye contact. Practice to ensure an effective presentation.

7. Learn eventually to emancipate yourself from your notes. You may surprise yourself by developing to the point of rarely needing to consult them. Work toward that end.

```
┌─────────────────────────────────────────┐
│ Intro.                                   │
│     Many do not consult instructors,     │
│         e.g. fearful girl.               │
│                                          │
│ Prop.: Simple procedures for cons.       │
│                                          │
│ Body                                     │
│     A. Office hours                      │
│        Choose time; knock; be clear;     │
│        Listen; time (e.g.)               │
│                                          │
│     B. Before class                      │
│        Come early; meet in front;        │
│        Be clear; time (e.g.)             │
│                                          │
│     C. Appointment                       │
│        Arrange (e.g.); suggestions       │
│        of "A" above                      │
│                                          │
│ Concl.                                   │
│     Not difficult; summary; try--        │
│     instructors expect; Steinbeck:       │
│     "I'm learnin' one thing good.        │
│     Learnin' it all a time, ever'        │
│     day. If you're in trouble, or        │
│     hurt or need--go to the poor         │
│     people. They're the only ones        │
│     that'll help--the only ones."        │
│     Not all teachers impoverished,       │
│     but they'll help.                    │
└─────────────────────────────────────────┘
```

Fig. 3–1   Facsimile of a 3x5 card containing speaking notes based on *Model Speech Outline 1*.

BASIC ASSIGNMENT

Prepare a speech using the plan explained in this chapter: Introduction, Proposition, Body, and Conclusion. Use an example (anecdote, case in point, or meaningful story) to support each main head.

Develop your introduction and conclusion by employing the methods suggested in this chapter that seem appropriate for your particular case.

Make a full outline to submit to your instructor.

Reminders:
1. Arrange your ideas carefully in order to help your audience to understand your ideas and their relationships.
2. Continue to improve your extemporaneous style by practicing the talk aloud several times before the day of presentation.
3. You can lessen stage fright by choosing a subject which is interesting and well known to you.

Suggested Exercise A

The following speech bodies are in some way poorly organized. Each one contains a major flaw. First, diagnose the difficulty; then, do the necessary rearranging.

Sample 1

II• *Proposition:*   Consider with me the ways in which television production has improved in the last ten years.

III• *Body*
    A. The programing is better.
        1. There is more variety.
        2. There is better quality.
    B. The technical aspects are better.
        1. Improved use of sound can be noted.
        2. More appropriate lighting methods are used.
        3. Refined camera techniques are used.
    C. The performers are better.
        1. The acting has improved.
        2. Announcers are more proficient.
        3. There are better musicians.
    D. Even the commercial announcers are better.
        1. They are more natural.
        2. They are less antagonistic.

Sample 2

II• *Proposition:*   Our last fishing trip was something less than a success.

III• *Body*
    A. We were up at 4:30 A.M.
        1. We awakened the neighbors.
        2. Ben could not find the car key.

    B. We were fishing by 7:30 A.M.
        1. I broke an expensive rod.
        2. We lost most of the bait.
        3. We caught only one small fish.
    C. We had a flat tire coming home.
        1. We started home at 2:30 P.M.
        2. Ben had no spare tire.
        3. We hitchhiked home.

Suggested Exercise B

Either outline these speech introductions and conclusions or draft outlines for the bodies, or do both.

Sample 1

   I• *Introduction*

      Last Thursday, while watching our basketball team practice in the gym, I started to think about the importance of physical education.

      Strong bodies and teamwork are needed in almost all phases of living. We work; we play; sometimes we defend our country.

      But down there on the court I saw only ten active people out of a student body of 5000. Where were the other 4990 getting their training? In physical education classes? Yes, and I learned later that several hundred take part in intramural athletics—organized, on-campus team competition.

      Are you, too, interested in developing physical skills, and in learning how to work better with others and having fun?

  II• *Proposition:* Let me tell you how to take part in the intramural athletic program.

 III• *Body*

 IV• *Conclusion*

      So you see it is not difficult at all. Just register with the director of activities, join a team or form one, and schedule your games.

      Everyone can play and have a good time. You may not be a Willie Mays, or a Jerry West of basketball fame, or a Johnny Unitas, but you will profit from the experience, especially if you remember the words of a wise old philosopher: "Learn to play when you are young, for without play in your life, work has no meaning."

Sample 2

I• *Introduction*

Remember the story of King Midas? Everything he touched turned to gold, and he was very happy until he found that his food, too, turned into indigestible chunks of gold. He was greedy, and his greed caused him no end of displeasure.

Now there are other more desirable types of the golden touch that can bring pleasure and satisfaction to us all.

Would you like to have a golden touch that would allow you to make one of the greatest contributions to humanity?

I am speaking of a very constructive kind that seems so necessary these days, the touch that has been lost by some parents—raising children properly.

II• *Proposition:*   Here is how you can begin to acquire this golden touch for able parenthood.

III• *Body*

IV• *Conclusion*

"As the twig is bent, so is the tree inclined." Give your children a proper start. Remember to love them, guide them, and provide for their physical needs.

The golden touch is not so magical after all, is it? There is no magic wand or secret formula. If any secret exists at all, it exists in the hearts of each parent and each prospective parent. The means to the end are there to be developed. Can you think of any more important end of human endeavor?

Suggested Exercise C

Each of the following series of main heads has a special characteristic (either topical order, time order, space order, or reason order). Label each in the series.

Sample 1

II• *Proposition:*   I want to describe what I consider to be a student's typical day.

III• *Body*
    A.   First, let us look at the morning hours—classes.
    B.   The afternoon hours are just as unexciting.
    C.   The evening hours are taken up with quiet study.

Sample 2

II• *Proposition:* Let us consider three important safety features found on many modern automobiles.

III• *Body*
    A. Collapsible steering wheels are used in some cars.
    B. Seat belts are standard equipment.
    C. Padded dashboards are common.

Sample 3

II• *Proposition:* It is not really difficult to understand why people act like people.

III• *Body*
    A. They do so because of their heredity.
    B. They do so because of their environment.

Sample 4

II• *Proposition:* Come along with me, and let us explore what many consider to be the most exciting sections of Disneyland.

III• *Body*
    A. Frontierland will take you back to early America.
    B. Tomorrowland will take you into the future.
    C. Adventureland will take you to foreign settings.

Suggested Exercise D
Write two, three, or four coordinate and nonoverlapping main heads for the following propositions:

    No. 1. These are my arguments, then, for urging you to read at least one good book a month.
    No. 2. I would recommend certain changes in our national election procedures.

Suggested Exercise E
In a brief talk, tell how the lack of organization thwarted some human effort. Your case need not refer to the speech field specifically. Consult your own experience or books, magazines, and so forth.

Suggested Exercise F
Shorten and make more concise the Model Speech Outline 2 that is found in this chapter. Rewrite it in the form of speaking notes.

Suggested Exercise G

Prepare a complete outline of Howard W. Runkel's speech, "Making Lincoln Live," found in Appendix A.

Suggested Exercise H

One experienced speech teacher suggests this exercise. Bring to class as many points as you can think of on the topic, "How to Buy a *Good* Used Car." The instructor will list all of the points on the board and together you will try to formulate a proposition and discover a logical grouping from which to build a sentence outline.

CHAPTER FOUR

Strengthening Your Thoughts

*. . . speech is a joint game by the talker and
the listener against the forces of confusion.*
—NORBERT WIENER [1]

The wisdom reflected in this quotation is surely nothing new to you
at this stage of your speech work. Look back to your earlier class work.
Why is it necessary to use a proposition that states your purpose in a
complete sentence? Why should it express only one idea? Why should
it be stated briefly? Why is it necessary to organize your ideas? You
know the answers: You must do these things in order to transmit your
ideas clearly and with some certainty. In order to communicate and to
conquer the forces of confusion, you must help the listener understand
your thoughts and let him know the direction they are taking.

Initially, then, you can work toward communication by being clear
in purpose and sound in arrangement. Also, there are factors besides
the speech itself with which the speaker must cope if he is to avoid confusion and lead listeners.

DYNAMICS OF THE AUDIENCE

That person or group of people with whom you speak, the audience,
is made up of an ever-changing, highly complex combination of elements. Imagine a speech situation, possibly your own class. It is Monday, and the first speaker of the day walks to the front of the room.
He looks out at the audience. What does he see? Does he see a group
of robots, each of whom is assuming exactly the same appearance and
position? Of course not; he sees a diverse array of individual persons
manifesting a variety of outward characteristics. Some are sitting up

[1] *The Human Use of Human Beings* (New York, 1956), p. 92.

straight in their chairs; some are semireclining; some are looking out the window, looking at the wall, or at a neighbor. He sees smiles and frowns, looks of anticipation and looks of lassitude, appearances of happiness, and appearances of unrest.

The speaker begins, and he soon observes changes in his audience. The one in the third row who seemed rather gloomy before now smiles at one of the speaker's comments. The fellow who was slouching down is now sitting more erectly. The blond girl in the back is looking out the window. Things are happening, but it is only the obvious evidence that can be noticed by the speaker.

What does he not know? What can he not see? Like viewing an iceberg—only to an enormously greater degree—the speaker sees but a fraction of the audience dynamics. He does not know that one of his listeners worked all night and is plagued by drowsiness, that another is worried about failing a history test, that another is thinking ahead to tonight's game, that another is remembering the appointment he forgot, and that another has broken up with her boy friend. It would be absurd to expect you as a speaker to know all such details about your audience, but it is imperative that you have a general realization of the "forces of confusion" with which you are dealing.

Among the multitude of human conditions that may intrude to challenge communication, six appear more frequently than many others. We discuss them here to indicate to you some of the behavioral characteristics of the people for whom speakers plan messages. Speakers ought to recognize the competition faced in attempting to establish a meeting of minds.

1. *Preoccupation.*   As implied above, people's minds may be captured either by worry over problems or by anticipation of some pleasure. They may be "a thousand miles away," as the saying goes. At a later point in the chapter, we shall offer some suggestions for meeting this condition.

2. *Indifference.*   Occasionally, certain members of an audience may be apathetic; they just may not care. A solution to apathy ought to start with subject choice and continue through all phases of preparation. Possibly your thorough planning (one way of showing that you care about your audience) will stimulate their interest in your proposal.

3. *Fatigue and Discomfort.*   Recognize the possibility of having a tired person in your audience—or someone who is not feeling well. Disposed either way, he will not be at his best. To compensate, you must make your best effort in the arts of communication.

4. *Bewilderment.*   Even intelligent people—college students, for instance—can lose track of a train of thought or become perplexed by specialized words or terms. We, as speakers—all of us—sometimes

digress. We occasionally cover thoughts too quickly. We at times use phrases that are totally foreign to others. They may be the right words to use, the only ones to carry the idea, but we are obliged to provide for clarity in their use.

5. *Lack of Confidence.*   Confusion can result from a listener's lack of confidence in his ability to understand. Now and then, and unbeknownst to anybody in the room, a speaker may face a member of an audience who, not believing in his powers to comprehend, is not able to keep his mind on the discourse. "Why try?" he unconsciously asks himself; "I am not able to understand it." The speaker's solution—his responsibility—is to show him that he can comprehend. How? By taking special care to make the speech comprehensible; means are available.

6. *Resistance.*   By *resistance* we mean the reluctance of one to exert himself to listen, his unwillingness to make the effort. Resistance, different from apathy, may be a conscious "dragging of the feet," or it may represent a "show me" attitude. In an extreme form, common in controversy, it manifests itself as hostility and may indicate fear of a threatening idea or antipathy toward the speaker or occasion.

This chapter will offer aids to help meet these competing conditions.

THE PHYSICAL ENVIRONMENT

In addition to the human element, every speaker needs to be aware of his physical surroundings, especially those which compete with his efforts to communicate. Let us go back to the speaker in front of his audience. As he talks, someone drops a book and attention is lost. An airplane flies low overhead. Carpenters are working next door. Someone comes into the room. The room is stuffy, or the room is too cold. The seats are uncomfortable and poorly arranged. Once again, we recognize forces of confusion at work; this time they are physical forces which challenge the speaker's attempts to communicate.

If no one can do anything to improve the physical environment, listeners and speaker must make the best adjustment possible. Both ought to ignore the existing distraction and bring to bear effective methods, even more assiduously than they ordinarily would.

THE ORAL MODE

Is it any wonder that speaking, with all its variables, is such a demanding activity? Now, in written communication the problems are quite different in some ways. The contact between originator and receiver is indirect, and the receiver of the message controls the experience. If distracted by an emotional or physical factor, the reader can reread a sentence or a paragraph. He can transport himself to a better environment, but a listener usually must stay where he is. If he is tired, the reader may put his book aside and go back to it at a later time; the fatigued listener has only the present opportunity to receive the message.

In oral communication, you, the speaker, are the one who makes decisions about how fast to go and when to review. You have ideas that you want to get across, and in order to do so, you must anticipate and contend with the various emotional and physical distractions. You must find ways to keep your listeners ever mindful of your "whereabouts," to clarify what you are saying, and to enforce your thoughts. How can you bring a wayward listener back into the stream of your thought? What methods can you use to compete with preoccupation, indifference, fatigue and discomfort, bewilderment, listeners' lack of confidence, resistance, and poor physical conditions? At this time, let us discuss four aids which are at your disposal for reducing the number and intensity of possible distractions: transition, restatement and repetition, definition, and explanation.

FOUR AIDS

Transition

One way to diminish confusion and to work for clarity and certainty in the expression of ideas is to show the relationships of your ideas as you move along during the presentation of a speech. In order to keep your audience continually aware of what you are saying and where you are taking them, link new thoughts to those previously offered. Connect and integrate new parts as you add them to the whole.

For example, if in one part of a speech you are discussing television as a teaching aid and your next point is television as a surveillance device in industry, you must indicate to your audience that you have stepped to another thought. Also, you ought to put the new thought in perspective, show how it fits in. You might say, "From the uses of television as a teaching aid, let us turn to television for industrial surveillance, a less important use, possibly, but one with increasing applications." Using the first model speech at the end of Chapter Three for reference, the speaker might begin his second main head by saying, "If you cannot see the instructor during an office hour, arrange to see him before class." These stepping stones between points are called transitions. They rarely add much new thought, yet they are essential aids in speaking. They serve to show listeners the progression of thought, how one idea is associated with another, and which ideas are emphasized and which are subordinated.

In order to compete with the various forces of confusion, you should guide your audience with the assistance of transitions throughout the entire talk.

1. *To the proposition.* Lead from the introduction to the proposition so that your purpose sentence seems to fall in place and logically seems to be the next thing to say.

2. *To the first main head.* As this point, tie in the first main head merely by repeating the essential thought of the proposition as you present the main head statement.

3. *To subheads.* These are not major transitions, and we mention them only to indicate that as speakers we link minor ideas, too. We use transitional aids to relate subheads of thought many times a day without realizing it. Usually, these are brief and oftentimes one-word conjunctions.

4. *To each new main head.* You can avoid considerable misunderstanding if you keep your listeners aware of your main points and their relationships. Let the audience know where you have been and where you are going. When you approach a new main head, show them how it relates to the proposition and other main heads. You may be able to fit in the new main head with a few words or a sentence; at other times you may need a full paragraph to integrate the idea.

5. *To the closing remarks.* In moving to their final remarks, many speakers seem hard-pressed for words. How many times have you heard the trite phrase, "In conclusion . . ."? It is easy to avoid such overused expressions if you will allow your purpose to dictate your wording. Ask yourself what thoughts or attitudes you want to convey. "What parting tone will help me to realize my goal?"

A person with an informative speech on uses of television may accomplish the transition by saying, as the first words of his conclusion, "These, then, are but three of the applications of television—in education, in industry, and in military operations."

A person with a persuasive speech on the same topic, perhaps with the same proposition, might begin his conclusion quite differently. For example, "Well, now, what can you and I do to convince others of the benefits of utilizing television in the schools, the factories, and the armed services?"

Probably you have concluded from these two examples that the transition to the closing remarks is a summary of the proposition and main heads. Quite right. It is the first point of the conclusion and a review of the principal statements of the speech as it unfolded.

Below is an illustration of the placement and wording of transitions in an abbreviated outline. Only major transitional statements are included. They are italicized. In the column to the right are brief explanations of the process at each point.

I• *Introduction*

There are many people and agencies active in our society with an intent to influence us in one way or another. Some want our allegiance; some want our vote; some want our money. *We come in contact with their methods every day, and we should be aware of them.*

This is the lead to the proposition, providing a short step to it.

II• *Proposition:*   Allow me to describe three techniques of propagandists.

III• *Body*

A. *The first device of the propagandist to recognize is* the bandwagon approach.

After stating the proposition, you move to the first main head with words that tell what point is coming and how it relates to the proposition. Then you discuss the point, the main head.

B. *Now, seeing that propagandists use the bandwagon technique to ensnare the unthinking, let us consider next* a language trick that fools many—the use of glittering generalities.

You take up B by showing its connection to A. You make it a part of the developing pattern of ideas by restating the essential thoughts of the proposition and main head A.

C. *If they have not put you on the bandwagon or captivated you with their high-sounding generalizations, they* may try a lesser-used technique—card stacking.

Again, aware of listeners' needs to be reminded of their whereabouts, you review prior major points as you bring forth a new one. Notice also, the slight subordination of C, the mentioning of "lesser-used."

IV• *Conclusion*

Hopefully, now, you will be able to recognize what prop-

Summary of the proposition. Note variety in word choice, providing *agandists are doing to you when they try the band-wagon approach or dazzle you with those shiny words or when they stack the deck in their dealings.*

(balance of the conclusion omitted)

interest and perhaps added understanding. Summary of the main heads. Note again the variety.

How would you finish the speech?

There are very few hard and fast rules of speaking which apply to all speakers, all speeches, all audiences, and all occasions. One, however, always will apply: *Your purpose will indicate why, where, and how frequently you should use a speaking technique.* This rule is relevant especially to the use of transitions. The following specific suggestions are pertinent also.

1. *Vary your word choice occasionally when relating one thought to another.* A synonym used in place of a frequently mentioned word can add variety and new meaning to a given thought. For instance, a "propaganda device" might at times be called a "tool" or "a technique" or "a trick." Consult your dictionary for synonyms, or better yet, a *thesaurus,* and get into the habit of enlivening your speaking with variety.

   Some overused transitional words and phrases are "and," "but," "so," "besides," "in addition to," "another," and so forth. Try different means of relating thought creatively, and in so doing, let the thought and your purpose tell you what pattern of words will be effective.

2. *Be natural and unmechanical in the employment of transitions.* Usually there is a tendency for people to be rigid and mechanical when first trying something. It happens when one drives a friend's car or when one first handles a tennis racquet. In either case, the person feels a bit rigid or awkward because he is not familiar with the object. This is true, also, with the initial *conscious* use of transition. At first, you may feel restricted, awkward, or otherwise, insecure, but with practice and the resulting familiarity, you will soon come to appreciate transitional aids. You will be able to use them gracefully and weave them into the total fabric of your oral effort.

Repetition and Restatement

Other means for contending with the forces of confusion are repetition and restatement. Repetition refers to repeating a term or sentence in the same form as first expressed. Restatement refers to expressing the thought again but with altered wording or form.

The values of these aids are apparent. If a listener is unimpressed with a vital point, repetition of it may cause him to recognize its significance. Repetition serves to emphasize, to stress. When used purposefully, for a reason, it is a recommended method of strengthening thought; when it is not a part of a conscious design and merely the result of a sparse vocabulary, it is valueless.

If a listener's mind has gone astray, restatement of an important point may bring him back and help him to apprehend the point. If a point is not clearly understood, restatement may bring light to it. Also, through variety, it can bring a freshness or new dimension to an idea.

Probably the most commonly repeated or restated thoughts in a speech are the major points, especially the proposition and main heads. This is not surprising. After all, they are the chief assertions of substance in a speech, the most important. Notice how repetition (reuse of identical words) strengthens the following thoughts.

> And while there may be some who say that the business of government is so important that it should not be confined to those who govern, in this free society of ours the consent and, may I say, the support of the citizens of this country is essential, if this, or any other piece of progressive legislation, is going to be passed. Make no mistake about it. *Make no mistake about it.*

> —*John F. Kennedy, to the National Council of Senior Citizens, in 1962, on an issue of medical care*

> This is a free country, my friends. Yes, *this is a free country,* though certain groups by their recent actions would deny it.

The following samples show the effect one can achieve in restating (recasting with new words) a point.

> Franklin D. Roosevelt had an ability to relate an anecdote. *He had a special knack for telling a story.*

> Smog limits visibility. *This haze occasionally prevents one from seeing clearly a hundred yards ahead. Certainly, polluted air can be as restricting to the vision as fog.*

> Physically speaking, we cannot separate. *We cannot remove our respective sections from each other nor build an impassable wall between them.* A husband and wife may be divorced and go out of the presence and beyond the reach of each other, but the *different parts of our country cannot do this.*

> —*Abraham Lincoln, First Inaugural Address*

> Today the supreme expression of historical irony is that the real war of extermination is possible, *the final destruction of the human species,* and just as the pressure of competitive need is withdrawn. We no longer need our neighbors' hunting grounds. The rationale of separate, desperate sovereignty has all but vanished in the last two or three decades. But just as the reason vanishes, *the means take over.* We can *wipe out*

the children of God just at the moment when, at last, the possibility of nourishing all of them begins to dawn. Irony of ironies!—The scientific means to end the need for war are twisted to ensure that *the war of final extermination at last becomes a possibility.*

> —*Adlai E. Stevenson, Charter Day, University of California, 1964*

Repetition and Restatement Combined

It is my purpose today to sound a note of caution and to say that we are in danger of building our expectations unsoundly and too high. There is no magic in education. *Those whose expectations are too high will be disillusioned;* it is quite possible that a wave of anti-intellectualism will follow *this disillusionment.* I repeat: *There is no magic in education!* What we need is a view of education that is crisp, clear, sure, unmagical.

> —*Dr. James M. Moudy, Chancellor of Texas Christian University, at his inauguration.*[2]

To get ahead in the world, you have to work. *You have to work to accomplish your goals. You have to work to make a name. You have to work to succeed.*

Definition

An all-too-frequent error in speaking is the assumption that one's chosen words will be understandable to all listeners. It is often hard for a person to realize that a certain word or phrase that he uses daily may not be meaningful to some listeners. A basic fact of our existence offers a prime explanation for the development of individualized modes of expression: the human tendency to identify with groups or subcultures. We set ourselves off in units of one kind or another and attempt our communicative exchanges with the language codes of those units. Such isolation can make communication in some situations difficult, for terms of one group may not have currency with another. Consider certain of the forms that isolation assumes.

First of all, we set ourselves off in family units where we develop our usage of distinct terms. Some terms used in a family may not be used at all by the family across the street or in another part of town. For instance, the members of one family may say "bumpershoot" and never umbrella; they may say "cornucopia" and never ice cream cone. Many families have retained the use of terms that members coined as babies—cute phraseology that "caught on" and is used for years by the family. From your experience, can you think of examples of individualized family speech?

Secondly, the social groupings of people can be powerful influences on word usage. In response to the accelerated pace of living and the

<hr>

[2] "Education Without Magic," *Vital Speeches of the Day,* XXXII (February 15, 1966), p. 275.

more impersonal aspects of society, we set ourselves off in smaller groups and develop a strong sense of belonging (identification) with the groups. We join car clubs, service clubs, and bridge clubs; we regularly attend Kaffeeklatsches, poker parties, and study sessions. Certain groups, especially those in which common interest and purpose are deepest and most compelling, often become marked by their unique language. Individualized language usage seems almost to be a ritual. So-called beatniks speak a language different in part from that of the larger society to which they are reacting. Some words are "in" with people in young adolescence, the junior high school "crowd"; some are used only by "squares." The "Jet Set," the "Mods," "Surfers," and numerous other classifications of persons—all have their special vocabularies. Almost any group with some cohesion has its in words and taboo words. Use of the former and avoidance of the latter gives the individual identification and status within the group. The status derives partly from the uniqueness of the group, that is, from its being *apart* from the larger society. The existence of certain groups represents a wish to reject the "Establishment" or the unattractive features and imposed standards of the general society. Language patterns of groups further their separation from the general society and act as instruments to accomplish the rejection. Some groups seem to say with their specialized vocabularies, "Get away, world; this is my realm; you cannot belong, for you are not one of us." In sum, the benefits of association with a smaller unit may be increased by dissociation from the larger. Such seems to be our nature. A problem arises only when a member of a subgroup attempts to communicate with members of other groups or with people at large. The solution is identification with the people *whom he is addressing* and a consciousness of the need to define specialized terms. Much may depend on a speaker's willingness or desire to address others on their ground, or on his ability to find a *common* ground—a better solution.

We also isolate ourselves geographically and learn to use words having meaning in the region in which we live. One student speaker in a college on the West Coast caused considerable consternation in his audience when, in a matter-of-fact manner, he mentioned "the dirty thirties" two or three times in a speech. Being from Kansas and often having heard Kansans refer to the terrible dust storms of the 1930s, the term was virtually a part of his life, but West Coast listeners had not had his experience.

In this day of intense specialization, we isolate ourselves in our fields of primary interest. We adopt the language of our specialties and upon occasion find it difficult to communicate with people in other fields. We talk "cybernetics," "cost accounting," "education," "IBM stenography," "supersonic flight," or "heatless cooking."

In order to be able to talk with people, it is first necessary to recognize your own areas of isolation and then to develop an awareness of the need for definition. Do not take it for granted that your audience is familiar with every word in your active vocabulary. Define your terms, especially the key terms and accompanying words. In addition to using mere synonyms, often insufficient, you can define in a number of ways:

1. *Classification.*   Define by telling the class to which the word or phrase belongs.

> A *hellgrammite,* much used as fish bait, is the larva of a certain insect, the dobson fly.
>
> A *novel* is a long, fictional work of prose.
>
>   Now, having said all these optimistic things, let me add one more article of faith: I hate *Pollyannas*—people who believe all these wonderful things will come to pass without any problems. I do not need to tell you, of all people, that the introduction of automation creates enormous problems . . ."
>   —*Thomas J. Watson, Jr., of IBM, to the National Conference of Editorial Writers, Milwaukee.*[3]

2. *Etymology.*   Define by telling the origin or derivation of the word or phrase.

> *Algebra* comes from the Arabian word "al-jabr" which meant the reduction of parts to a whole or reunion of broken parts or bonesetting.
>
> The *guillotine* was named after J. I. Guillotin, a French physician, who proposed that the instrument be used because other means of execution were inhumane.

3. *Example.*   Define by giving an example of what you mean.

> I can define *juvenile delinquent* best by illustration. Let us say that Roy X is a sixteen-year-old boy who consistently finds himself in trouble with the law as a result of his treatment of others and his treatment of the property of others. Roy X goes beyond plain mischief and into the realm of the criminal—car theft, slashing tires, assault, wrecking school property. Roy X is a juvenile delinquent.

4. *Negation.*   Define by telling what the term is not.

> By *outlawing war,* I do not mean effecting merely a weak international agreement. I do not mean compromising to limit arms or deciding to annihilate only military installations. I mean . . .
>
> The *heart of a business organization* is not the profit and loss statement, a battery of calculating machines, sales slogans, liberal expense accounts, or rich mahogany paneling. It is . . .

[3] "Automation," *Vital Speeches of the Day,* XXXII (November 1, 1965), p. 50.

5. *Statement of Criteria.*   Define by listing the conditions or require-ments that are necessary to qualify a term for use. A definition stating the necessary criteria often follows definition by classification and is more specific.

> A *mammal* is an animal [classification] that is warm-blooded, is a verte-brate, suckles its young, and has a thorax and abdomen separated by a diaphragm.
>
> To be called a *good talk*, a speech must be on an appropriate subject, be clear in purpose, be well organized, be well supported, and be ade-quately delivered.

6. *Authority.*   Define with the assistance of an authoritative source. Though a definition by itself may be one of the standard types, the reputation of the source gives it special character and effect.

> The *history of the world* is the record of a man in quest of his daily bread and butter.
>
> —*H. W. Van Loon,* The Story of Mankind
>
> A *good speaker* is a good man skilled in speaking.
>
> —*Cato*

Needless to say, speakers may find more than one type of definition valuable in clarifying a term. For instance, observe the strength result-ing from a combination of classification and negation in this definition:

> Basically, the standard TV documentary today misunderstands the mean-ing of the word, *objectivity.* Objectivity means judging each case or story or situation on its own merits, applying a powerfully schooled and disciplined judgment.
>
> Objectivity does not mean what present documentarians think it does: balancing each thought or statement with its opposite.
>
> —*Howard K. Smith, ABC News, to the National Conference on Broadcasting and Election Campaigns, Washington, D.C.*[4]

Explanation

Another process for purposefully contending with ambiguity and, possibly antipathy, is explanation. You will often find it valuable when discussing principles, conditions, concepts, or the operations of some-thing. A full explanation may be the answer to the resistance of an audience to a controversial proposal. It may show that no difference of opinion exists after all, that speaker and listener share the same belief. Once during a speech course a student speaker spoke on a rather con-troversial topic, and when he sat down, he found himself having to answer a great number of challenges to his ideas. After he clarified his position with an *explanation* of what he had meant, the class responded, almost in unison, "Why didn't you say that *in your*

---

[4] "Television in the Nation's Service," *Vital Speeches of the Day,* XXXII (Novem-ber 15, 1965), p. 80.

speech?" Speaker and listeners, it seemed, were not at odds on essential points. Yes, he should have explained more in his speech.

All of us sometimes take it for granted that listeners understand, that it is unnecessary to extend an idea or add ramifications. We should check our discourses for spots needing explication, for technicalities and other statements requiring interpretation. The following are examples of the use of explanation.

> . . . the undergraduate in a university of 20,000 or 30,000 students can be hopelessly and tragically lost. When he enters college at about 18, he is neither quite an adolescent nor quite an adult. He is searching for an identity of his own, to find out what kind of person he is, to see how he compares with others, and to establish his own philosophy of life. He wants desperately to be a participant in a community which cares about him. He believes that faculty members should worry at least as much about him as about the research projects they are pursuing with the aid of money from the Federal Government. He scorns the rules and regulations of the IBM machine type university, but at the same time is tortuously looking for help in forming his own moral code.
> —*Dr. Robert J. Wert of Stanford University, at a convocation, California State College, Los Angeles.*[5]

> The proposition is peace. Not peace through the medium of war; not peace to be hunted through the labyrinth of intricate and endless negotiations; but peace to arise out of universal discord, fomented from principle, in all parts of the empire; not peace to depend on the juridical determination of perplexing questions, or the precise marking of the shadowy boundaries of a complex government. It is simple peace, sought in its natural course and its ordinary haunts. It is peace sought in the spirit of peace, and laid in principles purely pacific.
> —*Edmund Burke, "On Conciliation with America,"* House of Commons, 1775

> Who are the working women? They represent about one-third of the women in our population. Of those between 18 and 24 years of age, 45 percent are employed—nearly one out of every two. These are traditionally the premarital years or the years of newlywed status, when the girl is trying out her job skills, acquiring a work record, and perhaps helping a young husband financially while he completes his education and strives for a foothold in his chosen field.
> —*Mary G. Roebling of the Trenton Trust Company, to Pennsylvania Federation of Women's Clubs, Pittsburgh*[6]

LET US SUMMARIZE

In that now famous speech that he gave 200 years ago, Patrick Henry said: "I have but one lamp by which my feet are guided; and that is the lamp of experience." Following the lead of that fiery patriot, we

[5] "The Restless Generation and Undergraduate Education," *Representative American Speeches: 1964–1965,* Lester Thonssen, ed. (New York, 1965), p. 52.

[6] "The Power and Influence of Women," *Vital Speeches of the Day,* XXXI (September 1, 1965), p. 690.

suggest that you take the advice suggested by the experience of speakers, past and present. A study of their works will demonstrate the value of the four aids that we have discussed. You can strengthen your thoughts by using transitions to relate one to another and to keep your audience constantly apprised of events. You can further reinforce your talk by repeating or restating key ideas, by defining terms in the way that you want them to be taken, and by clarifying with explanation. These are very important processes. Do not neglect them, for they can serve significantly in meeting the ever-present forces of confusion.

MODEL SPEECH OUTLINE 1

(In sentence form and with major transitions italicized)

Love Thyself in Order to Love Thy Neighbor

I• *Introduction*
  A. There are lots of unhappy people living in our time, a time that some call the "Age of Anxiety." (*Definition*)
  B. But there are many happy people, too.
  C. To get a firsthand view of the feelings of people, station yourself at some inconspicuous spot downtown and observe.
    1. Observe the behavior characteristics that indicate frustration, fear, insecurity, and general discontent.
    2. Observe the behavior characteristics that indicate confidence, security, satisfaction, and ability to cope with life. (*Example*)
  D. You may ask yourself *what it is that makes one person happy and another person unhappy.*

II• *Proposition:*   May I offer two underlying qualities of the happy person?

III• *Body*
  A. *His basic characteristic is that* he likes himself.
    1. He respects himself and recognizes his own worth. (*Restatement*)
    2. His love of self is wholesome and balanced, not of the type referred to by George Eliot: "He was like a cock who thought the sun had risen to hear him crow." (*Definition*)
    3. His love of self comes from self-analysis both of his strengths and weaker areas.
    4. There is a vast difference between having true self-

respect and being one's own worst enemy, as in the cases
of Albert and Ernest. (*Example*)

    B.   *If he likes himself, the happy person will have a second feature;* he will like other people.

        1.   By "like," I mean "get along with and accept." (*Definition*)

        2.   He will have a minimum of prejudice and hate. (*Example*)

        3.   He will be unafraid in his daily dealings with people.

IV• *Conclusion*

    A.   *The contented person has two prime qualities.*

        1.   *He likes himself.*

        2.   *He likes others.*

    B.   Knowledge is the real key to happiness.

        1.   Learn to accept yourself by learning about yourself.

        2.   Learn to accept people in general by studying the needs and motivations of people.

        3.   Appreciate the wisdom of Alexander Pope who said, "The proper study of mankind is man." (*Quotation*)

MODEL SPEECH OUTLINE 2

(In topic form, except for main heads which are written out to demonstrate applications of transitions, italicized)

The Grand Wagon

I• *Introduction*

    A.   Different types of cars from which to choose

        1.   Sports cars (*Example*)

        2.   Moderately-priced American cars (*Example*)

        3.   The big automobile (*Example*)

    B.   *The ideal all-around car: the station wagon*

II• *Proposition:* Let me suggest that you investigate the station wagon before you buy.

III• *Body*

    A.   *This versatile vehicle* is just the thing for daily use. (*Restatement*)

        1.   For shopping (*Explanation*)

        2.   For transporting children (*Example*)

        3.   For studying between classes with built-in desk (*Example*)

    B. *Such a car is not restricted to serve merely as a shopping cart or mobile office;* it can help you earn money.
       1. To help pay your way through school (*Restatement*)
       2. To distribute newspapers to a crew of paper boys (*Example,* including a *definition*)
       3. To deliver mail during Christmas season (*Example*)
       4. To transport children in recreation department work (*Example*)
    C. *If you do not need a station wagon to do daily chores and to earn money,* you will surely want one for vacation use.
       1. The best way to travel to the mountains or the seashore (*Restatement*)
       2. Space for camping gear (*Example*)
       3. Easy to unload

IV• *Conclusion*
    A. *Many benefits*
       1. *Daily benefits*
       2. *On your job*
       3. *On a vacation trip*
    B. Thousands of happy station-wagon owners
    C. The grand wagon

MODEL SPEECH

(Full text, based on OUTLINE 2) to illustrate the uses of methods and materials.

The Grand Wagon

Whenever you pass by a car lot or automobile show window, perhaps you are impressed, as I am, with the great variety of cars available for selection by the buying public. Among sports cars, alone, you have a wide choice of shapes, colors, and speed potential. I noticed this the other night at the European Mart. There were Triumphs, *Example* Simcas, Sunbeams, Jaguars, and all the rest; you know their names probably better than I do.

Just across the street was an acre of mod- *Example* erately priced American cars. These happened to be some of the different Plymouth models on the market.

And next door to the Plymouths was a Cadillac agency with a Coupe De Ville and a Sedan De Ville luxuriously displayed.

Example

What is your choice? Which one fits your needs? From my own experience, I have found that the ideal all-around car—the one meeting many common requirements— is the station wagon.

Transition

Let me suggest that you investigate the station wagon before you buy.

Proposition

This versatile vehicle is just the thing for daily use. For the many ways that we expect a car to serve us each day, the station wagon is the answer. When coming out of the supermarket loaded with groceries, all you have to do is open the big rear door and easily place the boxes and bags in the spacious compartment. Taking your children or sisters and brothers to lessons or taking the neighborhood children to the pool pose no space problems, if you have a station wagon.

Transition and *first main head*
Restatement

Explanation

Example

I know a college student who built in a desk in his station wagon. This was a veritable study center which he used for reading and writing, and so forth, between classes. He has a folding desk, a typewriter that can be pulled out on a sliding table, a small bookcase, and even a pencil sharpener mounted on the side. Maybe his grade point average influenced his purchase of a station wagon.

Example

Such a car is not restricted to serve merely as a shopping cart or mobile office; it can help you to earn money. It may help you pay your way through school, at least take care of tuition and books.

Transition and *second main head*
Restatement

For example, one of my best friends uses his station wagon on his job. He has a crew of boys whom he supplies with newspapers that they, in turn, deliver to their accounts. By "accounts," I mean home subscribers. His area covers about eight square miles in

Example

Definition

town, and he is responsible for nearly 1,000 papers so you see, he needs a car with a lot of room and one with convenient loading features.

Every Christmas season I work for the post office. Since they do not have enough of those red, white, and blue federal vehicles, I must use my own car. Of course, Uncle Sam pays mileage. I do not know how I would manage with my particular assignment, if I did not have my trusty wagon to use in delivery. All those big packages! Also, the bigger the load that I take, the more that is saved on mileage.

Example

One girl that I know works for the recreation department in the summer and uses her family's station wagon to transport children from Weeke's Park to Bishop Playground. And sometimes she takes groups out of town on field trips.

Example

If you do not need a station wagon to do daily chores and to earn money, you will surely want one for vacation use. This is the best way to travel to the mountains or to the seashore; you will have all sorts of advantages on a holiday trip. There is plenty of space for the camping gear and other important items. Suppose that you have a conventional car and that you and three or four friends are packing for a two-week camping trip to the Rockies. There you are in your garage at home, feverishly trying to fit in all of the necessary gear: the stove, tent, ax, bucket, clothing, food, fishing equipment, sleeping bags, lantern, shovel, fuel, hammock, cots, and so forth. You ultimately get it all in, but, wait, you forgot one thing: where will the people sit? Get a station wagon.

Transition and *third main head*

Restatement

Example

And a station wagon is easy to unload, too.

I hope that by now you have come to appreciate more the virtues of the station wagon and that you will give it considera-

Transition to final remarks (Summary)

tion the next time you are shopping for a car. Remember that it will be a benefit to you every day, whatever you ask of it; it may be a virtual necessity in handling some types of jobs; and on a vacation, it is just the car.

Thousands of people own them. Notice their great number the next time you watch the cars go by. Why not get with it, get in it, get on the grand wagon?

MODEL SPEECH OUTLINE 3

(In sentence form and with major transitions italicized)

By the Golden Gate

I• *Introduction*
   A. I would like to ask you if you have ever ridden on a cable car, or gone over a bridge 8¼ miles long, or been in the largest Chinese settlement outside of China.
   B. If your answer is "No," then probably you have not experienced *a singular American delight—San Francisco.*

II• *Proposition:*   Allow me to take you on a tour of selected points of interest in San Francisco.

III• *Body*
   A. *We shall start our Bay City trip with a* visit to Fisherman's Wharf.
      1. The atmosphere is authentic. (*Repetition*)
      2. The seafood is unequaled anywhere; today we shall lunch at Joe DiMaggio's. (*Example*)
   B. *After eating, we will go to* Golden Gate Park.
      1. Flowers and trees are in abundance.
      2. The Oriental Tea Garden is a major attraction. (*Example*)
      3. In the Steinhart Aquarium we will see thousands of fish from many seas. (*Example*)
   C. *We have fed ourselves on fish, and we have seen the live variety; our next stop will be* the downtown district.
      1. Shops of all kinds compel our attention.
      2. We see the pigeons and gulls in Union Square.
      3. Our exciting cable-car ride up Powell Street will be remembered forever. (*Example*)

D. *It has been quite a day of eating, riding, and viewing; let us indulge in the Oriental atmosphere once more and* visit Chinatown.
   1. Again the food lures us, and we decide to have dinner at the Shanghai Low. (*Example*)
   2. We might buy some gifts for the family at home. (*Example*)
   3. We notice the customs of the people.
   4. We listen to corner conversations in Chinese.

IV• *Conclusion*
   A. *As we prepare to leave, a map posted on the wall at the air-port reminds us of where we have been today.*
      1. *There on the map is Fisherman's Wharf.*
      2. *Across town to the west is Golden Gate Park.*
      3. *Between these two points is the downtown section.*
      4. *Not far from the heart of the city is Chinatown.*
   B. Someday we shall surely go back to San Francisco to see what we have not been able to include in this tour, such places as Nob Hill, the Mark Hopkins Hotel, the Yacht Harbor, the Mission, and Fleishacker Zoo.
   C. We shall surely go back to San Francisco. (*Restatement*)

BASIC ASSIGNMENT

Prepare a speech and include in it all of the details required in the Basic Assignment for Chapter Three. Use transitions at the key points as discussed in this chapter. Restate and repeat thoughts and define or explain terms which need clarification or emphasis.

Reminders:
1. Think of transitions, repetitions and restatements, explanations and definitions as natural helpers and not as mere mechanical devices.
2. The more demanding each new speech assignment becomes, the more it becomes necessary for you to prepare thoroughly. Compose carefully and rehearse sufficiently.

Suggested Exercise A
Listen for transitions as used by speakers who earn their livelihood by talking (radio and television commentators and newsmen, teachers, lawyers, salesmen, and so forth). To report on the effectiveness of usage, quote three actual major transitional statements used, and tell specifically what each transition did to further the speaker's efforts.

Suggested Exercise B

Be prepared for an oral class activity in which each class member will be asked to make a transition between the two headings below. Strive to make your wording different from that of the other speakers. Use your imagination.

1. History is the study of great men.
2. History is the study of great events.

Suggested Exercise C

Copy the following partial speech outline, and write in transitions at major points. Just for the experience of it, word your last transition in such a way as to make main head C the most significant point. In effect you will be subordinating A and B.

II• *Proposition:* Perhaps you believe as Francis Bacon did that some books should be read differently from others.

III• *Body*
    A. Some are to be tasted.
    B. Some are to be swallowed.
    C. Some are to be chewed and digested.

Suggested Exercise D

Select a term from your field of major interest that might not be meaningful to everyone. *Define* the term in a one-minute talk. Use one or more of the definition types explained in this chapter.

Suggested Exercise E

Select a concept or principle from your field of major interest, and *explain* it to the class.

Suggested Exercise F

Make a brief announcement about some coming event (game, dance, cake sale, television program, musical program, visiting lecturer, and so forth). For clarity and emphasis restate all the key factors: What it is, what day, what time, and where. For further help, turn to Chapter Thirteen.

Suggested Exercise G

Shorten and make more concise one of the three sample outlines found in this chapter. Rewrite it in the form of a speaking outline as specified by your instructor.

Suggested Exercise H

To complement your instruction on "meeting the forces of confusion," you may want to refer now to Chapter Nine, "Improving Listening Skills."

Suggested Exercise I

Though you may have read it before, read once again Ann Blasdell's speech, "The Waste of War," in *Appendix A,* this time looking for transitions. Knowing about certain of the difficulties that humans have in communicating, do you see how these aids may have helped Miss Blasdell to keep her audience oriented to her train of thought?

Suggested Exercise J

What ideas in Miss Blasdell's speech might be effectively heightened or made clearer with repetition or restatement?

CHAPTER FIVE

Developing Your Thoughts with Physical Materials

Let us begin by defining two principal terms of the chapter title. By "your thoughts," we mean your main ideas, your primary headings and subheadings, those points which make up the bare skeleton of your speech. For instance, the following speech outline consists of thoughts:

I• *Introduction*
   A.   Man has devised many ways to entertain himself.
   B.   Golf is one such means of enjoyment.
   C.   But considerable skill is required.

II• *Proposition:*   I would like to discuss with you the basic steps involved in hitting a golf ball.

III• *Body*
   A.   Grip the club.
      1.   Method No. 1 is used by some golfers.
      2.   Method No. 2 is used by others.
   B.   Approach the ball.
      1.   Your stance is important.
      2.   Maintain the correct distance of feet to ball.
   C.   Swing the club.
      1.   Keep leg movements to a minimum.
      2.   Arm movements are made in this manner.
      3.   Keep your eyes on the ball.
   D.   Follow through.

IV•   *Conclusion*

   A.   Now I shall summarize for you.
   B.   There are golf links close by.
   C.   Try golfing.

THE GENERAL AND THE SPECIFIC

The preceding outline consists of statements and partial statements, of rather general and unexplained headings, and when you read the outline, you get a *general* notion of the content as planned by the speaker. This is not the entire speech. It could take a speaker five minutes or perhaps a full half hour to deliver this speech, and yet you can read the outline aloud in thirty seconds. We can see that something is missing, and this leads us to another term in the title: "Developing."

To develop means to unfold more completely and to give greater meaning. Therefore, when you develop your thoughts, you expand on them and heighten or enhance or magnify or explain. You *support* your thoughts by giving them the backing of elaboration.

The golf outline has not been developed. The points have not been supported. It is but a skeleton and lacks those specific details which it needs to give it meaning and life. Thus we see that there are two primary types of data to be found in any speech—the general and the specific. General data are the framework, while specific data are those concrete materials which make the generalizations clear, important, or believable.

MATERIALS

Specific data are either physical or verbal. Physical materials are those which can be seen and sometimes felt or tasted, smelled, or heard. They make strong appeals to the senses. The speaker who wants to explain how to hit a golf ball would use some physical materials, at least a club and ball. He would develop the thoughts in his outline by demonstrating how to hold the club, how to address the ball, how to swing, and how to follow through. Imagine how much more effective this demonstration would be than merely *telling* how to do it. Movement is attention-compelling, and when you use physical materials, the listeners not only hear, but also *see*.

Verbal materials, which we shall discuss in the next chapter, are, as the name implies, made up of words. Even though they are such things as examples, statistics, and quotations and therefore not physical, a good speaker can prompt an audience to see, feel, taste, or smell, at least in their minds. For instance, a speaker's vivid illustration of a sizzling steak can cause a listener's mouth to water. Verbal materials, like physical materials, can evoke sensory reactions and otherwise make a speaker's generalizations meaningful.

Usefulness of Physical Materials

Many able speakers, knowing the limitations of verbal materials, recognize the value of well-chosen physical materials and use them when indicated. Yet occasionally, one will hear a speech that has real potential but is deficient for lack of visual aids. All speakers ought to know the value of physical materials.

1. *Getting attention and interest.* Well-chosen and relevant aids command attention. In some instances, this may be generated by colors or by the visible texture of an object. An unusually shaped object may catch interest. Or perhaps sound used as an accompaniment, as would be the case, if the regular beat of a metronome were used to support ideas in a speech on rhythm. People respond to visible movement. This has been known for a long time by persons whose responsibility it is to save human life. An American roadway with its variety and types of flashing lights, pendulum-like warning arms, and traffic signs is a pertinent example. Such stimuli arrest attention because they are strong and demanding. The speaker can captivate an audience by using materials which appeal directly to the senses.

2. *Clarifying.* Words are not always sufficient to the task of communication. You may have to show your idea. Sometime you may want to try this experiment on two friends. Describe to one, with words only, how to go to a certain place. Take the same amount of time in giving your directions to the second person, but this time use a sketch or drawing to help communicate the information. Ask each to give the directions back to you, and you will find that the second person probably will be more correct. Why? It will be obvious that the visual aid helped to clarify your ideas. The lesson is obvious to *us,* but surprisingly, some speakers, otherwise competent, neglect to use such means for making their messages clear.

3. *Impressing and causing listeners to remember.* Besides merely getting attention and interest and making thoughts clear, you often want your audience to retain ideas. When the people to whom you have spoken leave the speech setting and go their separate ways, you usually hope that they will take something of the message with them. A photograph of Winston Churchill making the famous victory V with two

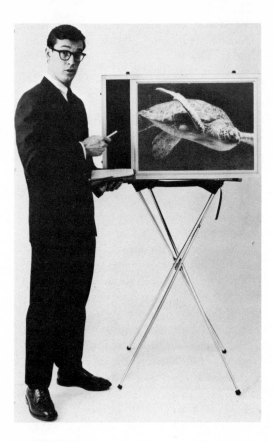

Fig. 5–1 The HPI Quadrapod, a light (4 pound) high (42 inches) stand that occupies 4 by 4 inches of floor space and is designed to travel anywhere. It easily supports the Groupshow rear projection screen. This screen folds flat into its own case and operates with any movie, filmstrip, or slide projector. *Photo courtesy of the Hudson Photographic Industries, Inc.*

fingers may cause an audience to remember the speaker's point about Sir Winston's mighty courage and resolve. After a number of years, several people who were members of one audience still remember the history of the McClellan saddle because the speaker had a saddle to refer to as he talked. Physical support for your verbal expression can help you to etch your ideas on the listeners' minds.

4. *Reducing fears.* When asked why he used a pointer while presenting all his speeches, one man replied, "My pointer helps me feel relaxed. I have something to hold and move." While we do not advocate using a pointer when delivering all speeches, we do think that the man has a point. Holding and manipulating an object does reduce tension for most speakers. Being active helps them to loosen up and be more natural and, therefore, better speakers. Also, the aid may remind the speaker of aspects of the speech that he intends to cover; consequently, it may increase his confidence.

VISUAL AIDS

Visual aids are all materials which can be seen, with the exception of those having a primary appeal to our hearing sense. Recall your own listening experiences, and make a mental list of the materials you have *seen* speakers use. On your list will be such items as charts, graphs, maps and globes, blackboard sketches, models, moving pictures, projected slides, and photographs. In addition, you may have remembered objects of different types which were used as special aids to support ideas in speeches. A list of such special aids would be at least as long as a list of speech topics. The biology teacher who shows the underside of a leaf to explain certain cell structure, uses an object, a special visual aid. The mechanic who manipulates and describes his customer's worn-out fuel pump employs such a special visual aid. In other words, visual materials can be all supporting objects that an audience is able to see.

Fig. 5–2   Here are two examples of various kinds of available equipment used to give audio support in speeches: the tape recorder and record player. These machines are easily operated, and in many schools, the a-v services put the equipment at the disposal of speech students. This photo and the following six are courtesy of Thomas Connelly, Audio-Visual Department, California State College at Hayward.

Guidelines for Use

1. *Use visual materials purposefully.* The only justification for including any item in a speech is that it will help you to further your purpose. A speaker does not sketch on the blackboard for his own enjoyment or because he has heard that some sketching may help him. He draws or writes on the blackboard because *he has a point to make,* and his purposeful sketching will help him make the point. An unnecessary aid is not only valueless but also is a possible distraction. Keep this in mind as you prepare oral assignments requiring some use of visual aids; start by choosing a subject that in development will necessitate the use of such materials. Be purposeful and be guided by the needs of *communication.*

2. *Be certain that all of your audience can see and appreciate your aid.* When sketching, for example, move aside occasionally to allow everyone a clear view. Also, it is often wise to change your sketching position from one side to the other during the speech. If you have been sketching and referring to the board from the left side for some time, move over to the right side. You can go back soon, should the left side be more comfortable for you. In any event, remember the sight lines. Speakers are most often neglectful of the sight lines of people who sit in the front rows at the ends—the front corners. Draw or write with large and broad lines; keep the drawing simple and not too detailed. Do not let the lectern or any other object block the view.

An object, too, must be used in such a way as to allow easy viewing. It should be large enough for all to appreciate and held at a satisfactory viewing height for as long as its presence is necessary. About chin high is a good height. But do not be satisfied with a general rule, for other factors such as your stature and room conditions may prescribe special handling. Resist any inclination that you might have to show the aid in the manner of a flash card; let it work for you. If it is important enough to include in the speech, you ought to use it carefully and get the most out of it. Occasionally it is necessary to walk out to the audience and move along in front of them as you demonstrate or display your object.

3. *Maintain contact as you use your aid.* In most cases, you will need to have a running commentary accompanying your use of visual aids. Words help to explain key points, and in addition words help to maintain interest. At times, pauses are unavoidable and even beneficial, but frequently they offer excuses for an audience to become rest-

less and even to engage in side conversations. Therefore, it is strongly suggested that you keep the thought flowing and interest growing by having enough to say as you present the visual phases of your speech.

Eye contact, too, should not suffer when you are employing a physical aid. There is a tendency when you are sketching or demonstrating to attend to your aid and neglect your listeners. Talk to the audience, not to the aid. Loss of valuable contact can be prevented by careful advance planning and practice.

4. *Control the use of your aid.* Avoid the danger of dividing attention. When planning how and where to use a given supporting device, ask yourself if timing is important. It frequently is. In mentioning timing, we refer to your having the materials handy and ready to use, introducing them at the proper place, and putting them aside after they have been used.

Fig. 5–3   Surrounding this student is a battery of different kinds of overhead projectors. Such equipment can be used by speakers to project drawings, overlays, photographs, maps, outlines, and so forth. These machines are easily operated by students.

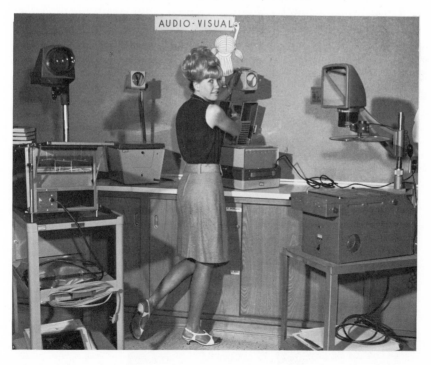

When you bring objects to a speaking situation, put them in some convenient location near the speaking area or keep them with you at your seat. They should be available and yet inconspicuous. Even though you find it necessary to keep them in a bag or box, do not have them so securely contained that you must struggle to remove them.

Introduce your sketch or object at the point in your speech where it will serve you best. Early "unveiling" may destroy some suspense value or be a distraction; late showing may provide nothing but a weak anticlimax. Again, the importance of rehearsal cannot be overemphasized.

Put the object aside (or, in the case of sketching, erase the board) when you have finished with it, unless you want to leave it on display for certain reasons. Only on rare occasions should you chance distracting the audience by passing an object among them during your speech. All too often the passed object gets the attention, while the speaker's ideas of the moment go unreceived.

If you wish to support your ideas with objects, the use of which requires more space than a room provides, it will be necessary to arrange for an outside speaking scene. Many speech teachers report that at least once during a course a student will bring a visual aid of unusual proportions. In this category are such prodigious supporting materials as automobiles, fishing (casting) equipment, motorcycles, archery equipment, and even horses.

Fig. 5–4 When speakers find it necessary to introduce a portion of a motion picture into a speech, the motion picture projector, such as this, comes to their aid. This highly developed speech aid requires, for its use, integration of the speech's subject matter with the film and practical experience in the use of the projector.

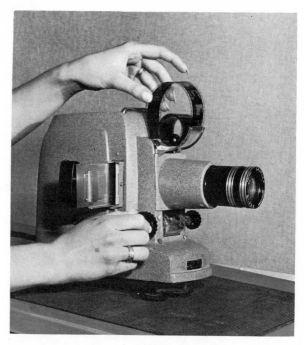

Fig. 5–5 An infrequently used speech aid is the film-strip projector. It is of greatest value when there is a need to show a continuous number of pictures—such as a series of related items.

AUDIO AIDS

Under this heading we put those devices which produce sound. Chiefly, they are tape recorders, record players, and musical instruments. Possibly a speaker plans to discuss the changes in popular music over the last ten years. He could illustrate each major stage in the development of popular music by playing recorded fragments. Of course, such record fragments should not take up an undue portion of the speaking time.

A speaker, in telling how to play the ukulele, might play the instrument to enhance his verbal explanation. He might even give a musical summary in his conclusion by playing an entire selection which could draw together all that he had discussed in the body of his talk.

Guidelines for using an audio aid are essentially the same as those for using a visual aid. First of all, employ the device to help you reach your goal. Plan your use of the aid, and sustain audience contact. Practice sufficiently to avoid wasteful pauses and any distracting activity.

TYPICAL SITUATIONS

Put yourself in these typical speaking situations, and consider possible solutions to problems posed. Most of the "take care" suggestions in any one of the typical situations will apply to other situations.

1. You plan to point out in a class speech the comparative percentages of student body money that is spent on athletics, the newspaper and yearbook, dances, special programs, student council expenses, and general expenses. How can you get your ideas across graphically to the

Fig. 5–6 In this sequence of photos (Figs. 5–6, 5–7a, 5–7b) the student is showing the necessary preparation for a speech utilizing a-v equipment. Fig. 5–6 shows the preparation of a photograph to be used as a visual aid in a speech. The illustration should be relevant, easily visible to all, and effectively displayed.

Fig. 5–7a, 5–7b If it fits the speaker's purpose, he may make a slide of the original p h o t o g r a p h, which he would show with a slide projector. Or he may choose to prepare a transparency to be shown on an overhead p r o j e c t o r (see bottom photo), another mechanical device available for presentation of visual aids. Notice that the speaker can sketch on the transparency (a picture, graph, drawing, and so forth), when he is speaking, as his purpose dictates.

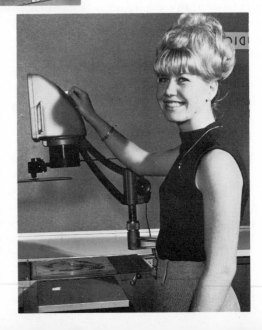

listeners? Why not *show* the percentages? Use a visual aid to help them understand immediately *and*, hopefully, retain the thought. A simple pie graph, boldly drawn (and without undue worry about "perfect-circle" precision) may be the answer. (See next page.)

The line graph or bar graph, are examples of other kinds of graphs that may be useful on occasion. (See next page.)

 Take care

To make the graph large, easy for all to see

To position the graph for convenient viewing. Scout the room in ad-vance to discover appropriate spots for placing your aids. You may need to bring tacks or tape for fixing them to a wall or board.

To plan and rehearse the presentation well, especially if you intend to sketch the graph as you speak. Perhaps you can put part of the work up before class starts and add detail to it as you speak.

To provide for a pointer if needed

2. Let us suppose that in planning a speech on the care of skis, you decide to discuss the process of waxing skis. Now, you might demon-strate waxing, asking your audience to pretend that a book is the ski's undersurface. But pretending is often half-hearted and weak. Instead, bring a ski; work with the real thing. Though the securing of an object may be a bother and may take time, your results with it will doubtless justify the effort.

 Take care

To have your object handy, ready for use

To move out to the audience with your aid if you wish them to take special note of some particular detail

To talk to your audience

3. Assume that the time is near Thanksgiving and you are preparing a talk in which you will tell your audience how to arrange a floral centerpiece. You realize that visual aids would be helpful, but you have not decided on the kind. Should you show a picture of the arrange-ment of ears of corn, gourds, pretty leaves, and so forth? Should you sketch in proper placement of objects with a blackboard sketch? Prob-ably the best solution would entail the use of real objects that you can pick up, manipulate, and place in the desired position as you tell what you are doing and why.

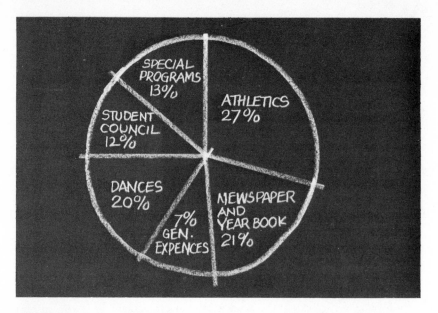

Fig. 5–8 Simple pie graph as it might be drawn on the blackboard.

 Take care

To plan for working space, one within everyone's visual range

To make relevant comment as you handle the physical materials

To make eye contact with the audience as much as possible. Let them know that this is something for them.

4. After spending a summer working in a cannery, you find that the subject choice for your visual aid speech is easy—as is the determination of supporting aids. With your purpose being to show the path of a peach from its entering the cannery to its entering the can, you

Fig. 5–9 Line graph showing comparison of plant personnel incomes.

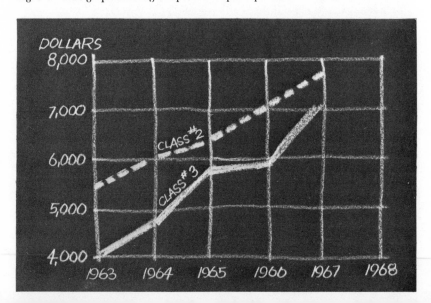

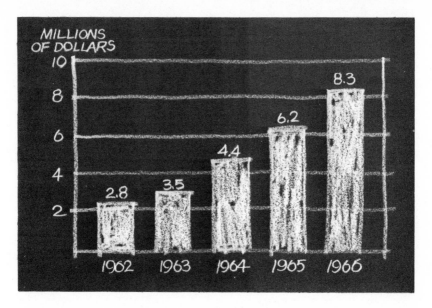

Fig. 5–10   Bar graph showing net corporate income for specified years.

decide to draw a sketch of the travels of the peach through the cannery. You can add to the sketch, let it build, as you progress in your verbal presentation.

   Take care

To focus on essential points only and to exclude minor detail or unnecessary complexity

Fig. 5–11   Sketch showing the processing of peaches through a cannery.

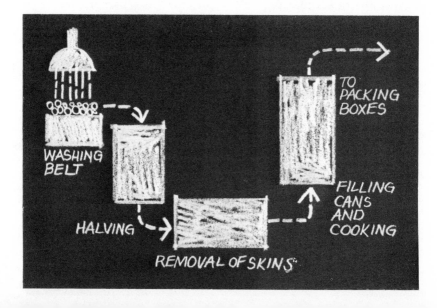

To avoid apology for your sketching. Fifty percent of speakers in speech classes will say something like, "I'm not much of an artist so bear with me." Be in the other 50 percent, those who are more worried about utility than artistic beauty.

To keep in touch with the audience, visually and verbally

5. With a proposition such as "I intend to reveal to you today the principal places on the underside of a car that require lubrication," you would doubtless find valuable a chart of the underside of a car. Perhaps you could borrow one from a service station. If not, you could draw it yourself on a piece of cardboard of ample size, using India ink or felt pen. A blackboard sketch would suffice in such an instance, yet a chart would free you for more constant eye contact with the audience.

Take care

To amplify details, perhaps by blowing them up with an augmenting sketch on the board—one to depict in greater size those aspects that are difficult to perceive; for example, some little but important valve or fitting

To stand clear of your aid, using a pointer or pencil if indicated

6. Let us imagine that a fire occurred recently in mountains close by. Having followed the course of events and being familiar with the fire-fighting equipment that the firemen used, you decide to speak on that topic. Which of the following might prove useful?—a forest service map of the area burned? Photographs of typical air and ground vehicles used in fire control? Representative pieces of hand equipment used? Protective clothing worn by the firemen? The answer, of course, is that any or all of these aids may serve at given places in the speech to enhance the verbal thought. Once again, the speaker's purpose at any point will dictate his mode of appeal and development.

Take care

To introduce the aids at points where they will serve best

To resist the temptation to pass articles around during the speech. If time allows, you may arrange to let your audience handle the articles when you finish speaking.

7. In another instance, for adequate explanation of the principles of flight, use a model airplane (or a sketch or chart). *Show* how the pressures above and under the wing cause it to lift when a source of power moves it through the air.

Similar types of aids might serve to reveal the principle of the internal combustion engine or the functioning of a photoelectric cell.

Take care

To avoid hurrying over ideas. Take pains to explain and show. Then, possibly, restate and reshow.

To prevent yourself from digressing to an interesting but unrelated area of thought. One can become so stimulated in using a visual aid that he wants to branch out, especially when he feels high interest in the audience. Resist the impulse; stay on the track as you have laid it out.

8. Perhaps you choose to explain the steps of a new dance. In strictly verbal treatment, your best means of clarification probably would be the analogy. You could say that the dance steps are like those of the rhumba, except that they go this way or that, and so forth. But a demonstration would be far better. Actually perform the steps with a partner. To add to the exposition and to clarify parts that the audience missed in the demonstration (could not see because of sight-line blocking or rapidity of movements), you might reshow the steps on a flannel board (felt board). Cut out pieces shaped like the bottom of feet; place and move them appropriately on the flannel board as you explain.

The flannel board has many uses for speakers whose presentations involve the placing, moving, and removing of elements. Besides relating dance steps, you can discuss game rules, the layouts of towns or buildings, the history of a word's development, comparisons and contrasts of a great variety of phenomena, the component parts of a large design (outlining, for instance), and so forth.

 Take care

To work where people can see the demonstration. You may have to rearrange the furniture into a circle or half circle.

To repeat complicated parts of the demonstration

To have your board set up before you start. A slight tilt backward will add assurance that the felt, flannel, or sandpaper-backed pieces will hang to the board.

LET US SUMMARIZE

Skillful use of audio and visual aids comes after extended experience, from watching others, and from ample practice on your own. Make it a point to note the techniques employed by some of your instructors and by other good speakers whom you observe. Notice how the use of these aids helps to get attention and interest, to clarify, to impress, and to reduce fears.

Allow audio and visual aids to further your sharing of thought.

1. Use your materials purposefully.
2. Be certain that all of your audience can see (or hear) and appreciate your aid.
3. Maintain contact as you use your aid.
4. Control the use of your aid.

Remember the question that Polonius put to Hamlet?—"What do you read, my lord?" And Hamlet's answer?—"Words, words, words." How many audiences would give Hamlet's answer if asked, "What do you hear, my listeners?" Some, certainly, upon occasion. Speakers want to avoid causing their audiences to give Hamlet's answer—or even to think it. They want their listeners to hear *ideas,* maybe a new idea now and then, or possibly a fresh perspective or provocative thought. Planned use of supporting materials is one positive measure for increasing chances of success.

MODEL SPEECH OUTLINE 1

(In sentence form)

The Housing Problem

I•   *Introduction*
   A.   Home is an important place in our lives.
      1.   "Be it ever so humble, there's no place like home." (*Quotation* from Payne)
      2.   "Home is where the heart is." (*Quotation* from Pliny)
      3.   "Home makes the man." (*Quotation* from Smiles)
   B.   Yes, home does make the man and the women and children, too.
   C.   One should build a home that will fit the needs of the whole family.
      1.   It should meet present requirements.
      2.   It should be planned to meet future requirements. (*Explanation*)

II•   *Proposition:*   The home-development plan that I shall show you should fit all needs.

III•   *Body*
   A.   When first married, start with a one-bedroom house like this one. (*Sketch*)
      1.   It is inexpensive.
      2.   It is attractive.
      3.   It is adaptable. (*Example*)

B. When children arrive, add on to the basic structure.
   1. One way is to add a bedroom in the rear. (*Sketch*)
   2. Other ways are possible. (*Sketch*)
C. If your family increases—by birth or by the arrival of a mother-in-law—make further adjustments. (*Sketch*)
   1. Costs can be moderate.
   2. Living can be normal during construction. (*Explanation* with references to sketch)

IV• *Conclusion*
   A. Adopt a basic plan.
   B. Add on as contingencies arise.
      1. Start with Phase No. 1. (Reference to sketch)
      2. Go to Phase No. 2. (Reference to sketch)
      3. If necessary, introduce Phase No. 3. (Reference to sketch)
   C. The development of a house is like one's development in speaking.
      1. You handle one phase at a time.
      2. You progress step by step.

MODEL SPEECH OUTLINE 2

(In sentence form)

Lesson in Bowling

I• *Introduction*
   A. You may recall Rip Van Winkle's meeting the little men who were bowling in the Catskill Mountains. (*Example*)
   B. The game of bowling has changed greatly in recent decades, especially in America.
      1. Ten pins are now the target, instead of nine.
      2. Automatic pinsetting machines are almost universal.
      3. There have been many other changes in equipment and general facilities.
   C. If you do not already take part, perhaps you are interested in learning the rudiments.
      1. You old hands may criticize—silently, I hope.
      2. You uninitiated ones are to pay close attention.

II• *Proposition:*   Here, then, is a short lesson in bowling, free of charge.

III• *Body*
   A. A good start in bowling depends on your finding a ball that is appropriate for you.

       1. The grip and fit are important.
         a. Some prefer the two-fingered grip. (*Demonstration with object*)
         b. Others like the three-fingered grip. (*Demonstration with object*)
       2. Determine what weight you can handle. (*Explanation*)

  B. Pay due regard to bodily behavior as you prepare to move forward with your chosen ball.
       1. Stand in this way, relaxed and with shoulders squared to the pins. (*Demonstration*)
       2. Step forward in a four- or five-step pattern.
         a. Attempt a rhythmical movement. (*Demonstration*)
         b. Move with full body coordination. (*Demonstration*)

  C. Smooth delivery of the ball is a natural consequence of a relaxed and easy approach.
       1. Slide up to the foul line. (*Sketch* and *demonstration*)
       2. Send the ball well out in front of the foul line.

  D. Finally, you cap off your execution of these three initial stages with a complete follow-through. (*Demonstration*)
       1. A natural follow-through helps avoid bad results caused by jerks of the arms.
       2. It may prevent putting the ball into the "gutter." (*Definition*)

IV• *Conclusion*

  A. Let us go over the lesson again.
       1. Pick a ball that has the right grip and weight for you.
       2. Relax and move forward in four or five steps.
       3. Slide to the foul line as you launch the ball beyond the line.
       4. Follow through.

  B. Now you should get some practice—lots of it.
       1. Facilities are operating in almost every community.
       2. More lanes are available in the middle of weekdays than at other times.

  C. I will see you at the Bowl!

SPEECH IDEAS

Below are representative topics for Basic Assignments 1 and 2. The topics suggest obvious use of physical material. Many topics with less obvious potential will be appropriate for these assignments.

Reading a Weather Map	Testing for Acids and Alkalis
Wedding Gowns of Today	The Rules of Soccer
Forms of Shelter Used by the Zulus	How to Clip a Poodle

Essentials of Mitosis   Making a Collage

Causes of Smog   Setting Up the Page of a Newspaper

Description of the Empire Dress   · First Steps in Reading Music

BASIC ASSIGNMENT NO. 1

Prepare a speech in which you develop each main head by use of an object or objects. The "Speech Ideas" above will indicate types of topics that you might choose. Demonstrate, manipulate, or show the object as you discuss each main head. You may use a single object or a number of such aids.

Use transitions at all major points. Restate, define, explain, or sketch on the blackboard whenever you feel it will help you to communicate.

Reminders:

1. Remember that the sole reason for using visual aids is to support your ideas; therefore, think of ideas first and of objects to explain those ideas second.
2. Some of the best supporting objects are those we use or observe everyday. Look around you.

BASIC ASSIGNMENT NO. 2

Prepare a speech in which you develop each main head by sketching on the blackboard. Do some sketching as you elaborate on each main head. You may use an independent sketch for each main head or add to a single sketch as the speech progresses.

Use transitions at all major points. Restate thoughts, explain, and define terms where it is necessary to do so.

Reminders:

1. If possible, practice your speech in a room equipped with a blackboard.
2. Review the section of the chapter on suggestions for using a blackboard.

Suggested Exercise A

In a one-minute chalk talk discuss one of the subjects listed below. This will be an opportunity for you to try out your sketching techniques.

How to Get to Some Interesting Place

A New Tower for the Campus

Types of Roofs on Houses

Driving Practices

Types of Moustaches

A Well-Planned Park

Hair Styles
What to Avoid in Making a Chalk Talk
Military Insignia
How to Write a Footnote

Suggested Exercise B

Report on the effectiveness of any special blackboard technique you have observed. One such special technique was used once by a student who was discussing three different ways to throw a bowling ball. He drew a separate bowling lane and set of pins for each main head. At the end of the speech, he said, "It makes no difference what type of ball you throw if you accomplish this—," and with one sweep of the eraser he leveled the pins on all three lanes. It was unusually effective.

Suggested Exercise C

In a one-minute talk, point out the uses, characteristics or disadvantages, and so forth, of an object that you bring to class. Attempt to observe the guidelines suggested in the chapter.

Suggested Exercise D

Report on a speech you have heard recently which included some type of visual material. Use the following questions as topics for your explanations:
1. Was the material pertinent to the speaker's ideas?
2. Did he make certain that everyone could see it to satisfaction?
3. Did he avoid long pauses in the use of it?
4. Was it ready and accessible at the time it was needed?

Suggested Exercise E

Observe carefully the use of visual aids by television announcers; the weather reporter, for example. Make a list of several techniques or skills that you judge to be effective. Your instructor may ask you to report your conclusions.

Suggested Exercise F

To complement your instruction on adapting ideas, read Chapter Eight, "Refining Speech Delivery."

Suggested Exercise G

Compare the time it takes you to read orally Model Speech Outline 2 following Chapter Four with the time that it takes to read orally the full text of the speech based on the outline. What conclusions can you draw from comparing the time?

CHAPTER SIX

Developing Your Thoughts with Verbal Materials

In the preceding chapter, our primary concern was with the use of physical materials, those specific supporting materials which can be seen, felt, or heard. Their concrete and tangible nature allows them to serve as excellent developers of generalized statements, especially for informative speeches; they help the speaker to anchor his thoughts to reality, to make his abstractions vivid and clear.

The topic for discussion in this chapter is very closely related to that covered in Chapter Five. This is merely a continuation and completion of our study of methods for developing ideas. (Consult Chapters Ten and Twelve for specialized discussions on the use of supporting materials.) Our attention now will be turned to those specifics that we call verbal materials. The word *verbal* is derived from the Latin *verbalis,* which means "consisting of words," and this is precisely what we shall discuss—developmental materials consisting of words. There are four main types: examples, statistics, quotations, and facts and opinions.

USEFULNESS OF VERBAL MATERIALS

Word developers of thoughts, like their physical counterparts, help to add meaning and believability to assertions in a basic speech outline. They help an audience to visualize the idea, to get a feeling of seeing, touching, or perhaps tasting and smelling. They help the listener to "get the picture," to understand or be moved by what the speaker is saying. Like physical aids they are useful in these ways:

1. In developing interest and establishing bases for understanding.
2. In clarifying thought.
3. In moving listeners to respond to thought.
4. In causing listeners to remember, to retain important thoughts.

The following discussion of the verbal developmental materials will elaborate on their usefulness.

Examples

In *Roget's Thesaurus* you will find, among others, the following synonyms for the word *example:* instance, exemplification, illustration, specimen, and sample. As indicated by these words, an example is an instance or case in point used to illustrate or to serve as a specimen or sample. For example:

> *General statement:* The rooting section went wild.
> *Example:* There was one elated man, for instance, who despite his more than sixty years, tossed his felt hat into the air with the abandon of a teenager. His team had scored, and his reaction was no less controlled than that of the freshmen and sophomores who surrounded him.

> *General statement:* Fishing is usually good on the North Fork of the Gorgona.
> *Example:* I went up there last week end armed with nothing but my father's old glass rod and an assortment of homemade flys. Despite my late start (the road was blocked by a tree at Willow Bend) the trip was successful. I arrived back home at six that night with eight rainbows, none of which measured less than eleven inches.

Examples assist in facilitating a coming together of speaker and listener. They promote the entertainment of an idea in the mind of the listener. The service of examples is accomplished through their—

Concreteness
References to the familiar
Color and variety
Stimulation of curiosity
Humor
Appeals to personal needs and emotions

For our purposes, there are two basic forms which the example can assume: the long, rather complete form which we shall call the *illustration* and the short, undeveloped form which we shall call the *instance.*

The *illustration* is used when the speaker needs to include many details in order to allow his listeners to participate extensively in the thought he is developing. The skillful speaker knows that in order to bring the audience "into his speech" he must offer supporting material which is in some way related to the lives and experiences of his audience. A good illustration with its specific details and richness of meaning has a broad and immediate appeal. It helps to make the point.

In the following development of a thought, the illustration capitalizes on elements of *description* to achieve its effect as a supporting aid.

General statement: Winter days are ideal for studying.

    Example (Illustration): Take, for example, last Saturday afternoon. Remember the downpour? Rain pounded the rooftops for five hours without ceasing and roared noisily down metal drain pipes, while gusts of wind made tall trees sway and whip. I sat studying in warm satisfaction in my bedroom on the north side of our house on Brandt Street. Piled on my old brown desk were all of the resources that I needed to make the day profitable—history and psychology textbooks, a dictionary, the *Columbia Encyclopedia,* pencils, a notebook or two, and other assorted tools of the student. There was nowhere to go; that was where I wanted to be. "Let it rain," I said. In those four or five hours I did the work of ten ordinary hours.

The illustration supporting the next point is a *narrative,* a story. We all enjoy well-told stories, and they can be effective means of support for ideas in speeches.

General statement: Complacency may lead to downfall.

    Example (Illustration): Take an illustration from the old Edinburgh Castle. Only once in the history of Scotland was it ever captured. And this is how it happened. The castle had a weak spot. Defenders guarded the spot. But the defenders thought that on one side the steepness of the rock made the castle inaccessible and impregnable and so they did not post sentries there. In the gray mist of an early morning a little party crept up that strong, unguarded, precipitous slope, surprised the garrison, and forced its surrender. You see, the defenders guarded the weak spot of the castle and so where the castle was weak, there it was strong; but the approaches they knew were strong, these they just forgot about, neglected, and so as it turned out, where the castle was strong, there it was weak.[1]

In a speech to the Greater Hartford Forum in 1965, Dr. Grayson Kirk, President of Columbia University, made use of an illustration to strengthen a point.[2]

General statement: Student unrest and activism have been a feature of higher education ever since its beginnings in Western Europe more than a thousand years ago.

    Example (Illustration): If you will read the history of the universities of Bologna, Paris, Oxford, and Cambridge, you will find a record of persistent friction among student groups, between the students and the administration, and, on many occasions, between the academic community and the officials of the secular government.

    On occasion the students dominated the institution completely, even levying fines upon professors whom the students had employed and who appeared to be falling behind in their courses of lectures. At other times, all students, no matter their maturity, were treated merely like

[1] Reverend Harold C. Phillips, "Religion—A Prop for the Weak?," *Representative American Speeches: 1950–1951,* A. Craig Baird, ed. (New York, 1951), p. 165.
[2] "Youth on the College Campus," *Vital Speeches of the Day,* XXXII (February 1, 1966), p. 249.

children and were subjected to corporal punishment if they violated institutional regulations. Over the centuries the students generally have been obliged to accept institutional regulations as a condition of their continued membership in the academic community, but they have seldom been docile or meek in their role.

These illustrations serve the purpose of giving strength and concreteness to assertions. They amplify and cause audiences to share in the thought. One person has described such examples as the "wings which carry ideas into a listener's consciousness."

The *instance* is usually shorter than the illustration, includes less detail, and is frequently used as one of a series of brief examples. A chain of instances can give an idea more believability than that provided by a single short example; there is usually more force and power in numbers.

General statement: Will Rogers commented on the foibles and follies of people and things where he found them.
　Instance: He flayed the anti-Jewish Ku Klux Klan back in the 1920s.
　Instance: He spoke against an income tax because he felt that a slick lawyer could help a person avoid heavy payment.
　Instance: Will Rogers was a thorn (humorous thorn) in the side of congressmen because he poked fun at the lawmakers' attempts to raise their own salaries, make political speeches, or "get something done."
　Instance: He once kiddingly referred to the New York Stock Exchange as a "racket."
　Instance: In 1934 he had occasion to discuss the Russians and came to the conclusion that they would never be as happy as we are. We have more things that provoke laughter in our country.
　Instance: Will once wondered if nudism were a religion. He felt that if it were, a lot of nudists would become atheists in the winter.

Note the many instances imbedded in this convincing passage from Jo Foxworth's speech to an advertisers' convention at Miami.[3]

General statement: Besides youth our business needs the creativity of seasoned talent.
　Instances: Michelangelo gave us his immortal "Pieta," "Bacchus" and "David" before he was thirty. But if the Pope had retired him at the age when we're putting too many of our advertising talents out to pasture, we would not have had his most glorious work, the Sistine Chapel ceiling which he did between the ages of 61 and 66. Thomas Edison, at 32, gave us the incandescent lamp but how wonderful that he kept going because, at 66, he produced talking motion pictures. At 26, Einstein originated his theory of relativity . . . and then when he was 60 he gave us, for better or worse, nuclear fission. A year beyond the mandatory retirement age in most business, an old codger named Winston Churchill got a stunned and despairing England up off her knees and

[3] "Our Creeping Idiot Savantism," *Vital Speeches of the Day,* XXXIII (July 15, 1966), p. 598.

was the dominant, young spirit in leading the free world to victory. Honoré de Balzac did not even begin to write novels until he was past 40 and Grandma Moses didn't start to paint until she was 70. When he was 59 and blind, Milton wrote "Paradise Lost" and when he was 63, "Paradise Regained." Verdi wrote *Aida* at 48, *Otello* at 74 and the incomparable *Falstaff*, the opera most often called our greatest, at 79!

An *illustration* coupled with a group of *instances* often provides stronger support than when either is used without the other. A most effective sequence of thought development consists of stating the point, giving an illustration to support it, and bolstering the point further with a series of instances.

General statement: Great men are versatile men.

Illustration: Benjamin Franklin, that shrewd and witty, self-educated American and citizen of the world, is a prime case in point. Name any area of human endeavor, and the chances are good that Ben Franklin delved there. What can we call him? Printer? Printer he was, but don't overlook his activities as economist and businessman, author (everyone remembers *Poor Richard's Almanac*) and editor, community leader and humanitarian, statesman and diplomat, scientist and inventor, philosopher, and bon vivant.

It took a broad and active man, indeed, to help establish America's first circulating library, the first fire and police departments, and a free hospital. He reformed the postal system, took part in setting up a college which became the University of Pennsylvania, and helped further the science of electricity. His home was cluttered with novel devices which he had contrived. Franklin was truly much more of a man than is represented by the kite and the key, or the Franklin stove, or the lightning rod.

Instance: Versatile, too, was the boisterous Italian Benvenuto Cellini, who carried his life beyond goldsmithing and into the fields of sculpture, music, literature, and politics.

Instance: Later in the sixteenth century Francis Bacon came on the scene and didn't leave until he had made an indelible mark as lawyer, statesman, developer of a scientific method, philosopher, and essayist.

Instance: John Locke pursued a medical career, but we do not remember him as a physician. To us he stands as one of the world's deepest thinkers. His mind was challenged and, as a result, it was productive—in economics, education, politics, philosophy, and literary expression.

Instance: We think of Goethe, and "author" comes to mind. This most universally renowned of all Germans held political offices, was a philosopher, art critic, and scientist who did brilliant work in classifying organisms in addition to earning his unsurpassed reputation as a man of letters—novelist, playwright, and poet.

Such a battery of examples gives a point the benefit of both specific detail and strength of numbers. What Bacon said of his own essays, we might say of ideas supported with an array of pertinent examples—they "come home to men's business and bosoms."

Special Characteristics of Examples

1. EXAMPLES TO COMPARE

The analogy is one of the most common and most fascinating of all materials of speechmaking. Much of our thinking and speaking is based on *analogy:* the resemblance between phenomena. For example, we hear statements like these every day: "The car that Brenda bought was a real *lemon.*" "Transitions are like *bridges.*" "Keep your mind on the *track of thought.*" "The speaker *delivered* a speech" (he made sound waves but he did not transfer or deliver some thing from himself to others). Many, many usages that we never stop to analyze are analogical.

When you compare two or more persons, agencies, ideas, or things, you point up their similarities, and the result is an analogy. If the two items are of the same class, your analogy is *literal*; if they are of different classes, your analogy is *figurative*.

> *General statement:* American society needs to be re-evaluated.
> > *Literal analogy* (comparison of two items from the same class, periods in history):
> > > There are those who say that America will go the way of the Roman Empire, that we are like the Romans in letting ourselves get soft, that our primary goal is to indulge ourselves and seek an undue amount of personal pleasure, that our society, too, shall decay.

> *General statement:* The system for electing our President must be changed because it is outdated.
> > *Figurative analogy* (two items that cannot be compared literally):
> > > The electoral college system is like an old jalopy. Oh yes, it "gets us there," usually; the people's will is expressed, usually. But *usually* is not satisfactory. Let's junk this obsolete, antiquated machine and put into use a smooth-running, precision instrument which will unfailingly convey the will of the voters.

Use caution in employing analogies. Be certain that the two elements are enough alike to justify the parallel. Moreover, you should recognize that an analogy alone usually does not "prove" a point. It is characteristically human: colorful and interesting, yet it serves but to clarify or to act as a base for adding real proof.

2. EXAMPLES TO CONTRAST

Illustrative material of this type is formed of two or more elements which have basic dissimilarities. They are put side by side to make the relevant thought interesting, graphic, or otherwise meaningful.

> *General statement:* The "good old days" were not so good.
> > *Example:* Consider the mortality factor, for instance. In 1890 there were no wonder drugs to combat pneumonia, no vaccine to prevent polio, no blood banks, no massage technique for stimulating a stopped heart, and no fast vehicle for getting a doctor to an injured child.

In developing a point to contrast styles of speaking, one might use the statement that Hugh Blair put in his *Lectures on Rhetoric and Belles Lettres.*

> *General statement:* Speaking styles varied among the ancients.
>> *Example:* The character of Demosthenes is vigour and austerity; that of Cicero is gentleness and insinuation. In the former you find more manliness; in the latter more ornament. The one is more harsh, but more spirited and cogent; the other more agreeable, but withal, looser and weaker.

3. HYPOTHETICAL EXAMPLES

Hypothetical cases are not actual, nor does the speaker present them as being actual. He asks his audience to imagine a possibility and introduces the example with, "Let us imagine . . ." or "Suppose that . . ." or "We will assume. . . ." When used with discretion, the hypothetical example can help to put an idea within an audience's reach.

> *General statement:* Don't use Highway 32 in bad weather.
>> *Hypothetical example:* Let's imagine what could happen. You're driving through the mountains on Route 32 in February, and it is snowing. You come to a point where you can go no further; the road is blocked. You attempt to turn around, but the road is narrow. You get off on the shoulder, and your wheels sink down. You attempt to maneuver out, but it is no use. You are stuck. What would you do? Where would you go? Such experiences occur quite frequently on Highway 32 in the winter.

Whether they are comparisons or contrasts or hypothetical cases, illustrations or instances, apt examples are the stock in trade of the speaker. Draw them from your experiences; "cast down your bucket where you are." Attune yourself to notice and remember the many interesting people, places, incidents, and objects with which you come in contact. Develop an appreciation for this most often-used type of supporting aid which can help you adapt your thoughts to the audience.

STATISTICS

There seems to be some confusion in the minds of many people about "facts" and "statistics." A fact may be statistical, or it may not be. Statistics are numerical data; something factual may be expressed either in statistics or in the form of a statement or actual example. We shall discuss facts in greater length at a later point in the chapter. We use many statistics daily. When we talk about mileage and distances, how much something weighs, what yardage the football team made, how many days are left in the month, salaries, percentages, and so on, we use statistics.

Numbers give weight and authority to your generalizations. The following points would mean little to an audience without the supporting statistics.

> *General statement:* The teen-age business market is big.
> *Statistics:* There are 20 million citizens between the ages of 12 and 20. They have over 10 billion dollars to spend a year and typically spend 170 million dollars a year for records and buy 3 billion gallons of gasoline.

Raymond Nakai used statistics effectively in discussing possible solutions to economic problems of the Navajo Indians of the Southwest.[4]

> *General statement:* Resourcefulness will help solve the problems.
> *Statistics:* Many years ago, just following the Second World War, the Krug Report stated the basis of the Navajo economic problem was that 75,000 people—it is nearer 100,000 now—were trying to eke out a living in an area with only enough resources to support 45,000. I reject such a short-sighted view. Switzerland, a land with even less resources, supports over 4 million people. Education and skill and hard work have accomplished this miracle. It cannot be done overnight, but it can be done—here.

President Kennedy was an able handler of statistics as this excerpt from his commencement address at American University reveals.[5]

> *General statement:* No nation in the history of battle ever suffered more than the Soviet Union suffered in the course of the Second World War.
> *Statistics.* At least 20 million lost their lives. Countless millions of homes and farms were burned or sacked. A third of the nation's territory, including nearly two thirds of its industrial base, was turned into a wasteland—a loss equivalent to the devastation of this country east of Chicago.

Suggestions for Handling Statistics

1. *Use round numbers when they are suitable.* If it is not important that the exact number be given, simplify and lighten your listener's burden. The statistics in the above samples are all approximate. Mr. Kennedy had no need to give the exact number of lives lost by the Russians in World War II, even if accurate figures could ever be compiled. While it is vital to report exactly the number of seconds and tenths of seconds that it took a man to run a quarter-mile, it is sufficient to know that the circulation of a daily newspaper which averages 124,891 is about 125,000.

2. *Use statistics sparingly.* A sure way to lose listeners is to overload a speech with numbers of pounds, dollars, and measurements. Would

[4] "Inaugural Address," *Representative American Speeches: 1963–1964,* Lester Thonssen, ed. (New York, 1964), pp. 53–54.

[5] *Representative American Speeches: 1963–1964,* p. 14.

you be willing (or able) to listen to a speech that went on and on like this?:

> An average of 973 people shop daily at each of the Midland Shopping Centers. Gross revenues at each average $8634.88 every day, except for Sundays when the figures dip to $5928.32. Of the 932,621 people in the greater market serviced by Midland Centers, at least 271,011 have shopped at one of our eighteen Centers during fiscal 1967–1968. These people represent 21,327 families, all living within an area of 207.56 square miles—unless you exclude the 2.77 square miles sometimes considered as a part of the Northborder market area. With the 2.77 square miles, the total area of the Northborder section would be 37.9 square miles.
>
> It is estimated that by 1975, 4,376,001 or perhaps 3,865,017 units of . . .

3. *Give them meaning.* Dramatize your statistics or relate them to something familiar. Instead of leaving your audience with the rather meaningless piece of knowledge that 132 million feet of cable was used in constructing a certain bridge, tell them that this equals approximately 25,000 miles or enough cable to gird the earth. When stating the distance that a home run hitter must travel around the bases, say that it is 360 feet, yes, but looking at it another way, say that it is 60 feet more than the length of a football field.

Note that Kennedy, in the sample above, stated the losses of the Russians in terms understandable to Americans. He allowed his audience to *visualize* the vastness of the waste. Nakai's usage was similar, employing the familiar case of little Switzerland as a point of reference.

4. *Use statistics judiciously.* Figures can lie or at least give false impressions. A town with an average per capita income of $4500 would seem to be quite prosperous, but remember that an average is found by getting a total and then dividing by the number of units. To get a $4500 average, you may be dealing with hundreds of incomes below $3000 or hundreds above $15,000.

Be frank with yourself in handling statistics. Know the full import of the material. A speaker in a speech class recently cited an authority which held that 97 percent of all American juveniles were law-abiding people. "This figure," said the speaker, "proves that America has no problem with juvenile delinquency." "Really?," asked people in the class. They suggested that he do some multiplying with the remaining three percent. Three percent of the conservative estimate of 20 million juveniles equals 600,000. No problem?

The sports page of a college newspaper one basketball season gave player Stan Clark's weight as 187 pounds. People acquainted with Stan Clark knew that his true weight was closer to 157 pounds. Magazines or newspapers, as well as most other sources, are not always accurate. A verification may spare embarrassment.

5. *Use recent statistics.* If your point is to show the need for more recreational facilities in your town, your case probably would not be strengthened if you used 1955 census figures, nor would your conscience leave you alone if you employed outdated statistics to argue against recreational development.

6. *Know well and cite the source of your statistics.* Did they come from an expert in the field, from some reliable agency, or from an unrecognized, questionable source? A man recently said that in fifty years the United States will suffer a major psychological breakdown. Would you not as a listener like to know who said it and how he should have knowledge of such an eventuality? Certainly you would. As good listeners we should demand to know if the author of the data uses a crystal ball or a more scientific measuring instrument.

The name of the compiler or source can augment the effect of the data. The mere mention of Albert Einstein as a source of statistics on some idea in physics or of George Beadle in genetics or of Clyde Kluck-hohn in anthropology, will add appeal to your statistics. In turn, you, of course, will want to interpret your experts' offerings fairly and not misconstrue or extend the data beyond logical limits.

QUOTATIONS

The words of others can lend authority, meaning, and appeal to your speeches; they can give your thoughts weight and help you to express them more aptly.

In the following sample, Senator Charles McGovern uses an authoritative quotation—one to add proof to an assertion. The senator made the speech in the Senate chamber.[6]

General statement: The arms race must be brought under control.
   Quotation: Speaking to the United Nations Assembly in 1961, President Kennedy said,
      "Today, every inhabitant of this planet must contemplate the day when it may no longer be habitable. Every man, woman, and child lives under a nuclear sword of Damocles, hanging by the slenderest of threads, capable of being cut at any moment by accident, miscalculation, or madness. The weapons of war must be abolished before they abolish us. . . . The risks inherent in disarmament pale in comparison to the risks inherent in an unlimited arms race."

Senator McGovern used such testimony extensively in this speech. At a point farther on, he called on the authority of the Secretary of Defense to enforce an argument with quoted evidence.

General statement: Our capacity to destroy is sufficient.
   Quotation: On February 6th of this year the Secretary said,

[6] "New Perspectives on American Security," *Representative American Speeches: 1963–64,* Lester Thonssen, ed. (New York, 1964), pp. 133–153.

"Allowing for losses from an initial enemy attack and attrition en-route to target, we calculate that our forces today could still destroy the Soviet Union without any help from the deployed tactical air units or carrier task forces or Thor or Jupiter IRBM's."

One searching for support in development of a philosophic point can find apt statements of qualified persons to assist him. The strength of the following two samples of thought development would depend on listeners' opinions of the sources, on their opinion of the speaker who selected the sources, or on his skill in handling the material.

General statement: Perfection is a myth.
   Quotation: Alfred de Musset tells us,
      Perfection does not exist. To understand it is the triumph of human intelligence; to desire to possess it is the most dangerous kind of madness.
   Quotation: In his *Essay on Criticism,* Alexander Pope agrees,
      Who ever thinks a faultless thing to see, Thinks what ne'er was, nor is, nor e'er shall be.
   Quotation: Further support is offered by Bayard Taylor,
      The maxims tell you to aim at perfection, which is well; but it's un-attainable, all the same.

General statement: Beauty is many things.
   Quotation: Keats wrote in his *Ode on a Grecian Urn,*
      Beauty is truth, truth beauty.
   Quotation: Charles Reade has said that
      Beauty is power; a smile is its sword.
   Quotation: Shakespeare, who had something to say about everything, gave his idea of beauty in *The Passionate Pilgrim,*
      Beauty is but a vain and doubtful good;
      A shining gloss that fadeth suddenly;
      A flower that dies when first
         it 'gins to bud;
      A brittle glass that's broken presently;
      A doubtful good, a gloss, a glass, a flower,
      Lost, faded, broken, dead within an hour.

For the final words of his speech to the Phi Beta Kappa Association on the role of the scholar in today's world, A. Craig Baird [7] used the words of Adlai Stevenson, a man whose life exemplified a statesmanlike yet practical approach to modern problems. Stevenson's appeal provided the speaker with a common ground on which to base a last word to his audience of scholars.

General statement (implied): The scholar has responsibilities in dealing with problems of the day.
   Quotation: Adlai Stevenson, at Salt Lake City, on October 20, 1952, said, "We are marked men, we Americans. We have been tapped by

[7] "The Scholar and the 'Alienated Generation,'" *Vital Speeches of the Day,* XXXII (July 15, 1966), p. 593.

fate—for which we should forever give thanks, not laments." Stevenson was obviously thinking of the problems of war and peace, finances, trade—the issues discussed by Aristotle and all thinkers since.

And Stevenson added with confidence, "What a day to live in!"

Suggestions for Handling Quotations

1. *Use the author's exact words when possible.* Be fair to the author of the quotation. If you are tempted to alter the wording, look for another quotation instead—one that gives more aptly the desired meaning. Should you decide to paraphrase (at times necessary with long quotations), be careful; avoid doing the disservice that comes from twisting the words around to the point of losing the shape of the original thought.

2. *Know the author's background.* Choose respected authority. Also, if the author is not commonly known, give his words extra vigor by telling your listeners who he is and why he is worthy of being quoted.

Is the author qualified to speak on your topic? Furthermore, does he have some vested interest that would make his statement useless to you? For example, a banker's opinion that depositing money in a savings and loan association is poor practice, would not be acceptable testimony to most audiences. Knowing that banks and savings and loan associations compete for deposits, the typical audience would question the banker's objectivity.

Some occasions will require a sentence or two of biography, but usually a parenthetical statement like, "director of Public Housing in Jackson County" or "author of *The Greek Way*" will suffice.

3. *If you take the quoted words out of context, be careful not to destroy the author's intent.* Words that the author placed before or after those that you have chosen relate to those chosen and affect their meaning. All are part of a larger "picture" of thought. Picture, incidentally, is a good analogy. Taking words out of context indiscriminately may be like showing the picture of cousin Tom that you have cut out of the family portrait. A viewer will miss Aunt Ella smiling approvingly at Tom or the look of worry on the face of Tom's wife as she stands next to him.

In his speech, "The Man with a Muckrake," Theodore Roosevelt, anticipating having his words taken out of context or otherwise distorted, warned listeners.

> An epidemic of indiscriminate assault upon character does no good, but very great harm. The soul of every scoundrel is gladdened whenever an honest man is assailed, or even when a scoundrel is untruthfully assailed.
> Now, it is easy to twist out of shape what I have just said, easy to affect to misunderstand it, and if it is slurred over in repetition, not

difficult really to misunderstand it. Some persons are sincerely incapable of understanding that to denounce mudslinging does not mean the endorsement of whitewashing; and both the interested individuals who need whitewashing and those others who practice mudslinging like to encourage such confusion of ideas.

Indeed, political enemies could have been tempted to overlook Roosevelt's larger purpose and to misconstrue by focusing on only a part of his message.

An unethical speaker might quote Abraham Lincoln as having said, "Force is all-conquering," but he would not do our sixteenth president justice unless he completed the quotation. The statement in full is: "Force is all-conquering, but its victories are short-lived."

4. *Use variety in introducing and closing a quotation.* Be certain that your audience knows when your quotation begins and ends; however, avoid overusing "Quote" and "Unquote" or "I have a quotation." To introduce a quotation appropriately, some speakers say, "In the words of Thomas Jefferson . . .," or "Washington once said . . .," or "Hamilton expressed it this way . . .," or "Listen to Madison's statement. . . ." They may close a quotation with, "That's the end of Hamilton's comment" or "So much for the view of Madison," and so forth. Look for fresh expressions.

Changes in vocal pitch or quality can be one of the best means for setting off quoted words. This skill can be perfected.

FACTS AND OPINIONS

The dictionary defines a fact as "Something that actually exists or has actually occurred; something known by observation or experience to be true or real: a scientific *fact*." To further clarify, facts are information that can be checked and verified. They may be in the form of statistics, or laws of science, or other types of statements about persons or things that may be corroborated by experience of qualified observers.

Sometimes facts are confused with opinions: beliefs not based on certainty, interpretations, or personal judgments of someone or of some source consulted. It is a *fact* that the Japanese attacked Pearl Harbor on December 7, 1941. Some people have the *opinion* that the United States government knew in advance of the coming attack. It is a *fact* that living organisms tend to seek an ecological balance, that is, to achieve a balance in nature. It is an *opinion* that man's interrupting the balance is wrong. It is a *fact* that the Civil War occurred. It is an *opinion* that it was inevitable.

Much of the substance of speeches is composed of facts and opinions. Samples of speaking ranging from daily conversations to formal public address will reveal the reliance of speakers on these types of data. Note the interweaving of fact and opinion in this representative sample of speaking:

> Henry Miller's books are definitely controversial (fact); moreover, they are not literature (opinion). Such books should be banned (opinion), for they corrupt the youth (opinion) and are topics of heated debate among many concerned people (fact). This would be a better world if books like *Tropic of Cancer* were not published (opinion); at least, that's what some serious people say (fact).

Distinguishing between fact and opinion is not always simple. Study the following excerpts from a speech given by Senator Jack Miller in Washington, D.C. to the Mississippi Valley Association. Which statements are factual? Which are opinions? Can you prevent being influenced by your personal beliefs as you categorize the statements?

> I well know that many businessmen have been complaining about too much government regulation, and I would agree that there has been a growing tendency—especially on the part of the federal government —to overregulate. The fuzzy application of the so-called wage-price guidelines is a current example of the trend. On the other hand, the complaining is generally muted when federal assistance is provided, especially when the businessman is the recipient of this assistance—be it in the form of a Small Business Administration loan, a liberalization of depreciation deductions or an investment tax credit for income tax purposes, or a government contract. Without such assistance private business would not have grown; or would not, at least, have grown as rapidly and, in fact, might never have started at all with respect to the particular activity being aided. Many of the job opportunities in private industry would not have opened up, and the economic growth of our nation would have been held back.[8]

Is it a fact that the government is tending to overregulate? How much regulation is overregulation? Is it a fact that without government aid private business would not have grown? Remember the marks of a fact: a fact exists or has actually happened; it is known by observation or experience; it can be verified. Opinions are estimations, personal views, or judgments based on likelihood.

Suggestions for Handling Facts and Opinions

1. *Distinguish between fact and opinion.* Attempt to apply the criteria that mark the differences. Know the nature of the materials with which you are dealing. Hopefully, you will assemble a respectable quantity of factual data for a given speech; but recognize the prevalence and value of good opinion. Do not condemn yourself or other speakers for using opinion. To do so is to condemn mankind.

2. *Know where to find facts.* Go to primary sources whenever pos-

---

[8] "National Transportation Policy," *Vital Speeches of the Day*, XXXII (March 1, 1966), p. 292.

sible. Investigate at firsthand the event, the document, or the person immediately involved. If you must go to a secondary source for facts or support for opinions, go to qualified persons or authoritative resources. Nearly every field has its established authorities: Richard Hofstadter, Carl L. Becker, Allan Nevins, and others in history; or Noam Chomsky, Otto Jespersen, and Edward Sapir and others in linguistics. Consult standard references like the *Dictionary of American Biography, Encyclopedia of the Social Sciences, Statistical Abstracts,* and *Encyclopaedia Britannica.*

3. *Check the reliability of facts and opinions.* Is the statement of one source corroborated by another? As historian Homer Carey Hockett advises, *"The statement of one person should never be regarded as establishing the truth of details."* [9] The agreement of two respected sources should give you considerable confidence in your data, especially if the two sources operated independently of one another. Furthermore, does the alleged fact seem to be consistent with other known facts? If it is inconsistent, can you explain the exception? A court not long ago convicted a young man of killing his parents, yet his action was entirely inconsistent with any known facts about his personality or prior behavior. Why the exceptions in his behavior pattern?

If you are dealing with an opinion, ask yourself if it is well-reasoned. Even though you cannot verify the item in a laboratory or other such "testing ground," you can test its logic and internal consistency. Are you able to be objective in your reasoning about the data? Can you keep personal involvements apart from your deliberation?

4. *Use facts and opinions judiciously.* Again, distinguish between the two, and avoid purporting an opinion to be factual. When you extend facts—when you extrapolate or project from the facts—you usually move to the realm of opinion. Know what you are doing; let your audience know. Let us assume that you are telling of an airplane that flew low over a nudist camp. A fact. But if you add that the pilot was anxiously making observations with binoculars, you extrapolate, give an opinion—unless, of course, you had firsthand knowledge.

You should acknowledge the origin of your data whenever it is proper to credit the source or whenever acknowledgment will add effect. Sir Alexander Fleming deserves to be recognized publicly as one of the prime sources on facts regarding penicillin; moreover, his published views are authoritative and command respect.

Criteria for Selecting Verbal Materials

1. *Select material that will allow adequate development of the idea.* Above all, make sure that any material you use relates directly to the point you are developing. The only justification for using a supporting

---

[9] *The Critical Method in Historical Writing* (New York, 1955), p. 68.

aid is that it backs up or explains a thought; therefore, it should be relevant to the thought.

Choose enough material to give you full support of the idea. Some speakers make the mistake of stopping short of satisfactory development. This is like getting off a ship before it docks. Others, though more rarely, belabor their ideas with too great a quantity of materials.

2. *Select material that will help you adapt your speech to the audience.* Beyond being meaningful and including the right quantity of detail, developmental materials should meet other standards.

Before settling on any example, statistic, quotation, or other material, ask yourself these questions: Will it appeal to the interests and motives of my listeners? Will it be immediately understood by my listeners? Will it help them to understand the point?

In using materials as evidence to support arguments in controversy, ask yourself questions about your material to check your faith in it. Is the source reliable? What is its reputation? Is it unbiased? If biased, is it of value to you? Is it known as a knowledgeable source? Is the material consistent with the standards of reliability that you hold and base your actions upon in daily affairs? Remember that when you adopt a piece of evidence, it becomes part of you—of your speech—and will orally represent you.

Are the materials accurate? Are the facts straight and the statistics correct? Are they consistent with other evidence? Are the words of the quotations exact? Do you have correct names of authors of testimony? Are your pronunciations of authors' names acceptable?

Is the material the most up-to-date? If recency is a criterion, do you have the latest statistics or the latest thinking of the experts? Philosophies and positions change. What is the current point of view?

3. *Select material that will meet the demands of the occasion.* Observe the purpose of the speech setting and follow along with the theme if there is one. In other words, be consistent with the tone or desired atmosphere established by those responsible for your speaking. This criterion will be especially important to remember should you ever be called upon to talk to a group who are meeting for an express purpose. A speech should relate to the over-all design of the occasion. Chapter Thirteen, "Preparing for Various Occasions," will be helpful in this regard.

FINDING MATERIALS

Where does one find materials to use in speeches? The main source, of course, is the reservoir of personal experience; what one has heard, seen, read, and done, and has taken time to ponder and assimilate is almost a part of him. Bits of this background in the form of stories, illustrations, vivid descriptions, and apt phrases can be used to develop the ideas that you wish to get across. Dip down into that reservoir, then, and continue to observe and store for the future.

Occasionally you may not have the exact wording of a quotation that supports a given idea, or you may need some fresh statistics. In such cases, you can go to a *common* reservoir—the library. To save time, you should be purposeful in your quest. Know what you are seeking, and enlist the librarian's aid if you cannot find it.

In addition to the standard books, magazines, and newspapers at your disposal, there are many specialized references such as encyclopedias of various kinds, books of important statistics, and books of quotations. Should your topic require more intensive exploration than most, consult the section, "Gathering Materials," in Chapter Ten for further guidance.

When you find your information, record it accurately on index cards. We all know how memories can fail, as Lewis Carroll vividly reminds us:

> "The horror of that moment," the King went on, "I shall never, *never* forget!"
> "You will, though," the Queen said, "if you don't make a memorandum of it." [10]

LET US SUMMARIZE

You cannot expect an audience to accept your ideas, to participate in their development, unless you justify the ideas with carefully chosen supporting data. Alert, thinking people ignore or challenge mere generalizations; they want specifics; they need grounds for responding favorably. When hearing a flat assertion, they mentally ask, "So what?" Find bases for sharing thought and causing listeners to grant your proposition a hearing; augment your thoughts with an ample supply of rich, pertinent, and appropriate examples, statistics, and quotations, accompanied by tested facts and opinions.

MODEL SPEECH OUTLINE 1

(In sentence form)

Man Against Man

I• *Introduction*
   A. It is my belief that war symbolizes the prime weaknesses of man.
      1. George Bernard Shaw seemed to agree; in *Man and Superman* he wrote: "In the arts of life man invents nothing;

---

[10] This quotation was found in *Bartlett's Familiar Quotations,* a volume that most libraries possess.

but in the arts of death he outdoes Nature herself, and produces by chemistry and machinery all the slaughter of plague, pestilence, and famine." (*Quotation*)

2. "War is hell," exclaimed W. T. Sherman. (*Quotation*)

B. We have had wars since the beginning of society.
   1. Cain and Abel started it all. (*Instance*)
   2. The Medes and Persians warred. (*Instance*)
   3. England and Spain fought bitterly. (*Instance*)
   4. We remember our own Civil War of the 1860s. (*Instance*)
   5. World Wars I and II, the Korean War, and the war in Vietnam are more recent examples. (*Instance*)

C. Many reasons are offered for the cause of war.

II• *Proposition:* I should like to discuss three causes of war.

III• *Body*
A. Nationalism is one reason for aggressive hostility between countries.
   1. By nationalism I mean a nation's dynamic and aggressive policy of striving for status and independence. (*Definition*)
   2. Germany under Hitler was a case in point. (*Illustration*)
   3. Mussolini's attack on Ethiopia was another case. (*Instance*)
   4. Nasser's Egypt is nationalistic. (*Instance*)
B. Warfare is provoked by "isms" other than the nationalism; imperialism is a second reason.
   1. This refers to the spirit and principle of empire. (*Definition*)
   2. Here we are talking about the creation and maintenance of colonies. (*Restatement*)
   3. The old British Empire was imperialistic. (*Illustration*)
   4. The Dutch were imperialists. (*Instance*)
   5. The French were imperialists. (*Instance*)
   6. The Spanish were imperialists. (*Instance*)
C. Some fight to assert themselves, others to acquire, and others because of militarism.
   1. A country may be fearful and anxious.
   2. It may face real or imagined military challenges.
   3. It engages in an arms race.
      a. Let us look at Europe prior to World War I. (*Illustration*)
      b. Then there was Germany under Hitler. (*Instance*)

    c. The East-West cold war is another such example. (*Instance*)

    d. Bismarck attempted to justify his actions: "I am accustomed to pay men back in their own coin." (*Quotation*)

IV• *Conclusion*

    A. Read today's headlines.

      1. Note the signs of nationalism.

      2. Note the signs of imperialism.

      3. Note the signs of militarism.

    B. We all have seen the waste of war.

      1. There have been twenty-four major wars in modern times. (*Statistics*)

      2. There were 15 million deaths in World War II (approximating the populations of New York, Chicago, and Los Angeles). (*Statistics*)

    C. Now may be our last chance to do something about it.

      1. The noted author, Philip Wylie, remarked in the *Science Digest:* "It is obvious to any physicist worth his salt, that man is not at the end of his weaponeering capabilities, but, rather, at a fresh beginning." (*Quotation*)

      2. If this is the genesis of war's potential, it may well be man's exodus.

MODEL SPEECH OUTLINE 2

(In sentence form)

Where to Live?

I• *Introduction*

    A. "In the choice of a horse and a wife," said George John Whyte-Melville, "a man must please himself, ignoring the opinion and advice of friends." (*Quotation*)

    B. But in other cases, as in choosing a place to live while going to college, you may need the advice of friends.

    C. Whether with good advice, bad advice, or no advice, students must make their decisions.

      1. Of the 5500 people who attend our college, over 3500 have decided (for one reason or another) to live at home. (*Statistics*)

      2. Nearly 1000 live in dorms. (*Statistics*)

      3. About 700 live with fellow students in apartments and other small dwellings. (*Statistics*)

      4. The balance live in rooming houses or hotels, and so forth. (*Statistics*)

  D. If you are not happily settled in your present quarters, my talk today may be of some help.

II• *Proposition:* Consider with me important factors to weigh in determining your place of residence while at college.

III• *Body*

  A. Find a place that fits your financial condition.

    1. Living at home may be the best alternative.
      a. Parents may be willing to pay the board and room.
      b. But you will have transportation costs. (*Statistics*)
      c. Of course, you married persons have solved this part of the problem.

    2. Some students economize by renting an apartment together.
      a. Three girls found an inexpensive and small apartment within walking distance from the school for only $60 a month. (*Illustration*)
      b. Some apartments may cost more. (*Instance*)
      c. Others are out of the question for most student budgets. (*Instance*)

    3. Include other options in your thinking.
      a. The dorms will cost more than sharing an apartment.
      b. The CO-OP is an economical place to live. (*Statistics*)
      c. A suitable rooming house may be the answer.

  B. When you have calculated your budget, decide if the conditions suit your personal habits.

    1. "Know that living away from home often tries a person's ability to get along with others," says the dean of students at our college. (*Quotation*)

    2. Decide in what situation you can study best.
      a. Family life has its distractions.
      b. Dorm life may be noisy.

    3. Assess your present level of maturity.
      a. Determine if you are ready for the independent life or if you should stay at home for a year or two.
      b. Compare yourself with Jill, who found the freedom of living away from home to be beneficial. (*Illustration*)
      c. Terry lived away from home. (*Instance*)

       d. Bradley lived away from home. (*Instance*)

       e. Theresa lived away from home. (*Instance*)

       f. But one young person's case was different. (*Example to contrast*)

   4. Keep in mind other relevant personal details.

       a. You may have to adjust your sleeping habits. (*Hypothetical example*)

       b. "Two out of three roommates have occasional problems in adjusting to their partners' personal habits," according to the head resident at the dorm. (*Quotation*)

       c. Some conditions may be like life in a submarine. (*Analogy*)

IV• *Conclusion*

   A. I have mentioned only two of the factors to think about when trying to select your residence.

      1. First, remember, is the **question of money.**

      2. Second, is your personal character and development.

   B. The old saying, "Experience is the best teacher," is applicable here. (*Quotation*)

   C. Ultimately, you will have to do as I did: try for yourself the mode of living that appeals to you. (*Illustration*)

MODEL SPEECH

(Full text, based on OUTLINE 2)

Where to Live?

"In the choice of a horse and a wife," said George John Whyte-Melville, British novelist and poet, "a man must please himself, ignoring the opinion and advice of friends." That's probably true, but in other cases, such as in choosing a place to live while going to college, one may need the advice of friends.

Quotation

With good advice, bad advice, or no advice, students make their decisions. Of the 5500 people who attend our college, over 3500 have decided, for one reason or another, to live at home. Nearly 1000 live in dormitories. About 700 live with fellow students in apartments and other small resi-

Statistics

dences. The balance live in rooming houses, hotels, and so forth.

Are you satisfied with your present quarters? Are you happily settled in? If not, my talk today—and I'm definitely not going to talk about horses or wives—may be of some help.

Restatement

Consider with me important factors to weigh in determining your place of residence while at college.

Certainly, you must find a place that fits your financial condition. "Do I have money to cover the costs?" is a major question. Living at home with your parents may be the best—if you are short of money. Perhaps the parents will be willing to pay the board and will not need compensation for your use of the room. But you will still have transportation costs, which, realistically, ought to be computed at about ten cents per mile traveled in a car, or in accordance with local bus fares. Of course, you married persons live at home and have solved this part of the problem.

Restatement

Statistics

Some students economize by renting an apartment together. Three girls who attend this college decided that they could save money this way and began looking for an inexpensive apartment close to school. After a week of looking, they found an apartment down on Fifth Street in the 600 block, which was available for only $60 a month. They follow a food budget very closely and take advantage of sales. They are very satisfied with their choice.

Illustration

Art Fisher and Bill Dickens had to pay more—$70, I believe. Other apartments near the college have a much higher rental fee, ranging from $100 to $250 a month— out of the question for most student budgets.

Instances

Include other options in your thinking. The dorms, though convenient, will cost more than sharing an apartment. The CO-OP is an economical place in which to live. The co-op—let me explain to those not familiar with its operation—is that dormitory-like building south of the gym, where the residents economize by buying wisely and in large quantities; they also share various responsibilities for maintaining the routine of the house. Expenses there, may amount, in some cases, to two thirds or half of those incurred in apartment living.

Explanation

Statistics

When you have calculated your budget, decide if the conditions suit your personal habits. In the term, "personal habits," I include temperament, personality, and so forth. The dean of students here at the college, whom I talked to last week, said, "Know that living away from home often tries a person's ability to get along with others." That's his view, and he's had much experience in these matters.

Definition

Quotation

With education as the main motivation for being in college, you should decide in what situation you can study best. Are you easily disturbed by noise? How much room do you need for books, typewriter, and other equipment? At what times of day do you study best? Everyone knows that family life has its distractions. And dorm life may be considered noisy to many people.

Explanation

Also, assess your present level of maturity as well as you are able. Try to determine if you are ready for the independent life or if you should stay at home for a year or two. You might compare yourself with Jill. She found the freedom of living away from home to be beneficial to her. At first, she was reluctant to strike out on her own, but it was her mother, a widow with three children younger than Jill, who convinced her that she would very likely gain maturity from the experience. And such was the case. She is less dependent on people now and more self-confident.

Restatement

Illustration

Terry found the adjustment to dorm life to be quite easy. Bradley, who has lived in many places in his life, had no difficulty in getting accustomed to life at the co-op. Theresa, too, found that she was ready to leave home. Add to the list the names of people whom you know who no longer need the various "comforts of home." But there are some college entrants who are home bodies. I once knew such a person. He had graduated from high school at sixteen, and while mature in some ways, needed much more time than most people in readying himself to go on his own. Accepting his parents' suggestion, he wisely chose to live at home for a year or two.

Instances

Example to contrast

You may have to adjust your sleeping habits. Suppose that your roommate likes to study late, and you like to go to bed early, or vice versa. What's to be done? Some adjustment may be required—of both of you. Just yesterday, the head resident at our dorm said, "Two out of three roommates have occasional problems in adjusting to their partners' personal habits." Some conditions may be like life in a submarine; the quarters can be very compact. In such a situation, people are bound to face a problem now and then.

Hypothetical example

Quotation

Analogy

I have mentioned just two of the factors to think about when trying to select your residence. First, is that all-important question of money. And second is your personal character and development, and so forth. According to an old saying, "Experience is the best teacher." These words probably are applicable to our discussion today. Ultimately you will have to try whatever mode of living seems to appeal to you. That's just what I did. A year ago I talked it over with the folks—very understanding people, I found—and decided to move to the dorm, even though my family lives only four miles

Quotation

Illustration

away. But I wanted to be closer to the college—be a part of college life: the library,
games, dances, and all. So I packed up and
moved into the dorm. For me, it was the
right decision, I believe. You, too, will have
to decide for yourself.

BASIC ASSIGNMENT NO. 1

Prepare a speech in which you use an illustration and a series of
instances (at least two) to support each main head. Be certain that your
instances support the illustration. Employ the following aids:
1. Relevant statistics
2. A quotation
3. Transitions at all major points

Use your own judgment about the use of restatement, definition, explanation, and visual aids.

Reminders:
1. This is probably the most demanding assignment you have had
   so far; therefore, get an early start. Begin your planning now,
   and let your speech grow and become a part of you.
2. If during practice you consistently go overtime, it may be necessary to limit the subject or shorten the length of your materials.

BASIC ASSIGNMENT NO. 2

Prepare a speech and include all the elements you have used in previous assignments: transitions, restatements, explanations, definitions,
visual aids (sketches or objects), examples, statistics, and quotations.
Use your own judgment to determine how many of each to use and
where to place them.

Reminder:
Consider your purpose carefully, and employ your materials with an
end toward achieving that purpose.

Suggested Exercise A

The following examples might be used to support points of speeches.
Consider the essential idea that each expresses to you, and write an
appropriate heading for it.

Sample 1

General Douglas MacArthur fought in World War I, was Chief of
Staff from 1930–1935, commanded the United States Armed Forces in

the Far East during World War II, and directed the Allied Occupation of Japan following the war.

Sample 2

According to a Hindu fable, six blind men came across an elephant. The first approached it, felt its side and said, "It's a wall." The second felt a tusk and pronounced it a spear. The third touched the trunk and called it a snake, while the fourth felt a knee and cried, "Tree!" The fifth touched an ear and thought it a fan. And the sixth swung on the tail, thinking it a rope.

Sample 3

When a young, would-be writer asked a well-known novelist the secret of choosing appealing themes for fiction, he was told to talk with people and determine their interests. The young man did so and found three themes to be universally attractive. And the next week he started his first novel, with the title, *Lincoln's Doctor's Dog*.

Suggested Exercise B

The following statistics and quotations might be used to support points of speeches. Consider the essential idea that each expresses to you, and write an appropriate heading for it.

1. Thirty percent of 12,154 top high school students indicated recently that they had selected teaching as a career. Of this 30 percent, 455 were boys and 3199 were girls.
2. In 1850 half of the family income went for food. In 1900 it was one third, and today we spend but one fourth of our salaries for food.
3. It is estimated that industrial injuries amount to a loss of 193 million man-days annually. This is enough to produce 100 million refrigerators, 200 million men's suits, 1.5 billion pairs of men's shoes, 26,000 jet bombers, 1 million six-room homes, or 2 billion tons of coal.
4. "Education is a companion no misfortune can depress, no crime destroy, no friend alienate, no despotism enslave; at home a friend, abroad an introduction, in solitude a solace, in society an ornament, in old age a comfort—without it, what is man?"

   —Author Unknown
5. "Our youth now love luxury; they have bad manners, contempt for authority; they show disrespect for elders and love chatter in the place of exercise. Children are now tyrants, not the servants of their households. They no longer rise when elders enter the room. They contradict their parents, chatter before company, gobble up their food, and tyrannize their teachers."

   —Socrates, fifth century B.C.
6. "That man's a fool who tries by art and skill to stem the torrent of

a woman's will: For if she will, she will; you may depend on't—And
if she won't, she won't—and there's an end on't."

—Author Unknown

Suggested Exercise C

Find two items of verbal supporting material for each of the following points. Use the "Criteria for Selecting Verbal Materials" in this
chapter to check the importance of each item. State the sources of your
materials. (Your instructor may want you to present one of these as a
one-point speech.)

1.   College athletics are no longer amateur athletics.
2.   People should spend more time in recreation.
3.   The number of farms in America is decreasing.
4.   The number of job opportunities for women is increasing.

Suggested Exercise D

Study one of the full speeches in Appendix A. List each item of verbal
material used, what point it develops, and tell how the material helped
in developing the point.

Suggested Exercise E

Develop one point in a one-minute talk. Use an example, a quotation, and statistics.

Suggested Exercise F

Study the two excerpts of speeches by Jeremiah S. Black and Jack I.
Straus in Appendix A. Write a critical analysis of the speakers' use of
examples, stressing techniques that seem especially commendable.

Suggested Exercise G

Of the following, which are facts? Which are opinions? Which are
inaccurate assertions? Your own logic may provide some of the answers.
For others you will have to consult authoritative sources.

1.   Darwin's *Origin of Species* was published in 1859.
2.   Freedom is the greatest source of happiness.
3.   T. S. Eliot wrote *Family Reunion*.
4.   The dogfish is a porpoise.
5.   Ty Cobb was the greatest baseball player of all time.
6.   Homer lived before 800 B.C.
7.   Christmas Island is in the Indian Ocean.
8.   Julius Caesar was a self-seeking opportunist.
9.   A dog is man's best friend.
10. Winston Churchill, the famous statesman and orator, was an
     American.

Suggested Exercise H

Find three different examples—an analogy, a hypothetical example, and one of contrast—to support the following general statement:

Shopping is one of woman's greatest joys.

Suggested Exercise I

Introduce and close the following quotation in three different and refreshing ways:

> "What this country really needs is a good five-cent cigar."
>
> *—T. R. Marshall*

PART II

COMPLEMENTARY
METHODS

CHAPTER SEVEN

Using Effective Language

People do not always say just what they want to say. Imagine a grandmother's bewilderment upon reading the following telegram: TWINS ARRIVED TONIGHT. MORE BY MAIL.

Then there was the foreign visitor who told a New York bus driver, "Vill you procrastinate me at ze baseball park?" "Huh?" questioned the driver. "Procrastinate me at ze baseball park! Here, I vill show you." He took out a pocket dictionary and pointed to *procrastinate* which was defined as "to put off." Ten blocks later he was put off at Yankee Stadium.

Little children offer some of the best examples of language difficulty. There is the story of Bobby, a second-grader, who asked his teacher how many people stayed in the "back tier" during America's pioneering days. His teacher was confused until she became aware of Bobby's reasoning: he thought of "back tier" as the opposite of "frontier."

Language is a system of symbols for use in communication. Its sounds, words, and phrases, represent the thoughts of messages when put together in patterns. But the symbols themselves are valueless, without content; their only substance is in the meaning that they carry. The word tree is not a growing thing with a trunk, branches, and leaves. The word *tree* is a symbol composed of four letters of the English alphabet and put together into a pattern which is intelligible to those of us who read English. Phonetically—according to sound—the word is made up of three *phonemes* (sound units).

"The map is not the territory," say the general semanticists. Words are not the things to which they refer. The word *snake* is an arrangement of symbols, not a slithering and venomous creature that may threaten one. Conceivably, some person exists somewhere who cannot bring himself even to utter the word *snake* because he confuses the idea with the word. Some snakes are harmful while others are quite useful. The word is *always* harmless, when one uses logic.

Most *politicians, Negroes, labor leaders, salesmen, jazz musicians, garbage collectors,* and *real-estate brokers* are moral beings *and* harmless—the reactions of some persons to the names, notwithstanding. One can spare himself and others much anguish in life, if he can learn to handle words operationally, that is, on the basis of how a thing or person operates or behaves and not by responding emotionally to the name of the general category. Words are only symbols.

AN AGREEMENT

A language system is organized and based on the agreement of people. In this sense, agreement means the acceptance and use of a language by people in a community (nation or culture). Of course, being born into a language, we do not enter individually into the agreement in a strict sense, but our culture over the centuries has adopted and "agreed upon" our language as a code for communication. Language used for social intercourse is necessarily a social agreement. It is true, as we discussed in Chapter Four, that some groups (ocean surfers, for example) use terms not agreed upon by the larger society. But "jams" (flowery swimming trunks), "hangs five" (have five toes over the front tip of the surfboard), "gremmy" (surfing novice), and "woodie" (wood-paneled station wagon) are terms agreed upon by the surfing society.

Moreover, the language is constantly changing. New words are coined daily, and words once used only by certain groups are adopted by the general society; for instance, the word *cool,* once the possession of jazz musicians. Modes of expression change. Splitting infinitives and ending a sentence with a preposition now seem to be acceptable informal oral usages in the eyes of most people.

Users of a language make other agreements. They conclude, for example, that certain language usages are *standard* (represesentative of the language of educated people) and that others are *substandard* (of the uneducated). The following are substandard expressions:

There's many people here.

He hits the ball good.

The runner was throwed out.

She sung a pretty song.

Get off'n the horse.

Furthermore, language use often varies with the social situation in which it is used. It may be *formal* or *informal,* depending on a speaker's reaction to a situation. The four expressions below are standard. Notice the greater degree of informality of those on the right.

They want no more.	They don't want any more.
Thank you for the drink.	Thanks for the drink.
I reside in an apartment.	I live in an apartment.
We met on the corner of 12th and Grove Streets.	We met at 12th and Grove.

Along with standards of acceptability and levels of formality, language has *rhetorical values*. In terms of practical usage, the rhetorical values in language include standards and levels of formality but are more basic. Rhetorical values have to do with audience acceptability and responses, with the effect that language has on the listener. Good language, rhetorically, is that which is suitable and adaptive in a given speaking situation; it is that which assists in achieving a meeting of minds with listeners and does not detract from the thought. Overly formal language or substandard language will detract on many occasions. If language is pedantic or highly scientific, unfamiliar or ungrammatical or threatening, it may interfere with communication. As communication theorists say, such language may constitute "noise" in the circuits of communication. But strange as it may seem, these same five types of language may, in rare instances, be entirely useful in conveying ideas. The prime variable is the situation—and the speaker's response to the demands of the situation. Effective language practice may depend less on criteria of right and wrong than on usefulness.

DENOTATION AND CONNOTATION

Words and terms have two kinds of meanings. The first is the logical, objective, dictionary meaning. This is the explicit meaning, that on which most people would be in agreement. For example, a *home* denotes a dwelling of a person or family. That is *denotative* meaning.

The second is the emotional, subjective, personal meaning. This is the meaning that an individual finds in the word, a special meaning. Home may connote a place of sadness where an invalid grandmother lies silently on a bed in a darkened room. That is a *connotative* meaning of home.

To one person, geometry may be that branch of mathematics that treats of space and its relations (denotative meaning). To someone else, it connotes a source of challenge and satisfaction; and to another, it is a bore. The meaning which first jumps into a person's mind when he meets a term is often the connotative or personal meaning; though upon reflection, he may be able to phrase a more exact and more widely accepted definition.

The more abstract the term, the more varied are our emotional reactions to it, that is, the more connotations it has. To illustrate: what is *wealth*? Who are *left-wingers*? What does it mean to *make a hit* with the girl's folks? Or to *sink or swim*? *America* may be the United States or the United States along with Canada, Mexico, and all countries to the south, but what does *America* mean to you? What does the word connote? Your connotation will vary with that of the person who sits next to you in class. What connotations do you find for words like *apathy, energy, bliss, marriage, speed, fear, time, friend, struggle,* and *promise*?

Let us examine some words in context. Study the language in the passage below, the words of a familiar song, "John Brown's Body."

He captured Harper's Ferry with his nineteen men so true,
And he frightened old Virginia till she trembled through and through.
They hung him for a traitor, themselves the traitor crew,
    But his soul is marching on!
    Glory, glory! Hallelujah!
    Glory, glory! Hallelujah!
    Glory, glory! Hallelujah!
His soul is marching on!

As in most songs, the words are strongly subjective. Feeling dominates. What are "true" men? Many connotations are possible. What does it mean to "frighten old Virginia" and make her "tremble"? The judgment that "they" are the "traitor crew" is a personal judgment, and "traitor crew" is a loaded term. The image of a soul "marching on" is a gloriously romantic picture. The song has very little objectivity and, of course, does not pretend to have.

Read next, the concluding paragraph from an article in a professional journal.[1]

> Of the several findings, the significant relationships of listening to teachers' grades and of reading to achievement scores seem the most important for further research. These results themselves should be checked through replications of the present experiment, for if accurate they are significant in several respects. They suggest, for instance, that achievement scores may be a better predictor of the ability to do independent study than are teachers' grades, they provide a possible explanation as to why grades are a good predictor of future academic success, and they suggest that listening and attractive personality factors may be related. Finally, these and other studies in this broad area eventually may help to determine which instructional materials should be presented through the spoken word and which should be made available in the printed form.

[1] Charles T. Brown, "Three Studies of the Listening of Children," *Speech Monographs*, XXXII (June, 1965), 129–138.

Some readers may fit the conclusions to their own experience and thus give connotations to certain phrases. But fundamentally, the language is more denotative. It is scientific and would be understood in the same way by most readers of the journal. Never would it stir and inspire as "John Brown's Body" once did.

But how would you analyze typical speaking? Most speaking probably would fall somewhere between the song and the scientific piece. Communication requires exactness and clarity; but needless to say, absolute precision is impossible. Moreover, even if it were possible, who would want to listen to it for very long? Speech must be clear, yes, but also *appealing*. It must have interest and color. It must be *popular*, in the best sense of the word: designed for reception by thinking and feeling people, people who respond to a substantial message best when it is conveyed with engaging language.

The passage below is from a speech by Lynn A. Townsend, President of the Chrysler Corporation. Notice the combination of subjective and objective elements.

> Perhaps one of the best examples of the search for this moral equivalent of war is the Peace Corps. I think it's fair to say that few programs ever proposed have been so skeptically considered by the older generation, or so beautifully made to work by the younger. A good number of my generation have had to eat crow about this program, which seemed to them too idealistic and impractical. But the results have been good for all of us. We've been shown a side of today's young people that we're happy to see—some sleeves have been rolled up and some hands have been dirtied. In the manner of the missionaries of a century ago and of today, these young people have extended a helping hand where there had been none before—doing practical and often very hard work to improve the lives of other people. Apparently they have come to understand that the essence of inhumanity is not to hate our fellow men, but to be indifferent to them. And they have expressed their understanding in a practical way.[2]

The speaker appeals to the good sense and to the emotions of his hearers (the graduating class and assembled guests at Alma College). The "practical and often very hard work" and the "results" of which he speaks can be verified. But his subjective references to his generation having "to eat crow," to "some sleeves" that "have been rolled up" and "dirty hands," to "missionaries," and so forth, are more connotative expressions. They enrich the discourse and add interest. In sum, he has a reasonable point and very likely communicated it with high audience interest.

[2] "Idealism without Illusions," *Vital Speeches of the Day*, XXXII (August 1, 1966), p. 627.

A COMMON GROUND IN USAGE

As we have suggested in nearly every chapter of the book, communication may depend on a speaker's willingness or ability to address others on their own ground or, better, on a *common* ground. One might say that speakers find listeners "as they find them"; that is to say, people are not made up as ideal organisms, ever ready to understand all that a speaker says—regardless of the value of the message. Some listen fairly well; others do not. Some may be prepared to grasp the ideas of a given speech; others may not. Some, but not all in an audience, may have certain experiences akin to the speaker's. Some, but certainly not all, may have connotations of the speaker's words that would square with his. All this is to lead to the premise that words can further the separation of speaker and listener, or they can bring the two closer together and thus enhance communication.

Good language is language adapted to the audience. "It is," writes linguist Robert A. Hall, Jr., "language which gets the desired effect with the least friction and difficulty for the user. That means, of course, that 'good' language is going to vary with the situation in which it is used." [3]

In choosing language, you the speaker, must consider the four familiar elements of speaking: yourself, your speech, your audience, and the occasion. When preparing and rehearsing your speeches, ask this question about your choice of language: "Is this word (or phrase or sentence) suitable for *me* to use in communicating *this thought* to *this audience* on *this occasion?"*

Use Language that Clarifies your Thoughts

1. USE SIMPLE, UNPRETENTIOUS LANGUAGE

Unless more complex wording is needed to get the message across, say it simply. Communication can often break down if the terminology is too technical, if a speaker uses "big words" for their own sake and lets the language become overly involved. The use of too many words and ornate or pretentious words may hamper communication and violate the criteria of clarity in speaking: directness, economy, and aptness.

Ralph Waldo Emerson tells us, "An orator or author is never successful until he has learned to make his words smaller than his ideas." The language found in John F. Kennedy's best speeches exemplifies an effective communicative style. He and those who helped him phrase his thoughts knew the importance of simplicity and straightforwardness in expression. This passage from his Inaugural Address is an example:

[3] *Linguistics and Your Language,* 2d ed. (New York, 1960), p. 27.

> To those peoples in the huts and villages across the globe struggling to break the bonds of mass misery, we pledge our best efforts to help them help themselves, for whatever period is required—not because the Communists may be doing it, not because we seek their votes, but because it is right. If a free society cannot help the many who are poor, it cannot save the few who are rich.

The simplest language is usually the most profound and practical, while flowery, glib, and profuse expressions distract listeners. When an audience is concerned about *how* it is being said instead of *what* is being said, communication suffers.

It is usually better to say:	*Instead of:*
lie	prevarication
name	cognomen
home	domicile
At this important ceremony . . .	At this august solemnization . . .
I am glad to be here with friends.	By virtue of the fact that we are all friends and have been for years, this moment is one of great joy to my heart.

By all means give your thoughts significance and meaning, but in so doing, be guided by the declaration of a wise man: "Clearness ornaments profound thoughts."

2. USE PRECISE LANGUAGE

We all recognize that the human organism is not a precision instrument. We make mistakes; we waste motion; we are often quite inefficient. And yet, paradoxically, we have distinguished ourselves despite our limiting human condition. As examples of notable oral communication, remember the Gettysburg Address, Patrick Henry's "Give me liberty or give me death," or even possibly the campaign speech of a candidate for student office.

Yes, it is truly remarkable that *human beings* using *human skills* are able to create mutual understanding. Actually, we are able to communicate, at best, only a fraction of any total thought or feeling. Since speech is used primarily to influence people, does it not seem logical that every speaker has an obligation to be as exact and precise as is humanly possible?

It is often better to say:	*Instead of:*
commendable, useful, beneficial, advantageous, choice, priceless, genuine, valuable, and so forth.	good

It is often better to say:	*Instead of:*
hardtop, sedan, convertible, *or* Chevrolet, *or* dark blue, 1967 fast-back Mustang	car
replied, stated, cried, commented, uttered	said
pretty, neat, grand, worthy, attractive, desirable, pleasant	fine
novel, text, anthology, pamphlet	book
river, creek, brook, millrace	stream

Especially plaguing are the vague words, *very, nice,* and *interesting.* To find more specific substitutes for these and other hazy terms, consult your dictionary or thesaurus. Mark Twain quite persuasively summed up the need for being exact: "The difference between the right word and the almost right word is the difference between lightning and the lightning bug."

The *euphemism* or roundabout word or expression is a special problem in imprecision. Speakers occasionally cast a euphemism when they wish to avoid being blunt or frank. This form of "soft-pedaling" an idea may be justified now and then, if the speaker does not sacrifice sincerity and honesty in the process. On the other hand, if use of euphemisms is extensive in a person's speaking or if he uses them to deceive, audiences doubtless will come to question his ideas or intent. Wishing to avoid an undesirable connotation of the words *death* or *dead,* and so forth, speakers often speak of "his passing," "the departed," "was called away," or "eternal rest." The cautious parent who finally works up enough courage to discuss the "facts of life" (a euphemism, itself) with his son or daughter may rely heavily on euphemisms. Soldiers in war may call a retreat a "strategic withdrawal." A politician, when challenged regarding his position on a controversial policy, may say, "The over-all impact on the economy will not be inconsiderable." He knows that the impact will be heavy and that saying so directly will arouse hostility.

Though audiences and purposes vary—

It might be better to say:	*Instead of:*
The company fired Bill.	The company gave Bill his termination notice.
The mob decided to kill Frankie.	The mob decided to remove Frankie from the scene.
He got out of the house.	He arranged for alternate lodging.

It might be better to say:	*Instead of:*
I like your idea—or—	I am not unsympathetic to your
I do not like your idea.	proposal.
Stephen eats too much.	Stephen is a victim of overzealousness at the dinner table.
I have bad news.	I have just heard something that will not be the most welcome information.

Check your language habits. Excessive or imprudent use of euphemisms can make for flabby expression, and it can raise doubts about your purpose.

Use Language that Enlivens your Thoughts

1. USE LANGUAGE THAT APPEALS TO THE SENSES

Paint word pictures that connote impressions of form, texture, and color. Put life into your speaking, and use words that help you to achieve your purpose. In his Inaugural Address, Kennedy appealed to the senses of his listeners through language, influencing them to share in his ideas, to identify with them. Note in the selected portion below, the specific appeals to movement, to light, to texture, and to taste. The result is a spirit-lifting and exciting statement of resolve. It is strong, youthful, and inviting.

> We dare not forget today that we are the heirs of that first revolution. Let the word go forth from this time and place, to friend and foe alike, that the torch has been passed to a new generation of Americans—born in this century, tempered by war, disciplined by a hard and bitter peace, proud of our ancient heritage—and unwilling to witness or permit the slow undoing of those human rights to which this nation has always been committed, and to which we are committed today at home and around the world.

Not everyone can reach the standard of John Kennedy. Nor does everyone find himself in situations similar to those that he faced; however, we are all communicators, and in our realms have significant ideas to share.

It might be better to say:	*Instead of:*
A blue-eyed, sprightly girl of four tossed her blond pigtails into the air as she skipped and bounced across the flat, clay schoolyard.	The girl played.
The s.s. *"Artemus,"* decaying and weary after forty years of unfailing service between James Island and the mainland, settled to the dark,	The old ship sank.

It might be better to say:	*Instead of:*
muddy bottom of the harbor noiselessly and peacefully.	

2. USE FIGURATIVE LANGUAGE

A fitting figure of speech can animate an abstract idea and enable a speaker to attain richness of expression and listener involvement. Although many such gems of language are available to the speaker, simile, metaphor, personification, and irony are especially useful.

A *simile* is a short comparison introduced with *like* or *as*.

It might be better to say:	*Instead of:*
Like wild wind on a March day, her presence put everyone on edge.	Her presence put everyone on edge.
Running down the road as if tormented by a hornet, Raymond outdistanced his sister.	Running down the road, Raymond outdistanced his sister.

A *metaphor* is an implied comparison in which something is spoken of as being something else. The words *like* and *as* are not used.

In the excerpts from Kennedy's Inaugural that follow, observe the graphic and persuasive metaphors. The first is a stern and unmistakable warning to tyrants; the second is a figure expressing hope, appealing to all who yearn for a fresh start and who seek a reaffirmation of faith in the future.

> But we shall always hope to find them [new nations] strongly supporting their own freedom—and to remember that, in the past, *those who foolishly sought power by riding the back of the tiger ended up inside.*
>
> And if *a beachhead of cooperation may push back the jungle of suspicion,* let both sides join in creating a new endeavor, not a new balance of power, but a new world of law, where the strong are just and the weak secure and the peace preserved.

It might be better to say:	*Instead of:*
History is the gateway to the trodden field of man's recorded experience.	History introduces one to man's recorded experience.
He was a caged lion, walking to and fro.	He walked to and fro.
"The torch has been passed to a new generation."	A new generation is now leading.

Personification gives human qualities to inanimate objects.

It might be better to say:	*Instead of:*
The pines whispered.	The wind in the pines made soft noises.

It might be better to say:	*Instead of:*
Law is a spokesman for every man.	Law is for the protection of every man.

Irony is a figure of speech in which the intended meaning is opposite to that indicated by the words used. It is often sarcastic.

It might be better to say:	*Instead of:*
You know how children hate watermelon.	Children love watermelon.
Oh no, we just twiddled our thumbs on the ranch last summer.	We worked very hard on the ranch last summer.

Use Language that Lends Variety

1. USE DIVERSIFIED LANGUAGE

We like variety in our lives. William Cowper once observed, "Variety's the very spice of life, that gives it all its flavour." We vary the placement of our living-room furniture, our choice of current songs to sing, our wearing apparel, and our sources of entertainment. We should do more to vary our language in speaking.

How can the desired variety be achieved?

First of all, you can try varying the shaping of sentences. If you characteristically employ long and loosely constructed sentences, it would be well for you to break up the pattern with a short, emphatic sentence now and then. If your habit is to use an overabundance of simple sentences that usually begin with the subject, you can add variety by introducing an occasional periodic sentence—that is, one that withholds the important thought until the end. If your practice is to rely almost entirely upon declarative and imperative sentences, perhaps you should put a question into your discourse at times.

Occasionally it might be better to say:	*Instead of:*
From now on we will lock our doors. (Periodic)	We will lock our doors from now on.
Since its formation in 1945, the United Nations has helped to promote peace throughout the world. (Periodic)	The United Nations has helped to promote world peace since its formation in 1945.
What standards should be set down?	These standards should be set down.
How long has it been since our salaries were raised?	You know how long it has been since our salaries were raised.

Seek changes from your usual thought patterning by occasionally introducing alternate forms of expression. Among them are climax, parallelism, alliteration, and repetition. Develop a sensitivity to them, and learn to use them well—and unselfconsciously.

Climax is a building of interest within a passage. The speaker arranges elements to achieve an increase of force or impact, seeking a corresponding increase of listener attention to his thought. The final sentence in this section of President Kennedy's Inaugural Address is the climactic statement.

> To our sister republics south of our border, we offer a special pledge —to convert our good words into good deeds, in a new alliance for progress, to assist free men and free governments in casting off the chains of poverty. But this peaceful revolution of hope cannot become the prey of hostile powers. Let all our neighbors know that we shall join with them to oppose aggression or subversion anywhere in the Americas. And let every other power know that this hemisphere intends to remain the master of its own house.

Parallelism is a form of structuring that sets one phrase or clause against another in a balanced relationship. In form, each is equal to the other. The symmetry appeals to listeners' sense of proportion. Remember the balanced clauses of Julius Caesar's report of victory?— "I came, I saw, I conquered." Here is a sampling of parallel structure from Kennedy's speech:

> If a free society cannot help the many who are poor, it cannot save the few who are rich.
> United, there is little we cannot do in a host of cooperative ventures. Divided, there is little we can do . . . .
> Let us never negotiate out of fear. But let us never fear to negotiate.

Alliteration is the artful repetition of sounds in a passage. It, too, adds variety and is designed to heighten the force of an idea. A speaker who wishes forcibly to say, "The community, shocked by disaster, attempted to regain its normal operations," might communicate his thoughts more effectively by saying: "The community, *t*orn by *t*ension and *t*error, attempted to right itself."

We discussed *repetition* in Chapter Four but reintroduce the concept here to emphasize its value as a form of language usage for stimulating audience interest and stressing thought. Again, Kennedy's speech is our model:

> Let both sides explore what problems unite us instead of laboring those problems which divide us.
> Let both sides, for the first time, formulate serious and precise proposals for the inspection and control of arms—and bring the absolute power to destroy other nations under the absolute control of all nations.

Let both sides seek to invoke the wonders of science instead of its terrors. Together let us explore the stars, conquer the deserts, eradicate disease, tap the ocean depths, and encourage the arts and commerce.

Let both sides unite to heed in all corners of the earth the command of Isaiah—to "undo the heavy burdens and to let the oppressed go free."

2. USE FRESH LANGUAGE

Vary your use of individual words and phrases, too. In informal speaking situations, it is appropriate for you to add variety by including contractions and other acceptable colloquialisms. Be wary, though, of the *unacceptable* expression. Unfortunately some clichés and slang expressions which seem to serve us well on some occasions create listening blocks on other occasions. Certain old sayings that once were attractive are worn-out and useless now; others, especially some slang terms, are repulsive or meaningless to many listeners.

From your own experience as a listener, can you think of terms that you find grating and cause you to be distracted? Such distractions can be costly, indeed, when the speaker is a salesman, a politician seeking votes, or a young man being interviewed for a job. A word or phrase is acceptable if it does not call attention to itself and if it helps to communicate the ideas. When in doubt, you should ask yourself this key question: "Will *this wording* help me to communicate *this idea* to *this audience* on *this occasion?*"

Usually it would be better to say:	*Instead of:*
girl, lady, or woman	a member of the fair sex
He is growing rapidly.	He is growing like a weed.
finally or last on the list	last but not least
terrible or distasteful, and so forth.	gosh awful
poor, dreadful, imperfect, shocking, destructive, and so forth.	lousy
truly, true, actual, honestly, and so forth.	for real

Use Language that is Appropriate

1. USE LANGUAGE APPROPRIATE TO THE OCCASION

In addition to being overused, some of the words and phrases in the right column of the section above would be unacceptable in certain situations on any count—for instance, "lousy," "for real," and "gosh awful." Our main concern at this point lies with acceptability of word choice and usage. Now, one might appeal for better language usage by building a case for showing pride in the beauty of our language, but there is a more cogent and practical reason for advocating that speakers use language with care. It is that many listeners are bothered by speakers' lapses in adjustment to the level of formality of an occasion. When speakers are overly formal or overly informal, listeners' minds have a tendency to leave the message and focus on the expression.

Depending on the level of formality of the occasion—

It might be better to say:	Instead of:
man or boy	guy
I will not be long.	I shan't be long.
finished or completed	finalized
I shop at Safeway.	I shop Safeway.
Where are you going?	Where are you going to?
I am not related to him.	He's no kin of mine.
Am I to go with you?	Aren't I to accompany you?

2. USE STANDARD LANGUAGE

As mentioned earlier in the chapter, linguists often classify language as standard or substandard. The language of the educated is standard, the language which you will doubtless find most useful in your life. In the great majority of your oral exchanges, substandard expression probably is, and certainly will be increasingly, a hindrance. If a listener hears, "We was . . .," he is moved to judge, not the idea, but the person delivering the idea. As unfair as it may seem, his judgment may be against both the speaker and the idea.

As you study the samples in the two columns below, you will probably discover that most of your modes of expression can be found in the left column. Should you find that you habitually use any of those in the right column, take it as a sign of need to review and revise your language practice.

It is always appropriate to say:	Instead of:
We accepted the invitation.	We excepted the invitation.
regardless	irregardless
this	this here
broke	busted
cannot	can't hardly
his	his'n

It is always appropriate to say:	*Instead of:*
rather *or* somewhat	kind of
He did it.	He done it.
I am going to lie down.	I am going to lay down.
It is very hot today.	It is real hot today.

USE YOUR LANGUAGE

Use clear, vivid, and undistracting language, yes, but use *your* language. Improve your use of English, yes, but start from the foundation you have been laying these past years. Take yourself where you are, and start your program of self-improvement. Do not think in terms of a major overhaul but of gradual and steady development toward ever-increasing skill in the use of language. Avoid attempting a radical change in style. Instead, occasionally substitute new words, improved phrasing, and more appropriate forms for weaker and less effective units of expression. Such action will enable you to present yourself as yourself and to obviate the fear that so many seem to have: "If I do not make some English errors, my friends will think I am a stuffed shirt; if I change my speaking habits, I will not be able to talk with some people." Growth and personal appeal need not be incompatible.

 Listen.

Learn to listen to yourself. And listen to the practices of users of standard English. Compare your language with theirs, and weed out undesired words and forms. But, listen to compare and to check yourself with the standard, not to find a *new* style of speaking.

 Read.

Read as widely and as avidly as your time and inclination will allow. Read without consciously thinking about language development. Just read. In the process, you will painlessly acquaint yourself with varied and useful forms of expression and possibly increase your appreciation of each man's unique way of developing thought through language.

 Write.

Though certainly harder work than listening or reading, writing will sharpen your sensitivity to language usage. The practice of casting a sentence on paper and then recasting it, and recasting it once more, is an invaluable builder of the discipline of shaping ideas in language. The benefits may be well worth the required rigor.

 Speak.

Take advantage of every opportunity to speak. Say, "Yes," when asked to chair a meeting, conduct a forum, or make an announcement. Language is tied to thinking processes and, therefore, to your ability to think before people. Experiences in speaking will add to your ability to cope with situations that require competence in thinking and casting ideas into effective language.

DO YOU REALLY WANT TO IMPROVE?

It is one thing to read about how to develop language skills, but do you *really* want to improve? This is a basic question. Without the desire, it cannot be done. Without your recognition of the need for lucid and rich expression, the job cannot be started. It is much like a fundamental premise held by psychologists: If the patient himself does not want to be helped, he cannot be helped.

LET US SUMMARIZE

Assuming that you do wish to help yourself, where do you start? First of all, make an accounting of your strengths and weaknesses. Become conscious of your usage, and gradually replace the less effective.

1. Use simple and precise language which clarifies your thoughts.
2. Use sense-appealing and figurative language which enlivens your thoughts.
3. Use diversified and fresh language that lends variety.
4. Use standard language that is appropriate for the occasion.
5. Use *your* language.

Above all, remember that the *thought* is supreme; it is the thought that you wish to communicate. Yet language, necessarily associated with the thought and its oral representation (or misrepresentation), deserves a full share of our attention.

Consider one last case in point, a not so serious, but relevant, reminder about using effective language.

Dear William,
    Are you still upset about last night? If I could I would like to clarify that it was really in jest when I told you I really didn't mean what I told

you about changing my mind about not reconsidering my decision. These are my sincere feelings.

Yours always,
Marjorie Y.

Perhaps William and Marjorie's understanding of one another is sufficient to allow them to communicate in spite of the apparent verbal confusion. If so, one would wish that all senders and receivers of the language had a sizable portion of such common understanding. But they do not. We must use effective language to create it.

AIDS IN LANGUAGE USAGE

To a speaker or writer (and who is not?), there are three essential books: a good dictionary, an English handbook, and a book of synonyms and antonyms, or thesaurus.

Dictionaries

The American College Dictionary (New York, 1964).
Standard College Dictionary (New York, 1963).
Webster's New Collegiate Dictionary, 7th ed. (Springfield, Mass., 1965).
Webster's New World Dictionary of the American Language (Cleveland, 1966).

Handbooks of English

Buckler, William E. and William C. McAvoy, *American College Handbook of English Fundamentals* (New York, 1965).
Shaw, Harry, and Richard H. Dodge, *The Shorter Handbook of College Composition* (New York, 1965).
Watt, William W., *An American Rhetoric,* 3d ed. (New York, 1964).
Wilson, Harris W., and Louis G. Locke, *The University Handbook,* 2d ed. (New York, 1966).

Thesauri

Dutch, Robert A., *Roget's Thesaurus of English Words and Phrases,* rev. ed. (New York, 1964).
Lewis, Norman, *Thesaurus of Synonyms* (New York, 1965).

Suggested Exercise A

Write, word for word, a short speech to be read instead of delivered extemporaneously. Include all the basic elements called for in preparing speeches and whatever developmental materials you need. Give special attention to the language factors discussed in this chapter:

1. Simplicity
2. Preciseness
3. Vividness

4. Variety
5. Appropriateness
6. Naturalness

Suggested Exercise B

Prepare a speech in which you include the basic elements of speaking and whatever materials that are needed to develop your ideas. Use each of the four figures of speech discussed in this chapter at least once. Write them into your outline.

During one practice session record your speech and analyze your use of language by answering the following questions after you play it back:

1. Was the wording simple and precise? What wording was not?
2. Can the language be made more vivid? How?
3. Were there any overused words or phrases?
4. Was any inappropriate slang used?
5. Were there any distracting ungrammatical expressions?
6. Was the language natural and representative?

During your next practice session, revise the speech on the basis of your answers to the questions.

Suggested Exercise C

Listen to a speech of a known public figure. Analyze it, using the six questions stated in *Suggested Exercise B.*

Suggested Exercise D

Read a printed speech from *Appendix A* or from a source such as *Representative American Speeches* or *Vital Speeches,* and cite ten specific uses of language that helped the speaker express his thoughts vividly and clearly.

Suggested Exercise E

Write ten terms or sentences that would be inappropriate (substandard, or not on the appropriate level of formality) for use before your class. Be prepared to justify your selection.

Suggested Exercise F

Make two lists, one headed "Overused Terms" and the other headed "Ambiguous or Meaningless Terms." Develop the lists either by recalling terms you have heard or by listening closely to the speech of people with whom you come in contact.

Your instructor may want you to prepare an oral report on your project, or he may want to make a master list from written class reports of all the students.

Suggested Exercise G

Compose four figures of speech, each one of a different type, and explain how each might be used to help express a thought.

Suggested Exercise H

Using a thesaurus, make a list of all the synonyms for *nice* (meaning "pleasing"), *very,* and *thing.*

Suggested Exercise I

Prepare a two-minute speech in which you make as many appeals to the senses as possible.

Suggested Exercise J

Without spending too much time in thought, list the connotations that come immediately to mind for these terms.

happiness	pencil
steam shovel	rapture
tension	spirit

Suggested Exercise K

Become conscious of the prevalence of euphemisms by recording each one that you hear during one day. Your instructor may wish to have you report your findings in class.

Suggested Exercise L

Name any audience of people who assemble for a mutual purpose, for example the Daughters of the American Revolution, the Democratic party, the Teamsters Union, and so forth. List ten samples of language usage that would probably help to establish a *common ground* for communicating with them.

CHAPTER EIGHT

Refining Speech Delivery

Which is more important in speechmaking, content or delivery? Is what a speaker says more important than the way in which he says it? This question is debated with surprising frequency. Truly the frequency is surprising, for the question can never be resolved either way. Both content and delivery are important. *Neither* should be neglected. Now, one might say that content is more important because it is attended to first and it *is* the message; yet, without adequate delivery, the message will not be communicated. Giving attention to one while neglecting the other will lead to defeat of the ends of communication.

ADAPTING

The concept of *adapting* helps one to understand the important (the essential) service of delivery in cooperatively functioning with content in speechmaking. To *adapt,* according to *Webster's Collegiate Dictionary,* means "to make suitable; to fit, or suit; to adjust." A speaker is successful to the extent that he is able to adapt his ideas to his audience.

In the predelivery stages of speech work, one makes major steps toward adapting by planning and composing thoughtfully. One attempts to adjust his ideas or to make them suitable and fitting in the following ways:

1. By choosing a suitable subject.
2. By carefully wording a purpose.
3. By analyzing and arranging his thoughts.
4. By strengthening and supporting his thoughts.
5. By preparing to use effective language.

Finally, one must adapt his prepared thoughts and deliver them to his audience directly. A speaker is much like a house painter at this point. The speaker has composed a speech, and the painter has mixed his paint. Now each has the job of applying his "content." Will the painter make efforts to work his paint into the wood, to adapt his paint? Will the speaker make efforts to work his ideas into the minds and hearts of his listeners, to adapt his ideas? In each case, a conscientious worker would make such efforts. Whether he is a painter or speaker, the experienced craftsman knows that if he is to be effective, his material must be accepted, assimilated, and in some cases retained. Delivery, for the speaker, is primarily a matter of adapting ideas.

As a speaker, you have one instrument to use in delivering your thoughts and feelings, and that is *you*. As parts of the total, integrated you, however, there are four elements which offer themselves for study: your personality, your body, your voice, and your processes of articulation. None of these elements is independent; each one is related to the others. To gain a better understanding of the complete process of delivery, let us isolate them and examine them one at a time.

PERSONALITY

Personality can be defined as the sum total of one's body, mind, and emotional characteristics; it is those patterns of behavior, interests, temperaments, attitudes, values, and motives that distinguish one person from another.

What are the specific features of *your* personality? What are *your* distinguishing characteristics of body, mind, and emotions? Do you know what they are? Are you an outgoing person who enters into many social activities, or does your temperament influence you to minimize your social life? Are you generally liberal or rather conservative? Are you ambitious or easygoing, optimistic or frequently more pessimistic? Whatever your personal qualities are, it is important for you to recognize them, to begin to know yourself. Self-improvement is based upon self-knowledge.

Effectiveness in speaking requires your acceptance of yourself, in addition to understanding yourself. Now, *acceptance* does not mean overlooking personal needs. Certainly you wish to continue a program of self-improvement until you have come to terms with yourself. After all, every human being who desires to better his personality is to be commended. No one, however, should refuse to recognize and accept his basic and important personal assets. Too many people totally reject themselves. As a result of this preoccupation with the negative, they cut down their own efficiency in speaking—indeed, in any social situation. When a person is apologetic and otherwise gives the impression that what he has to say is not worthwhile, the audience might believe him. If this happens, both the speaker and the audience lose. On this point Joshua Loth Liebman wrote in *Peace of Mind:* "Self-understand-ing rather than self-condemnation is the way to inner peace and mature conscience." It is also a way to more effective speaking.

Free yourself, and let your best self and whole self come forward to help you deliver your ideas. People usually respect other people who are willing to accept themselves and release their thoughts and feelings. From such willingness it follows that their ideas, too, will stand a better chance of being respected. We really cannot separate a person from his ideas; moreover, great thinkers—from Aristotle to most contemporary experts—have found that a speaker's strongest point is himself. Do not be afraid to be yourself. Will Rogers was a man who knew thousands of people and yet was able to say, "I never met a man I didn't like." Nonetheless, it would be misleading to imply that everyone who is him-self will be liked. Obviously, such is not the case. But by the same logic, you can be sure that being oneself and freeing oneself for speaking are not conditions for necessarily provoking enmity. There is no better place to start gaining true freedom of personal expression than in your speech class.

BODY

Your bodily actions are also agents of expression, and here, once again, we find differences among people. From each individual person-ality come individual forms of physical activity. Some people are ex-tremely active and seem to move constantly, while others exhibit a minimum of action.

Which pattern is the right one for a speaker, the active or inactive? Actually, neither is right nor wrong. The right pattern for you is the one which is a reflection of you. Express yourself with as much bodily action as is consistent with both your personality and the ideas that you are communicating. If you use physical movement extensively, you will probably use arm gestures and other movements automatically if, on any given occasion, you happen to be delivering a strong point. Bodily activity, whether limited or extensive, is a part of the language of expressing ideas. An arm movement may add punctuation or empha-sis. A nodding of the head or a step forward may actually "say" some-thing to the listeners. To assist in achieving desired ends, speakers subconsciously let their bodies engage compatibly with other elements of the total act of oral communication. The slightest movement, in a strict sense, becomes a part of the message. Movement that is consistent with the content enhances development of thought.

There is, then, no formula for either bodily action or use of gestures that can be applied to all people. If you have a deep desire to communicate, and are sure of your thoughts, usually your body will respond naturally to help you communicate. One of America's outstanding speakers of the last century, Robert G. Ingersoll, said that "if you really understand what you say, emphasis, tone and gesture will take care of themselves. All these should come from the inside." [1] Your nature, associated with the content of your speech, will dictate the forms of your physical response.

Nonetheless, a degree of control may be called for at times. No element of delivery should call attention to itself since delivery is important only insofar as it assists in communicating the content of a speech. Therefore, you should avoid wasteful pacing, shifting weight from one foot to another, uncomfortable stances, window gazing, "waltzing" with the speakers' stand, toying with a pencil, anxiously handling your notes, and slouchy posture.

Heavy reliance on notes is another obstacle to communication. Ample practice along with real concern for reaching your audience will help you to escape this pitfall. Your notes should be as brief as possible, and for some speeches, perhaps, recorded only in your head. Whenever you can get by without notes, you will have removed one more source of potential distraction. For a reminder of suggestions on the use of notes, turn back to the Model Speaking Notes and explanation for their use in Chapter Three.

Eye contact performs extremely significant functions in speechmaking. Looking at one's listeners is part and parcel of talking *with* them. It is a mode of address that audiences expect to accompany the discussion. Audiences anticipate eye contact and are bothered when speakers do not look at them regularly. They expect a speaker to recognize their presence—and not by mechanically fixing his eyes at some point over their heads. Genuine eye contact can be accomplished only when a speaker *wants* to consult his audience visually.

Additionally, eye contact can tell you how you are doing. By signs like smiles, frowns, head movements, and seat shifting, audiences will indicate their responses to your speech. You can learn to use this feedback as indication of ways to adjust your message. It may tell you that a point needs more explanation, or that you are belaboring a point, or that you have pleased them with an idea, and so forth. If face-to-face communication is more effective than communication by radio or television, it is primarily because of the presence of live, reacting people who are sending messages back to the speaker as he sends his. Able

---

[1] *The Works of Robert G. Ingersoll*, Dresden ed., C. P. Farrell, ed. (New York, 1900), VIII, p. 594.

speakers react to listeners' messages by making adjustments and thereby enhancing the total effort. Competence in exploiting feedback should be the goal of all speakers.

Give your body a chance to help you in speech delivery. Use your body naturally to reflect your personality and your ideas and, yet, control your movements to minimize distracting elements.

VOICE AND ARTICULATION

A general understanding of the physiological aspects of speech should be established before we discuss voice and articulation, the third and fourth elements of delivery. There are five steps in the production of speech: the mental phase, breathing, phonation, resonation, and articulation. We shall call them *steps* in examining the process, but, actually, they are so closely interrelated and complex that it is difficult to say where one step ends and another begins.

Producing Speech

Like most bodily functions, producing speech is a complicated act; so complex, in fact, that explanation of it necessitates oversimplification. Bear that in mind as you read on. At this point, the purpose of our digression is to draft a rough sketch of the speaking process; one that is reasonably accurate in its simplicity, in order to establish increased appreciation of the act.[2]

THE MENTAL STEP

You possess certain thoughts or emotions that you wish to communicate. Possibly you speak to answer a question, to scold, to ask a question, to comment on a pretty sight, to express fear, or to instruct. For some reason or other, you are moved to speak; therefore, the act of speaking starts as a mental process with its origin and control in the brain.

THE BREATHING STEP

Our need to get air into and out of the lungs is "exploited" by the speech function. Producing speech is dependent upon this flow of air since the outgoing breath is utilized as the power for producing sound.

When one inhales, nerve impulses from the brain cause the muscular partition (the diaphragm) that horizontally divides the body to be

---

[2] For a more complete explanation consult a full treatment of the subject; for example, Theodore D. Hanley and Wayne L. Thurman, *Developing Vocal Skills* (New York, 1962) or Lyman S. V. Judson and Andrew Thomas Weaver, *Voice Science,* 2d ed. (New York, 1965).

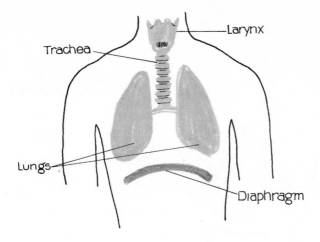

Fig. 8-1   Lower Speech Organs

pulled down and pushed against the stomach organs. At the same time, the rib muscles contract to pull the ribs up and out. As a result, the chest cavity is given greater capacity, and a vacuum is created. Since nature abhors a vacuum, air immediately rushes in from the mouth or nose openings and down the trachea (windpipe) into the lungs.

Exhalation is characterized by a gradual relaxation of the parts that are active in inhalation. The diaphragm relaxes and is forced upward by the pressure of the crowded stomach organs. Rib muscles relax, too, and the ribs descend and draw in. The inward and downward force of the ribs and the upward force of the diaphragm cause air to be squeezed out of the lungs and up the trachea. This action is sometimes compared to that of a bellows forcing air out of its spout.

THE PHONATION STEP

At the top of the trachea is the larynx, or voice box. The larynx, the front part of which is frequently referred to as the Adam's apple, is the cartilage structure which houses the vocal folds. The vocal folds, sometimes called vocal cords, are a pair of membranes fixed in a horizontal position in the larynx. The vocal membranes are like two lips whose smooth, rounded edges face one another. Their length—stretching from the front to the back of the interior of the larynx—is less than one inch. Their coming together and parting is analogous to the action of a type of valve.

All air which is inhaled or exhaled must pass between them. Air forced up from the lungs, passes between the tightened folds and

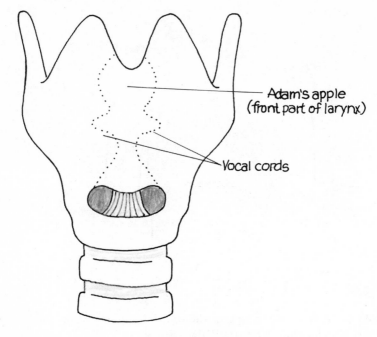

Adam's apple (front part of larynx)

Vocal cords

Fig. 8–2   The Larynx.

vibrates these vocal membranes. This vibration produces sound waves —the raw material of what will eventually be speech.

THE RESONATION STEP

The sound made by the vibrating vocal folds is weak and lacks richness. To be amplified and enriched, the original sound is sent into the pharynx (throat), mouth, and nasal passages. In these hollow places, it is allowed to resonate and reverberate and thus attain volume and a distinctive quality.

One resonator, the mouth, has another very important duty. By changing its shape and size during the production of speech it creates the vowels. Just as changes in the size and shape of automobile mufflers alter the original sound, changes in the mouth alter the sound of a person's voice. The movement of facial muscles and of the tongue within the mouth create variations in the structure of the resonator. For instance, the "ee" in "see" is commonly made by stretching the lips to form a small opening and arching the tongue. In forming the "o" of "go," the resonator is changed to a hollowed shape; the lips are rounded, and extra enlargement is given to the cavity by a drawing back of the tongue.

We shall not consider the formation of each vowel, but remember

Fig. 8–3   The Vocal Cords: open,   ajar, closed.

that the function of resonation does more than enhance and strengthen the original tone; it is also responsible for vowel production.

THE ARTICULATION STEP

At this point we have voice—resonated sound waves—but we do not have speech. The last phase, which we call articulation, has to do with forming consonants and joining or blending them with vowels and other consonants. Principally involved in this process are the tongue, lips, teeth, and palate. These articulators perform their highly important tasks mainly by channeling and altering the passage of breath through the mouth and nose. Such is the nature of articulation, the final step in the production of speech; and as we shall see at a later point, the source of the most common speaking disorders.

Fig. 8–4   Upper Speech Organs.

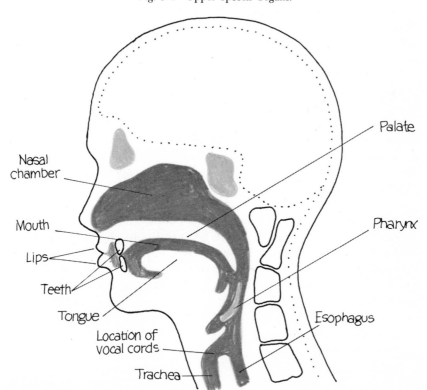

The Voice

Voice production is concerned with breathing, phonation, and resonation. It is during these phases that distinguishing vocal characteristics of pitch, volume, duration, and quality are developed.

Pitch, or frequency, as it is sometimes called, is the characteristic of a sound as it relates to the musical scale, the frequency with which the sound-producing object vibrates. The greater the number of vibrations, the higher the pitch.

Each person's voice has a certain pitch level that may be considered high, low, or medium. The level depends upon the *tension, length,* and *weight* of the vocal folds. It is because of differences in these three features that women's voices are unlike men's; female cords are shorter. On the average, women's vocal cords are a half-inch in length, while those of men average three-fourths of an inch. Then, too, female cords are stretched more tightly and weigh less.

Basically, there are three pitch conditions which can call attention to one's speaking and cause communication to suffer:

1. When it is too high;
2. When it is too low;
3. When it lacks variety and is monotonous.

Volume, or loudness, is another factor that characterizes a voice. It is dependent upon the amount of a person's *breath power* and degree of *amplification given by the resonators.* There are three conditions of volume that give speakers difficulty:

1. When it is too great (not adjusted to the room size, for example);
2. When it is too weak (especially at the ends of words or thoughts);
3. When it lacks variety.

Duration is the length of time a sound lasts; in particular, the vowel sounds. An extending or prolonging of the vowels results in a drawn out characteristic commonly called a *drawl.* An omitting or cropping of the vowels results in a rapid or possibly staccato speech pattern. The two chief problems, then, are:

1. Overlengthening of the vowels;
2. Eliminating or shortening of the vowels.

Quality is difficult to explain in a few words, but perhaps we can be helped by a statement of two writers on the subject. They explain quality as "that element of voice which makes one voice recognizably different from another or which makes it possible for us, upon hearing a voice, to say to whom it belongs." [3] Quality is that vocal characteristic most like a fingerprint; no two people have identical voice quality.

---

[3] Roy C. McCall and Herman Cohen, *Fundamentals of Speech,* 2d ed. (New York, 1963), p. 182.

Quality is determined by the nature of the sound waves you produce. Some sound waves have more noise elements, and some have more harmonious or musical elements. The greater the degree of harmony, the better the quality. Five common faults are:

1. Nasality (too much resonance in the nasal passages)
2. Denasality (too little nasal resonance, for example, when you have a cold)
3. Harshness
4. Hoarseness
5. Breathiness

What should you do if a study of your voice indicates certain faults? First of all, consult your speech teacher for advice. It may be that what you consider to be faults really do not interfere with your communication. On the other hand, if your problem is a serious one, perhaps a program of correction can be set up for you, or you can take a special course in vocal improvement. Should you seek appropriate guidance and follow it earnestly, you can be assured that your chances for betterment are great.

Articulation

Articulation, you remember, is that phase of speech production during which the consonants are formed and joined with vowels. In a way, the articulators have a function similar to that of a football quarterback. It is up to him to decide on the manner of advancing the ball, and it is up to the articulators to call the signals for advancing (emitting) the breath stream. If a "t" is to be uttered, the tongue tip is placed against the upper teeth or gum ridge; for an "m," the lips are placed together momentarily. The main inconsistency in our football analogy is that the articulators "call more plays" in a minute of speaking than a quarterback calls during an entire game. The average college student delivering a speech utters about 150 or 160 words per minute, and the average word is made up of four or five sounds. Therefore, the speech mechanism must handle at least 600 sound units in a minute. Knowing the complexities of the articulatory process makes it easier for us to understand why it may break down under fatigue or emotional stress. It is no wonder that the articulators fumble a sound occasionally.

Misarticulation is different from mispronunciation. Pronunciation has to do with standards of acceptability—either the standards of a region or a dictionary standard—while articulation has to do with the distinctness or clarity of the utterance. Paul L. Soper contrasts the processes well: "We mispronounce words when we do not know how to pronounce them; we misarticulate words when we know how to pronounce them correctly but do not."[4] Therefore, if you say "mis-CHEE-ve-us" for mischievous you are mispronouncing a word. If you say "ny-stays" for United States you are guilty of misarticulation.

But any standard based on custom and common agreement is arbitrary. Acceptable articulation in one region or social environment may be unacceptable elsewhere. Usually, an occasion marked by a high level of formality calls for more careful articulation. The speaker accommodates his bearing to the character of the environment—probably automatically, without conscious control. Just as speakers adapt their ideas to audiences and occasions, they also adapt themselves and their modes of utterance to audiences and occasions. An unavoidable standard, then, is that imposed by the situation in which the speaker puts himself. He makes whatever adjustments to the situation that his personal standards, predispositions, and collection of habits will allow.

The concept of "sociability of speaking" is applicable here. Most effective speakers are sociable, that is, willing to respond to occasions' demands—to the extent that their own standards permit. A person moving from Massachusetts to Texas probably does not plan on learning to say "y'all," but after a period of living in Texas among Texans, he will very likely come to say "y'all." His speech will come to fit in, to make the adjustment. Perhaps you would never pronounce "horse" HOSS or "iron" EYE-un, but if you lived in certain parts of the East or South for a time, you might come to adopt these pronunciations. The *NBC Handbook of Pronunciation* recognizes varying standards and observes, "Americans have never consented to have 'correct' pronunciation laid down for them by a government academy, as is done in several other nations." The handbook's advice to broadcasters is well-taken for other persons who find themselves before different types of audiences:

> That pronunciation is best which is most readily understood, and that pronunciation is most readily understood which is used by most people. Thus a standard of pronunciation for the American radio and television broadcaster is reasonably based upon the speech heard and used by the audience that the broadcaster reaches. This means that the broadcaster would use the pronunciation that is spoken by the educated people of the area served by the station. If the station is a local one, the broadcaster would do well to pronounce words as the educated people of his community pronounce them. Otherwise he might be difficult to comprehend and might even alienate a part of his audience.[5]

Be true to yourself and to your personal standards, yet at the same time, accept your tendency to be "sociable" orally in the scenes in which you function.

[4] Paul L. Soper, *Basic Public Speaking*, 2d ed. (New York, 1965), p. 163.
[5] Thomas Lee Crowell, Jr., *NBC Handbook of Pronunciation*, 3d ed. (New York, 1963), p. ix.

With adjustment to the environment as a backdrop and with speech of the educated in a community as a norm, let us turn to a discussion of misarticulation and mispronunciation in general terms; acknowledging that many times one cannot dismiss as always wrong some vocal patterns or forms of expression.

The most common reasons for poor articulation and faulty pronunciation are habit, carelessness, and, occasionally, indifference. People become accustomed to certain patterns and forms, frequently without awareness of deviation. In childhood, one learns to speak by listening to others. By adopting the characteristics of those around him and by fusing them with his own personality, he develops a pattern of expression. It may be a pattern which has a minimum of articulation faults, or it may be sprinkled with many unacceptable practices.

Articulation problems constitute the most common speech disorders; and since they are so prevalent, it is possible that you have difficulty with certain sounds or words. What are your problem spots? Let us ask some specific questions.

1. Do you ever create a possible distraction by *substituting* one sound for another?

d *for* th—	dat *for* that, da *for* the, dis *for* this
d *for* t—	liddle *for* little, starded *for* started
th *for* s—	betht *for* best, mitht *for* mist
u *for* aw—	yur *for* your, fur *for* for
uh *for* oo—	tuhday *for* today, ought tuh *for* ought to, yuh *for* you
uh *for* o—	winduh *for* window, yelluh *for* yellow
eh *for* ā—	pel *for* pail
ih *for* uh—	jist *for* just
ih *for* eh—	git *for* get
in *for* ing—	runnin *for* running

2. Do you ever *insert* extra sounds?

ath-*uh*-lete—athlete	umb*er*-ella—umbrella
Ap-*er*-il—April	acrosst—across
fil-*um*—film	e*k*scape—escape

3. Do you ever *omit* certain sounds?

em—them	er—her
hep—help	kep—kept
slep—slept	libary—library
at—that	guvment—government
cross—across	thurly—thoroughly
probly—probably	worl—world
plitical—political	actshly—actually
pitcher—picture	

4. Do you ever misplace an accent?
    the-A-ter—THE-a-ter
    im-PIE-ous—IM-pi-ous
    re-SPITE—RES-pit
    pre-FER-a-ble—PREF-er-a-ble
    com-PAIR-able—COM-par-a-ble
    HO-tel—ho-TEL

Indistinctness and incorrectness are even more apparent when observed in continuous discourse. You have heard utterances similar to the following:

"Jeet?"—Did you eat?

"Wutchadoonigh?"—What are you doing tonight?

"Ahm gonna cuz uh hafta."—I am going to because I have to.

"Hev ya lef yer pinny on a teble?"—Have you left your penny on the table?

Improving Your Expression

Force of habit, indifference, and carelessness cause people to give a poor representation of themselves. Faulty expression may not be a detriment to communication in the early years of one's life when one's guiding standard is that of the "gang" or the neighborhood. Nevertheless, most people, and certainly those acquiring an advanced education, want to achieve success in their chosen fields. In the majority of occupations, advancement depends considerably upon skill in communication. At a certain rung on the ladder of success, a person begins to realize that he must speak correctly and clearly. It may happen when he receives a promotion or when he is selected to represent his company.

What do you want for yourself? How far do you want to go? You may be able to go further than you presently realize, and it is time to make preparations for the future. In addition to preparing yourself in accounting, engineering, social work, sales, or music, and so forth, attend to your speech habits—your voice, pronunciation, and articulation. Become conscious of any vocal problems and of the sounds you omit, substitute, insert, or accent improperly. Torture yourself a bit by consciously reminding yourself of the need to put the "ern" syllable in "government" or an "ng" in "running." Strive for more vocal variety and expressiveness. You may feel awkward and self-conscious at first, but with willingness and work you can make clear, distinct speech a part of you.

Begin your program of improvement now—with your next occasion for speaking. After thoroughly preparing the content of the speech, make definite preparations for the moment of delivery by following these steps in rehearsal.

1. Read the outline aloud several times, diligently trying to fix the main ideas in your mind. Read it through each time without stopping. Your immediate purpose is to get a grasp of the whole speech—the main ideas and their relationships. You might be astonished to know the number of people who give speeches without fully realizing the basic meaning or significance of their thoughts.

2. Find a vacant classroom and practice the entire speech with the aid of the outline, consulting it as frequently as necessary. Once again, go right through; do not stop. Repeat the process. Your purpose at this point is to fix the ideas in mind and become acquainted with words that may be useful in final delivery of thought.

3. After sufficient practice with the full outline, deliver the speech two or three times with the aid of speaking notes only. At the end of each such rehearsal, consult the full outline to see if you have omitted any significant detail. Perhaps a friend will be willing to listen to a rehearsal and give his reactions.

4. Practice with or without notes to the point of being able to give the speech freely and effectively.

When it is your turn to speak, move to the front of the room confidently and in a manner fitting the occasion and your purpose in speaking. Remember, your speech starts from the moment that you leave your seat. Find your position before the audience, take a few seconds to get set, and begin your exchange of thought with self-assurance.

Preparing for good delivery

As we have seen, delivering ideas involves a speaker's total self—especially his personality, his outward bodily movements, his voice, his articulation, and his pronunciation. Consequently, what a speaker is and what a speaker does determine whether he will be effective in delivering his message. What should *you* be and what should *you* do in order to be successful?

1. *Have the welfare of your audience at heart.* We cannot separate character and intent from speaking, nor can we say that one who seeks to delude or deceive is a good speaker. It is true that charlatans and swindlers seem to be quite effective for a time, but eventually people are able to see through the false front and, as a result, reject their ideas. Honesty, sincerity, and respect for others are elements of good delivery. As one criterion, we have the provocative point of view held by Quintilian and other renowned speech scholars: *the good speaker is the good man speaking well.*

2. *Have something that you want to say.* Ideas coupled with a desire to convey the ideas are prerequisites to good delivery. The famous speaker, Booker T. Washington, expressed strong conviction on this

subject: "I do not believe that one should speak unless, down deep in his heart, he feels convinced that he has a message to deliver. When one feels, from the bottom of his feet to the top of his head, that he has something to say that is going to help some individual or some cause, then let him say it. . . ." [6] Your subject matter and how you feel about it should influence the manner in which you express it. Good delivery, then, should be a natural response to a yearning to communicate your ideas.

3. *Make a personal investment.* Assuming that you have chosen the content that you want to deliver, you should let your personality, body, and voice speak out for you in your delivery. Let yourself go. You may be amazed at how effective you can be when you are able to free your real self. One who gives little, gets little in return, and willingness to invest yourself in the speaking situation will bring you truly satisfying rewards. Booker T. Washington wrote, "I always make it a rule to make especial preparation for each separate audience. No two audiences are exactly alike. It is my aim to reach and talk to the heart of each individual audience, taking it into my confidence very much as I would a person." [7]

4. *Try to remove distracting elements when practicing.* A sincere speaker who concentrates upon delivering his ideas to his audience does about all that can be asked of him at the moment. You should remember that when you face the audience your program of self-improvement is suspended for the time being. Your purpose then is communication, not correction of errors. Correct yourself in practice— in private. Work on your problems of pronunciation and articulation during rehearsals periods only, for they are *your* problems, not your listeners'. At the time of delivery, your attention and your listeners' attention should be given to your speech and its purpose.

LET US SUMMARIZE

When one makes a speech, one's personality, body, and voice should work naturally and harmoniously together. Only during rehearsal should one be concerned with improving his techniques of delivery. As one gives the speech, his concern should be with ideas. Good delivery places four basic demands upon you:

1. You should have the welfare of your audience at heart.
2. You should have something that you want to say.
3. You should make a personal investment.
4. You should do nothing that calls attention to itself.

---

[6] *Up From Slavery: An Autobiography* (New York, 1901), p. 243.

[7] Washington, *Up From Slavery,* p. 214.

When asked what advice he would give to a young man who wanted to become a successful speaker, Robert G. Ingersoll responded: "In the first place, I would advise him to have something to say—something worth saying—something that people will be glad to hear. This is the important thing. Back of the art of speaking must be the power to think. Without thought words are empty purses." [8]

Start with a body of well-conceived thought—well-selected, organized, and developed; then, give deserved attention to its delivery.

PHONETIC ALPHABET

In the alphabet that we use for writing, a number of different symbols often stand for a single sound. For example, the ē sound may appear as "ey" in "key," as "ee" in "tee," as "i" in "machine," as "ei" in "receive," as "ie" in "believe," and "uay" in "quay." To overcome confusion in noting sounds, experts devised the International Phonetic Alphabet, a system of symbols to stand for the sounds of speech. Unlike standard alphabetical symbols, the phonetic alphabet assigns only one sound to a symbol. As a result, the easily learned phonetic alphabet allows one to study speech sounds rather precisely and to tabulate on paper the sounds of a word or sentence. The following are symbols of the IPA, key words containing the sounds, and phonetic transcriptions of the words.

Vowels

IPA Symbol	Key Words	IPA Transcriptions
[i]	heat	[hit]
	meet	[mit]
[ɪ]	sit	[sɪt]
	tryst	[trɪst]
[e]	say	[se]
	rein	[ren]
[ɛ]	never	[nɛvð]
	quest	[kwɛst]
[æ]	hat	[hæt]
	blast	[blæst]
[a]	ask	[ask]
	bath	[baθ]
[u]	spoon	[spun]
	true	[tru]
[ʊ]	book	[bʊk]

[8] *The Works of Robert G. Ingersoll,* Dresden ed., C. P. Farrell, ed. (New York, 1900), VIII, 594.

IPA Symbol	Key Words	IPA Transcriptions	
	would	[wʊd]	
[o]	total	[totl̩]	
	odor	[odɤ]	
[ɔ]	law	[lɔ]	
	cough	[kɔf]	
[ɒ]	soften	[sɒfən]	
	calm	[kɒm]	
[ɑ]	father	[fɑðɤ]	
	ah	[ɑ]	
[ʌ]	custom	[kʌstəm]	(accented "uh")
	above	[əbʌv]	
[ə]	custom	[kʌstəm]	(unaccented "uh")
	above	[əbʌv]	
[ɝ]	first	[fɝst]	(accented, with "ur" sounded)
	bird	[bɝd]	
[ɜ]	first	[fɜst]	(accented, with "ur" not sounded—as in Eastern and Southern speech)
	bird	[bɜd]	
[ðʲ]	hasher	[hæʃðʲ]	(unaccented, with "ur" sounded)
	weather	[wɛðð]	
[ɑɪ]	lime	[lɑɪm]	
	white	[hwɑɪt]	
[ɔɪ]	toy	[tɔɪ]	
	adroit	[ədrɔɪt]	
[ɑʊ]	sound	[sɑʊnd]	
	cow	[kɑʊ]	

Consonants

[p]	paper	[pepð]	
[b]	baby	[bebɪ]	
[m]	mime	[mɑɪm]	
[n]	name	[nem]	
[ŋ]	running	[rʌnɪŋ]	
	ink	[ɪŋk]	
[t]	ten	[tɛn]	
[d]	hid	[hɪd]	
[θ]	thin	[θɪn]	
[ð]	this	[ðɪs]	
[f]	fifty	[fɪftɪ]	

IPA Symbol	Key Words	IPA Transcriptions
[v]	glo*v*e	[glʌv]
[k]	*c*li*ck*	[klɪk]
[g]	*g*ood	[gʊd]
[s]	*s*i*s*	[sɪs]
[z]	hi*s*	[hɪz]
	*z*oo	[zu]
[ʃ]	*sh*all	[ʃæl]
	*s*ure	[ʃʊr]
[ʒ]	mea*s*ure	[meʒð]
[tʃ]	*ch*ur*ch*	[tʃɝtʃ]
[dʒ]	*j*u*dg*e	[dʒʌdʒ]
[hw]	*wh*ere	[hwɛr]
[w]	*w*as	[wʌz]
[j]	*y*ou	[ju]
[r]	*r*ed	[rɛd]
	ta*r*	[tɑr]
[l]	*l*ed	[lɛd]
	tab*l*e	[tebl̩]

(the dot under the "l" indicates that the "l" is sounded as a full syllable: "ul")

[h]	*h*ard	[hɑrd]

Suggested Exercise A

Analyze your delivery characteristics. Do you have speaking habits (other than those which require specialized attention, such as stuttering) which call attention to themselves? Enlist the services of your friends, the instructor, your family, or a tape recorder to help you in the analysis.

Make specific suggestions for improvement under three headings: Voice, Body, and Articulation-Pronunciation.

Sample
Voice
1. Needs more variety; should bring out the full color of my ideas.
2. In too much of a hurry; should take time to express the meaning.
Body
1. Constantly shift my weight from one foot to the other. This takes the listener's mind off my speech.
2. I twist the ring on my finger. Probably half the class could describe my ring!

Articulation-Pronunciation
1. *Substitutions:* git (get), jist (just), fur (for), yur (your), becuz (because)
2. *Additions:* Aperil (April), acrost (across)
3. *Omissions:* lenth (length), kep (kept), probly (probably)
4. *Misplaced accents:* luh-MENT-uh-ble (LAM-en-tuh-ble)

Suggested Exercise B

Make a list of sentences which include examples of your pronunciation and articulation faults. Practice by saying each sentence twice; first, incorrectly and then, correctly. Do this until the appropriate expression comes easily.

Suggested Exercise C

Listen to a speaker (someone outside the class) and analyze his vocal, body movement, pronunciation, and articulation characteristics. List the features that seem to call attention to themselves.

Suggested Exercise D

Practice reading one of the following speech excerpts. Put yourself into the reading in order to bring out the full meaning; invest yourself—your personality, your voice, and your body. Sound the words clearly and expressively. Have a partner comment on the variety of your expression—specifically regarding pitch, rate, and force.

Practice many times until you are convinced that you are adequately expressing the content. A tape recording will help you to determine how successful you are.

> With malice toward none; with charity for all; with firmness in the right, as God gives us to see the right, let us strive on to finish the work we are in; to bind up the nation's wounds; to care for him who shall have borne the battle, and for his widow, and his orphan—to do all which may achieve and cherish a just and lasting peace among ourselves, and with all nations.
> —Abraham Lincoln, *Second Inaugural Address,* 1865

> The unity of government which constitutes you one people is also now dear to you. It is justly so, for it is a main pillar in the edifice of your real independence, the support of your tranquility at home, your peace abroad, of your safety, of your prosperity, of that very liberty which you so highly prize. But as it is easy to foresee that from different causes and from different quarters much pains will be taken, many artifices employed to weaken in your minds the conviction of this truth, as this is the point in your political fortress against which the batteries of internal and external enemies will be most constantly and actively

(though often covertly and insidiously) directed, it is of infinite moment that you should properly estimate the immense value of your national union to your collective and individual happiness; that you should cherish a cordial, habitual, and immovable attachment to it; accustoming yourselves to think and speak of it as the paladium of your political safety and prosperity; watching for its preservation with jealous anxiety; discountenancing whatever may suggest even a suspicion that it can in any event be abandoned, and indignantly frowning upon the first dawning of every attempt to alienate any portion of our country from the rest or to enfeeble the sacred ties which now link together the various parts.

—George Washington, *Farewell Address*, 1796

My urgent advice to you would be, not only always to think first of America, but always, also, to think first of humanity. You do not love humanity if you seek to divide humanity into jealous camps. Humanity can be welded together only by love, by sympathy, by justice, not by jealousy and hatred. I am sorry for the man who seeks to make personal capital out of the passions of his fellow-men. He has lost the touch and ideal of America, for America was created to unite mankind by those passions which lift and not by the passions which separate and debase. We came to America, either ourselves or in the persons of our ancestors, to better the ideals of men, to make them see finer things than they had seen before, to get rid of the things that divide and to make sure of the things that unite. It was but an historical accident no doubt that this great country was called the "United States"; yet I am very thankful that it has the word "United" in its title, and the man who seeks to divide man from man, group from group, interest from interest in this great Union is striking at its very heart.

—Woodrow Wilson, *Address to Foreign-born Citizens*, 1915

In the future days, which we seek to make secure, we look forward to a world founded upon four essential human freedoms.

The first is freedom of speech and expression—everywhere in the world.

The second is freedom of every person to worship God in his own way—everywhere in the world.

The third is freedom from want—which, translated into world terms, means economic understanding which will secure to every nation a healthy peacetime life for its inhabitants—everywhere in the world.

The fourth is freedom from fear—which, translated into world terms, means a world-wide reduction of armaments to such point and in such a thorough fashion that no nation will be in a position to commit an act of physical aggression against any neighbor—anywhere in the world.

This is no vision of a distant millennium. It is a definite basis for a kind of world attainable in our own time and generation.

—Franklin D. Roosevelt, *Message to Congress*, January 6, 1941

Suggested Exercise E

How many of the words listed below are troublesome to you? Do you sound them distinctly and accurately? Can you add some words to the list? Write an anecdote in which you include those most difficult for you. Spell them according to sound, perhaps using the International Phonetic Alphabet. Review the exercise daily and be ready to read it when the instructor calls on you.

acquiesce	hiccough
adversary	human
agile	infamous
alacrity	inference
arduous	insurance
armistice	integral
bade	irrevocable
barbarous	Italian
cello	library
cement	maintenance
chaste	municipal
comparable	naive
copious	novice
corps	orgy
dearth	propitious
decadent	recess
defense	rendezvous
detail	respite
discretion	saga
docile	salmon
efficacy	schizophrenia
emaciate	scion
epitome	servile
exquisite	solace
gala	subtle
genuine	suite
gesture	superfluous
grievous	tyrannical
gross	vehement
hearth	wane
height	zoology

Suggested Exercise F

Read aloud the Key Words that are listed for the symbols of the International Phonetic Alphabet. Ask a partner to note any deviations from standard enunciation. In addition, you can record the words with a tape recorder and make a self-check of vocal and articulatory habits. Put the Key Words in phrases and sentences and recheck your enunciation.

Suggested Exercise G

Each of the following sentences contains a selected consonant sound in all three possible positions: at the beginning of a word (initial position), in the middle of a word (medial position), and at the end of a word (final position). Use the sentences either for practice in learning to discriminate sounds or for drill.

1. [p]   Paul prepared to clip the paper tape.
2. [b]   The drab ebony board was buried above the neighbor's lab.
3. [m]   Lemons made Tom remember many moments of gloom.
4. [n]   One never knows how many cannons are necessary.
5. [ŋ]   Running ink I think is instinctive.
6. [t]   Peter takes teeter-tottering too seriously to get fun out of it.
7. [d]   Heed Dora's words, Edward, and do not demand the guarded hoard.
8. [θ]   An unthoughtful but enthusiastic thinker in math gave baby Thelma a bath.
9. [ð]   That boy could not bathe because his father put the leather there.
10. [f]   Fifty-five and one-half fifes filled Phil's safe.
11. [v]   "Very lovely voice," averred Ev from above.
12. [k]   Kirkwood carried the cake quickly and cackled at the cook.
13. [g]   Glenna's toes wiggled as she giggled at the whirligig.
14. [s]   Save all excess sassafras, sister.
15. [z]   Because of Zeb's raising pigs, the zebras became lazy.
16. [ʃ]   Should a ration of sugar, hash, or shoe polish be assured?
17. [ʒ]   I had a vision of the treasure of rouge put in the garage by Jean (who pronounces his name the French way).
18. [tʃ]   Chimpanzees lurched in bunches by the church but did not chortle much.
19. [dʒ]   George jumped over Roger to juggle the gauge.
20. [hw] Which whippersnapper shall I whip somewhere on the pinwheel?
21. [w]   Walter, overweight but unworried, ate Wilma's sandwich willfully.
22. [j]   Hey, you, can you make W's brilliantly?
23. [r]   The terrible rapids passed the bar very readily.
24. [l]   Lazy Lola laughed and trilled on the hill and in the dale.
25. [h]   The left-handed hermit followed the fox hunter uphill.

Suggested Exercise H

This exercise will help you to develop breath control. Take in a supply of breath; then, let it out while making the "sh" sound. Can you sustain a good full sound for ten seconds? Try the exercise again, this time with "s."

Suggested Exercise I

This exercise, too, will assist in developing breath control. With a normal supply of breath, read aloud the first sentence in Suggested Exercise G two times without taking in a new breath supply. Next do it three times on one supply, then four. Try the same exercise with other sentences in the series.

Suggested Exercise J

This exercise is designed to enhance resonance and to develop consciousness of the process. With an open throat, read sentence number two in Suggested Exercise G. As you read, prolong the vowel sounds and build them with resonance in the throat. Can you feel the shaping of the vowels? Repeat the exercise with sentence number four.

Suggested Exercise K

Of all speakers whom you have heard, which one has the most "ideal" delivery? Think before you commit yourself, for your answer will reveal a great deal about your knowledge and opinion of what constitutes good delivery.

Improving Listening Skills

An ancient proverb tells us, "He who speaks, sows; who listens, reaps." Now while we might argue that he who speaks also reaps and makes accomplishments through his speaking, we must credit and examine the other vital aspect of oral communication—listening.

When does a good listener do his "reaping"? Whenever he listens, of course, which is more frequently than most people realize. Paul Rankin at The Ohio State University found that adults spend about 70 percent of their daytime hours engaging in communication activities. They devote 9 percent of this time to writing, 16 percent to reading, 30 percent to speaking, and *45 percent to listening*. The study indicates that about a third of our lives is spent in listening. More recently, an Illinois publication on communication acknowledged that over 85 percent of all human communication is carried on by speaking *and* listening. Also, they report an estimate that 90 percent of all learning happens through the speaking-listening medium.[1]

HOW IMPORTANT IS LISTENING?

In the classroom and in one's everyday life, effective listening helps one to get along and to learn. Wilson Mizner expresses it humorously: "A good listener is not only popular everywhere, but after awhile he knows something." Getting the most out of our leisure hours requires adequate listening habits. Watching television, seeing plays and movies and getting the maximum benefits from such experiences becomes important—because these days, we spend so much time with these entertainment media. Then, too, rearing a family, carrying out civic obligations, and being successful on the job demand proper listening. "Nobody ever listened himself out of a job," remarked Calvin Coolidge. The benefits of good listening cannot be overrated wherever we find a message worthy of our attention.

[1] *Communication in the High School Curriculum* (Springfield, Illinois, 1961), p. 3.

WHAT IS LISTENING?

To listen is to do more than to hear. Hearing is a physiological function and involves *receiving* a message; listening is a mental function which involves *perceiving* a message. After a sound or series of sounds is picked up by the auditory mechanism and transmitted to the higher nerve centers (after it is heard) it must be interpreted and given meaning. Once the message is received, skill in listening is dependent upon how well the message is translated and understood.

We are dealing then, with a mental process. Actually, there are two mental processes to be considered. Listening is part of a two-way act between the one who originates the message and the one for whom the message is intended. To effect real communication, speaker and listener must work *in concert;* that is, the two participants in the exchange must mentally engage one another in shaping the message. They cooperatively build thought and determine meaning and significance. If the listener invests nothing in the enterprise, communication will suffer.

Speaking, we see, is elliptical, partially developed; therefore, listeners must "fill" in the gaps with their understanding and experience. For example, if a speaker says, without explanation, "Darwin's *Origin of Species* changed the course of thinking in the biological sciences," the listener immediately "helps" the speaker by bringing to bear his own knowledge of evolution—based, perhaps, on natural selection and the struggle for survival. If the listener is "tuned in" to the speaker's purpose, he can supply the data that is necessary for adequate completion of thought, and fulfill the speaker's purpose: to evoke appropriate responses from the listener.

Each agency in the transaction should have a purpose. A speaker's goal will be to entertain, to inform, or to persuade, but what is the listener's goal? Since he and the speaker are "in it together," it is logical to assume that his purpose is determined by that of the speaker, and he must adjust himself accordingly. Though speakers and, therefore, listeners have multiple and overlapping general goals, let us discuss three main ones.

Listening for Enjoyment

We listen to stories, after-dinner speeches, poetry reading, or dramatic programs mainly to be entertained. The usual attitude that we assume in such a situation might be called one of attentive relaxation. Our listening behavior is guided by our tastes, by what we as individuals appreciate.

Listening for Understanding

This is a basic listening goal. To understand does not mean to accept but merely to know what the speaker means. We listen to understand sermons, class lectures, newscasts, debates, and conversations. We may want to remember a speaker's ideas, either to apply or reject them, but first, we must understand what he is saying.

Evaluative Listening

Critical listening places heavy demands upon the listener, a burden that we who live in a free country must carry. We are guaranteed freedom of speech, which means that a person can say nearly anything he wishes. Yet, we do not have to condone every speaker or accept all of his ideas. In fact, one of our prime democratic responsibilities is to develop an ability to judge, to learn how to think critically. In American society, thoughtful critics help to maintain a wholesome spirit of checks and balances. Listening to evaluate (critical listening) is everybody's daily business.

HOW DOES LISTENING BREAK DOWN?

Many studies have been made in recent years to find out how well people listen. The results indicate that there is much room for improvement of listening skills; people do not listen as well as they should. Tests show that, at best, the average person retains only 60 to 70 percent of what he has heard, and after a lapse of time the percentage scores drop markedly. From a study of many such cases, Drs. Ralph G. Nichols and Thomas R. Lewis, leaders in speech education and listening research, conclude that "after a lapse of two months or more, learning through listening seldom operates at more than a 25-percent level of efficiency." [2]

There are several critical factors to be analyzed in the study of listening. The difficulty may be traced back to the speaker, to the physical environment, to the listener, or to a combination of these elements. If the speaker does not do his part, he cannot expect the audience to listen to him. When there are extraneous noises and other environmental conditions competing with the listener and speaker, there is a definite possibility of breakdown in the listening process. Finally, the fault can rest with the listener himself. If communication is to occur, he must do more than occupy a seat. He must be willing to accept an active role.

[2] Ralph G. Nichols and Thomas R. Lewis, *Listening and Speaking* (Dubuque, Iowa, 1954), p. 4.

Six Problem Conditions

Our observations reveal six principal problem conditions contributing to the breakdown of listening which you also may have noticed. They comprise the following listing, but not necessarily in order of frequency or weight.

1. LACK OF DESIGN. The listener who does not know what he should listen for or who does not know his function, profits little. This kind of behavior might be represented by the listener's silent testimony, "Here I am; do something for me." With the speaker's help, he should work to see the purpose, to visualize the structure of thought, to perceive relationships or comparative value of the significant ideas, and so forth. He should participate *purposefully*.

2. MENTAL WANDERLUST. Needless to say, when a member of an audience is preoccupied or in a daze, he does not function with the speaker in effective communication. He is presumably unable to control his listening behavior because of a competing force—perhaps emotional, or perhaps his mental wandering is habitual and reflective of inadequate training in listening. Explanations are as numerous as the cases.

3. INDIFFERENCE. In the case of indifference, the listener is inactive or apathetic. He lacks interest and *chooses* to remain uninvolved. Consequently, he offers nothing in response. The nonparticipating member of an audience neither gives nor receives. Why does indifference occur? Perhaps at times it is a manifestation of quiet resistance or a "show me" attitude. Certainly we must acknowledge, realistically, that some occasions are boring; they give one some justification for a "ho hum" position. Nonetheless, the listener must always ask himself if he is doing his part.

4. IMPATIENCE. Sometimes listeners are in too great a hurry. They get fidgety and challenge the speaker's pace or mode of developing thought; they are unwilling to hear him out. Admittedly, some speakers have problems in "getting on with it" and in finding their central thoughts; yet most of the time, listeners are socially obliged to indulge such a speaker's propensities. They may hope that the speaker will eventually undertake a program of speech improvement, but for the moment, they will have to do their best in helping him.

5. FAULTFINDING ATTITUDE. Hypercritical behavior is worse than impatience. Occasionally one will encounter a member of an audience who is unable to listen because he allows his perceptive faculties to be blocked by his observations of "faults." For example, he may be critical of aspects of the occasion, the time for which the meeting was called. He may take issue with the speaker's use of words—even minor samples of them. He may unfairly criticize the speaker's mode of dress, voice, or

bodily behavior. To sum it up, he unfortunately focuses on petty features and cannot accept them or prevent their taking a central position in his mind.

6. FEAR. This feeling can be related to indifference, impatience, or faultfinding. Here the problem is strong intolerance of the speaker's thought. It may be prejudice. It may take shape as a covert rebellion based on the threat of the speaker's ideas. For instance, a person may be hard pressed to listen well when the speaker makes a comment that seems to threaten his status or challenge a held value or belief. He may find himself shutting out the thought or being overcome with wrath. Now, he could have good reason for being fearful, but if he is so overcome that his listening is hampered, he will not be able effectively to challenge the speaker in a question-and-answer period or whenever he has a chance to reply.

HOW CAN LISTENING BE IMPROVED?

Let us look on the positive side of the problem and consider the three elements of the previously mentioned communicative process as they apply to you.

The Speaker's Responsibility

The speaker, of course, must assume his share of the responsibility for establishing communication. By this time, you are becoming increasingly aware of the specific criteria that you follow in preparing and delivering a talk, and we need not review them now. In general, though, you have three basic obligations:

1. To choose your ideas wisely;
2. To use proven methods of composition;
3. To adapt your speech to the audience.

Environment and Atmosphere

The physical environment should be conducive to good listening. We all know how important it is to have a fitting atmosphere accompanying any activity. Somehow, a steak eaten in a restaurant by candlelight, with soft music playing in the background, tastes better than it would if it were eaten in a brightly illuminated and noisy setting. It is the atmosphere that makes the difference. When you are a chairman or are otherwise responsible for a speaker-listener situation, it is your obligation to set up and maintain an atmosphere appropriate for the occasion.

Plan carefully; think through all details relating to the arrangement of the setting. Be sure to contact all the people involved. For example, get an understanding with the people in charge about your access to the room, the availability and use of facilities, length of time for your use, and so forth. If a band is scheduled to play outside during your meeting, determine what you can do about it. In short, do all in your power to make communication possible. Specifically, you can enhance the possibilities of success by:

1. Controlling distracting noises;
2. Providing ample ventilation;
3. Controlling the temperature of the room;
4. Providing comfortable and properly arranged seating;
5. Providing a speaker's stand;
6. Providing for the unobtrusive entrance of latecomers;
7. Making the environment attractive.

The Listener's Responsibility

The listener, as a partner in the communication enterprise, should hold up his end of the unwritten compact that he has with the speaker. Attentiveness is dictated by simple courtesy, if not also by the possible benefits of knowledge and enjoyment that can be gained from a speaker. In fairness to the speaker, to the audience as a whole, and to yourself as a listener, you have the following responsibilities. Let us call them Guides to Good Listening.

1. *Come with a desire to participate.* Be ready and willing to be a listener. The speaker needs you, and it is very likely that he will have something to offer in return for your participation. Find something of value in his remarks. Come to all speaking occasions with that intent.

2. *Choose an appropriate seat.* Find a spot which will allow you to see and hear comfortably. If you are one of the 4–6 percent who have serious hearing losses, you will want to seat yourself close to the speaker.

3. *Handle distractions.* Some distractions are unavoidable while others can be eliminated. If the construction gang down the corridor cannot be asked to desist, you must do your best to "listen louder than they are pounding." Whisperers, however, can be given courteous suggestions to be quiet; doors and windows can be opened or closed depending on the need, and lights can be turned on. It should be each listener's duty to help curtail distracting physical elements and to ignore those which cannot be eliminated.

Distractions that are emotional in nature may be even more bothersome. A listener brings with him a complex of feelings. On Monday he may be confident and secure, but on Wednesday he may come plagued with certain anxieties and extensive self-concern (even though he does not have to speak that day). How can he put aside his personal disturbances and pay attention to the speaker? The answer is not a simple one, nor do we presume that you will solve the problem by reading a chapter on listening. Nonetheless, there are some possible starting points. First of all, some people find that they can side-step their own feelings by plunging themselves wholeheartedly into a speaker's speech, by giving their keen attention to the speech, and eventually by forgetting about themselves. Others achieve success by self-analysis. They attempt to determine why they feel as they do, why their personal problems are more stimulating than the speaker's ideas. A listener's competing feelings constitute one of the major obstacles to communication.

Do not be distracted by a speaker's seeming "strangeness," his individual characteristics or mannerisms. In a large American city there is a man so skilled in speaking that hundreds come to hear him. The fact that he has a decided lisp does not deter his listeners. Because he has something to say and the ability to say it, and because his audiences are unwilling to be distracted, all participants profit. Listen for ideas, and ignore the minor, seemingly peculiar characteristics that you may notice.

4. *Give the speaker a fair chance to reach you.* Give the speaker the courtesy of a hearing; go along with him as far as you can go. Look at him, and acknowledge his comments; let him know that you are with him. Be confident; let your mind entertain the ideas—even the threatening ones. Repress your prejudices and preconceived ideas. Try to be patient, and avoid drawing conclusions too hastily. After you hear him out and understand his ideas, then you can decide upon what ideas to accept and what ideas to reject.

5. *Analyze.* Make an over-all running analysis during the speech. First of all, be alert, and grasp the speaker's purpose. Remember that it may be stated directly or merely implied. Continually ask, especially on controversial subjects, "What is he saying, *really?*" "What does he want, *really?*" Listen to determine his intent and what he seeks from you—whether it be your vote, your allegiance, or merely your interest in some innocuous idea.

When you have perceived his purpose, work along with the speaker by mentally outlining the points and subpoints he sets down in developing the purpose. To help reconstruct the broad structure of his speech, you should observe little cues which indicate his movement from thought to thought. Such transitional aids are usually verbal, but very often they are enhanced by vocal inflection or body movements. Since seeing is a part of listening, facial expressions and gestures can assist you in following the flow of ideas.

Immediately after the speech, analyze it further. Think back to the speaker, the reasoning he used, and the conclusions he drew. Ask yourself some key questions. Was his appeal basically emotional or did he reinforce his talk with logic? Did he have enough evidence to support his generalizations? Did he have an ax to grind? Is he a man of character? Can you believe in him? All speeches should be subjected to this type of "post mortem" but especially those that are intended to change our beliefs and influence our actions.

LET US SUMMARIZE

Perhaps the only activity which takes up more of our time than listening is sleeping. Since listening is such a frequent and vital function and *can be improved,* it is indeed a waste of human resources when neglected. How much have you missed in your life because of your listening habits? How many times have you responded to the persuasive efforts of speakers only to be sorry later that you had been so gullible? Realistically, it is impossible for us to measure what we have wasted by our mistakes and perhaps foolish to do so anyway. The truly hopeful prospect is that it is not too late. You can strengthen your ability to enjoy oral presentations, to understand, and to evaluate. To do so, you should:

1. Do your part in setting up and in maintaining appropriate surroundings and conditions;
2. Come with a view toward listening;
3. Choose an appropriate seat;
4. Handle distractions;
5. Give the speaker a fair chance to reach you;
6. Analyze during and after the speech.

As Professor Ralph G. Nichols, acknowledged authority on listening, has said, "Most of us are destined to hear at least twenty speeches for every one we give."[3] Based on that statement, the need for our concern is obvious.

Suggested Exercise A

Make an honest and objective analysis of your own listening characteristics. As you analyze, keep in mind typical speaker-audience situations in which you might find yourself. Include in the report answers to the following questions:

1. On what basis do you choose your seat?
2. What factors might cause a lack of desire to listen or closed-mind attitude on your part?
3. What methods have you devised for handling your own distracting emotions?
4. In what situations might you deny speakers your full participation?

[3] "Listening," in *Introduction to the Field of Speech,* Ronald F. Reid, ed. (Chicago, 1965), pp. 148–161.

5. Are you usually able to grasp a speaker's purpose and main ideas?
6. Are you usually able to determine when a speaker is employing a transitional aid?
7. What are some characteristics of delivery and language usage that you have allowed to distract you recently?
8. What is your usual practice in analyzing a speaker's reasoning, judgments, character, and personal interests?

Suggested Exercise B

Toward the end of the hour on a day of student speaking, your instructor may test your listening by asking you to answer key questions about the speeches. Be ready!

Sample

1. *May's speech:* What was the proposition?
2. *John's speech:* What were the main heads?
3. *Roger's speech:* Where did he neglect to employ a needed transition?
4. *Marjorie's speech:* What samples of sound reasoning did you note?
5. *Sam's speech:* Which supporting materials seemed especially effective?

Suggested Exercise C

Observe an off-campus audience and list the weaker listening habits they exhibit as you see them. You may be asked to use your list as the basis for a short speech or discussion.

Suggested Exercise D

Your instructor will read to the class an article containing controversial ideas. Attempt to follow the thoughts faithfully during the presentation.

1. After the reading, *interpret* what the author wrote by listing his main ideas.
2. Next, *evaluate* each idea by telling why you agree or disagree with it. Show fairness in interpretation and intelligence in evaluation.
3. Is there a difference between your interpretation and your evaluation?

Suggested Exercise E

Listen to a controversial radio or television news analyst. After you have heard him, repeat the directions in Suggested Exercise D.

Suggested Exercise F

Analyze the environment of a speaker–audience situation you have been in recently.

1. Was the ventilation adequate? If not, how might it have been improved?
2. Were there distracting noises? If so, how might they have been handled?
3. Was the room temperature satisfactory? Too hot? Too cold?
4. Were the seats reasonably comfortable and well arranged? If not, what improvements would you have made?
5. Were the speaker's needs met? If necessary, did he have a properly functioning microphone and a lectern? Was he placed in a satisfactory location from which to address the audience?

Suggested Exercise G

Your instructor may wish to assign class members to cross-examine speeches of other students. Such training in discerning and testing arguments can contribute to improved listening.

PART III

SUPPLEMENTARY
METHODS

CHAPTER TEN

Participating in Group Discussion

Where there is no mastery of the medium for exchanging ideas, ideas cease to play a part in human life.

—MORTIMER J. ADLER

This chapter is about discussion, exchanging ideas with others in a group. This we do quite frequently and in all sorts of settings. An interesting discussion took place just recently in a student council meeting:

HANK: Well, I got the word just a few minutes ago. They aren't coming!

EARL: Who isn't coming?

HANK: The jazz group for our show on the 20th.

PATTY: Not coming? Why, they can't do that! We've had this arranged for a month.

HANK: I know, I know, but what can you say when the booking agent tells you, "Sorry, but Mr. Raine's group will be playing at the University of Washington on February 20th"?

EARL: And just ten days to go! We've got a problem!

HANK: That's life, one problem after another!

Even though we sympathize with Hank, that *is* life—one problem after another. Some problems are easy; some are difficult, but we all have them.

EXCHANGING IDEAS

Of course we attempt to answer most of life's perplexing questions ourselves by using past experiences and our powers of reasoning and investigation. To a large degree, a person's growth and maturity are dependent upon his learning to handle his own affairs; a mature person cannot expect someone else to solve all of his problems. Nevertheless, there are times when group action is necessary. The problem-solving process is often more democratic and more effective that way. One student cannot be given the sole responsibility for allocating student body funds, for example. The job is too big and, besides, others deserve to have a voice in the matter. Many points of view must be represented and expressed. "How much money should be spent on athletics?" "What can we cut in order to balance the budget?" "Should we grant the band an extra $800?" If you have ever been a part of such an important group, you know the problems involved. Hours of our time must be spent in deliberation if fair and intelligent decisions are to be made.

Group discussion is necessary in all phases of life—social, political, economic, educational, and religious. The family assembles to talk things over. A senator calls his committee together. The school board convenes. Church leaders hold a meeting. Or a group of friends informally sit down to work out a solution to a mutual problem; several heads are better than one. It behooves everyone to understand this frequently-used and effective democratic process.

THE DISCUSSION PROCESS

Before going on, let us make a distinction. The main oral assignments for this unit of work will call for participation in those forms of public discussion presented before audiences—panel, symposium, lecture-panel. Except when one has occasion to appear in a discussion before a class, or at a PTA meeting, or at a union meeting, and so forth, discussion experiences are informal or nonpublic—for example, committee meetings, family deliberations, and planning sessions of a club. These are not discussions that belong on television or before audiences, for the groups' problems concern only the people involved. Even though your discussion experiences are largely informal, training in public discussion will help to prepare you for them as well as formal discussion situations of daily life.

Now, a discussion designed to determine a plan or reach a solution is more than aimless talk. As with other forms of speech with which you are familiar, there should be a purpose for speaking. The discussion method of oral communication is but another type of speechmaking, a type set up as a problem-solving or information-getting venture. When a number of people discuss a question in a group, they build a speech together. Each member contributes his part to the total group effort. The speakers are guided by a leader who helps them move along in an organized manner toward the desired goal. They have a reason for deliberating, and they know that success depends upon their use of a proven method. Just as in making an individual speech, there are techniques to follow in making a "collective speech." There are fitting ways to start a discussion, to develop the body of it, and to conclude. All purposeful speech calls for a planned procedure.

The Subject

Obviously, in day-to-day affairs, the selection of problems for discussion poses no difficulty, for they continually "rear their heads" without our effort. Consequently, unless a certain concern is the cause for starting a discussion, a subject must be selected. Therefore, after you have formed a group, in class, your next step is to choose a subject. How do you make the choice? You should, of course, choose a subject that fits you (your group), the audience, the amount of preparation time available, and the occasion. Let us be more specific.

1. *Your subject should be meaningful and interesting to all parties.* Avoid selecting an insignificant subject. Choose an area that touches upon the lives of the discussion members and the audience. What of importance is happening in the school, community, state, nation, or world at this time? Is there a question of contemporary interest that is worthy of investigation and consideration? What are the present problems facing the student body or the city? Campus politics? Recreation? Elections? Juvenile delinquency? Is there a national matter of special significance to you? Draft laws? The vote for eighteen-year-olds? Narcotics laws?

2. *Your subject should be one with which you can increase your familiarity.* Can you learn more about it? To insure a worthwhile discussion, it is necessary to investigate, to find new information; therefore, it is necessary also to know if new information is available. You should survey possible sources of material before settling upon your subject.

3. *Your subject should be one with which you can become conversant in a limited time.* Ordinarily you do not have a long period of time in which to prepare for a discussion. In class, a group may typically be allowed only a few days to ready itself. Now, if you know that certain vital materials on a given subject will not be available for at least two weeks, doubtless your only alternative is to choose another problem

area. Or, if adequate exploration can be expected, realistically, to take an extended time and perhaps cause last minute pressure in preparation, a change of subject seems indicated.

4. *Your subject should be appropriate for the occasion.* In class, the setting usually remains the same unless a hypothetical situation is set up. If you plan a discussion for presentation elsewhere, you will be expected to adhere to the demands of the occasion, just as you would for any oral presentation. Know what is expected of you, exactly how much time is allotted to your group, and all pertinent details about the purpose and plans for the meeting.

Narrowing the Subject

Take a close look at your subject, and decide if it is too broad to be treated in the allotted time. How much time has your instructor allowed for your group's discussion in class? Do you have the full period, or has the instructor reserved a few minutes at the end of the hour for class evaluation of your discussion? Has he planned for a second discussion group to precede or follow yours? Know what time is available to you, and scale your scope accordingly. You may need to select a portion or division of a subject as your area for consideration.

Wording the Question

The specific question, or proposition, is worded to indicate the scope of the discussion. Like all propositions, it should contain one idea, worded clearly and briefly. Unlike many propositions, it is frequently stated in the form of a question. A question suggests that the matter is up for discussion and unsolved at the present; it is open for consideration.

State the question fairly without bias or prejudice for a particular point of view. An unfair question suggests that the group already agrees on the answer or solution. With such a question, the members cannot talk impartially, for they are prejudiced from the beginning. This violates the basic characteristic of group discussion: *an honest search for the solution to an important problem.* The inclusion of the italicized word in the following question makes it unworthy:

How can our *wayward* teenagers spend their time profitably?

Could a group in your class carry on an impartial search for a solution to this problem? It is not likely. The question makes a biased assumption, and a full hour could be spent in debate over the one word. These questions, also, are not worded fairly:

Should the *useless* system of giving final examinations be abolished?
What can be done to improve our *backward* school system?

Then, too, you should word the question in a way that will avoid setting up sides. If a discussion results in one side upholding the "con" and another side the "pro," you do not have a discussion; you have a debate; and the fault often lies in the wording of the question. Notice how these sentences suggest debate rather than cooperative problem-solving:

Should all U.S. citizens be encouraged to live abroad for a year?
Should capital punishment be abolished?
Should speech be a required course?

Instead of discarding them, let us restate each one in a way which should encourage cooperative discussion:

What can we do to improve world understanding?
How should we punish those who commit the most serious crimes?
What can we do to provide training in oral communication for all students?

FACT-VALUE-POLICY

Depending on the nature of the subject and the group's goals, discussion questions are worded to promote deliberations seeking either factual information, assessment of value, or determination of policy. Discussion problems can thus be classified as questions of *fact, value,* or *policy*. The first problem involves a search for information regarding present conditions, actual accomplishments, the historical facts, definitions, requirements, and so forth. The second is to evaluate a condition, program, idea, or course of action—to ask if something is good, beneficial, or effective. The third, policy, is perhaps the most commonly used in the speech classroom. With this type of question, the members' purpose is to work out a suitable policy for solving the problem at hand.

The following questions will further illustrate the three types.

Fact
1. What is the meaning of the term "political extremism"?
2. Are ethics and successful business practices compatible?
3. What led to the adoption of the Code of the National Association of Broadcasters?

Value
1. What are benefits of the quarter system over the semester system?
2. How important is it to require aliens seeking naturalization to pass tests in United States history?
3. Is the electoral college useful?

Policy
1. How can colleges discourage academic dishonesty?
2. What system of law enforcement will help promote support of the people?
3. How should the United States select men for military service?

In summary, these are the marks of a good discussion question:
1. It contains one idea.
2. It is brief.
3. It is worded clearly.
4. It is usually worded in the form of a question.
5. It is worded fairly.
6. It is designed to encourage discussion, whether classed as fact, value, or policy.

ORGANIZING THE DISCUSSION

How do you start? What steps are followed? Since good discussion is based upon sound reasoning, it follows that the steps in the process should be related to the process of thinking. Most systems for organizing a discussion are offsprings of John Dewey's pattern for reflective thinking which we can interpret as follows:
1. Recognition of a problem condition;
2. Analysis (definition, limitation, causes and effects of the problem);
3. Consideration of possible solutions;
4. Selection of a satisfactory solution;
5. Implementation of the solution.
You can apply this rational pattern in organizing a discussion.

Furthermore, you can accommodate the pattern to the familiar four-part plan for speaking that is detailed in Chapters Two through Six. The following outline is an extension and adaptation of Dewey's steps from reflective thinking to the standard speaking formula.

I• *Introduction* (presented by the leader)
    A. The area of difficulty
    B. General background

II• *Proposition* (statement of the problem as presently visualized)

III• *Body*
   A. Analysis of the problem
      1. Determining the extent of the problem; limiting and defining
      2. Citing causes and effects
   B. Considerations of possible solutions
      1. Strengths
      2. Weaknesses

IV• *Conclusion*
   A. Selection of a satisfactory solution
   B. Determining a course of action to put the solution into effect.

DETERMINING FORM OF THE DISCUSSION

There are various forms which a discussion may take. Some are quite formal; others are more informal. Some demand much of the leader; others give the members a greater burden. Some call for a "guest expert"; others depend solely upon the original group. The one you use should be one that provides the best framework for achieving your goals.

As we mentioned earlier, informal forms are used frequently by the leaders of business, churches, and clubs to solve the internal problems of their organizations or to seek enlightenment on a topic. These are not public discussions because the officers or executives deliberate among themselves without the presence of an audience. Different names are often attached to such forms. Some may call them conferences. Others may refer to them as round tables, committee meetings, councils, or merely meetings.

Three very useful forms for public discussion are the panel, the symposium, and the lecture-panel.

The Panel

The *panel* is probably what most people have in mind when they think of public group discussion. The participants assemble themselves before an audience in positions which will allow visual and oral contact with the audience and among the group. This may be accomplished by arranging the chairs in a semicircle or by placing the chairs around a table. The leader seats himself in a central position in view of the audience and panel members.

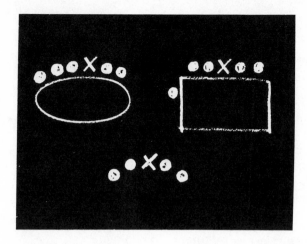

Fig. 10–1 Hypothetical panel groups, X represents the leader.

The panel is usually composed of four to seven persons, who, under the guidance of a leader, set about to resolve a difficulty in an orderly fashion. There are no set speeches. Each person taking part has studied the question carefully, and he may make contributions freely, based on his thorough preparation. This is not to say that he may talk of anything at any time. For the benefit of everyone concerned, all remarks should be pertinent to what is being discussed at a given moment. To help the group avoid straying from the point, the leader keeps an outline before him as a constant reminder of their over-all plan. The outline, prepared in pre-discussion consultation with all members of the group, is a plan of *probable* movement of the discussion. It is an elaboration or filling out (as prescribed by the topic) of the Dewey pattern or of the standard, four-part formula suggesting the main areas to be delved into and an order of progression.

Take note of one word of caution regarding use of the outline. It should be an "assistant," not a "dictator." Use it; let it help you, but do not allow it to handcuff you. You know how an outline functions in individual speaking. Occasionally you change some bit of your speech as you are speaking. You omit a certain example or add one. You think of a good statistic on the spur of the moment and decide to include it. You make adjustments because the situation seems to demand changes. Fresh thinking increases effectiveness. Maintain the basic structure of your discussion, but permit worthwhile alterations.

To illustrate a panel in action, let us examine a hypothetical case. We shall assume that Donna, Ron, Ruth, Vickie, and George have selected "How can we increase the attractiveness of the Guest Speaker Forum on our campus?" as the question for their panel and that George was chosen to lead it. They held two preliminary planning meetings, and each person, including the leader, studied the problem thoroughly. In one column below you see the general outline and beside it a summary of the discussion as it developed.

OUTLINE	ACTUAL DEVELOPMENT
I• *Introduction* (Recognition of a Problem) A. The area of difficulty B. General background	George introduced the panel members and explained why the topic was up for discussion. He said that there had been some dissatisfaction among the student body with the Guest Speaker Forum and that such an essential part of school life should not be neglected.
II• *Proposition*	Let us consider the matter of improving the Guest Speaker Forum.
III• *Body* (Analysis and Possible Solutions) A. Analysis of the problem 1. Extent of: limiting and defining	George asked Donna if she felt that conditions were serious. Donna gave statistics to show that attendance had dropped 50 percent in the past two years. Ron cited two examples of poorly attended programs. Ruth and Vickie agreed that the problem was serious and widespread, but all agreed that they should discuss G.S.F.-sponsored programs only, and not events arranged by other groups.
2. Citing causes and effects	"What are the causes?" asked George. Vickie presented the results of a poll she had taken of the student body which brought out two reasons for the disinterest: (1) too many local speakers and (2) week-night scheduling. Ruth and Ron added two more causes: (1) competition with other community events and (2) lack of publicity. Donna disagreed with the charge that there was insufficient publicity. She worked on the *Red and White* and had personally written several articles publicizing the events. Ron said that other means of publicity had not been used. George asked if there were any

OUTLINE

ACTUAL DEVELOPMENT

more possible causes, and Ruth stated that the gymnasium acoustics were poor for listening to speakers.

B. Consideration of possible solutions

Donna spoke for having more nationally-known speakers. Ron brought out the factor of cost. He cited figures to show why the student body could not afford it. Ruth got off the subject, and George reminded her of the present topic. Vickie agreed with Ron about the cost being great.

1. First solution: strengths and weaknesses.

2. Second solution: strengths and weaknesses.

"Why not hold the Forum at midday during the week?" Ruth volunteered. Ron mentioned conflicts with classes. Donna said that a person rarely has classes at all midday hours. "We could schedule some speakers at 11 A.M., some at 12 P.M., and others at 1 P.M.," she added. "This way, everybody could hear some." Vickie agreed and pointed up the need to work out a schedule early in the year. Ron went back to the subject of prominent speakers for a moment but showed how it applied to the present topic.

George, who had been asking occasional questions and otherwise helping them along, summarized the two proposed solutions.

3. Third solution: strengths and weaknesses.

"What else can be done?" George asked.

Vickie asked the group to consider giving a trophy at the end of the year to the class having the largest representation at the G.S.F. programs. Ron praised the idea, but when Donna talked about dif-

OUTLINE	ACTUAL DEVELOPMENT
	ficulties in recording attendance, and so forth, he changed his mind.
4. Fourth solution: strengths and weaknesses.	Ron felt that more publicity would help. Vickie did not think that it was so vital in this case. George, noticing that Ruth had been silent for a long time, spoke to her. "Ruth, we would like to hear your views on this idea." Ruth disagreed with Vickie, stressing the necessity for publicity.
IV• *Conclusion* (A Solution and Course of Action)	Before summarizing, George made certain that no one had any more important contributions.
A. Selection of a satisfactory solution	"What is our best solution?" questioned George. The group weighed and evaluated each proposal they had made. They ruled out the trophy idea and finally decided upon a combination of the first, second, and fourth solutions: well-publicized G.S.F. programs, with more prominent speakers, held on alternate midday hours.
B. Determining a course of action	George restated the solution and announced, "All right, we have a solution, but what are we going to do with it? How can we put it into effect?" All agreed that the only way was to present their idea to the student council.
	That afternoon George arranged for a hearing before the student council.

This is only a summary of a hypothetical panel discussion. Just the highlights were presented, and you can fill in the details mentally. We did not repeat all the examples, statistics, quotations, and other materials that might have been used. We did not go into the finer points of leadership which George might have employed.

Nor did we suggest how much time elapsed during the discussion.

Timing depends upon the peculiarities of the problem. For some questions it may take the majority of your allotted minutes developing the problem. Others require a longer consideration of solutions. Assuming that the preceding discussion lasted thirty minutes, the following is a *possible* distribution of time:

Area of difficulty and general background	3 minutes
Analysis of the problem	8 minutes
Consideration of possible solutions	11 minutes
Selecting a satisfactory solution	5 minutes
Determining a course of action	3 minutes

The Symposium

The *symposium* follows the same pattern of organization as the panel but differs in other ways. The panel is characterized by free exchange of ideas within the pattern; whereas the symposium is composed mainly of prepared speeches on phases or subtopics of the total problem. With the exception of the conclusion, a symposium is made up of a series of speeches similar to the ones discussed in the first chapters of this book. The conclusion in a symposium may be the same as in a panel discussion.

If we assigned George, Ron, Ruth, Vickie, and Donna to a thirty-minute symposium, their parts might be distributed as follows:

Area of difficulty and general background	George (Chairman): 3 minutes
Analysis of the problem	Vickie: prepared speech, 6 minutes
First solution	Donna: prepared speech, 4 minutes
Second solution	Ruth: prepared speech, 4 minutes
Third solution	Ron: prepared speech, 4 minutes
Selecting a satisfactory solution and a course of action	Entire membership: panel discussion, 9 minutes

In addition to introducing the general background for discussion and guiding the concluding discussion, George has the responsibility of tying each speech together with effective transitions. For example, following Vickie's speech, he would summarize the problem briefly and introduce Donna who would offer the first solution.

The Lecture-Panel

The *lecture-panel* is a third discussion form. This variation calls for a resource speaker—someone who has a close acquaintanceship with the question—to deliver a prepared speech.

After the leader introduces the problem topic area and the speaker, the speaker analyzes the nature of the problem and presents possible solutions. During the panel discussion which follows, the members may ask questions of the resource speaker, make comments of their own, and discuss any aspect of the matter among themselves. They may accept, reject, or modify any of the offered solutions. Finally, with a solution in mind, the members may work out a plan for putting the solution into practice.

The nature of the problem will dictate your selection of a resource speaker. He may be from outside the class, or he may be one of your class members who is well versed on the subject. Outside resource people often invited are police department members, recreation department personnel, radio and television authorities, athletic coaches, teachers, lawyers, businessmen, agriculturists, and newspaper personnel.

If an outside person is not available, do not despair. Someone in your class can be encouraged to come to your rescue. He may have to make a careful study of the subject, but, of course, you will too. Here is a sample time distribution plan for a thirty-minute lecture-panel.

Area of difficulty, general background, and introduction of the speaker	Leader, 3 minutes
Analysis of the problem and possible solutions	Resource speaker, 15 minutes
Questions, comments, and selection of a satisfactory solution and course of action	Panel members, 12 minutes

Incidentally, one common variation is the lecture-forum, in which full audience participation is substituted for the panel. (Weigh the possible usefulness of this form as we consider audience participation.)

Audience Participation

In our explanation of discussion forms, the audience should not be forgotten. The listeners are participants, also, in that they actively follow the course of the discussion. They, too, have an interest in the problem and, therefore, must be alert in their efforts to understand, consider, and evaluate.

Public discussion forms provide for oral audience participation after the group has concluded. This part of the program is called a *forum*. A forum in Rome was the market place, a large public square where public or private affairs were discussed, speeches delivered, and courts of law held. Today we use the word to indicate an occasion at which everyone has a right to express his ideas. Actually, when the audience is allowed to speak following a discussion, the entire program is called a forum. Thus we have the panel forum, the symposium forum, and the lecture-panel forum.

Audience members may ask questions of specific discussion speakers or of the group as a whole. They may refer to some phase of the subject and make statements of their own. A question from the audience is directed to the leader who, in turn, submits it to the group or to a certain member for response.

GATHERING MATERIALS

A critic once defined discussion as "pooled ignorance." Possibly this definition would apply to some situations, but certainly not to a well-informed, alert group. You can become informed on your subject by collecting pertinent data. Where should you look for your materials?

CHECK YOUR OWN EXPERIENCE FIRST.

Perhaps you have had some contact with the subject area. A summer job might have introduced you to labor-management relations. Baby-sitting could have provided you with knowledge about raising children. What have you read about the subject? What have you seen that pertains to it? What have you heard well-informed people say about it?

VISIT THE SCENE OF ACTION RELATED TO YOUR SUBJECT.

One of the best ways to become well informed is to make firsthand observations. If you will be discussing "Community Recreation," visit the playgrounds, the pools, and other facilities. Make the field trip a worthwhile one by planning carefully in advance and by keeping your purpose uppermost in your mind.

Arrange an interview with an authority. The head of the recreation department, for example, would be glad to help you. Make an appointment; be prompt; and prepare your questions in advance.

USE THE LIBRARY SERVICES.

Here is a source of materials on almost any subject. The library is valuable not only because so much information is deposited there but, also, because the librarian can be of great assistance in helping you to find it.

Become familiar with and use the research aids found in the library.

a. The *card catalog,* contained in a filing cabinet, lists every book in the library alphabetically. You can find the information card for a

Fig. 10-2 Sample Cards.

Need for Recreation Facilities in Our Town

"Our present recreation facilities are too meager to serve our growing town. The population has nearly doubled in twenty years, yet we have not increased our services. "Something must be done soon to correct this difficulty."

Anderson, Howard F., head of the Johnstown Recreation Department, in an interview on March 5.

How to Interest the Public in Recreation Needs

"A well-organized student speakers' bureau helped a community in the state of Washington to wake up to the importance of having an active, wholesome recreation program."

Braydon, Samuel A., Spending Leisure Hours, New York, Riordan Press, 1968, p. 39.

Benefits of a Good Recreation Program

Towns have already observed decreases in juvenile delinquency rates after instituting good programs.
        Springfield--down 10% after 5 years
        Clayton--down 12% after 4 years
        Newton--down 21% after 6 years

The Johnstown Daily Herald, editorial, March 11.

certain book by title, author, or subject; each work is listed in these three ways.

b. The *Reader's Guide to Periodical Literature* is an index of articles published in many magazines. The listings in this aid, too, are by author, subject, and title. If you are not acquainted with the *Reader's Guide,* learn how it can work for you.

c. Many students find the library pamphlet file to be extremely helpful in preparing for a discussion. Ask your librarian about it.

d. Newspapers, encyclopedias, dictionaries, yearbooks (including almanacs), or biographical dictionaries may be of use to you. Browse around the reference section and notice the varied volumes on the shelves. In addition to the standard encyclopedias and dictionaries, you will find special aids which treat specific areas of knowledge. For example, there is an encyclopedia of music and one of social science.

e. The United States Government Printing Office publishes thousands of pamphlets and books on a wide variety of subjects. Ask the librarian for a catalog pertaining to your subject.

RECORDING DATA

Assuming that you are now ready to gather information from your personal experiences, from field trips, and from the library, how will you record your data? You will need to proceed systematically. A method is necessary in order to make the fruits of your research usable at the time of discussion.

The best plan calls for recording your materials on 3 x 5 or 4 x 6 cards. Observe the following suggestions:

1. Use a different card for each new subject.
2. Include a topic heading.
3. Record the material accurately.
4. Enclose quoted material with quotation marks.
5. Include the author, source, and date.

CHECKING THE MATERIALS

You will recall from previous speech activities that you were asked to test the value of your materials. This same sort of checking is needed to evaluate discussion materials. Ask these questions:

1. Do I have enough to make my share of contributions in the discussion?
2. Have I gathered an ample amount of data from all sides of the question?
3. Are the data related to probable subtopics of the discussion?
4. Are the statistics accurate?

5. Are my quotations authoritative?
6. Are any of my sources prejudiced or biased?
7. Are my materials not likely to arouse needless debate?

USING REASONING

You cannot expect to contribute effectively to a discussion without collecting a store of well-tested materials, nor can you neglect your reasoning. It is not sufficient to offer an example of something or some authority's quotation without *reasoning* that reveals the material's practicability or applicability. After all, the only purpose for introducing materials is to develop ideas and reach conclusions; therefore, you must reason whether your data show their significance and come to valid and acceptable conclusions. In other words, use logical processes in establishing your ideas and in relating them to the ideas of your fellow participants. The two principal modes of reasoning are *induction* and *deduction*.

Induction

Inductive reasoning is the process of deriving a general premise from a consideration of specific data, sometimes called evidence. This following example illustrates a form of induction called *generalization*.

Jones, a successful salesman, has had training in persuasive speaking. Smith, a successful salesman, has had training in persuasive speaking. Brown, a successful salesman, has had training in persuasive speaking. Therefore, training in persuasive speaking probably helps one to be a successful salesman.

Is this reasoning sound? To check the validity of a generalization reached inductively, you should ask yourself three questions:
1. Do I have a sufficient number of instances?
2. Are my instances typical or representative?
3. If contradictory instances exist, can they be explained?
Causal reasoning, a form of induction, is commonly used in discussion. Here are some types and samples:

1. Reasoning from cause to effect:

    Oily rags (*cause*) piled in corners of garages may start fires (*effect*).

2. Reasoning from effect to cause:

    The bridge collapsed (*effect*) because its main span was too long (*cause*).

3. Reasoning from effect to effect:

Peterson's Department Store is having a sale, and the fact that the store is crowded today (*effect of a sale*) indicates that by tomorrow the merchandise will be well-picked over (*second effect*).

To check the accuracy of a conclusion reached by causal reasoning, you should ask yourself the following questions:

1. Is there more than a chance relationship between cause and effect?
2. Was the cause sufficient to produce the effect?
3. Have I considered other possible causes?

Reasoning by *analogy* is another form of induction—one with which the speaker attempts to make a point by comparing two phenomena. If you reason that the honor system that has worked at Stanford University should be instituted at your school, you develop the point by analogy. To make your argument acceptable you must show that conditions at the two institutions are similar enough to warrant your conclusion. Because of all the varying and intangible factors, reasoning by analogy is risky business. On the other hand, when extreme care is taken to choose closely related phenomena the use of analogy can be helpful, especially in clarifying.

Test the validity of an analogy with these questions:
1. Are the cases similar in all vital aspects?
2. Can dissimilarities be explained?

Deduction

Deduction is the process of reasoning by which a general premise is applied to a specific case in order to reach a conclusion. In formal logic, a sample of deductive reasoning is called a *syllogism*. Study the following types of syllogisms and accompanying samples:

1. *Categorical*

MAJOR PREMISE: All automobiles are subject to mechanical failure.
MINOR PREMISE: The Rolls Royce is an automobile.
CONCLUSION: Therefore, the Rolls Royce is subject to mechanical failure.

2. *Hypothetical*

MAJOR PREMISE: If the carload of grain has arrived, we must work overtime.
MINOR PREMISE: The carload of grain has arrived.
CONCLUSION: Therefore, we must work overtime.

3. *Disjunctive*

MAJOR PREMISE: Fisk is either a hero or an imposter.
MINOR PREMISE: Fisk is not a hero.
CONCLUSION: Fisk is an imposter.

Typically, formal three-part syllogisms are not presented as such in discussions; however, they can serve as skeletal plans to be expanded upon in developing ideas. They can serve, also, as tests to check the validity of reasoning.

Verifying the accuracy of a syllogism depends upon the type of syllogism, and we shall not discuss the technical details here. Nonetheless, there are three questions that you can ask which apply to all methods of deductive reasoning:

1. Is the generalization sound? In a discussion, the generalization is a main idea or assertion; in the syllogism, it is the major premise.
2. Is the specific case—the evidence or supporting data, the minor premise in a syllogism—relevant to the generalization? (See "Checking the Materials" section in this chapter.)
3. From the premises offered, does the conclusion logically follow?

The Enthymeme. Much more common in discussion—in fact in all speaking—is the *enthymeme*. This is a kind of syllogism that more often than not typifies the thinking of people and characterizes almost all of our daily deliberations. The enthymeme has two contrasting marks: (1) it deals in probabilities and (2) it is usually stated with fewer than three premises.

While the syllogism is used to reason about certainties or absolutes, the enthymeme is used to reason about probabilities. Only rarely are people—whether they be teachers, lawyers, students, businessmen, or politicians—able to reason together about certainties. For example: the *certainty* of solving the school dropout problem; the *positive fact* of jealousy as the cause for a murder; the *infallibility* of memorization as a method of study for an examination; the *absolute assurance* of a coming boom in business; the *inevitability* of a political party's defeat. No, regardless of how confident we may appear, we usually find ourselves reasoning about possibilities and probabilities and likelihoods. For example, we may reason that if a library has well-trained librarians such as ours has, it serves its patrons better than libraries with ill-trained personnel. Or, since it is likely that the weather will be fair on June 6th, we should hold the annual art sale outdoors. But we cannot be *sure* in either case of these two instances; neither gives us certainty. You will notice that: (1) both of the preceding samples of reasoning are based on probabilities; (2) both make tacit assumptions about the listener's previous knowledge of the situations.

Check these assumptions using the form of a regular syllogism.

MAJOR PREMISE: Libraries with well-trained librarians offer better service than those that are poorly staffed.

MINOR PREMISE: Our library has well-trained personnel.

CONCLUSION [assumed but not stated]: Our library offers better service than those that are poorly staffed.

In the preceding enthymeme—structured as a syllogism for purposes of analysis—the missing step is the conclusion. The speaker did not feel obliged to state the conclusion; for he implied it strongly. Moreover, we assume that he was talking with a listener who was sympathetic and also loyal to the local public library. Hopefully, the listener drew the conclusion for the speaker.

Check the dynamics of the second enthymeme.

MAJOR PREMISE: [assumed but not stated]: An art show should be held outdoors only in fair weather.

MINOR PREMISE: On the date of our show, June 6th, the weather will be fair.

CONCLUSION: We should plan to hold the art show outdoors on June 6th.

In this instance, the premise assumed and supplied by the listener is the major premise. It was not necessary for the speaker to state it because the listener knew what he meant. In other words, why use a full syllogistic form and run the risk of boring the listener or appearing to speak down to the listener?

To enhance your understanding of the enthymeme in practice, note how it functions in the following fragment of a discussion. The italicized portions are enthymemes, whose structure you might test by casting them in the form of syllogisms. All but one of them omit a premise.

RICK: No, I don't believe in censorship. *No board of censors is wise enough to tell a person what he shall or shall not read, and that's just what the proposed board will do.*

ALICE: But what about little children? *All children need guidance in significant aspects of their training. Since reading is a significant aspect, children need guidance in it.*

MARTHA: *I think that both of you are taking extreme positions, and all extreme positions are to be questioned.*

RICK: Extreme or not, *our present system is best; it's democratic.*

If you keep in mind that your expectations ought to be for a reasonable degree of probability (depending on the subject in question), you can check enthymemes with the same tests listed following the discussion of syllogisms.

A New Perspective in Reasoning

Until recent years, students of speech went about studying reasoning with almost exclusive reference to classical structuring of induction and deduction (*see* preceding discussion). Recognizing the possibility that one's understanding may be increased by introduction of a new perspective, let us examine briefly a system developed recently by Stephen Toulmin, an English logician.

The new system enables one to examine more microscopically and operationally the elements in a line of reasoning, elements that might not be apparent in the structure of an enthymeme or syllogism. It can help you to check your own reasoning patterns and those of other people. Now to illustrate the workings of the Toulmin system. Let us suppose that in preparation for a discussion you determine that mental illness affects 10 percent of all Americans. Furthermore, you reason that since these 10 percent influence the lives of millions of other people, mental illness is the nation's major health problem. Using the new method and its terms—*data* (evidence), *conclusion,* and *warrant* (connecting or supporting commentary)—this is the way that you would structure the line of thought diagrammatically:

(Data)	therefore (Conclusion)
Mental illness affects 10 percent of Americans	**mental illness is the nation's major health problem**

Since
(Warrant)

these 10 percent influence millions

As you see, *data* are specific materials, facts, or evidence; the *warrant* is the link in the chain of thinking that gives justification for drawing the *conclusion.*

The preceding diagram shows graphically how a simple pattern of reasoning might unfold. Let us add two elements to it: a *backing* for the warrant (in the form of added evidence or reasoning), and a *qualifier* (to note the temper or strength of the conclusion). Written in paragraph form, the full line of reasoning would appear as follows:

Mental illness affects 10 percent of all Americans; since these 10 percent influence the lives of millions of other people—the family, friends, and employer of the ill person, for example, (*backing*)—

probably (*qualifier*) mental illness is the nation's major health problem.

Charting the course of thought we can see it more clearly.

		therefore	
(Data)		**(Qualifier)**	**(Conclusion)**
		probably	
Mental illness affects			
10 percent of Americans			**mental illness**
			is the nation's
			major health
	Since		**problem**
	(Warrant)		
	these 10 percent		
	influence millions		
	(Backing for the warrant)		
	family, friends, and em-		
	ployer, for example		

Just one more element, a *reservation*,[1] may be added if the reasoner needs to account for exceptions or limitations to the conclusion. For instance, you would add a reservation if you chose to modify the conclusion by saying, "Mental illness is the nation's major health problem *unless* one classifies certain ailments like heart disease as strictly physical ailments." On the diagram, a reservation to a conclusion is sketched in below the conclusion.

                              (Conclusion)

                              Unless

                              (Reservation)
                              we classify ailments
                              like heart disease
                              as strictly physical

Suppose that someone (possibly you) in a discussion offered the line of reasoning on world population that appears in the following extract.

> Experts testify that the problem of population in the world is reaching dangerous proportions, as technology has so reduced death rates that we face a tripling of the population in the next fifty years. Many countries, facing misery and hunger among their peoples, are helpless in meeting the problem. Numerous countries in Asia with their teeming millions, are examples. Since individual nations have not solved the problem, the United Nations is probably the only agency with sufficient strength to be effective in meeting the crisis. Yet we must recognize that

[1] "Reservation" is the term used by Douglas Ehninger and Wayne Brockriede in *Decision by Debate* (New York, 1963).

in dealing with peoples of varying beliefs and customs, an outside agency like the U.N. may find its efforts resisted or thwarted.

How would you begin to examine or analyze this reasoning? Try laying it out with the Toulmin model. The charting may result in increased understanding of the developed thought and increased capability in responding to it. Though the diagramming is sometimes hard work, the final picture of the reasoning may make the effort worthwhile.

Fallacies in reasoning, whether inductive or deductive, should be avoided, and you should be able to detect those made by others. There are many errors of reasoning; here are the most common types:

1. Hasty generalization (jumping to conclusions):
   I saw a drunk on Main Street and another on Front Street. This town is full of drunks.

2. Coincidence of events ("after this, therefore, because of this"):
   Everett's bad grades are due to his disappointment in losing his scholarship last year.

3. No relationship (a connection of "unconnectable" phenomena):
   The new courthouse in the next county is beautiful. They must have an efficient system of government.

4. Insufficient relationship (false analogy):
   Since New York and Seattle are cities with important harbors, they have similar bus transportation problems.

5. Either-or (offering only two solutions when others are possible):
   Either we levy a sales tax or endure our present financial struggle.

6. Begging the question (false or dubious assumption):
   Now we all know that war is inevitable [Do we?] so let us reason from there and plan . . .

7. Personalizing (referring to irrelevant personal characteristics):
   I would not vote for Greta Hammond. You cannot trust a woman who wears her hair that way.

8. Arguing in a circle (using a point to "prove" the point):
   Dr. Carson, who has lectured far and wide on animal husbandry, is well known in the field because he talks to many large and small groups.

BEING A GOOD MEMBER

If you appreciate the purpose of discussion and understand its methods and applicable forms of reasoning, you are almost ready to participate. Before starting, study the following injunctions for discussion members and keep them in mind as you do your work.

1. *Make thorough preparation.* Preparation is the member's prime responsibility. Some people have the false notion that preparation means doing a little thinking about the subject and getting ready to offer an opinion here and there in the discussion. No view is more ridiculous or more revealing of a lack of training in the process of group discussion. Not until he has analyzed the problem rationally, organized his thoughts, and gathered substantial materials, is the member ready to contribute constructively to the development of the group effort.

2. *Adopt a cooperative spirit.* Recognize the need for a cooperative spirit in achieving a successful discussion. You may not always agree with the ideas of others, but be tolerant and willing to try to understand all points of view.

Acknowledge your prejudices. Anyone may have a prejudice, but not everyone has that special kind of courage it takes to admit it to himself. A good member examines his own opinions and attempts to weed out those that are based on mere prejudice.

3. *Avoid needless debate.* This is not to say that a person should refrain from supporting his convictions. It merely means that the good discussion speaker knows that extended debate can incur strong feeling and perhaps cause the discussion to bog down. Persistent debating forces people to take sides and rules out open-mindedness and objectivity. Know when to stop, when to yield for the sake of the discussion as a whole.

4. *Contribute your share.* The occasion is not one for long, time-consuming speeches. Contributions should be short, clear, and relevant. Regardless of how wise and fluent a member may be, if he is considerate he will avoid taking up an unreasonable share of time. Discussion is a *group* effort.

Then, too, the good member avoids the opposite extreme—that of too little participation. You must realize that any solution reached cannot be yours if you have had no part in finding it. Some people underestimate their own value as much as others seem to overestimate theirs. In addition to the right to speak, you have an obligation to speak. Involve yourself actively in the discussion, and commit yourself to its purpose.

5. *Be tactful.* Discuss *ideas* and avoid personal ridicule. Use tact, and do not injure the feelings of others. A good member guards against making remarks—unintentional or otherwise—which will antagonize or offend. In other words, social propriety is the guiding standard.

6. *Accept the leader's guidance.* Remember the importance of the

orderly progression of thought for which the leader is responsible. Respect the leader's actions, and refrain from getting ahead of the discussion. For example, you should not insist on discussing solutions when the group is still considering the problem.

7. *Use appropriate language.* Communication among the members is based on concrete and accurate speaking. Vague and abstract thoughts usually mean very little to others. The good member adapts his ideas to the lives and experiences of his listeners.

8. *Be a capable listener.* Be conscientious in following the flow of discussion and attempt to understand and interpret comments before referring to them. The effective speaker ignores emotional and physical distractions and listens intelligently.

When in doubt about what to do in a discussion, ask yourself this question: "What can I do for the good of the discussion?" If you are undecided about expressing a given thought, ask yourself, "Will it help or hinder the progress of the discussion?" In all cases, be guided by a desire to make the group efforts successful.

BEING A GOOD LEADER

As mentioned earlier in this chapter, a discussion is a collective speech. It is the task of each member to make contributions to the development of the discussion. You can see quite readily that another agent is needed in the process—someone who must act as a guide in order to make the activity a purposeful one. This person, of course, is the leader. His job begins in the planning period when he leads the group in selecting and narrowing the subject, wording the question, determining the form, and preparing an outline of the main points to be discussed.

What are the requirements for leadership?

1. *Make thorough preparation.* As a leader, you should have substantial over-all knowledge of the subject. After all, you are responsible for the development of the discussion. A captain must know the whole ship in order to coordinate the work of the various officers. Your reading and specific preparation should be at least as extensive as that of the members.

2. *Adopt a cooperative spirit.* You must have deep respect for the discussion process, an awareness of the "working together" nature of discussion. Be honest, tactful, friendly, and impartial. Avoid being an overlord, and yet be firm when necessary. Use your intelligence and your sense of humor. Have an attitude which will enable the group to have confidence in you. Remember that you are the leader and not a member; as such, you offer leadership but not your views on the topic, ordinarily.

3. *Provide an appropriate beginning.* Open the program in much the same way as you would commence any speech. An example might be used or, possibly, a quotation, or a statistic. Work in an explanation of the subject's importance along with background information. Introduce the individual participants, and announce the procedure which will be followed.

4. *Give guidance to your group.* This is your main job. It is your duty to insure orderly progress toward the final goal. You may clarify or ask for definitions and restatements. You should summarize whenever the group needs to be reminded of what it has accomplished. Occasionally ask questions to keep the discussion moving or to bring out key points. Recognize the key points presented, and see that they get sufficient emphasis. For example, if Betty made a significant contribution, say, "I think Betty made a significant point," and so forth.

Be sure to encourage all members to participate. Help the quiet member by asking for his ideas. He has something to share, too. When Betty has not spoken for a time, you may need to say, "We have not heard your thinking in this area, Betty." On the other hand, be ready to deal with the overtalkative member. Be gentle and tactful, and maintain a balanced discussion.

5. *Provide an appropriate ending.* Include a summary of what has been accomplished, along with other remarks designed to round out the discussion. If the audience is to take part, remind them that they may ask questions of individual discussion speakers, or of the group as a body, and that they may make comments of their own. Guide the forum period, and bring the program to a smooth conclusion.

LET US SUMMARIZE

Discussion—the medium for exchanging ideas and solving problems —is part of all phases of life. Whenever group action is called for, this method can be utilized to implement the proceedings. Discussion can be a trusted form of communication if it is appreciated and used wisely, if users—

1. know and respect discussion processes and forms,
2. have substantial thought and materials to exchange,
3. are able to analyze and check patterns of thinking, including their own,
4. know and adhere to their functions as members, and provide for capable leadership.

Thomas Macaulay once said: "Men are never so likely to settle a question rightly, as when they discuss it freely." You will find occasion upon occasion for settling questions through discussion. Learn to use it.

SUGGESTED QUESTIONS FOR DISCUSSION

1. How should we deal with academic dishonesty?
2. How can automobile accidents be reduced?
3. What can be done to reduce campus parking problems?
4. How should an individual plan to meet his medical needs?
5. How can more students be provided with a college education?
6. What can be done to make more part-time jobs available?
7. What should a family do to help either a boy or a girl or both with personal problems?
8. What standards should guide a person in choosing his lifework?
9. What should be the minimum voting age?
10. What can be done to achieve harmony among nations?
11. How can the teacher shortage be alleviated?
12. How can the number of divorces be reduced?
13. What should be the parents' policy regarding the reading of comic books by their children?
14. What should be the age limit for compulsory education?
15. What should be the high school's policy regarding the matter of sex education?
16. How can we improve the mental health of the nation?

SUGGESTED TOPICS FOR DISCUSSION

The following may be shaped as questions for discussion.

Labor-Management Relations	Uses of Folk Music
The School Paper	Tolerance among People
Air Travel	Popular Music
Advertising Methods	Modern Fashions
Extracurricular Activities	Student Government
Natural Resources	City Planning
Overcoming Emotional Problems	Going Steady
European Unification	Increased Population
Slum Clearance	College Entrance Requirements
Outlawing War	Propaganda
Military Service	Taxation
Homemaking	The United Nations
Women in Industry	Rearing Children
Providing for the Future	Spending Leisure Time
Crowded Highways	Choosing a Major
Air Pollution	Problems of Alcoholism
Using Personal Talents	Dating
	Teaching Methods

Keeping the Campus Clean	Preparing for Examinations
Buying a Car	Raising Money for a Club
Alienation in Society	Choosing a Play

Suggested Exercise A

Organize your class into discussion groups of five or six, and select a qualified leader for each. The leader will guide the group in choosing and narrowing the subject, wording the question, determining the form, and preparing an outline of the points to be discussed. Allow time for a forum period if you plan to have audience participation.

Before starting to do research, review the sections of this chapter on "Gathering Materials" and "Checking the Materials." Prior to the time for which your discussion is scheduled, review the sections on "Being a Good Member" and "Being a Good Leader."

Suggested Exercise B

Analyze your efforts as a participant in the group discussion by commenting upon these questions:

1. Did you have a discussion attitude? (Were you cooperative, willing, and responsible?)
2. Were you prepared? (Did you do enough thinking and investigating?)
3. Did you contribute your share of ideas? (Did you present enough ideas? Did you do more than you should have?)
4. Were you tactful? (Did you respect the feelings of others?)
5. Did you use appropriate language? (Did you avoid ambiguous words and phrases?)
6. Were you a good listener? (Did you understand and interpret correctly the thoughts of others? Were you able to ignore distractions?)
7. If you were a leader, did you guide the discussion adequately?
   a. Did you provide an appropriate beginning and ending?
   b. Did you introduce the question and the participants?
   c. Did you clarify, summarize, and ask questions when necessary?
   d. Did you recognize key points when they were presented?
   e. Did you encourage participation?
   f. Did you guide the forum period successfully?

Suggested Exercise C

As a discussion observer, analyze the efforts of a group presenting a discussion in your class. Comment constructively and fully.

1. Was the subject well chosen?
2. Was the spirit of discussion appreciated?

3. Was the question clearly stated?
4. Were the form and organization suitable?
5. Were the materials well chosen?
6. Were the members effective?
7. Was the leader capable?
8. Were the goals realized?

Suggested Exercise D

Participate in an informal class discussion of how you may use group discussion in the future: in business; in family affairs; in civic affairs; in your lodge or club; or in your church.

Suggested Exercise E

Find two enthymemes from a speech. (For copies of speeches consult *Vital Speeches of the Day, Representative American Speeches,* or an anthology of speeches.) In a written or oral report, analyze each line of reasoning in syllogistic form and discuss the possible response and mental participation of the listener in each instance. Before proceeding, review "Deduction," the section of the chapter which deals with the enthymeme.

Suggested Exercise F

Find an extended line of reasoning in a speech. In a written or oral report, analyze the line of reasoning with a Toulmin diagram. From the layout, discuss weak points or gaps in the reasoning and possible ways to strengthen it.

Suggested Exercise G

Arrange for the recording in class of a discussion in which you participate. Use the Toulmin method to analyze samples of *your own* reasoning as you listen to the playback. What recommendations in reasoning would you make to yourself?

CHAPTER ELEVEN

Applying Parliamentary Law

Centuries of human experience have shown that the affairs of men must be governed by law. We have learned, and sometimes at great cost, that the absence of law results not only in anarchy and chaos but also in tyranny and widespread violence. Laws protect men and serve as standards of guidance; a code of just laws is the foundation of a free state. "Where there is no law, but every man does what is right in his own eyes, there is the least of real liberty," declared Henry M. Robert.[1]

The accepted set of procedures for the operation of deliberative bodies—whether they be special-interest clubs, social fraternities, professional associations, or the United States Senate—is called parliamentary law. These procedures are based on customs and rules that have been used for centuries in the English Parliament and other deliberative assemblies. To meet changing needs, men have modified and adapted parliamentary law over the years. Thomas Jefferson, as presiding officer of the United States Senate, wrote a manual of parliamentary law, adapting procedures of the House of Commons to requirements of the legislature in America. The rules of order that you observe in your club are those that fit your needs. Those adhered to by the United States Senate are necessarily more complex and detailed. Regardless of the group's purpose or size, people who deliberate in organized groups need a governing system. It is the purpose of this chapter to explain the main elements of the system. If you think of parliamentary procedure as something too complicated and mysterious to master, we ask that you put aside this preconceived notion and seriously attempt to learn the fundamental rules. Do not use these rules as "intellectual" devices for making a pretentious show or for confusing people. Regard them as valuable tools which, when used simply and conscientiously, work for the welfare of your group. Put to practice by

[1] *Robert's Rules of Order*, rev. ed. (Chicago, 1951), pp. 13–14.

a well-intentioned and informed membership, procedure for governing group action can provide the necessary code for functioning effectively.

Specifically, there are three basic services which parliamentary law has to offer:

1. *It provides means for orderly deliberation* by demanding that elements of business be handled one at a time, according to priority.
2. *It encourages courtesy and dignified action* by demanding civility and use of reason.
3. *It implements democratic principles* by demanding recognition of majority rule and respect for minority rights.

BEING A GOOD CHAIRMAN

The presiding officer of any association—whether he be called chairman, president, or by some other title—should be a responsible and intelligent person in whom the membership can have confidence. In large measure the success or failure of the organization depends upon him. We shall make repeated references to the role of chairman in this chapter, but at the outset let us set down four requirements of chairmanship.

1. *Keep yourself informed.* You must know the history and traditions of your organization as well as the current operational procedure. A workable knowledge of parliamentary law is, of course, indispensable.

2. *Conduct business in the proper order.* Follow a sequence prescribed by your organization. The following is a typical *order of business:*

Call to order
[Roll]
Reading of minutes
Committee reports
Unfinished business
New business
Announcements
Adjournment

3. *Guide the deliberations of the group.* Open meetings promptly. In maintaining order, be fair and tactful; yet firm and sure. To indicate objectivity, refer to yourself as "the chair." For example, you may say, "The chair stands corrected," or "The chair recognizes Jim Albright." Keeping discussion going and confining it to the question at hand, clarifying, and giving all members a chance to speak are obligations of the presiding officer. The chairman does not participate in the actual discussion except when he steps down and allows the vice president or another member to occupy the chair temporarily.

4. *Handle the voting effectively.* Restate a motion before putting it to a vote and allow ample discussion on debatable questions. The chairman himself does not vote, except in the case of a tie or when voting is by ballot. Immediately after the voting, he announces the result.

BEING A GOOD MEMBER

Standards of good membership, although not as stringent as those to be met by the presiding officer, are important for us to consider. Associations are not formed merely to elect officers and to have an occasional meeting. They are formed for a greater purpose, and as a member, you should do all that you can to further that purpose.

1. *Keep yourself informed.* Like the chairman, you must know the nature of your organization's business and be able to use parliamentary procedure efficiently.

2. *Know how to obtain the floor when you want to speak.* Stand or raise your hand, and when recognized by the chairman, say, "Mr. Chairman" or "Mr. President." A good member is patient and waits his turn; nonetheless, he should not allow himself to be frightened out of making a helpful contribution merely because he has difficulty in obtaining the floor.

3. *Know how to share your ideas.* First of all, be willing to participate and share. A member should address all remarks to the chair and not engage in side conservations. Of course, he should confine all discussions to the question before the house. The correct wording to use in making motions is: "I move that . . ." or "I move to . . . ," and *never,* "I make a motion . . . ."

MOTIONS

In a group governed by parliamentary procedure, business is presented in the form of a *motion.* A motion is a proposition or proposal that is offered to the membership for consideration of action. Being similar to a speech proposition, it is simply worded and contains only one item of business—the question under consideration. This is the order followed in presenting and disposing of most simple motions:

1. After a member obtains the floor, he states his motion.
2. Another must second it.
3. The chairman announces: "It has been moved and seconded that . . . ," (the full and accurate wording of the motion).
4. The chairman asks: "Is there any discussion?"
5. After allowing ample discussion time, the chairman puts the question to a vote: "All those in favor, say 'Aye.' All those opposed, say 'No.' "
6. The chairman announces the result.

Main motions or ordinary motions are the most common. Having the lowest priority status, a main motion can be made only when no other motion is before the house. "I move that we donate $5 to the Community Chest" and "I move that we send our president to the annual convention" are main motions.

Subsidiary motions relate to other motions being considered by the group. They are used either to handle or dispose of other motions. Following are seven of the most important subsidiary motions, listed according to rank. Sample motions and rules of order governing their usage follow the italicized titles.

1. *To lay on the table* (Either to delay or to suppress action on a question)

    SAMPLE: "Mr. Chairman, I move that the motion to raise dues be laid on the table [or tabled]."

    RULES: Seconded; Not debatable; Not amendable; Majority vote.

2. *Previous question* (To stop debate and vote on the pending question. Sometimes this is called "To close debate." If this motion carries, the pending motion is voted on immediately.)

    SAMPLE: "Mr. Chairman, I move the previous question" or "I move that we close debate and vote immediately on the pending question."

    RULES: Seconded; Not debatable; Not amendable; Two-thirds vote.

3. *To limit debate* (To restrict discussion time)

    SAMPLE: "Mr. Chairman, I move to limit debate on this question to one half hour." "Mr. Chairman, I move to limit the time of each speaker on this question to two minutes."

    RULES: Seconded; Not debatable; Amendable; Two-thirds vote.

4. *To postpone to a certain time* (To defer action for purposes of getting needed information or for rallying support, and so forth)

    SAMPLE: "Mr. Chairman, I move to postpone further consideration of this motion until our next regular meeting."

    RULES: Seconded; Debatable; Amendable; Majority vote.

5. *To refer to committee* (To allow further study of the question without taking the time of the full membership)

    SAMPLE: "Mr. Chairman, I move that the chair appoint a committee of three to investigate this matter and report at our next regular meeting."

RULES: Seconded; Debatable; Amendable; Majority vote.

6. *To amend* (To modify the motion)

MAIN MOTION: I move that we invite the principal officers of the Sociology Club to attend our forum.

SAMPLE AMENDMENTS:
(1) "Mr. Chairman, I move to amend the motion by striking out 'principal.' "
(2) "I move to amend the motion by adding 'to be held in November.' "
(3) "I move to amend by substituting 'entire memmership' for 'principal officers.' "

RULES: Seconded; Debatable; Amendable; Majority vote.

7. *To postpone indefinitely* (To reject or suppress a main motion without running the risk of taking a direct vote)

SAMPLE: "Mr. Chairman, I move that the matter of changing our club name be postponed indefinitely."

RULES: Seconded; Debatable; Not amendable; Majority vote.

Since a subsidiary motion takes precedence over the motion to which it refers, it must be voted on before action can be taken on the main motion. In keeping with the rules of precedence (or rank), when a given subsidiary motion is before the house, the only additional subsidiary motion that can be made is one of higher rank. For example, when the motion to lay on the table is pending, no other subsidiary motions can be attached to the main motion. The motion to lay on the table has the highest ranking among the subsidiary motions.

To illustrate further, let us imagine that someone on the student council has moved that "the student body buy a color television set for the lounge." The motion is seconded. During the discussion of this main motion, an economy-minded member obtains the floor and says, "I move to amend by striking out 'color.' " After being seconded, the motion to amend is discussed. Perhaps it is believed by some that the council is acting too hastily. One member states: "I move to postpone further action on this question until our next council meeting." Since the motion to postpone is of higher rank than the pending motion to amend, the president allows it to be introduced. It is seconded. At this time, any of the three subsidiary motions of higher rank than the motion to postpone would be in order. They are: to lay on the table; the previous question; and to limit debate.

Assuming that no other motions are presented, the group disposes of its three pending motions in this manner:

1. Ample time is allowed for the motion of highest rank (the last one made) to be discussed; then it is voted upon. It is, of course, the question on postponement. If it loses, the motion next highest in rank is brought up for consideration. If the postponement question carries, the other pending motions are automatically disposed of along with it for the duration of the postponement.
2. Assuming that the postponement motion loses, the pending motion (to amend) is put before the house. The chairman allows time for further debate, and puts it to a vote. If it carries, the question before the house is the main motion as amended. If it does not carry, the question to be discussed and voted on is the original motion.

Before leaving subsidiary motions, let us add a word regarding motions to amend. Only two motions to amend may be pending at any given time: the first motion to amend, and another to amend the amendment.

For example:

MAIN MOTION: "I move that we take funds from the treasury to send President Rogers to the convention in Dallas."

AMENDMENT: "I move to amend by inserting 'to the amount of $100' after the word 'funds.'"

AMENDMENT TO THE AMENDMENT: "I move to amend the amendment by substituting '$125' for '$100.'"

Neither amendment should alter the intent of the motion to which it refers. They are disposed of in the reverse order of presentation; that is, the motion to amend the amendment is taken up first.

Incidental motions also relate to pending motions or to matters of procedure. They may interrupt other business, and they have precedence over the motions to which they relate. The following incidental motions are frequently used.

To withdraw a motion (To cancel a motion you have made)

SAMPLE: "Mr. Chairman, I wish to withdraw my motion."

RULES: If there is no objection, the request is handled informally. If there is objection, a formal motion must be made.
No second; Not debatable; Not amendable; Majority vote.

To suspend a rule temporarily (To deviate from following an accepted rule. It must not be in conflict with the constitution or by-laws.)

SAMPLE: "Mr. Chairman, I move that we suspend our order of business rules and hear the nominating committee's report after we discuss unfinished business."

RULES: Seconded; Not debatable; Not amendable; Two-thirds vote.

Point of order (To question use of parliamentary law, point of business, and so forth)

SAMPLE: "Mr. Chairman, I rise to a point of order." The chairman responds: "State your point of order," and after it has been stated, he rules on it.

RULES: No second; Not debatable; Not amendable; Chair rules.

To appeal from a decision of the chair (To question a decision of the chairman)

SAMPLE: "Mr. Chairman, I appeal from the decision of the chair." The chairman responds after the second: "Shall the decision of the chair be upheld?"

RULES: Seconded; Debatable; Not amendable; Majority vote.

Privileged motions, unlike subsidiary and incidental motions, are not related to other motions being considered by the group. They are important enough to be allowed at any time. The only restriction is that such proposals cannot be made when another privileged motion of higher rank is before the house. These are the most common privileged motions:

1. *To fix the time of the next meeting*

    SAMPLE: "Mr. Chairman, I move that we set the time of our next meeting at 7 P.M., January 28."

    RULES: Seconded; Debatable (if no business is pending); Amendable; Majority vote.

2. *To adjourn*

    SAMPLE: "Mr. Chairman, I move that we adjourn."

    RULES: Seconded; Not debatable; Not amendable; Majority vote.

3. *Questions of privilege* (To close the windows, bring in more chairs, raise the volume of the public address system, and so forth.)

    SAMPLE: "Mr. Chairman, I rise to a question of privilege." The chair responds: "State your question."

    RULES: Not seconded; Not debatable; Not Amendable; Chair rules.

4. *To call for the orders of the day* (To remind the chairman of an item of business that he has omitted. He may have neglected to call for a reading of the minutes, or perhaps he failed to ask for a scheduled committee report.)

    SAMPLE: "Mr. Chairman, I call for the orders of the day."

RULES: Not seconded; Not debatable; Not amendable; Not voted on.

The *unclassified motions* listed below are used to bring matters which have either been tabled or otherwise dispensed with back to the floor. They may be made whenever another motion is not pending.

To take from the table (To bring back a tabled motion for deliberation)

SAMPLE: "Mr. Chairman, I move to take from the table the motion to paint the clubhouse."

RULES: Seconded; Not debatable; Not amendable; Majority vote.

To reconsider (To discuss and vote on a question previously decided)

SAMPLE: "Mr. Chairman, I move to reconsider the decision to raise membership dues."

RULES: Can be made only by someone who originally voted with the majority and must be made during the meeting or session when vote was taken.
Seconded; Debatable (if the motion to which it refers is debatable); Not amendable; Majority vote.

To rescind (To reverse a decision previously made)

SAMPLE: "Mr. Chairman, I move to rescind the action taken at our meeting of March 1st regarding membership regulations."

RULES: Seconded; Debatable; Not amendable; Majority vote (if previous notice has been given; otherwise a two-thirds vote is needed). Only the unexecuted part of the motion may be rescinded.

VOTING

Most motions are passed by a simple majority vote, that is, more than half of the votes cast. Others require a two-thirds majority vote, and some are decided by the chairman.

There are good reasons for requiring a two-thirds majority vote to pass certain motions. In this chapter the two-thirds majority rule applies to these motions: to limit debate, the previous question, to suspend a rule, and to rescind. Motions to limit debate and stop debate (the previous question) curtail speaking time and would be undemocratic actions if a great majority did not agree to the measures. Motions to suspend rules and to rescind are made to repeal some decision, and no deliberative body should be allowed to alter its decisions because of whim or fancy. There must be certainty that the action is desired by the larger majority.

In addition to the common voice vote, other types of voting are available to groups. For example, when the chair is in doubt about the results of a voice vote, it can ask for a show of hands. Another means for more accurate counting is the rising vote, often called division of the house. If for any reason a member wishes the voting membership to "stand up and be counted," he has but to gain the floor and call for a division of the house.

In elections, the usual voting is by written ballots prepared in advance of the meeting with provisions for efficient and accurate tallying.

RECORDING BUSINESS

Realizing the extent of business conducted by many organizations, it is easy to understand the need for an able secretary. His minutes are a valuable document of the group and ought to be prepared with care.

Minutes are a summary of group business; they should include only essential data:

1. Name of the group
2. Kind of meeting (whether regular or special, and so forth), place, date, and time
3. Presiding officer
4. Essentials of reports
5. Motions passed
6. Details of adjournment

The following is a model of minutes:

> The regular meeting of the Quintilian Club was held in Room 192 in the Humanities Building, on February 26, 1968, with President Raymond Cranston calling the meeting to order at 3:10.
>
> Minutes of the meeting of February 12 were read and approved.
>
> Treasurer Caldecott reported a balance of $101 in the treasury.
>
> The program committee reported that plans for the debate with the Hellenes (philosophy club) are going well, but noted minor disagreement between the clubs regarding phrasing of the question. The debate will be held, as originally scheduled, on March 12, at 12:00, in the Forensics Chamber.
>
> As unfinished business, the group discussed whether to adopt the proposed club insignia. Herb Stott moved that the insignia, rendered in red and white, be adopted. Alice Chandler moved to amend by substituting "cardinal" for "red." The amendment and the motion as amended passed.
>
> Tracy Bothwell moved that the time of regular meetings be changed from 3:00 to 12:00. The motion failed.
>
> The meeting was adjourned at 4:35.
>
> Pam Gregner, Secretary

STARTING AN ORGANIZATION

How do you get an interest group or club started? What are the commonly accepted steps or procedures that you should follow? First of all, you ought to determine if others are interested in the idea. Next, contact all potentially concerned parties, set a time and place for an organizational meeting, and designate someone to act as convener of the meeting. Besides calling the meeting to order, he will make the motion to elect a temporary chairman.

At the organizational meeting, the convener calls the meeting to order and announces: "I move that Harvey Craig be elected temporary chairman." Someone seconds the motion and the vote is taken. Should Harvey Craig not be elected (an unusual circumstance), the convener will entertain a motion to elect another person.

The newly elected temporary chairman takes the chair and entertains a motion for election of a temporary secretary. The form of this motion and its disposition are identical to those for electing a temporary chairman.

The temporary chairman calls on a person present (who is probably prepared for the function) to state the reason for the meeting and the probable aims and purposes of the group. Following discussion of aims and purposes, the chair entertains a resolution that a group be formed.

The wording of the resolution should include the nature and purposes of the proposed organization and might be presented with the words, "Mr. Chairman, I move the adoption of the following resolution: 'That in order to enhance the speaking abilities of its members and in order to create campus-wide appreciation of the values of oral communication, that a speech club be formed for students on this campus.' " After someone seconds the resolution, the assembly will discuss it, make amendments if it chooses, and finally vote on it.

Before adjournment, the temporary chairman ordinarily will appoint a committee—or the group will elect one—to draft a constitution and by-laws. Very likely the committee will be charged to present the draft for adoption at the next meeting.

At the next meeting, the group will discuss each section of the constitution and by-laws presented by the committee, using parliamentary procedures to make any necessary amendments as it moves through the document. Lastly, the membership will vote on the entire document as finally shaped.

The membership will then elect permanent officers as prescribed by the constitution.

LET US SUMMARIZE

For handy reference you can consult the chart on the opposite page which lists motions and the main rules governing their use.

As you apply parliamentary procedures in class exercises and in your clubs and associations, keep in mind the purpose of the rules of order. Make them work for the general welfare and never against it. Wise

Types of Motions	Rank	Seconded	Debatable	Amendable	Vote
MAIN	12	Yes	Yes	Yes	M
SUBSIDIARY					
To postpone indefinitely	11	Yes	Yes	No	M
To amend	10	Yes	Yes	Yes	M
To refer to committee	9	Yes	Yes	Yes	M
To postpone to a certain time	8	Yes	Yes	Yes	M
To limit debate	7	Yes	No	Yes	2/3
Previous question	6	Yes	No	Yes	2/3
To lay on the table	5	Yes	No	No	M
INCIDENTAL Have precedence over motions to which they refer					
Withdraw a motion		No	No	No	M
To suspend a rule temporarily		Yes	No	No	2/3
Point of order		No	No	No	Chair
Appeal from a decision of the chair		Yes	Yes	No	M
PRIVILEGED					
To call for the orders of the day	4	No	No	No	None
Questions of privilege	3	No	No	No	Chair
To adjourn	2	Yes	No	No	M
To fix time of next meeting	1	Yes	Yes, if no business pending	Yes	M
UNCLASSIFIED May be made when another motion is not pending					
To take from the table		Yes	No	No	M
To reconsider		Yes	Yes, if motion it refers to is debatable	No	M
To rescind		Yes	Yes	No	2/3 (M if previous notice given)

usage of parliamentary law by the leaders and members of any organization will ensure orderly handling of business, and courteous, dignified, and democratic operation.

MODEL CLUB CONSTITUTION AND BY-LAWS

ARTICLE I●   NAME

The name of this organization shall be the Quintilian Club.

ARTICLE II●   PURPOSE

The purpose of the club shall be to increase the speaking proficiency of its members and to create a campus-wide appreciation of the values of oral communication.

ARTICLE III●   MEMBERSHIP

Membership shall be extended to all student body card holders.

ARTICLE IV●   OFFICERS

Section 1. The officers of this club shall be a president, a vice president, a secretary, a treasurer, and an historian.

Section 2. Officers shall be elected at the second meeting of each new year.

Section 3. Vacancies in office shall be filled by a special election.

ARTICLE V●   MEETINGS

Section 1. The club shall have biweekly meetings during the regular school year.

Section 2. Special meetings may be called by the president or by a majority vote at a regular meeting.

ARTICLE VI●   AMENDMENTS

Section 1. This constitution may be amended at any regular meeting of the club by a two-thirds vote of the members, provided that the amendments have been submitted in writing and read at a previous regular meeting.

BY-LAWS

ARTICLE I●   DUES

The dues of the club shall be $2 a year, payable at the second meeting of the year.

ARTICLE II●   OFFICERS

Section 1. A nominating committee of three members shall be elected to nominate one or more candidates for each office.

Section 2. The duties of the officers shall be those that are implied by their titles and prescribed in *Robert's Rules of Order.*

ARTICLE III•   COMMITTEES

Section 1. The president shall appoint standing committees.

Section 2. The membership committee is responsible for acquiring new members.

Section 3. The program committee is responsible for planning and presenting the club activities during the year.

ARTICLE IV•   PARLIAMENTARY AUTHORITY

Robert's Rules of Order shall be the final parliamentary authority of this club.

ARTICLE V•   QUORUM

One third of the active membership of this club shall constitute a quorum.

ARTICLE VI•   AMENDMENTS

These by-laws may be amended at any regular meeting of the club by a majority of the members present, provided that the amendments have been presented in writing at a prior meeting.

Suggested Exercise A

Set up a hypothetical club or legislative assembly in your class. Your instructor will lead while you nominate and elect a presiding officer. Under the leadership of your elected chairman, conduct a business meeting in which you make and dispose of main motions and various types of subsidiary motions only. When half the period has expired, nominate and elect a new chairman and continue. During this second "meeting," include an occasional privileged motion.

By restricting your use during the first meeting to main and subsidiary motions, you can avoid some of the confusion in learning parliamentary law. This principle reflects a theme of the book: mastery of basics and then gradual introduction of advanced procedures in a step-by-step progression.

Suggested Exercise B

Have each member of the hypothetical club compose a club constitution. Elect a committee to study those constitutions submitted, and select one to present to the "club" for adoption.

Suggested Exercise C

Define these parliamentary terms:

before the house	rank
debate	second
deliberation	simple majority

motion	the chair
obtaining the floor	the floor
pending	the question
precedence	to dispose of
previous question	

Suggested Exercise D

What motions would you present to meet the following conditions?

1. To improve some part of a main motion.
2. To dispose of a motion for an indefinite time.
3. To cancel a motion you have made.
4. To ask the chairman to allow discussion before a certain subsidiary motion has been seconded.
5. To propose that a smaller group investigate a question.
6. To postpone a decision on a proposal until the next meeting.
7. To correct the chairman when he rules incorrectly on a point of order.
8. To restrict the time for discussing a measure.
9. To put the ventilating system in operation.
10. To reverse a decision of the group on a proposal.
11. To consider a tabled motion.
12. To bring a motion (on which you voted with the prevailing side) previously disposed of, back for deliberation.
13. To stop discussion and take a vote.
14. To require the chairman to follow the prescribed order of business.

CHAPTER TWELVE

Finding Bases of Persuasion

The subject of this chapter is persuasion: a study of the ways in which speakers affect the thinking, feeling, and behavior of people. In a sense, a separate chapter on persuasion is not needed, for all communication is a social act, and consequently, potentially persuasive. People are affected by the acts of others. Who is to say, for example, that a simple speech on taking good lecture notes will not affect a listener's future behavior? People speak to cause response from others, not merely to exercise their vocal apparatus. And people do respond; speakers move them, act upon them, are persuasive with them. Nonetheless, we have a separate chapter on persuasion to discuss in greater depth some of the particular modes of reaching people through speech.

THREE ASSUMPTIONS

The chapter rests on three assumptions:

1. That citizens in a democracy are obliged to function as users of persuasion, as social critics or social commentators;
2. That they will find the bases of their persuasive comment in the minds of their listeners; and,
3. That listeners are affected by any or all features of the total speaking situation.

Let us discuss each assumption.

Our society needs speechmaking. The United States was built as surely by talk as by use of concrete and steel. It was built by people hammering out decisions through debate and discussion and agitation. It was built up from the resolution of conflict and controversy—from persuasive acts and counter-persuasive acts of dissent. The story of America is one of people speaking out, making their views known, and answering challenges. It is a story of social checks and balances through free and willing speaking.

And the talk must go on. Preservation of the system demands that people continue to function as developers of ideas and as critics of ideas. Such is the citizen's responsibility. He must speak his opinions to others. Out of the dialogue will emerge, hopefully, something of use that is just and good for the society.

We should recognize, of course, that some persons do rely upon unethical means to sway others; furthermore, people will occasionally use this fact as an excuse for blanketly condemning the process of persuasion. But cases of unethical behavior should offer a challenge to responsible citizens, not despair or cynicism. Ethical persuasion is never needed more than when unethical persuasion is being used. Do not blame the process of persuasion when you hear a speaker insincerely play upon the sorrow of mothers whose children are on crutches. Blame the one who is speaking, and do your part to prevent him from being effective.

A society needs persuasion and counter-persuasion for promoting and testing ideas for the collective good.

Speakers reach and influence listeners on the listeners' ground. Accepting this, we come to an obvious conclusion: a speaker must know about his audiences, that is, about people. Only when he is aware of where they stand—of their feelings and beliefs—will he be able to bridge the gap between his proposal as he has conceived it and their natures or wishes. And it is the gaps with which we are especially concerned at this point. Speaking of the gaps, psychologist Daniel Katz[1] wrote:

> The individual lives in a private world of his own perception, emotion and thought . . . . To the extent that his perceptions, feelings and thoughts arise from similar contacts with similar aspects of reality as experienced by others, the private world can be shared and lose something of its private character.

To varying degrees, people are, necessarily, caught up in their own lives and patterns of habit and thought. We might call them the private "provinces of experience," and one who would communicate with us must recognize our "provincial" nature and meet us in our province. The speaker will start from where the listeners stand and select common elements from his and their provinces of thinking and experience. Moreover, in order to communicate, the speaker in some way will *reveal* this kinship to his audience. Good communication—persuasion —is based on a transaction between speaker and audience featuring means by which the parties involved can cooperate. The successful speaker first discerns where he and his audience are divided. Then he discovers ways to act together, ways of unity—grounds of agreement.

---

[1] "Psychological Barriers to Communication," *Annals of the American Academy of Politics and Social Science*, CCL (March, 1947), pp. 17–25.

The areas of agreement are found in the same places as the areas of disagreements: in concepts, methods, attitudes, words, customs, and so forth. Here, psychologist Katz[2] offers a solution:

> Though groups may differ in their experiences, there is generally more of a common core of psychological reality between them than their language indicates. A neglected aspect of communication is the identification of these areas of common understanding.

It was that identification of areas of common understanding that Abraham Lincoln sought in his Second Inaugural Address. Remember that the Civil War was nearing its end, and Lincoln was concerned about the nation's future unity. Accordingly, he made frequent reference to the common ideals and concerns of the entire nation. At one point, he mentioned that both parties to the conflict "read the same Bible and pray to the same God." He further identified, using the biblical injunction, "let us judge not, that we be not judged." Not losing sight of his goal, he reiterated in his conclusion the grounds for unity and cooperation:

> With malice toward none, with charity for all, with firmness in the right as God gives us to see the right, let us strive on to finish the work we are in, to bind up the nation's wounds, to care for him who shall have borne the battle and for his widow and his orphan, to do all which may achieve and cherish a just and lasting peace among ourselves and with all nations.

Though facing far less consequential situations, all effective speakers are similarly motivated to find materials or methods to dispel differences with their audiences. Elmer E. Ferris, sales manager of a large company, identified his thought with that of New York Advertising Club members in these words:

> GENTLEMEN OF THE ADVERTISING CLUB: It is a pleasure to speak before you tonight because you and I stand on common ground. Sales is the essence of advertising. The gist of salesmanship is getting the other person to take your point of view and act accordingly. That is also the gist of what the advertising man is trying to do. Furthermore, this matter of judging and handling men, which lies at the heart of personal contacts, is just as essential a part of advertising skill as of sales ability, and so right at the outset of this talk I can confidently claim your interest because the subject itself ought to hold you.[3]

Identification with the listener is your end whenever you discard a certain word for one more precise or choose a certain example instead of another, or alter your sequence of ideas from that originally planned.

---

[2] *Annals of the American Academy of Politics and Social Science,* CCL, pp. 17–25.
[3] "The Art of Personal Contact," in *Modern Speeches,* Homer D. Lindgren, comp. (New York, 1926), p. 434.

These are decisions to enhance effectiveness and to increase opportunities of securing favorable responses.

All features of the speaking situation influence listeners' responses. Audiences are affected by the speaker's ideas, yes, but they are also affected by the words he uses to convey ideas and by his personal bearing, his mode of organization, his delivery, and by any other attribute perceived by the listeners. Thus, the speaker has many avenues to use in relating to the province of his listeners' thinking and expectations.

Now oftentimes, speakers "strike the right chord" with their audiences without consciously thinking about method. This is no surprise, surely. Speech is a social act, and socially responsive people know something about getting along with others and addressing themselves to them. In other words, part of the job of accommodating a message to the listeners' minds involves nothing more than sociality. These are the means that people use in their daily dealings with people, means which the socially aware speaker uses without conscious thought. The speaker's looking at the listener while he speaks, speaking at the listener's level and not over or below him, treating him with respect, showing concern for his comfort, acknowledging his personal or professional identity through direct and thoughtful reference ("I know that as parents you have interests in . . ."), noting common feelings and beliefs about conditions of life experienced by all ("None of us enjoys standing in line. . . ."), attempting to fit the message to the listener's pattern of thinking and reaction—all these acts and many more arise from social consciousness. They are common practices and they facilitate a meeting of minds.

Let us turn now to a discussion of four specific areas of the process of persuasion in which speakers find bases for communicating: modes of appeal, patterns of organization, language, and delivery.

BASES IN THE MODES OF APPEAL

Starting with Aristotle and including writers in our day, theorists of speechmaking have discussed the basic means of persuasion under three headings: logical appeal (*logos*), psychological appeal (*pathos*), and personal appeal (*ethos*).

Logical Appeals

Logical appeals—those based on reasoning—can provide a sound foundation for communication, and, consequently, deserve primary status in a discussion of persuasion. One cannot expect to move a thinking audience unless he reasons with them and makes his ideas logically acceptable. Now, making ideas logically acceptable usually does not mean that a speaker must show an idea to be absolutely "foolproof" logically. Nor does it mean that a speaker's line of reasoning necessarily leads to an inevitable or "absolutely final" conclusion. No. Only rarely in our communication do we find ourselves in areas of absolute truth or inevitability. The most important and (therefore) most discussed ideas are unresolved, still open for consideration. They are matters in dispute: labor-management problems, government programs for farmers, meeting a nation's medical needs, admission standards for colleges, reducing highway accidents, making a successful marriage, systems of drafting for military service, and so forth. Whose arguments in any of these problem areas are final and foolproof? Usually the best judgment that any of us are able to make of an idea is that its value is "highly probable," or that it "seems quite reasonable," or "suggests a strong likelihood," and so forth. Thus, *logically acceptable* means that an audience finds the speaker's thoughts to be reasonable or convincing.

THE ENTHYMEME.

One prime means in persuasion for showing a line of thought to be convincing is the enthymeme. Aristotle called the enthymeme a rhetorical syllogism, that is, a form of deductive reasoning for practical speechmaking. As we observed in Chapter Ten, speakers rarely have occasion to use fully constructed formal syllogisms, the ones based on certainties. Instead, they use *enthymemes,* arguments based on probabilities and designed for audience acceptance.

Besides being based on a probability, an enthymeme usually is "open" at some point, meaning that one step in the reasoning is not fully spelled out. If a speaker and audience are thinking together, the speaker does not have to delineate every step; a good enthymeme is a base for persuasion on which both parties to the communicative exchange can think along together. For example, a book salesman talking to a group of history teachers probably should not say, "All history teachers want to use the best books; you are history teachers; you want to use the best books." No, that is the complete form of the syllogism. But he might reason, informally, with an enthymeme: "As history teachers, you want to use the best books." The audience realizes and accepts, perhaps subconsciously, the omitted steps in the chain of reasoning.

Analyze the following enthymeme from Patrick Henry's speech, "Call to Arms." Does he include all the steps as he reasons to a conclusion? What ideas or premises was the audience expected to bring to the argument? Was the speaker in a province of thinking compatible to his listeners'?

> If we wish to be free—if we mean to preserve inviolate those inestimable privileges for which we have been so long contending—if we mean not basely to abandon the noble struggle in which we have been so long

engaged, and which we have pledged ourselves never to abandon until the glorious object of our contest shall be obtained, we must fight!

The following argument, also cast as an enthymeme, is from John F. Kennedy's Inaugural Address. It is quite brief. What is the full statement of his thinking as you might have perceived it as a listener? Do you imagine that most people in the audience knew what he meant? Do you imagine that they responded to his reasoning?

> We dare not tempt them [those nations who would make themselves our adversary] with weakness. For only when our arms are sufficient beyond doubt can we be certain beyond doubt that they will never be employed.

INDUCTION.

Besides the enthymeme—a deductive form of reasoning—speakers may avail themselves of inductive forms. Induction (as contrasted with deduction) is reasoning from specifics to a generalization. The speaker cites an instance or several of them and draws a conclusion. Again, you might wish to refer to Chapter Ten for another view of the process.

President Franklin Roosevelt used inductive reasoning in his speech of December 8, 1941, calling for a declaration of war with Japan. After mentioning the attack on the Hawaiian Islands and on American ships at sea, he detailed specific instances and drew a conclusion from them.

> Yesterday the Japanese Government also launched an attack against Malaya.
> Last night Japanese forces attacked Hong Kong.
> Last night Japanese forces attacked Guam.
> Last night Japanese forces attacked the Philippine Islands.
> Last night the Japanese attacked Wake Island.
> Last night the Japanese attacked Midway Island.
> Japan has, therefore, undertaken a surprise offensive extending throughout the Pacific area.

When you reason that since on a certain school day the Post Office, banks, and most stores will be closed, it should also be a school holiday, you reason inductively. This type of induction is reasoning by analogy. You base your case on some kind of similarity between the school and the other institutions.

Casual reasoning is also inductive. Claire Boothe Luce used reasoning from effect to cause in this argument, developed in a speech at Wilson College in Pennsylvania:

> . . . America in this century has twice failed, with a third time threatening, to prevent the outbreak of world war as our moral duty and our prime task as the world's strongest nation. America failed because the Public Will would seldom support a foreign policy or a diplomacy which would permit our statesmen to introduce the subject of the war-making capacity of the United States into the normal conduct of international

negotiations. We would not allow—we positively forbade—our diplomats to convert our tremendous physical power into diplomatic or political victories for peace.[4]

When Secretary of State Dean Rusk talked to the Association of the United States Army in Washington, D.C., at one point he reasoned from cause to effect, expressing the fears of many. He was speaking of the war in Vietnam:

> . . . we must take care not to use more force than is necessary. Now, as in previous conflicts and crises during the last two decades, there are those who want to go all out—apply maximum power and get it over with. That would be a perilous course, which conceivably would escalate into the thermonuclear exchange which no rational man could want.[5]

After a speaker has satisfied himself that his arguments are reasonable and accommodative to listeners' needs and views, he should check them for fallacies. The list of fallacies in Chapter Ten will be helpful in checking arguments. Remember that sound, clear thinking can be the surest road to achieving favorable responses from listeners.

SUPPORTING EVIDENCE.

Whether building a line of reasoning deductively or inductively, a speaker needs materials to support his thought. (The topic of finding and using materials for developing ideas is discussed fully in Chapters Five and Six, and you are strongly urged to review those chapters before beginning preparation of assignments in persuasion.) Examples, statistics, quoted testimony, physical materials, fact and opinion are the "stuff" of speeches. Since they make up the bulk of the content, it behooves speakers to find a sufficient quantity of them, to check them for relevance, clarity, appeal, and appropriateness. At a later point (when detailing means of holding attention) we shall return to developmental materials.

Psychological Appeals

The second mode of appeal available as a base for persuasion is the psychological mode. In this category, we shall consider elements with emotional overtones: appeals to human motivations, to feelings and values. Probably you will see, as you read along, that logical and psychological appeals never can be completely separated. They usually overlap and do not exist in isolation. Nevertheless, motivating an audience and causing it to share your view of your proposition often re-

---

[4] "American Morality in Nuclear Diplomacy," in *The Dolphin Book of Speeches*, George W. Hibbitt, ed. (New York, 1965), pp. 338–343.
[5] "Organizing the Peace," *Vital Speeches of the Day* (November 15, 1966), pp. 67–71.

quires more than reasoning. People have values and emotions, and very frequently, their responses to a speaker's proposal are influenced by these elements.

Listeners want to know how a given policy will affect them before they decide to accept it or act upon it. "Will his suggested plan to change the company's hiring system endanger my security?" the personnel manager asks himself. "What good is that life insurance program to me?" asks a student of an insurance agent. "Why should I vote for Smith, a Democrat?" questions Jones, a Republican. People want to know how they personally will be affected.

COMMON NEEDS, POSSESSIONS, AND BEHAVIOR.

We once asked groups of college freshmen and sophomores to draw upon their own observations and experiences, and list common human characteristics of which they thought speakers should be aware. Their suggestions were excellent and probably quite useful to students of speech. We have classified them under three headings: What Most People Want and Need; What Most People Share; and, What Most People Do.

What Most People Want and Need
> To be accepted, to be loved, to be needed, to be respected
> To be competent socially, to get along well with others
> Security (economic, personal, and family, "a place to settle down")
> Knowledge and education
> To communicate with others (to relate to others)
> To see justice done
> To acquire material goods and "wealth"
> To succeed and be "prosperous" (at work, home, school, and so forth)
> Longevity—long life
> Good health
> The "good life" (as variously viewed)
> Peace (personal, community, national, international)
> Happiness
> Friendship and companionship

What Most People Share or Possess
> A natural interest in other people (their natures, their customs, habits, tragedies, joys, ideals, common problems, and so forth)
> An interest in the arts and other creative expressions (visual arts, music, literature, or dance)
> Interest in matters relating to sex, courtship, and marriage
> Emotional "stores" (love, hate, anger, fear, jealousy, pride, hope, and so forth)

A common origin

A sense of immortality

Interests in children (hopes for, love for, desire to procreate, and so forth)

Interests in pets and other animals

An interest in weather

Loyalties and pride of citizenship in a nation, a region, a community, and so forth

Beliefs in democracy and various freedoms and rights

Feelings of mutuality with people of the same sex, age group, and racial group; with people who have common problems, common socio-economic backgrounds, education, beliefs, and so forth

Strong feelings for home and family (love, security of, security in, and so forth

What Most People Do

Manifest needs, beliefs, and expressions of religion (varied though the manifestations are)

Appreciate humor

Experience certain activities of daily living (eating, working, sleeping, wearing clothes, being in a dwelling)

Make mistakes ("To err is human")

Experience sadness and mental strife

Respond to beauty (of nature, of the human body, and so forth)

Enjoy sports, games, puzzles, and other such forms of leisure and recreation

Respond to reason (to intelligent discourse, to logic)

Doubtless, if a speaker allowed himself to be guided by the knowledge represented in the list, he would increase his chances for finding understanding and influence with his listeners. The items are bases (many of them universal in application) for appealing to people and therefore useful to the speaker as he weighs means of interesting an audience in his ideas. With thought and some sensitivity, he may find ways to make his ideas reasonably compatible with those of his listeners. That is the ultimate in persuasion, the discovery that speaker and listener are together in thought.

Recall Patrick Henry's speech as you look again at the list of human characteristics. It is no wonder that the speech has such strong appeal, for it is laden with heartfelt and sincere references to justice, peace, happiness, the value of knowledge, loyalty, freedom, God and religion, mental strife, and other items found in the preceding catalog. Examine the speeches of Winston Churchill, Franklin Roosevelt, other speakers, and—closer to home—those found in an Appendix of this book. Such an examination will reveal how speakers have recognized in their communications the common attitudes and experiences of people.

The human motives and characteristics to be taken into account in persuasion depend, in large measure, upon the people to whom you are speaking. The analysis of your prospective audience will give you guidance in the selection of effective appeals. We shall treat audience analysis further on.

But where are appeals to be placed in the speech? In your introductory remarks and throughout the entire talk you should augment the development of your thoughts with appeals to values and motives. Consider them in your choice of language, and weave them into the fabric of your ideas as you elaborate.

Some cautions and suggestions are in order. It is strongly suggested that you vary your approach by using a variety of appeals. Then, too, you should avoid being obvious when you use persuasive methods. A wise man once said that the best artist is the one who conceals his artistry. Be sincere, and never be guilty of misrepresentation.

Consider, briefly, two opposing views regarding the use of emotional appeals in persuasive speaking. The first might be stated in this way: "People are gullible, easy to fool or flatter. If you find their weak spots, you can lead them around by the nose." This cynical outlook reflects a rather dismal picture of mankind in general. In contrast, we have the second point of view: "People can be moved when they are offered satisfaction of their needs and desires and answers to their expectations; they can be led to better their opinions and improve their ways of doing."

What is the essential difference between these two views? Both agree that motivational persuasion is *effective,* but the second statement suggests that it can and should be *responsible* also. Persuasive speaking is responsible if the listener is respected as a dignified human being. Conversely, persuasive speaking is irresponsible if the listener is shown the disrespect of being subjected to heartless, crude, or unprincipled appeals.

In responsible speaking, the emphasis is not on "tool-using" in the ugly sense of manipulating people. The most responsible and ultimately most effective persuasion is that which finds the greatest mutual benefit.

THE MAKEUP OF THE SPECIFIC AUDIENCE.

How should a speaker go about analyzing the particular audience he will be facing? It is true that some success can come from knowing the general nature of people or the "average man," but without an earnest effort to learn what the immediate audience requires and expects, you

may not gain your end. Be guided by the following suggestions in analyzing your prospective audience:

1. *Learn their backgrounds.* What is the predominant age level and
sex? Your approach to a group of teen-agers would vary greatly from
your approach to middle-aged people; what might be pertinent at a
men's club meeting perhaps would not stir an assembly of women.

For additional assistance in planning your talk, you should try to
ascertain their family status as well as their educational, economic,
political, social, and religious backgrounds. You can sympathize with
the speaker who found out later that he had presented his lecture on
"Go to Church on Sunday" to a gathering at least half of whom cele-
brate their Sabbath on Saturday. He did not know his audience.

2. *Learn how much they know about the subject.* Determine the
extent of their familiarity with the subject and whether the acquaintanceship is from formal study or direct experience. If the audience
knows something of electronics, is it based on classroom training, practical experience, or both? Such an analysis will help you to come into
the lives of your listeners at the proper point: the point to which their
learning has advanced.

3. *Learn about their attitudes toward the subject.* An audience that
might become uneasy at the slightest mention of certain subjects can
make the speaker's task formidable. You should know what emotional
involvements the audience has in your subject area and if they are
likely to be either favorably or unfavorably disposed or indifferent.

In areas of controversy, attempt to assess the nature and extent of
their sympathies and hostilities. How deep is their feeling? What is
the history of their convictions regarding the subject? Are their stands
unalterable?

4. *Learn about their attitudes toward you.* Learn how much they
are likely to know about you and what their opinion is of you. This
information will tell you how much time should be spent in getting
acquainted and in establishing good will. Listeners who respect a
speaker tend to respect his ideas. Do they know you? What is your
reputation with them?

5. *Face up to your reactions to them.* Are they people with whom
you can be "sociable"? Can you work easy with them and be free to
adapt to them? Or do you have some reserve or rigidity regarding
them? Do you have any hostility toward them? These very important
questions must be answered, for a rapport, or working relationship, is
essential for adaptation of your lines of thought to your listeners'
thinking and motivations. Do you really want to speak to the audience?
If the answer is no, you face a problem of adjusting your attitude, your
subject, or some other condition. The best solution may lie in further

assessment of the total situation and, from that, in finding some good reason for welcoming the chance to speak before them. Intelligent and sincere human beings are capable of discovering workable answers to most social problems.

HOLDING THE AUDIENCE'S ATTENTION.

Most means of holding attention relate to intelligent handling of materials. In persuasion, we sometimes call these specific data *evidence,* but regardless of the name, the types are similar for all speaking: examples, quotations, statistics, physical aids, and so forth. Following are five admonitions to which successful speakers adhere when composing their speeches.

1. *Be concrete and specific.* Include particulars in your illustrative material. Instead of supporting a point with an abstract instance, give detail. To illustrate, do not be satisfied with an example of a local overcrowded freeway in which you say, "During rush hours, the cars are bumper-to-bumper for blocks." Introduce specifics: "At 5 P.M. on the freeway, on the three-mile stretch between High and Davis Streets, you won't find space enough between the front of one car and the back of another to insert a pillow. Though the angry drivers snarl with impatience, their crawling at a rate under five miles per hour prevents many a rear-end collision. That's the harried freeway driver's only consolation."

2. *Refer to the familiar.* Faraway places with strange-sounding names may appeal to some audiences, but the well-known things of life are more meaningful and give us a greater feeling of security. If, for instance, you are looking for an analogy to heighten a discussion of the prolonged process of registering for classes, you should not compare it to the pace of a relatively obscure phenomenon. Choose an analogue with meaning. Perhaps you would consider "a snail's pace" too trite to use. If so, try developing an analogy that compares registration to the length of a day in the Arctic (a faraway place but sufficiently known) or to a local mountain that has been standing patiently over the ages— more patiently than any student at registration.

3. *Introduce color and variety.* Be lively. Paint full word pictures, and vary your technique. People respond to richness and movement. The freeway example above has some color and life, though one could enhance it by mentioning the "haggard and drawn" faces of the drivers, the words they mutter, or the steam arising from car radiators, and so forth. Anticipate and adapt to listeners' needs and inclinations.

4. *Stir up curiosity.* Build up suspense. On some speech occasion try leaving at least one of your minor ideas partially veiled; notice the listeners' reactions. Too, you might say at the outset of a given talk

that you will make a prediction or important announcement later on in the speech. Do not let the audience down!

Be strategic in the placement of material.

5. *Use humor.* Relieve your listeners' tensions and put them in a receptive mood by bringing in an occasional short funny story or quip that seems relevant. Though you may have an intense and serious desire to persuade, you should realize that a little lightness may help you reach the goal.

One might even find something humorous in a speech on crowded freeways or mile-long registration lines. Choose humor that is suitable to your audience and valuable in furthering your end.

Personal Appeals

The third mode of appeal, called *ethos* by the ancient Greeks, may on occasion be the most potent force in persuasion. Ethos is personal appeal: the speaker's influence on audiences—either positive or negative—and what he represents in their minds.

One's reputation, appearance, personality, and character affect an audience and influence their analysis of one's ideas. If the audience is favorably impressed by the speaker, they will be moved to give him and his ideas a fair hearing; if they suspect or fear the speaker, he has the necessary chore before him of creating an attitude of confidence and friendliness. When an audience is kindly disposed toward the speaker, it will be kindly disposed toward his speech.

In a certain sense, the personal element in speaking represents "content," for it conveys a message and "says something" to the audience. In other words, it carries substance. Successful speakers are able to show that their substance—what they stand for—is akin to their listeners' substance. The outcome of the exchange between speaker and audience will very likely depend on the audience's acceptability of the speaker's bearing and being, on the speaker's ability to identify his way with theirs by showing a kinship in idea or spirit.

Good speeches are replete with instances of speakers' attempts to show that they identify themselves with their audiences. Let us examine some samples.

Secretary of State Dean Rusk wished to identify himself with the Association of the United States Army when he said to them at a banquet in Washington, D.C., "This great dinner revives many personal memories of a connection with the Army which began when I was twelve years old—with ROTC training in Boys High School in Atlanta." [6] With this and similar references, Rusk began building a relationship for communication.

[6] *Vital Speeches of the Day* (November 15, 1966), pp. 67–71.

Paul H. Nitze, United States Secretary of the Navy, recently spoke to an audience at the University of Edinburgh, Scotland, attempting to offer a base for understanding between Europe and America regarding military strategy in the Atlantic community. At the end of his speech he had his last chance to identify his way (America's) with Europe's. He did so by referring to mutual acceptance of ideas, a common heritage, and common conditions of freedom:

> . . . this is what I believe. With the joint application of American and European academic talents to this problem, I feel certain that a mutually acceptable body of thought of great value can be hammered out. For after all, what could be more within the great intellectual heritage which was handed down by Europe, and particularly by Great Britain, to the United States? Do not we believe that we are free men who can, by the exercise of our own intellects, work out for ourselves a better life here and now, on this earth, in our time? The way lies open before us.[7]

When Admiral R. C. Colbert talked about NATO to the Norfolk, Virginia Rotary Club, he opened his speech with material designed to unify speaker and audience (and the speaker's subject and audience):

> I am delighted to be with you here at Rotary today. When I was asked to speak to you on the subject of "International Cooperation for Peace," I felt it was important that I accept. My NATO experience is so closely associated with the goal of peace through international cooperation that it seemed important that I come here today and tell you a story—the story of SACLANT and NATO and how all of us in the NATO organization—civilian and military—are working to achieve the goal in which you here in Rotary are so interested.[8]

At a later point in the speech, Admiral Colbert employed the same strategy. It is an excellent example of identification of a speaker's goals with the listeners' goals:

> In reading your book on the "Seven Paths to Peace" I was interested in the policy of Rotary International on international service. One tenet of this policy especially struck me: "You will look beyond patriotism and consider yourself as sharing responsibility for the advancement of international understanding, good will and peace." Gentlemen, that principle could apply as well to all of us of the NATO team—whether civilian or military.[9]

DEVELOPING PERSONAL PROOF.

How does a speaker develop this element of persuasion known as personal proof? We have five suggestions—none of which is an easily

[7] "The Issues of World Power," *Vital Speeches of the Day*, XXXIII (December 1, 1966), pp. 98–103.

[8] "North Atlantic Treaty Organization," *Vital Speeches of the Day*, XXXIII (December 1, 1966), pp. 125–128.

[9] *Vital Speeches of the Day*, XXXIII (December 1, 1966), pp. 125–128.

applied, magic key to success, for refining the many components that make up personal proof may be a lifetime project.

1. *Continue to build a good reputation.* What people think of you affects their reception of everything you say. A known and respected person has fewer obstacles of audience indifference or negativeness to surmount than others who are not as fortunate. A good name is important for effective public speaking.

2. *Attend to your physical appearance.* We need not expand upon the importance of neatness and grooming for the speaker who desires to persuade. You should be acceptable in appearance and appropriately dressed. Do be careful, though, of fashion extremes. Clothing that is too dapper or too chic may cause some audiences to be suspicious and unwilling to put their trust in you. If this seems unfair to you, then you will sympathize with those whose occupations involve the handling of other people's money. Bankers and investment brokers, you know, are expected to dress quite conservatively.

3. *Find ways with your audience to show common substance.* On your own speaking occasions, follow the lead of the speakers quoted above. Make it known to your audience that their problems are yours, that their hopes and aspirations are yours. It may not be too extreme to say that any person before any audience can discover elements of a common substance. Of course, speakers who belong to the same club as listeners, or to the same political party, or live in the same neighborhood, and so forth, have an easier job. Conversely, the more divided are speaker and audience—the more alien or separate in thought—the greater is the difficulty in finding unity in spirit. Nonetheless, grounds can be found in most instances, if they be nothing more specific than a common hope for peace among men or for economic betterment for all, and so forth.

4. *Give evidence of your personal merit.* Modestly and humbly work into your discourse an occasional remark referring to your worth as a person speaking on the chosen subject. Along with other commendable characteristics, you might show that you have a sense of humor, self-confidence, sound character, and knowledge of your material. Following are some excerpts from actual speeches which show the use of this type of personal proof. Note evidence of modesty, regard for audience values, competence, sincerity and authority.

> I am little accustomed, gentlemen, to the part which I am now attempting to perform.
> I hope I have too much regard for justice, and too much respect for my own character, to attempt . . .
> Though I could well have wished to shun this occasion I have not felt at liberty to withhold my professional assistance . . . .
> —*Daniel Webster, prosecution of the Knapp-White murder case*

And I should like to say to my friends of the press and radio that I regret that I have no manuscript and have therefore been unable to give them an advance on what I shall say. What I shall say, therefore, shall be spoken from the heart and not from a piece of paper.

Four years ago, when I had the honor to be the temporary chairman of the Democratic convention in Philadelphia and to deliver the keynote address . . .

—former Vice President Alben Barkley

5. *Show respect for your audience.* If you have studied the audience beforehand, you can avoid such poor practices as speaking down to them or over their heads. Show respect for your listeners by accepting them as partners in the communicative enterprise. As you speak for your proposition, be tactful, keep your audience's welfare uppermost in your mind, and manifest a feeling of goodwill toward them.

BASES IN ORGANIZATION

Through appropriate arrangement speakers can also accommodate their thought to listeners' expectations. Like personal appeal, organization is—in a sense—substantial; that is, it carries a message. Clear organization bespeaks clear thinking and concern for audience welfare. Lack of arrangement may tell of the speaker's confused thinking or of his lack of real interest. In lending clarity to your speech and in complimenting listeners, good organization is persuasive.

In the organization of ideas in persuasive speaking, you should take into account both logic and psychology. You need to develop your thoughts in a sequence which is—on the one hand—logically sound and—on the other hand—psychologically advantageous. It is folly to stand and aimlessly cast ideas in all directions; you must proceed in an orderly manner with a well-conceived plan.

Deductive Patterns

A deductive plan for organizing speeches was discussed in Chapter Three; it is the Introduction-Proposition-Body-Conclusion formula with which you are so familiar. The essential characteristic of the deductive plan (based on deductive reasoning) is that it involves a movement from the general to the specific in thought development. General points are presented before specific supporting details are offered.

It is a practical plan, certainly logical, and easy to handle. It is excellent for achieving clarity and directness in expression. As with any system, care should be taken to make it work right. The proposition and main heads must be worked out with a particular audience in mind. To illustrate: "I will convince you that Harry Haskell is the man to elect to the City Council" in some speech situations would be a poorly worded purpose sentence. It is a challenge and could bring forth a wave of hostility. Instead, one might say, "Let us consider the qualifications of Candidate Haskell" or "I would like to discuss what Mr. Haskell will do for our city—for you and me." Most audiences cannot be forced to accept a proposal, but they can be encouraged to give it a hearing.

Persuasive speeches set up according to this deductive plan frequently include only two main heads: Problem and Solution. One popular variation is a five-part pattern based upon John Dewey's problem-solving formula (see Chapter Ten). The five-part pattern is valuable, for it impels the listener to move along with the speaker from one step to the next. The listener tends to become arrested by the sequence of thought as one section flows to the next. The plan seems to parallel logical thought patterns. If the listener agrees with the speaker during presentation of Parts One and Two, he will more than likely go along with him as he introduces the next logical step. This is the five-part plan:

I• *Attention*
   A. Stimulation of interest
   B. Recognition of a problem condition

II• *Problem*
   A. The extent of the problem
       1. Limitation
       2. Definition
   B. Causes and effects

III• *Possible Solutions*
   A. Strengths
   B. Weaknesses

IV• *The Most Satisfactory Solution*
   A. Interpretation
   B. Values

V• *Action on the Solution*
   A. An appeal for overt action to put the solution into effect
       or—
   B. An appeal for change in belief

Before going on to another system of idea arrangement, let us offer one additional suggestion about the use of the five-part plan: have a thorough knowledge of your problem. Many persuasive speeches break down because the speaker really does not understand the problem that he is attempting to treat. Be sure that you know the history, extent, causes, and effects of the problem.

Inductive Patterns

Some authorities consider the inductive plan to be psychologically more effective at times than the deductive. This is the upside-down system of arrangement in which the proposition is placed near the end of the speech along with the conclusion. The speaker presents a brief opening, develops the main heads, and finally unveils his proposition. Development of the individual main heads may be done deductively—the most familiar to you—or it may be done inductively. If accomplished inductively, the speaker presents all of his supporting material for a given main head before he states the main head. The main head comes as a conclusion to the gathered evidence.

The inductive approach, which allows the speaker to withhold the statement of his objective until the last minute, makes two accommodations to listeners' behavior: (1) it minimizes the development of negative feelings against the proposal, and (2) it adds suspense to the speech. The following outline is one that a friend of Harry Haskell might use to support his candidacy for the City Council:

1. You will make a major decision next Tuesday.
2. This is the most important city election to be held in many years.
    a. The man we elect will handle 13 million taxpayers' dollars annually. (*Statistics*)
    b. He will vote on several new traffic safety measures. (*Example*)
    c. He will be charged with helping to set policies for the police and fire departments. (*Example*)

Main head A.   Therefore, the man we elect must be *responsible.*

1. Our new city councilman will help decide on a plan to rezone certain areas for light industry. (*Example*)
2. The next five years will see this city either remain at a standstill or progress like such cities as Northborough and Sexton. (*Example*)
3. Judge Waite always said, "The progress of a city depends upon the vision of her leaders." (*Quotation*)

Main head B.   Therefore, the man we elect must be *forward-looking.*

Proposition-Conclusion: The candidate who is both responsible and forward-looking is (Need I tell you?) Harry Haskell—the man our city needs!

For further study of systems of speech organization, see the model speech outlines that follow this chapter.

BASES IN LANGUAGE

The language used in persuasion can help or hinder the speaker. If poorly chosen, it either will be of little use to the speaker as he goes about attempting to adapt his thought to his audience, or, worse; it will widen the breach between speaker and listener and hasten failure of the exchange. If well chosen, language can help to relate the thinking of a speaker and listener and lead to discovery of unity of belief and purpose.

As you remember from the discussion in Chapter Seven, useful language is clear, lively, varied, and appropriate. Actually, we can cluster all of these criteria of usage under one term: "rhetorical value." Whenever he consciously checks himself on style and language usage, the speaker must eventually come to ask one question: "Will this word (or phrase or way of casting the thought, and so forth) help me to gain the desired response from this audience on this occasion?" In other words, "What is the rhetorical value of the language?" Asked in more basic terms, the question is: "Will this word (or other element) help to unite my purpose with my listeners' interests and aims, and so forth?"

The ideas in persuasion are affected by the language used with them. Let us review the four criteria and introduce examples of speeches that illustrate them.

Clarity

Abraham Lincoln's style in speaking was simple and unornate. And he was effective; he succeeded often in uniting his purposes with his listeners' interests and intents. In February of 1860, he gave his views on the Slavery Question at Cooper Institute in New York City. The speech greatly added to the Illinois man's prestige in the East and contributed to his eventual election to the presidency. Clarity of expression is a prime attribute of the speech. For example,

> Now, and here, let me guard a little against being misunderstood. I do not mean to say we are bound to follow implicitly in whatever our fathers did. To do so would be to discard all the lights of current experience—to reject all progress, all improvement. What I do say is that if we would supplant the opinions and policy of our fathers in any case, we should do so upon evidence so conclusive and argument so clear, that even their great authority, fairly considered and weighed cannot stand . . .

Such style represented Lincoln as a lucid thinker, and as a direct and respectful man. Clear language helped communicate his virtues, as well as his beliefs.

Liveliness

We use "liveliness" to cover a discussion of sense-appealing and figurative language, but the word really does not bring out the full import of the topic. Appeals through the senses and figures of speech do add liveliness to thought—and more. They are of great value in crossing over to the listeners' province of belief and interest and finding a common province for communication.

Lincoln evoked enthusiastic response from the New York audience at Cooper Institute with an extended and lively side statement which he called "a few words to the Southern people." Observe the appealing language in the following brief but vivid passage.

> And now, if they would listen—as I suppose they will not—I would address a few words to the Southern people. I would say to them: You consider yourselves a reasonable and a just people; and I consider that in the general qualities of reason and justice you are not inferior to any other people. Still, when you speak of us Republicans, you do so only to denounce us as reptiles, or, at the best, as no better than outlaws. You will grant a hearing to pirates or murderers, but nothing like it to "Black Republicans." In all your contentions with one another, each of you deems an unconditional condemnation of "Black Republicanism" as the first thing to be attended to. Indeed, such condemnation of us seems to be an indispensable prerequisite—license, so to speak—among you to be admitted or permitted to speak at all. Now can you or not be prevailed upon to pause and to consider whether this is quite just to us, or even to yourselves? Bring forward your charges and specifications, and then be patient long enough to hear us deny or justify.

Still talking to the South, Lincoln finds an analogy useful in making his point.

> But you will not abide the election of a Republican president! In that supposed event, you say, you will destroy the Union; and then, you say, the great crime of having destroyed it will be upon us! That is cool. A highwayman holds a pistol to my ear and mutters through his teeth, "Stand and deliver, or I shall kill you, and then you will be a murderer!"

You can imagine the reactions of the stout Abolitionists in the New York audience to that figure of speech.

Variety

Audiences like variety. Said negatively, they are repelled by cliché and redundancy of mode of expression—for example, overused word patterns and sameness in sentence structure. Lincoln knew the natures and expectations of people. Accordingly, he diversified his employment of language elements and usually could be counted on to find a fresh way of verbalizing an idea. The important Cooper Institute speech is a mine of information for practices in variety of expression. Lincoln relied not on the declarative sentence alone but stimulated the audience with an occasional rhetorical question. He varied the length of his sentences—switching from balanced to periodic sentences and then to short, emphatic sentences. These and other methods served to heighten interest and cause the listeners to "go right along" with the speaker.

Appropriateness

What language does the occasion prescribe? The speaker should suit his style to the tone (or demands) of the occasion. Not only what he says but also the manner of expression should be in keeping with the occasion—not solely because it *should* be done but because it will help effect the audience's identification of the message. Audiences, having certain images of themselves, tend to resent and reject usages that do not fit their image. The self-image held by Lions Club members, of course, differs from that of the Peace Officers Association. What kind of formality is indicated? What are the expectations of the group whom you will face? Can you "get away" with a bit of slang or will the occasion's formality forbid it? Can you use certain modes of expression that set so well with your close friends, or would the audience reject them?

At Cooper Institute, Abraham Lincoln, the gaunt, roughhewn orator from the backwoods, apparently had no problems in adapting to his occasion in the big-city atmosphere of New York. He knew his audience and the character of the occasion. He adapted; for his overriding purpose was to effect oneness in spirit with them. To have shown ignorance or disrespect of the occasion would have alienated speaker from listener, and alienation is the antithesis of communication.

BASES IN DELIVERY

The character of the delivery, too, can advance or retard the speaker's purpose. As with other elements of persuasion, vocal and bodily behavior ought not to run counter to audience expectations and the nature of the occasion.

Probably the best examples of what to avoid come from instances of speakers who ignore social convention. Now and then one will observe a speaker whose mannerisms seem to be entirely out of keeping with the tenor of the program or, in fact, out of keeping with the age or culture! At a recent service club speech contest, one young male contestant fell into a "cultural trap." He had prepared his speech well in all ways, but for some reason or other he decided to employ flowery mannerisms of voice and gesture, some of which were quite reminiscent of certain old-time speakers. His bearing was an anachronism before his modern audience, a throwback of a time decades ago when such embellishment was welcomed. His manner distracted from his thought and communication did not occur.

Actually, the young man was acting a part. His fundamental problem—in common with many who have any difficulty in delivery—stemmed from a misunderstanding of the purpose of speechmaking.

Speechmaking is not acting; it is not an exhibition or display. It is a purposeful exchange of thought. James Albert Winans had advice that might have helped the young contestant: "Do not look upon public speaking as a performance, but as genuine dealing with men." Men— and women—respond favorably only when elements of the exchange offer bases for mutual respect and welding of belief.

(For additional study in delivery, refer to Chapter Eight, "Refining Speech Delivery.")

LET US SUMMARIZE

Comments of two highly respected men might serve to emphasize what has been our focus in this chapter on persuasion. First, the great Frenchman, Alexis de Toqueville speaks: "Feelings and opinions are recruited, the heart enlarged, and the human mind is developed only by the reciprocal influences of men upon one another." He is talking about persuasion and is acknowledging its significance. The second man is Reinhold Neibuhr of this century. Note carefully his idea: "Men, acting in classes, races, and nations, might achieve a tolerable harmony with their fellows only by arbitrating their competitions by standards of discriminate justice, *or by stratagems that would discover the point of concurrence between the more parochial and the more universal interests.*" [10] Like de Toqueville, Niebuhr recognizes the social goals of men. The portion of Niebuhr's statement that we have put in italics is a speaker's fundamental aim, the theme of this chapter. The speaker must find the means for reaching the parochial or provincial lives of listeners. He seeks the universal or common interests on which he can build a line of reasoning, and he finds them—the bases of communication—in ideas and modes of appeal, organization, language, and delivery.

Perhaps any assembled group can be unified on some ground. The speaker who would find the ground must needs write his speech "sitting in the audience," figuratively speaking. He should "be with them" as he prepares his thought for them. He should look around and ask himself questions: "Whom do I see? Who are they? What do they want? Where do their ideas and mine coincide? How can I reach them? What can I do for them?"

Hubert H. Humphrey, a master in the art of communicating with people, has a very practical and moral view of persuasion. Features of his plan—one requiring conviction, hard work, and knowledge of people—are worth studying.

[10] "Some Things I Have Learned," *Saturday Review*, XLVIII (November 6, 1965), pp. 21–24, 63–64.

My basic aim as a speaker is to make others understand, to educate, to challenge others, to think deeply about the matters which I consider so important and significant.

. . .

The necessary components to build a speech are:
1. A full and detailed understanding of the facts.
2. A thorough understanding of the particular audience to be addressed.
3. A deep and thorough belief in what one is saying.

. . .

I do not try to hide a difference of philosophy or attitudes between myself and the group to which or to whom I am speaking. Usually, I find that this method earns me respect, if not agreement. But it is seldom that I cannot, in some way point out areas of agreement.[11]

THEMES FOR PERSUASIVE SPEECHES

Television is not meeting the public needs.
Our government is moving toward socialism.
As an American, you should not tip.
Donate to the March of Dimes.
Join the Speech Club on campus.
Religious instruction has no place in the public schools.
The Post Office should be operated as a private business.
Everyone should subscribe to the *Saturday Review*.
Organized labor is becoming too powerful.
Join a fraternity (or sorority).
Attend religious services regularly.
Buy a small automobile.
Improve your study habits.
All women should take courses in home economics.
Resist the fashion trends.
Poor mental health is our most serious problem.
Participation in athletics builds citizenship.
Take a course in geology.
The jury system should be abolished.
This political party (Democratic or Republican) will win at the next election.
Go fishing during your next vacation.
A liberal education is rewarding.
The proper study of mankind is man.
Enlist in the Marine Corps.
Drive safely.
Learn to play bridge.

[11] Ben Padrow, "Hubert H. Humphrey: The Glandular Zephyr," in *Today's Speech*, XII (September, 1964), pp. 2–3.

A man should be a dog's best friend.
Be a responsible speaker.
The greatest virtue is prudence.
Know thyself.
Give every man equal opportunities.
In speaking, practice ought to be preceded by theory.
Start to build a record collection.
Avoid overeating.
The good businessman is ethical in his actions.
Learn to detect fallacies in reasoning.
The meek shall inherit the earth.
Learn to appreciate good music.
A student should go away to college.
Lou Gehrig was the greatest baseball player of all time.
Take an active part in politics.
Recognize the extent of Aristotle's teachings.
All young men should have some military training.
Poetry is the highest form of literary art.
Improve your listening.
Take a vacation in Oregon.
Buy more life insurance.
Study a foreign language.
Procrastination is a thief of time.

MODEL SPEECH OUTLINE 1

(The five-part plan in sentence form)

A Helping Hand

I• *Attention*
  A. We Americans enjoy our way of life.
      1. Our supermarkets are laden.
      2. Our homes are comfortable. (*Example*)
      3. Our schools are outstanding.
  B. Some people of other countries, especially children, have never known how it feels to have their stomachs filled or their minds properly trained.

II• *Problem*
  A. Many are homeless.
      1. There are thousands of homeless orphans in Korea. (*Example*)
      2. India has a similar problem. (*Example*)
  B. Many are hungry.

       1. Natural disasters frequently cut off the food supply in the Orient. (*Example*)

       2. Poor farming methods impede agricultural output.

       3. There are merely too many mouths to feed in some countries. (*Examples*)

   C. Many are uneducated.

       1. There is too little money for schools. (*Statistics*)

       2. Pagan beliefs hold back educational progress in parts of Africa. (*Examples*)

       3. Many youths, such as Francisco Santillan of the Philippines, must forego school in order to earn a living. (*Example*)

III• *Possible Solutions*

   A. We could relax our immigration restrictions.

   B. We could send more experts abroad to offer assistance.

   C. We could make personal contributions.

IV• *The Most Satisfactory Solution*

   A. The problem must be met immediately.

   B. I would like to suggest that we consider the possibility of making personal contributions through the Children's Aid Plan.

       1. One may "adopt" (support) a boy or girl in an orphanage in one of twenty-eight different countries.

       2. His benefactor receives the child's history and may correspond with him.

       3. The plan is nonpolitical and nonsectarian.

       4. The support is nonobligatory, that is, it may be withdrawn at any time.

       5. The cost for one month is $15.

V• *Action on the Solution*

   A. This is not much money from an individual or from a group.

       1. Less than $3.75 a week will help to provide a young and innocent victim of circumstance with nutritious food, adequate shelter, and proper schooling.

       2. The average American wastes this much each week. (*Statistics*)

   B. As an individual or member of a group, you can make your contributions with very little inconvenience.

       1. Just write to Children's Aid, New York, N. Y.

       2. Jean de la Bruyere said, "Liberality consists less in giving a great deal than in gifts well timed." (*Quotation*)

3. Now is the time to help our world's hungry children—before they become hungry men.

MODEL SPEECH OUTLINE 2

(The five-part plan in topic form)

Our Not-so-Fair City

I• *Attention*
   A. The Willow Avenue neighborhood
      1. Trim and comfortable houses
      2. Happy, healthy families having fun
      3. Spacious playgrounds and modern schools
   B. The Front Street district
      1. Shacks and decaying apartment dwellings
      2. Filth and disease
      3. Junk-littered lots and bleak school buildings

II• *Problem*
   A. The economic problem in the district
      1. Inadequate housing accommodations
         a. Only thirteen new houses since 1959 (*Statistics*)
         b. Bath facilities for but 50 percent of the families (*Statistics*)
         c. A family of ten in a three-room shack (*Example*)
      2. Other squalid features
         a. Cheap, rundown business places (*Examples*)
         b. Two elementary schools with average class size of forty-two (*Statistics*)
         c. Narrow streets and filthy alleys
   B. The social problem in the district
      1. Juvenile delinquency
         a. 25 percent incidence (*Statistics*)
         b. The case of Tom C. (*Example*)
      2. Drunkenness
         a. 120 beer and wine licensees (*Statistics*)
         b. 200 drunks arrested weekly (*Statistics*)
         c. Liquor affecting home life (*Examples*)
      3. Crime
         a. Five stabbings, forty-one burglaries, and eleven brawls in December (*Statistics*)
         b. Tuesday night's barroom gun fight (*Example*)

III• *Possible Solutions*
   A. Education

    B.   More social work
    C.   Removal of slums

IV•   *The Most Satisfactory Solution*
    A.   More than one approach needed
    B.   A combined attack
        1.   A program of enlightenment as carried on in other cities (*Examples*)
        2.   Along with more attention from the Social Welfare Department
        3.   Plus gradual replacement of substandard buildings (*Hypothetical Example*)

V•   *Action on the Solution*
    A.   Must be initiated by you, the responsible citizen
        1.   By talking to city council members and others of influence
        2.   By writing letters to the newspaper
        3.   By voting for improvement measures and persuading others to do so
    B.   Benefits to you, the responsible citizen
        1.   Pride in your city
        2.   Financial gain from our increased wealth
        3.   Security when your children are out at night

MODEL SPEECH OUTLINE 3

(The inductive plan in sentence form)

Leisure and Learning

1. At the end of Spring, thousands of people will flock to the lakes, rivers, and seashore.
2. In Winter, the mountain slopes are crawling with skiers. (*Statistics*)
3. Some fortunate souls, like Ralph Simpson, take trips to Europe. (*Example*)
4. There are those like my father who have fun puttering around the yard. (*Example*)

Main head A.   One thing is certain, then, people desire pleasure.

1. In a different vein, consider the case of Mr. Nellis, my neighbor, who attends school three nights a week. (*Example*)
2. In this city, 200 people meet in various study groups each week. (*Statistics*)
3. The Community Forum was attended by over 600 people last week. (*Statistics*)

4. The enrollment of our college has doubled in the past ten years. (*Statistics*)
5. Only last Wednesday, Professor Hunter said, "Never before have I seen such a clamor at the school gates." (*Quotation*)

Main head B. This activity indicates that people desire an education.

Proposition-Conclusion: Like Ralph Simpson and Mr. Nellis you can help to satisfy your yearnings for pleasure and learning by joining a Great Books Discussion Group.

1. The enjoyment and knowledge that is gained by people in groups all over the country can be yours, too. (*Explanation*)
2. Complete information is here in this brochure, and I have copies for each of you. (*Visual Aid*)
3. You are invited to attend an introductory meeting in the library tomorrow night at eight.
4. As Sophocles, one of our Great Books' authors, observed, "Though a man be wise, it is no shame for him to live and learn." (*Quotation*)
5. I shall be looking for you tomorrow night.

MODEL SPEECH OUTLINE 4

(The inductive plan in sentence form)

Therapy is Available

1. Wilma was unsuccessful in talking herself out of fearing high places. (*Example*)
2. Marvin failed in using reason to fight his serious emotional problem. (*Example*)
3. Other resolutions to "get better" are often broken. (*Examples*)

Main head A. Therefore, will power does not cure serious mental disturbances.

1. Well-meaning family members may worsen conditions. (*Hypothetical example*)
2. A friend tried to help someone but gave up in disgust. (*Example*)
3. Thomas à Kempis: "Be not angry that you cannot make others as you wish them to be, since you cannot make yourself as you wish to be." (*Quotation*)

Main head B. The advice of associates does little to allay deep-seated emotional problems.

1. There are meaningless generalizations in some popular do-it-yourself psychology publications. (*Quotations*)
2. Ed was not helped even after reading seventeen books (3927 pages) on popular psychology. (*Example* and *statistics*)

Main head C. To those severely plagued, articles and books offer little therapy.

Proposition-Conclusion

1. You have seen the ineffectiveness of an exercise of will, the counsel of friends, and the use of written materials; the answer to the emotionally afflicted lies in psychotherapy.
    a. Consult a psychologist, psychiatrist, or psychoanalyst. (*Definitions*)
    b. There are many cases of successful therapy. (*Examples*)
    c. Fees may not be exhorbitant. (*Statistics*)
2. Get names of qualified therapists:
    a. Call the local university or college counseling office;
    b. Call the Family Service Agency;
    c. Call the Health Department;
    d. Call medical or psychological associations.

Suggested Exercise A

Prepare a speech designed either to alter the thinking of your audience or to influence their behavior. Use a deductive pattern of organization, either the four- or five-part plan.

Before selecting your subject, prepare a list of beliefs and values which you hold in common with your audience. After selecting the subject, prepare another such list, this one based on ideas regarding the chosen subject. Constantly remind yourself of these bases for communication as you plan every phase of the speech.

Suggested Exercise B

Select another proposal and repeat *Suggested Exercise A*, using the inductive pattern of organization.

Suggested Exercise C

Reword the following statements to make them propositions of deductive persuasive speeches which would be acceptable to your class as an audience.

1. You are duty-bound to attend all of our basketball games.
2. Fraternities and sororities should be banned from all college campuses.
3. Teaching by television will replace "live teaching."
4. The ideas of the ancient Greeks are too impractical for the twentieth century.
5. Every instructor should require his students to write a 2500-word term paper.
6. If America is to survive, you must spend less time in leisure and more in work.

Suggested Exercise D

Listen to a speaker, either on or off the campus. Analyze the effectiveness of his logical, psychological, and personal appeal. What specific means did he use to hold attention and build interest? What other techniques were particularly effective?

Suggested Exercise E

Study a written speech from *Vital Speeches, Representative American Speeches,* or other speech anthologies. Discover examples of enthymemes and inductive reasoning used by the speaker.

Suggested Exercise F

Recast the following enthymemes in the *form* of syllogisms in order to get an understanding of the line of reasoning used. Underline the missing premise of each one (the premise that the audience would be expected to supply).

1.   The Coast Guard spotted an oil slick at a certain point in the ocean. The missing submarine must have gone down there.
2.   John Baxman is the Republican party chairman in this county; he could not have voted for the Democratic candidate.

Suggested Exercise G

Note the contents of three television or radio commercials. List the human motives to which the messages appealed. With what type of audience would each commercial be likely to have been effective?

Suggested Exercise H

Let us assume that you are planning to give a speech at an assembly of the high school that you attended. You want to convince your audience that the automobile is the greatest invention of all time. What would be your principal arguments? What might you say to enhance your personal appeal (ethos)?

In contrast, if your audience were composed of retired men and women, would the arguments be the same? Or, would you use the same arguments but merely vary your treatment of them? How might you enhance your personal appeal?

Suggested Exercise I

What speaker currently on the scene stands out in your mind as one who manifests strong personal worth? What specific qualities give him this enviable asset?

Suggested Exercise J

What persuasive speaking practices that you have noticed do you consider unethical? Submit the list to your instructor. He may wish to discuss the topic in class.

Suggested Exercise K

Review the section on fallacies in Chapter Ten and then name the fallacy in each of the following examples:

1. I have seen a lot of cheating around this campus; all students cheat.
2. Have you noticed the new football uniforms? We will have a great team.
3. He has had a siege of bad luck as a result of walking under a painter's ladder last Spring.
4. The little man does not have a chance these days. He must play ball with the big operators or perish.
5. It is his name that bothers me. Do you want a President named Ziggleton?
6. Our economic situation here in Kansas is just like the one they had on San Cristobal Island in 1915.
7. We all understand, of course, that engineering is the most important profession, but it is an underpaid profession also.
8. Arthur, who reads Einstein's works, must be very intelligent because he has read nearly all of the great man's writings.

Suggested Exercise L

What gaps in understanding or experience might possibly exist between the following people?

1. Immigrant parents from Europe and their American-born teen-age offspring
2. A machinists union and the factory management
3. Catholic laymen and Methodist laymen
4. A socialist and a capitalist

What common grounds might each find for communicating with the other on certain critical topics suggested by their respective identifications?

Suggested Exercise M

How might people set apart by their "uniforms" or office reveal substance possessed in common with an audience of college students? Consider, for example, the problems of people who are police officers, clergymen, deans of men or women, court judges, and military officers.

Suggested Exercise N

Analyze the delivery of a speaker whom you have heard recently. Did the character of the delivery itself "carry a message"? That is, did it seem to present thoughts in addition to those verbalized by the speaker? What did it say to you? Was the message of the delivery consistent with the speaker's purpose and what he intended to convey?

Suggested Exercise O

Find the printed text of a speech, and write a brief description of the audience and the occasion. Then analyze the supporting material (evidence consisting of examples, testimony, statistics, and so forth). Is the evidence always relevant to the point under discussion? Is the quantity sufficient? Does it seem to be clear and understandable? Do you suppose that it appealed to the interests and motives of the listeners? Does it seem to be fitting for the occasion.

CHAPTER THIRTEEN

Preparing for Various Occasions

The shaping of any speech that you plan to make will be determined by your assessment of the entire situation. In effect, you must ask yourself, "What kind of speech should I make to this audience on this occasion?" Fundamentally, all types of original speeches are similar. All require thoughtful consideration of the subject, formulation of a definite purpose, sound organization, adequate development of ideas, and effective delivery.

Some occasions, however, demand more than the application of fundamental principles. For example, if you are called upon to speak at some gathering without benefit of extensive preparation, it will be necessary for you to gather your thoughts immediately. Making an announcement, presenting a guest speaker to your club members, nominating a candidate for office, giving a speech to offer a token of honor to one who is leaving the community, accepting an award for service to your school, speaking as official host to a visiting delegation—all such events have special peculiarities to which you must adapt. At some time during your life you will have occasion to deliver one of these speeches.

THE IMPROMPTU SPEECH

The impromptu speech is a short talk given on the spur of the moment. Does the thought of making such a talk frighten you? Actually, the main difference between the requirements of impromptu speaking and other types of speechmaking is the amount of preparation time. We shall not attempt to convince you that this difference is insignificant because that would not be accurate. Yet, every speech that you have made can be thought of as a preparatory experience for making future impromptu speeches. In all of your speaking you have been getting ready to give speeches of limited preparation for a special occasion. Since much of the groundwork has been laid, the job now is to carry over to that special occasion what you have learned about composition and delivery. You will find this less difficult than you now think.

The following instructions will help you to implement your knowledge of speaking and be successful in the impromptu situation:

1. *Give thought to your subject.* On some occasions you may be allowed to choose your own subject, while at other times you will be expected to adhere to an imposed subject. When the choice is yours, it is always wise to choose a significant subject. Speak about the occasion: its purposes, high points, or humorous aspects. Speak about the people assembled: their successes, future plans, or other group interests. Current events can offer impromptu topics such as popular fads, or recent happenings in the community. Do not attempt to cover a wide area; limit your scope.

2. *Plan your course.* Decide immediately upon your proposition or theme, and select two or three main heads for developing it. The proposition might suggest that the main heads be topical, spatial, or chronological; or they may be set up as reasons, or in a problem-solution pattern. Pairs of opposites are frequently quite handy "pillars of thought": for example, East and West, ups and downs, right and wrong, or past and future.

3. *Select materials as you speak.* During the time that it takes you to push back your chair and assume your speaking position, you can be gathering together a few introductory words. Make no apologies about "being unaccustomed to giving impromptu speeches." At a banquet you can refer to the beautiful table decorations, to a timely conversation that you had a minute ago, possibly to the committee's excellent work in arranging the program, or you can tell an appropriate story.

After leading into your proposition, state it. Present your first main idea; elaborate on it with a story or example, some statistics, or a quotation if one should come to you at the time. Available visual aids might be used as means of development. One person, in fact, used a knife, fork, and spoon upon which to base his entire talk. He discussed "cutting through red tape" (with his knife), "spearing the main facts" (with his fork), and "scooping out details" (with his spoon). Use your imagination; capitalize on the tone of the occasion and factors related to it.

Before sitting down, perhaps you should summarize, make an appeal —or work both in together. In speaking before an organization, it is often appropriate to close with pertinent comments about the group's goals and aspirations, their unsolved problems, future gatherings, or noteworthy efforts of the officers and members.

4. *Guard against speciousness.* Reference is made here to a danger that may present itself to a person who has had enough impromptu

speaking experience to give him a feeling of overconfidence, but not enough to convince him of the need to have a significant message. Glibness and smoothness do not necessarily indicate effectiveness. If the impromptu speaker has a worthy message and presents it sincerely, he will avoid becoming "inebriated with the exuberance of his own verbosity."

THE ANNOUNCEMENT

Whether given as an impromptu speech or based upon extensive planning, the announcement speech is often poorly made. This is probably due to its not being thought of as a "speech"; some persons seem to think that only formal public addresses require careful preparation.

What are the "rules" for making announcements?

1. Plan your talk.
2. Open with an attention-getting sentence.
3. Relate all of the essential information—who, what, when, where, and how much—succinctly and clearly.
4. Be enthusiastic; make the subject inviting; emphasize its importance.
5. Repeat the essential information briefly.
6. Be seated!

The following is a sample outline:

I• *Introduction*
  A. Don't save your money.
  B. Bring it with you next Wednesday, and throw it away.

II• *Proposition:* Throw it away at the Jester Club's Annual Candy Sale to be held all day Wednesday along the arcade.

III• *Body*
  A. We will have creamy homemade fudge.
  B. We will have heavenly divinity.
  C. We will have mouth-watering peanut brittle.

IV• *Conclusion*
  A. Each generously filled bag will cost you a mere 25 cents.
  B. Remember that Wednesday is candy day along the arcade.

THE SPEECH OF INTRODUCTION

If you have had the uncomfortable experience of being thrown into a group at a party without benefit of introduction, you will certainly appreciate the fact that guest speakers deserve appropriate speeches of introduction. The loneliest and most anxious time in a speaker's experience can be that period during which he waits to become acquainted with the audience. He may wonder what they have heard about him, what they think of him, or if they have heard of him at all. These typical thoughts of concern may pass through his mind: "Will my ideas be accepted? Can I get across to them? I wish I were more familiar with them and they with me."

Speeches of introduction are important. They help to create a friendly relationship between the speaker and his audience, dispel fear, and effect a "shaking of hands." Vital though they are, such talks occasionally are mishandled. When you have the opportunity to acquaint a speaker with an audience and help him to get started, follow these suggestions:

1. *Know your function.* You are to make a speech; however, you are not the *main* speaker. Like the waiter in a restaurant, you provide a service, but like the waiter, again, what you introduce is the more important element. Subordinate yourself on this occasion and, like a good host, give the main speaker his rightful position of prominence. Rarely would you be justified in speaking longer than two or three minutes. In fact, the introduction of a very well-known person might be accomplished in a few seconds with, "Ladies and Gentlemen, our president, Dr. Wagner."

2. *Learn about the speaker.* Study his background by consulting printed sources and people who know him. If possible, arrange to have a personal talk with him well ahead of the speaking time. Be certain that all of your information is accurate, including, of course, his proper title and the pronunciation of his name.

3. *Include appropriate data.* Remember now, that *he* is the speaker. Avoid trespassing very far into his subject area. General comments that show how the subject relates to the occasion or that summarize the speaker's work in his field are appropriate. Your knowledge or personal philosophy of the subject normally should not be included. For a hilarious example of a speaker finding himself with nothing to say because preceding speakers had used all of his ideas, see "Stolen Thunder" in Appendix B of this book.

Specifically, what information is to be presented? Though occasions vary, usually you would summarize his qualifications, tell why everyone anticipates his speech. Capitalize on the background data that are especially meaningful to the audience.

Point out primary accomplishments of the speaker, yet do not overburden your introduction with many statistics and facts. Use humor if you wish, but use care and good taste in so doing. Build him up, yet not to an embarrassing extent. You can sympathize certainly with a person who is introduced as "the greatest speaker in Ohio." You may envy his announced reputation, but you would not want to be in his position of having to live up to it.

On the other hand, if he is your second choice, you should not embarrass him by revealing the fact. It would be most uncomplimentary to say, for instance, that you had tried to get Mr. Wilson but that Mr. Rogers, here, will surely give a good speech.

4. *Organize your remarks.* Like any other oral effort, the speech of introduction should be properly arranged. Many people like to use the inductive or upside-down plan. It involves making a brief opening to get attention and interest, developing two or three main heads, and finishing with a combination Proposition-Conclusion. Here is a sample outline:

I• *Introduction*
    A.   Some people say that television will replace radio.
    B.   Those of us who enjoy popular music would, indeed, debate that point.
    C.   The point would be debated also by the prominent man who is to speak to us today.

II• *Body*
    A.   He has fourteen years of experience in broadcasting.
        1.   He started out as a script writer for KRRL.
        2.   He worked for them as a disc jockey for three years.
        3.   After extended experience in other capacities, he became manager of KRRL.
    B.   Our speaker believes that radio has more potential today than it ever had.
        1.   He has proven this in our community.
        2.   He has more new ideas about the future of radio, some of which he will describe to us today.

III• *Proposition-Conclusion*
    Ladies and gentlemen, I present, speaking on the topic "Radio and You," the man who makes of air a tangible commodity—the manager of KRRL, Tom Barber.

5. *Present the speaker.* As indicated in the sample outline, you should make an appropriate statement to tell the speaker that *his* time has come. Sometimes a speaker is embarrassed because the introducer fails to present him properly to the audience. After the presentation, turn his way, and lead the applause.

THE AFTER-DINNER SPEECH

Unlike some banquet speeches—which may be quite serious in purpose and development—the traditional after-dinner speech is humorous. It is a "special breed" of talk, presented to give pleasure following a dinner. But along with the fun and beneath the laughter, the audience usually expects to find a message of some sort. A theme ought to run through the speech, carrying a significant idea.

One of America's most celebrated after-dinner speakers was Mark Twain. Perhaps you have read his "A 'Littery' Episode" in which (at the birthday celebration of John Greenleaf Whittier in 1877) he poked fun at the literary works of Emerson, Longfellow, and Oliver Wendell Holmes—all of whom were present. His "New England Weather" and "The Babies" are also famous samples of his after-dinner wit.

Once a student in Oregon had occasion at a dinner gathering to speak on the topic "South of the Border." He found his humor in subtopics related to California: the smog, driving the freeways, Hollywood, crowded classrooms, and so forth. Everybody enjoyed his fun with the sister state "south of the border." He concluded with a tribute to California for efforts to solve its growth problems.

On another occasion, a teacher of twenty years recalled funny experiences in a classroom of those days, as he followed a theme relating to new demands being placed on students in this day. At a forensics award banquet, a speaker humorously characterized varying types of student debaters: the "fast-talking lawyer type"; the "frowner"—always grim and deeply serious, believing the world is coming to an end; and the "lion," who paces as though in a cage and who consequently wears out a pair of shoes at each speech tournament. Accompanying the speaker's humor was an acknowledgement of the values of debating experience.

After-dinner speakers use all types of humor. Stories are favored by some. A speaker once provoked considerable laughter with this story:

> A minister was invited one Sunday to eat at the farm home of the best cook in the congregation. Besides liking good food, he enjoyed tossing off funny expressions. When handed a huge plate of fried chicken, he quipped, "Here's one chicken that's going into the ministry."
>
> But, not to be outdone, the twelve-year old son of the family replied, "I hope that she does better than she did in lay work."

Having fun with the provincial nature of people, a speaker on one occasion successfully appealed to listeners when he told the following:

> It seems that two ladies from Boston were visiting Disneyland on a hot day. One of them, showing marked discomfort, gasped, "Boston never has weather like this."
>
> "It certainly does not," puffed the other, "but you must remember that here we are 3,000 miles from the ocean."

The fabricated personal-experience story sometimes fits in very well. This is the sort of narrative that often begins with "A funny thing happened to me on the way to the banquet this evening." Or, "When I was in Washington last week, I happened to run into the President waiting for a bus. . . ." After the opening, the speaker fabricates some fantastic story to fit his purpose of the moment. You might try it some-time.

Puns and other plays on words may be useful. The samples below may prove funny (or may not, depending on the speaker and audience).

> "Do you like books?" the professor asked the student.
> "Yes, I like books," the student replied. "I like *Little Women*. In fact, I like them better than books."

> In Detroit there is a very popular Italian restaurant called "The Tower of Pizza." But from all reports it's a very upright establishment.

> Did you know that speeches are like animal's tails? For example, some are like cat's tails—fur to the end. Others are like rat's tails—straight and to the point. Or like dog's tails—bound to occur. Or rabbit's— just a suggestion.

Among the many other types of mirth-stimulating material are humorous verse, witty descriptions and illustrations, and entertaining allusions to famous persons and events or local persons and topics. Free your imaginative spirit, and all kinds of possibilities for raising a laugh will come to mind.

In addition to following proven practices of speech preparation, you ought to consider the following suggestions when preparing the after-dinner speech:

1. Choose a theme that is suitable to the audience and the occasion.
2. Plan carefully and follow the selected theme; avoid irrelevant detail.
3. Develop the theme with appropriate material, being careful to eliminate any which may offend persons or respected institutions.
4. Give special attention to transitions—devices that connect and give coherence to ideas and materials.
5. Use only *your* kind of story or piece of humor, the type that is easy for *you* to carry off.
6. Be brief, especially if in doubt as to amount of allotted time.

NOMINATING SPEECHES

Most of the recommendations for giving speeches of introduction apply to speeches designed to nominate a candidate for office. However, you should pay special attention to the following points:

1. Mention the requirements of the office and how your candidate is qualified to meet them.
2. Be positive in your approach; avoid sarcasm and ridicule if you must refer to other candidates running for the office.
3. You might include a memory point—a catchy phrase or slogan that the voters will be likely to remember. The famous "I like

Ike" was enormously helpful to Dwight Eisenhower during his first campaign for the presidency.

4. Deliver the speech with conviction and enthusiasm.

Though written for the fun of it, Will Rogers' "Nominating Calvin Coolidge," found in *Appendix A,* suggests a useful form for shaping nominating speeches.

SPEECHES OF PRESENTATION

Many organizations, communities, and companies have established the practice of presenting symbols of acknowledgment to praiseworthy persons or institutions. Such presentations may be made to give public recognition of long or exemplary service, scholastic or athletic accomplishment, or to commemorate an event.

Since the occasion is of considerable importance, the accompanying speech should serve to carry it off in the proper spirit. If this speaking opportunity ever arises for you, what should you do?

1. Do not use notes.
2. Discuss reasons for the presentation and what the symbol being offered represents.
3. Discuss the characteristics and qualifications of the recipient.
4. Be sincere in expressing the genuine pleasure felt by those giving the award or gift.
5. Maintain the proper spirit of bestowing an honor, yet avoid making embarrassing exaggerations.

In a public ceremony on February 23, 1962, President Kennedy presented Colonel John H. Glenn, Jr., with a medal for his accomplishment as the first American to fly a spacecraft in orbit. The speech here printed in full may be a helpful model.

> Now Colonel Glenn, will you step forward.
>
> Seventeen years ago today, a group of marines put the American flag on Mount Surabachi, so it's very appropriate that today we decorate Colonel Glenn of the United States Marine Corps and also realize that in the not too distant future a marine or a naval man or an Air Force man will put the American flag on the moon.
>
> I present this citation:
>
> "The President of the United States takes pleasure in awarding the National Aeronautics and Space Administration Distinguished Service Medal to Lieutenant Colonel John H. Glenn Jr., United States Marine Corps, for services set forth in the following:
>
> "For exceptionally meritorious service to the Government of the United States in a duty of great responsibility as the first American astronaut to perform orbital flight.
>
> "Lieutenant Colonel Glenn's orbital flight on Feb. 20, 1962, made an outstanding contribution to the advancement of human knowledge, of space technology and in demonstration of man's capabilities in space flight.

"His performance was marked by his great professional skill, his skill as a test pilot, his unflinching courage and his extraordinary ability to perform most difficult tasks under conditions of great physical stress and personal danger.

"His performance in fulfillment of this most dangerous assignment reflects the highest credit upon himself and the United States."

Colonel, we appreciate what you've done.

SPEECHES OF ACCEPTANCE

A speech given to accept an award or gift is usually an impromptu effort. Even though the recipient may have advance notice of the event, he must adapt his remarks to those of the presenter. The nature of the occasion, the type of symbol offered, and the preceding formalities will influence your response. However, there are certain general guideposts that apply to most speeches of acceptance:

1. Speak briefly, unless a long speech is expected.
2. Discuss the importance of the award to you; show your appreciation.
3. Modestly discuss significant and relevant facts that led to the honor being paid to you; discuss the roles played by other persons.
4. Pay tribute to those responsible for the presentation.

Notice how Colonel Glenn follows all four of the guideposts in his response to President Kennedy's presentation.

All right. Fine. Thank you.

Sit down, please.

I can't express my appreciation adequately to be here in accepting this when I know how many thousand people all over the country were involved in helping accomplish what we did last Tuesday and knowing how—particularly this group here at the Cape and many of the groups here on the platform, our own group of astronauts who were scattered all around the world and who performed their functions here at the Cape also—we all acted literally and figuratively as a team and it was a real team effort all the way.

We have stressed the team effort in Project Mercury. It goes across the board, I think, sort of a crosscut of Americana of Industry and military and Civil Service, Governmental workers, contractors, the—almost a crosscut of American effort in the technical field, I think. It wasn't specialized by any one particular group.

It was headed up by NASA, of course, but thousands and thousands of people have contributed certainly as much or more than I have to the project.

I would like to consider that I was sort of a figurehead for this whole big tremendous effort and I'm very proud of the medal I have on my lapel here for all of us—you included—because I think it represents all of our efforts, not just mine.

Thank you very much and thank you, Mr. President.

SPEECHES OF WELCOME

Noted groups or individuals who visit your school, community, church gathering, or club should be accorded the courtesy of a welcoming speech. Similarly, new members of a professional or social organization ought to be so treated. Allow these suggestions to guide you in handling this type of speaking assignment:

1. Do not use notes.
2. Discuss the nature of the occasion.
3. Discuss complimentary and interesting traits or characteristics of your visitor(s) or new member(s).
4. Discuss pertinent features of the welcoming group (your group).
5. Be a genial and cordial ambassador of good will; put out the welcome mat.

Observe the spirit of cordiality and respect in President Johnson's welcoming of British Prime Minister Douglas-Home to the White House on February 12, 1964.

> Mr. Prime Minister, you do this land and this house great honor by your visit. Mrs. Johnson and I welcome you, Lady Douglas-Home, the Foreign Secretary, Mrs. Butler, and other members of your party to the United States and to the White House.
>
> This visit only continues a tradition that is both auspicious and warm. Meetings between American Presidents and British Prime Ministers were first firmly established by our great President, Franklin Roosevelt, and your legendary Prime Minister—and now our fellow American— Sir Winston Churchill.
>
> No matter the political complexion of our two Governments, this tradition has remained happily unbroken for more than a quarter of a century.
>
> During these years we have had our differences, but these differences have passed away. They have passed away because of a very special reason: There is between our two countries the invisible cords of a mingled respect and understanding and affection, much as two brothers who may differ but whose ties are too strong to ever break.
>
> So we meet today as Presidents and Prime Ministers of two countries, as they have always met with friendship and high resolve to face our common problems and to try to settle them for the common good. Together our nations are secure. They are strong enough to win any fight, and we hope they are wise enough to prevent one. Together we search for hope, we search for peace.
>
> In that spirit and with that aim, Mr. Prime Minister, we welcome you. We welcome you to this house and to this land, and may God bless our work together.

The Response to a Speech of Welcome

Occasionally when welcomed, you are expected to respond briefly. You ought to consider the following recommendations:

1. Graciously acknowledge the host's extended courtesy.
2. Bring greetings from the group that you represent (if you are a representative), and point up common bonds.
3. Sincerely praise the welcoming organization.

Prime Minister Douglas-Home's fitting response to President Johnson's welcome follows:

> Mr. President, I would like to thank you very much for the warmth of your welcome to my wife and myself and to the Foreign Secretary and Mrs. Butler, and to say how much we are looking forward to our exchange of views with you.
>
> We are engaged, as you have so clearly and graphically put it the other day, in the pursuits of peace, and much of our talks will undoubtedly be concerned with how we can improve the situation in a difficult and dangerous world, and we in Britain are particularly conscious now of its difficulties and its dangers because we are engaged, as you know, far afield in trying to help to maintain stability and order which is, I know, your concern, too, as a great power.
>
> Since, as you say, this is one of a sequence of meetings which have always been of great benefit to our own countries, I would like you to know that my firm desire is to keep as close as we can to the United States as partners and as allies and as two countries upon which the peace of the world may well depend.
>
> So, Sir, I would like once more to thank you. We are going to enjoy ourselves in Washington, and we brought the sun with us and that may be a good omen.
>
> I would once more only say that anything that I can do in our talks and my Government can do to help to keep the relations between Britain and the United States close and harmonious will be done with the full support of all of our countrymen.
>
> Thank you very much.

LET US SUMMARIZE

We have discussed specific peculiarities of several varying speech types: the impromptu speech, the announcement, the speech to introduce a speaker, the nomination speech, the after-dinner speech; along with speeches of presentation and acceptance, welcome speeches, and response to speeches of welcome. There is a type of speech for nearly every special occasion, and realistically we could not consider all of them in this chapter. When making any speech for a special occasion, remember three governing principles:

1. Know the demands of the occasion.
2. Employ sound speaking fundamentals.
3. Adapt the speech to the occasion.

Suggested Exercise A

Arrange to have a series of impromptu talks in your class. The instructor may ask you to suggest either some topics or areas of general knowledge from which topics can be drawn.

Suggested Exercise B

Prepare a brief announcement about a subject of special importance to you—a dance to be held soon, an interesting television program, motion picture, or book, a cake sale, formation of a new club, or an athletic or speech contest, and so forth.

Suggested Exercise C

Arrange to introduce a speaker in your class during the next series of assigned speeches.

Suggested Exercise D

Divide the class into two equal sections. One section is to make speeches of presentation for hypothetical (but serious) occasions, and the other section is to respond with speeches of acceptance.

Suggested Exercise E

Arrange to have a friend visit your class. Receive him with a short welcoming speech.

Suggested Exercise F

Attend an event where one of the speeches discussed in this chapter is likely to be made. Analyze the effectiveness of the speech.
1.   Did the speaker employ sound speaking fundamentals? Explain.
2.   Did he adapt to the occasion? Explain.

Suggested Exercise G

Attend the next assembly held to nominate student body officers. If you were a speech consultant for the speakers, what "do's" and "don'ts" would you offer them for future consideration?

CHAPTER FOURTEEN

Reading Aloud

"I plead for more reading aloud. It is a friendly, quiet and thoroughly refreshing thing to do. It makes us participants rather than spectators. Instead of sitting by to let the professionals amuse or enlighten us, *we* can get into the act, make contact with new ideas, exercise our imaginations."[1] These are the words of the late Charles Laughton, who was a recognized authority on the art of reading aloud.

Oral reading is an art—and a practical skill. The experience it offers can help one to become not only a better reader but also a better speaker. Have you ever noted how much actual reading is necessary in some types of speechmaking? Many speeches call for the use of quoted material such as poetry, statistics, and prose passages, in great quantity. For accuracy and convenience, speakers usually read material of this kind.

Perhaps you have also observed that speakers frequently do not handle their quoted content to full advantage. If the material used were put to full advantage, there would always be evidence of careful preparation. We would not hear, as we do occasionally, the distracting contrast between the delivery of what is read and what is presented extemporaneously. Also, we as listeners would not be disturbed by lack of eye contact, monotony, mispronunciations, and embarrassing stumblings. The speaker who does not attend to this phase of his job is all too common. As a result of neglecting to prepare those portions of the speech that are to be read, he limits his total effectiveness.

OPPORTUNITIES TO READ ALOUD

In addition to the many opportunities one has to apply reading ability in typical speaking situations, there are scores of practical and artistic uses not associated with speechmaking as such. Consider, for

[1] Charles Laughton, *This Week Magazine,* November 19, 1950.

instance, the variety of reading experiences that one person may have during one week. On Monday morning, let us say, Frank read a newspaper article to his family at breakfast. Later in the morning at work, he read a safety bulletin to his staff, and at 3 P.M. that afternoon, his superintendent listened to his oral presentation of a written report on plant operations. Before his two children went to bed that night, he amused them with a reading from *Winnie-the-Pooh*. He read some new regulations to his platoon at the Naval Reserve meeting on Tuesday night. Wednesday evening, as secretary of the Men's Club, he reviewed the minutes of the last meeting. Late Thursday afternoon, Frank was called upon to read a policy statement to new employees at the plant. Friday night he came upon a familiar Robert Frost poem, and he read it to his wife; he knew that she would enjoy it. On Saturday, the Cub Scouts were delighted with his rendition of a *Huck Finn* episode. The next morning he read to his Sunday School class.

Frank's experiences are hypothetical, but they are not unusual. They are typical of people's experiences everywhere, for all of us have opportunities to read aloud.

What types of reading aloud will be required of you in your future life? Are you a good oral reader? Consider these questions as you study this chapter.

THE READER'S ROLE

Your reading assignments in this class are designed to help you gain increased reading skill and develop an appreciation for the art. Your role, in some ways, will be similar to your role as a speechmaker. The two activities overlap at points: (1) both original speaking and oral reading require thoughtful subject matter selection; (2) both demand that you determine and analyze a purpose or central idea; (3) attention to organization is a key factor in both activities; (4) the use of introductions and transitions can apply to both; (5) the same instruments of delivery are utilized in each case, of course, and (6) both require ample practice before actual presentation.

The major difference between the roles of the original speaker and the oral reader is in content. In the first you develop your own thoughts and feelings, while in the second you *interpret* the thoughts and feelings of someone else. As a speechmaker, you speak for yourself; as a reader, you speak for the author who wrote what you are reading. You interpret what he has written and attempt to convey the content of his work to your listeners. We might think of the oral interpreter as a translator who deciphers the alphabetical symbols on a printed page and relays the message to his listeners. From his familiarity with the author's work, he is able to bring out the ideas and feelings contained therein.

The interpreter has three instruments at his command to use in presenting his reading: personality, voice, and body. The voice is the primary means by which the essence of a selection is communicated. Heavy reliance upon only one instrument limits the reader, yet reading is a limited speech form. It is quite different from impersonation, or acting on the stage. No costumes, properties, or make-up are employed in true oral interpretation. It is not acting. It is a unique type of activity. You can imagine how ridiculous it would be for a left fielder in a baseball game to play in a football uniform or for a couple to attempt dancing a tango when the band plays a waltz. Those things are not done—except possibly in humorous stunts. Baseball is baseball, and waltzing is waltzing. The same holds true for reading aloud. Reading is reading. It is not acting or dancing, and the reader is himself, not a character in a play or skit.

In Chapter Eight we discussed the vocal characteristics: pitch, loudness, duration, and quality. It is—to a great degree—in the variation of these four factors that the reader is able to interpret his selected material for his audience. Essentially, here is what happens: The reader studies his selection thoroughly in order to master the meaning and grasp the feeling. With this knowledge and understanding of the material, he reads it aloud. While reading, the pitch, loudness, duration, and quality of his voice vary as his mind and "heart" respond to the content of the selection. Please note, however, that he does not consciously vary his pitch in certain places or add extra loudness in other places. He allows his knowledge of and inward feelings for the material to inspire the appropriate vocal variation. Thus the oral interpreter avoids a mechanical recital of the author's words; he is assured that his expression will be natural and true, a salutary response to the author's work.

The reader's bodily actions, too, must stem from an inner relationship with the material. If the content is humorous, the interpreter will surely be moved to smile; on the other hand, a sad story will provoke a facial response which reflects the mood. The expressions, head movements, and gestures that *naturally* accompany faithful interpretations of literature can help the audience to understand the selection.

Empathy

The reader's responses, based on his feelings for and understanding of the material, will lead him to suggest comparable responses in his listeners. The audience will tend to *empathize* with the material in accordance with his treatment of it and will be moved to respond in kind to his visual, verbal, and vocal expressions. "Feeling into" the reader's interpretation of a selection—showing empathy—the listeners will mirror his frown, muscular tension, acceleration of tempo, relaxed mood, somber attitude, and so forth—either outwardly or inwardly. A common example of empathy in action is the yawn that occurs when one sees someone else yawning. In a real sense, the reader gets from his audience what he asks for. As he practices, he should be aware of the cues that his interpretation suggests, capitalizing on those designed to promote appropriate empathy, while eliminating the irrelevant or distracting cues.

Esthetic Distance

Though working to promote a real empathic response from his listeners, the reader must not overstep the bounds of the art. He must remember that his purpose is not to effect a complete feeling into his presentation or a full removal of the realities of the occasion. As a listener participates with him and the selection, the listener may get "caught up" in the material, but if he fully loses himself in it, art suffers. Ideally, the listener, while empathizing, participates "at some distance"; the extent depending on the reader's design of the moment. This is called maintaining esthetic distance. Control of that distance is another of the problems to be studied and solved by the reader.

In summary, at this point we should say that the role of the oral reader is to communicate the author's ideas and emotions to his listeners. He must do it sincerely and naturally by allowing his personality, voice, and body to reveal what he feels and what he has learned about the selection.

In other words, his job is to act as the author's faithful representative and to do so within the limitations of the specialized activity.

FINDING AN APPROPRIATE SELECTION

Not every piece of literature can be read aloud well, and material that may be appropriate for one person may not be appropriate for you. In situations where you have a choice of materials, you should choose a selection because you *want* to read it and not because you feel duty bound to tackle a work that is accepted as great writing. If, for example, neither the poetry of T. S. Eliot nor the prose of O. Henry appeals to you, try the work of another author. In literature there are selections for everyone; make a search, and you will find some that are suitable to your needs. Here are specific suggestions to assist you in making your decision.

1. Choose material that you appreciate and desire to study.
2. Choose material that you can cause your audience to appreciate and understand.

3. Choose material that has inherent human appeal—warmth, feeling, and interesting development.
4. Choose material that is worthy of being read aloud, material which makes you feel that it ought to be passed on to others.

PROSE AND POETRY

Most of the reading that you have done since acquiring that skill is written in prose form. Newspaper and magazine articles, short stories, novels, and textbooks are written in prose form. But what about poetry? Have you avoided poetry? Are you poetry shy? Has fear caused you to miss one of the most pleasurable human experiences? If you have a genuine desire to increase your appreciation of poetry, you can do it. Many students quite like yourself have gained their first respect for poetry by reading it aloud. Others who were once quietly tolerant of such literature are now ardent enthusiasts.

How would you define poetry? Arriving at a succinct and acceptable definition is one of the most perplexing problems in the study of literature. Even such a poet as Edwin Arlington Robinson is unable to offer an exact definition. He says: "Poetry is a language that tells us, through a more or less emotional reaction, something that cannot be said."

Though poetry may defy definition, it can be understood better when compared to prose. Prose does not have a rhyme scheme or obvious meter. Prose is set up in paragraph units while poetry is organized in stanzas. Finally, it has been said that while some prose has a degree of poetic appeal, it speaks mainly to our heads. Poetry speaks "to our heads through ideas, to our hearts through feelings, to our ears through music, to our eyes through pictures, and to our bodies through rhythm." With such a diverse appeal, it is no wonder that poetry has been recognized as the highest form of literary expression.

Let us now examine several types of prose and poetry which are suited particularly to our purpose of studying oral reading. Though the classifications may overlap in some cases, certain essential distinctions justify our studying them separately. As an oral interpreter, you should have some experience in reading each of these types.

Narrative Literature

Narrative literature tells a story. If it is poetry, it is a story in verse form. Here are some examples:

RICHARD CORY

Whenever Richard Cory went down town,
We people on the pavement looked at him:

He was a gentleman from sole to crown,
Clean favored, and imperially slim.

And he was always quietly arrayed,
And he was always human when he talked;
But still he fluttered pulses when he said,
"Good morning," and he glittered when he walked.

And he was rich—yes, richer than a king—
And admirably schooled in every grace:
In fine, we thought that he was every thing
To make us wish that we were in his place.

So on we worked, and waited for the light,
And went without the meat, and cursed the bread;
And Richard Cory, one calm summer night,
Went home and put a bullet through his head.

> "Richard Cory" is reprinted with the
> permission of Charles Scribner's Sons
> from *The Children of the Night* by
> Edwin Arlington Robinson

THE BALLAD OF THE OYSTERMAN

It was a tall young oysterman lived by the riverside,
His shop was just upon the bank, his boat was on the tide;
The daughter of a fisherman, that was so straight and slim,
Lived over on the other bank, right opposite to him.

It was the pensive oysterman that saw a lovely maid,
Upon a moonlight evening, a-sitting in the shade;
He saw her wave a handkerchief, as much as if to say,
"I'm wide awake, young oysterman, and all the folks away."

Then up arose the oysterman, and to himself said he,
"I guess I'll leave the skiff at home, for fear that folks should see;
I read it in the story book, that, for to kiss his dear,
Leander swam the Hellespont—and I will swim this here."

And he has leaped into the waves, and crossed the shining stream,
And he has clambered up the bank, all in the moonlight gleam;
Oh, there are kisses sweet as dew, and words as soft as rain—
But they have heard her father's steps, and in he leaps again!

Out spoke the ancient fisherman: "Oh, what was that, my daughter?"
" 'Twas nothing but a pebble, sir, I threw into the water."

"And what is that, pray tell me, love, that paddles off so fast?"
"It's nothing but a porpoise, sir, that's been a-swimming past."

Out spoke the ancient fisherman: "Now bring me my harpoon!
I'll get into my fishing boat, and fix the fellow soon."
Down fell the pretty innocent, as falls a snow-white lamb;
Her hair drooped round her pallid cheeks, like seaweed on a clam.

Alas for those two loving ones! she waked not from her swound,
And he was taken with the cramp, and in the waves was drowned;
But Fate has metamorphosed them, in pity of their woe,
And now they keep an oyster shop for mermaids down below.

—Oliver Wendell Holmes

"THERE SHE BLOWS!"

"There she blows!—there she blows! A hump like a snow-hill! It is Moby Dick!"

Fired by the cry which seemed simultaneously taken up by the three lookouts, the men on deck rushed to the rigging to behold the famous whale they had so long been pursuing. Ahab had now gained his final perch, some feet above the other lookouts, Tashtego standing just beneath him on the cap of the top-gallant-mast, so that the Indian's head was almost on a level with Ahab's heel. From this height the whale was now seen some mile or so ahead, at every roll of the sea revealing his high sparkling hump, and regularly jetting his silent spout into the air. To the credulous mariners it seemed the same silent spout they had so long ago beheld in the moonlit Atlantic and Indian Oceans.

"And did none of ye see it before?" cried Ahab, hailing the perched men all around him.

"I saw him almost that same instant, sir, that Captain Ahab did, and I cried out," said Tashtego.

"Not the same instant; not the same—no, the doubloon is mine. Fate reserved the doubloon for me. *I* only; none of ye could have raised the White Whale first. There she blows!—there she blows! There again!—there again!" he cried, in a long-drawn, lingering, methodic tone, attuned to the gradual prolongings of the whale's visible jets. "He's going to sound! In stun'-sails! Down top-gallant-sails! Stand by three boats. Mr. Starbuck, remember, stay on board, and keep the ship. Helm there! Luff, luff a point! So; steady, man, steady! There go flukes! No, no; only black water! All ready the boats there? Stand by, stand by! Lower me, Mr. Starbuck; lower, lower,—quick, quicker!" and he slid through the air to the deck.

"He is heading straight to leeward, sir," cried Stubb; "right away from us; cannot have seen the ship yet."

"Be dumb, man! Stand by the braces! Hard down the helm!—brace up! Shiver her! So; well that! Boats, boats!"

Soon all the boats but Starbuck's were dropped; all the boat-sails set —all the paddles plying; with rippling swiftness, shooting to leeward; and Ahab heading the onset. A pale, death-glimmer lit up Fedallah's sunken eyes; a hideous motion gnawed his mouth.

—Herman Melville, from *Moby Dick*

Folklore and Dialect

Our second category, folklore and dialect literature, includes stories, legends, and songs that tell the customs, beliefs, and experiences of distinctive individuals or groups. Such material is suggested for reading aloud because its frankness, openness, and spontaneity should inspire the reader to respond in kind—to let go.

Then, too, there is something about reading a folk tale or dialect selection that gives one a feeling of respect for the people whom the piece represents. One learns that all men have like feelings, even though certain of their cultural, language, or physical features may differ. One learns that we are all human. As Gertrude E. Johnson said: "Dialect is the language of the heart and of the emotions, and we react naturally to its appeal." [2] Such an appeal cannot be ignored as an aid in the improvement of oral reading and as a delight to listeners. The following selections are representative.

MIA CARLOTTA

Giuseppe, da barber, ees greata for "mash,"
He gotta da bigga, da blacka mustache,
Good clo'es an' good styla an' playnta good cash.

W'enevra Giuseppe ees walk on da street,
Da people dey talka, "How nobby! how neat!
How softa da hands, how smalla da feet."

He raisa hees hat an' he shaka hees curls,
An' smila weeth teetha so shiny like pearls;
O! many da heart of da seelly young girls
            He gotta
      Yes playnta he gotta—
          But notta
          Carlotta!

[2] *Studies in the Art of Interpretation* (New York, 1940).

Giuseppe, da barber, he maka da eye,
An' lika da steam engine puffa an' sigh,
For catcha Carlotta w'en she ees go by.

Carlotta she walks weeth nose in da air,
An' look through Giuseppe weeth far-away stare,
As eef she no sees dere ees som'body dere.

Giuseppe, da barber, he gotta da cash,
He gotta da clo'es an' da bigga mustache,
He gotta da seelly young girls for da "mash,"
                    But notta—
            You bat my life, notta—
                Carlotta.
                I gotta!

DAN'L

Well, this-yer Smiley had rat-tarriers, and chicken cocks, and tom-cats, and all them kind of things, till you couldn't rest, and you couldn't fetch nothing for him to bet on but he'd match you. He ketched a frog one day, and took him home, and said he cal'klated to edercate him; and so he never done nothing for three months but set in his back yard and learn that frog to jump. And you bet he *did* learn him, too. He'd give him a little punch behind, and the next minute you'd see that frog whirling in the air like a doughnut—see him turn one summerset, or may be a couple, if he got a good start, and come down flat-footed and all right, like a cat. He got him up so in the matter of catching flies, and kept him in practice so constant, that he'd nail a fly every time as far as he could see him. Smiley said all a frog wanted was education, and he could do most anything—and I believe him. Why, I've seen him set Dan'l Webster down here on this floor—Dan'l Webster was the name of the frog—and sing out, 'Flies, Dan'l, flies!' and quicker'n you could wink, he'd spring straight up, and snake a fly off'n the counter there, and flop down on the floor again as solid as a gob of mud, and fall to scratching the side of his head with his hind foot as indifferent as if he hadn't no idea he'd been doin' any more'n any frog might do. You never see a frog so modest and straight-for'ard as he was, for all he was so gifted. And when it come to fair and square jumping on a dead level, he could get over more ground at one straddle than any animal of his breed you ever see. Jumping on a dead level was his strong suit, you understand; and when it come to that, Smiley would ante up money on him as long as he had a red. Smiley was monstrous proud of his frog, and well he might be, for fellers that had traveled and been everywhere, all said he laid over any frog that ever *they* see.

—Samuel Clemens, from *The Celebrated Jumping Frog of Calaveras County*

DAVY CROCKETT, SPEECHMAKER

I made many apologies and tried to get off, for I knowed I had a man to run against who could speak prime, and I knowed too that I wa'n't able to shuffle and cut with him. He was there, and knowing my ignorance as well as I did myself, he also urged me to make a speech. The truth is, he thought my being a candidate was a mere matter of sport, and didn't think for a moment that he was in any danger from an ignorant backwoods bear hunter. But I found I couldn't get off, and so I determined just to go ahead, and leave it to chance what I should say. I got up and told the people I reckoned they knowed what I come for, but if not, I could tell them. I had come for their votes, and if they didn't watch mighty close, I'd get them too. But the worst of all was, that I couldn't tell them anything about government. I tried to speak about something, and I cared very little what, until I choked up as bad as if my mouth had been jammed and crammed chock-full of dry mush. There the people stood, listening all the while, with their eyes, mouths, and ears all open to catch every word I would speak.

At last I told them I was like a fellow I had heard of not long before. He was beating on the head of an empty barrel near the roadside when a traveler who was passing along asked him what he was doing that for. The fellow replied that there was some cider in that barrel a few days before and he was trying to see if there was any then, but if there was, he couldn't get at it. I told them that there had been a little bit of speech in me awhile ago, but I believed I couldn't get it out. They all roared out in a mighty laugh and I told some other anecdotes, equally amusing to them; and believing I had them in a first-rate way, I quit and got down, thanking the people for their attention. But I took care to remark that I was dry as a powder horn and that I thought it was time for us to wet our whistles a little; and so I put off to the liquor stand and was followed by the greater part of the crowd.

I felt certain this was necessary, for I knowed my competitor could open government matters to them as easy as he pleased. He had, however, mighty few left to hear him as I continued with the crowd, now and then taking a horn and telling good-humored stories till he was done speaking. I found I was good for the votes at the hunt, and when we broke up, I went on to the town of Vernon, which was the same they wanted me to move. Here they pressed me again on the subject, and I found I could get either party by agreeing with them. But I told them I didn't know whether it would be right or not, and so couldn't promise either way.

Their court commenced on the next Monday, as the barbecue was on a Saturday, and the candidates for governor and for Congress as well as my competitor and myself all attended.

The thought of having to make a speech made my knees feel mighty weak and set my heart to fluttering almost as bad as my first love scrape with the Quaker's niece. But as good luck would have it, these big candidates spoke nearly all day, and when they quit, the people were worn out with fatigue, which afforded me a good apology for not discussing the government. But I listened mighty close to them, and was learning pretty fast about political matters. When they were all done, I got up and told some laughable story and quit. I found I was safe in those parts, and so I went home and didn't go back again till after the election was over. But to cut this matter, short, I was elected, doubling my competitor and nine votes over.

A short time after this, I was in Pulaski, where I met with Colonel Polk, now a member of Congress from Tennessee. He was at that time a member elected to the Legislature as well as myself; and in a large company he said to me, "Well, Colonel, I suppose we shall have a radical change of the judiciary at the next session of the Legislature." "Very likely, sir," says I, and I put out quicker, for I was a afraid some one would ask me what the judiciary was; and if I knowed I wish I may be shot. I don't indeed believe I had ever before heard that there was any such thing in all nature, but still I was not willing that the people there should know how ignorant I was of it.

When the time for meeting of the Legislature arrived, I went on, and before I had been there long, I could have told what the judiciary was, and what the government was too; and many other things that I had known nothing about before.

> —David Crockett, from *A Narrative of
> the Life of David Crockett*

THE SOCIETY UPON THE STANISLAUS

I reside at Table Mountain, and my name is Truthful James;
I am not up to small deceit or any sinful games;

And I'll tell in simple language what I know about the row
That broke up our Society upon the Stanislow.

But first I would remark, that it is not a proper plan
For any scientific gent to whale his fellow-man,
And, if a member don't agree with his peculiar whim,
To lay for that same member for to "put a head" on him.

Now nothing could be finer or more beautiful to see
Than the first six months' proceedings of that same Society,
Till Brown of Calaveras brought a lot of fossil bones
That he found within a tunnel near the tenement of Jones.

Then Brown he read a paper, and he reconstructed there,
From those same bones, an animal that was extremely rare;
And Jones then asked the Chair for a suspension of the rules,
Till he could prove that those same bones was one of his lost mules.

Then Brown he smiled a bitter smile, and said he was at fault.
It seemed he had been trespassing on Jones's family vault;
He was a most sarcastic man, this quiet Mr. Brown,
And on several occasions he had cleaned out the town.

Now I hold it is not decent for a scientific gent
To say another is an ass,—at least, to all intent;
Nor should the individual who happens to be meant
Reply by heaving rocks at him, to any great extent.

Then Abner Dean of Angel's raised a point of order, when
A chunk of old red sandstone took him in the abdomen,
And he smiled a kind of sickly smile, and curled up on the floor,
And the subsequent proceedings interested him no more.

For, in less time than I write it, every member did engage
In a warfare with the remnants of a palaeozoic age;
And the way they heaved those fossils in their anger was a sin,
Till the skull of an old mammoth caved the head of Thompson in.

And this is all I have to say of these improper games,
For I live at Table Mountain, and my name is Truthful James;
And I've told in simple language what I know about the row
That broke up our Society upon the Stanislow.

—Bret Harte

Children's Literature

Children's literature is included here not only because most people have occasion to read to youngsters but also because this type of material facilitates the development of oral reading skills. There is feeling and life in a good children's selection, and the reader is impelled to respond accordingly.

THE ELEPHANT'S CHILD

" 'Scuse me," said the Elephant's Child most politely, "but do you happen to have seen a Crocodile in these promiscuous parts?"

Then the Crocodile winked the other eye, and lifted half his tail out of the mud; and the Elephant's Child stepped back most politely, because he did not wish to be spanked again.

"Come hither, Little One," said the Crocodile. "Why do you ask such things?"

" 'Scuse me," said the Elephant's Child most politely, "but my father has spanked me, my mother has spanked me, not to mention my tall aunt, the Ostrich, and my tall uncle, the Giraffe, who can kick ever so hard, as well as my broad aunt, the Hippopotamus, and my hairy uncle, the Baboon, *and* including the Bi-Coloured-Python-Rock-Snake, with the scalesome, flailsome tail, just up the bank, who spanks harder than any of them; and *so* if it's quite all the same to you, I don't want to be spanked any more."

"Come hither, Little One," said the Crocodile, "for I am the Crocodile," and he wept crocodile-tears to show it was quite true.

Then the Elephant's Child grew all breathless, and panted, and kneeled down on the bank and said, "You are the very person I have been looking for all these long days. Will you please tell me what you have for dinner?"

"Come hither, Little One," said the Crocodile, "and I'll whisper."

Then the Elephant's Child put his head down close to the Crocodile's musky, tusky mouth, and the Crocodile caught him by his little nose, which up to that very week, day, hour, and minute, had been no bigger than a boot, though much more useful.

"I think," said the Crocodile—and he said it between his teeth, like this—"I think to-day I will begin with Elephant's Child!"

—Rudyard Kipling, from *Just So Stories*

JIM HAWKINS FINDS BEN GUNN

From the side of the hill, which was here steep and stony, a spout of gravel was dislodged, and fell rattling and bounding through the trees.

My eyes turned instinctively in that direction, and I saw a figure leap with great rapidity behind the trunk of a pine. What it was, whether bear or man or monkey, I could in nowise tell. It seemed dark and shaggy; more I knew not. But the terror of this new apparition brought me to a stand.

I was now, it seemed, cut off upon both sides; behind me the murderers, before me this lurking nondescript. And immediately I began to prefer the dangers that I knew to those I knew not. Silver himself appeared less terrible in contrast with this creature of the woods, and I turned on my heel, and, looking sharply behind me over my shoulder, began to retrace my steps in the direction of the boats.

Instantly the figure reappeared, and, making a wide circuit, began to head me off. I was tired, at any rate; but had I been as fresh as when I rose, I could see it was in vain for me to contend in speed with such an adversary. From trunk to trunk the creature flitted like a deer, running manlike on two legs, but unlike any man that I had ever seen, stooping almost double as it ran. Yet a man it was, I could no longer be in doubt about that.

I began to recall what I had heard of cannibals. I was within an ace of calling for help. But the mere fact that he was a man, however wild, had somewhat reassured me, and my fear of Silver began to revive in proportion. I stood still, therefore, and cast about for some method of escape; and as I was so thinking, the recollection of my pistol flashed into my mind. As soon as I remembered I was not defenseless, courage glowed again in my heart; and I set my face resolutely for this man of the island, and walked briskly toward him.

He was concealed by this time behind another tree trunk; but he must have been watching me closely, for as soon as I began to move in his direction he reappeared and took a step to meet me. Then he hesitated, drew back, came forward again, and at last, to my wonder and confusion, threw himself on his knees and held out his clasped hands in supplication.

At that I once more stopped.

"Who are you?" I asked.

"Ben Gunn," he answered, . . .

—Robert Louis Stevenson, from *Treasure Island*

WYNKEN, BLYNKEN, AND NOD

Wynken, Blynken, and Nod one night
   Sailed off in a wooden shoe,—
Sailed on a river of crystal light
   Into a sea of dew.

"Where are you going, and what do you wish?"
   The old moon asked the three.
"We have come to fish for the herring fish
   That live in this beautiful sea;
Nets of silver and gold have we!"
         Said Wynken,
         Blynken,
         And Nod.

The old moon laughed and sang a song,
   As they rocked in the wooden shoe;
And the wind that sped them all night long
   Ruffled the waves of dew.
The little stars were the herring fish
   That lived in that beautiful sea—
"Now cast your nets wherever you wish,—
   Never afeard are we!"
So cried the stars to the fishermen three,
         Wynken,
         Blynken,
         And Nod.

All night long their nets they threw
   To the stars in the twinkling foam,—
Then down from the skies came the wooden shoe,
   Bringing the fishermen home:
'Twas all so pretty a sail, it seemed
   As if it could not be;
And some folk thought 'twas a dream they'd dreamed
   Of sailing that beautiful sea;
   But I shall name you the fishermen three:
         Wynken,
         Blynken,
         And Nod.

Wynken and Blynken are two little eyes,
   And Nod is a little head,
And the wooden shoe that sailed the skies
   Is a wee one's trundle-bed;
So shut your eyes while Mother sings
   Of wonderful sights that be,
And you shall see the beautiful things
      As you rock in the misty sea
      Where the old shoe rocked the fishermen three:—

Wynken,
Blynken,
And Nod.

—Eugene Field

Lyric Poetry

Lyric poetry differs from narrative poetry in that it reveals feelings and moods more than it tells a story. Such poetry gives us the collected impressions of the author on certain aspects of life; it is an expression of the poet's mood or viewpoint and often corresponds to our own unexpressed emotions. In reading lyric poems, particular emphasis should be placed upon the latent beauty, music, and color in the poem.

DELIGHT IN DISORDER

A sweet disorder in the dress
Kindles in clothes a wantonness.
A lawn about the shoulders thrown
Into a fine distraction;
An erring lace, which here and there
Enthralls the crimson stomacher;
A cuff neglectful, and thereby
Ribbons to flow confusedly;
A winning wave, deserving note,
In the tempestuous petticoat;
A careless shoestring, in whose tie
I see wild civility;
Do more bewitch me than when art
Is too precise in every part.

—Robert Herrick

THE WORLD IS TOO MUCH WITH US; LATE AND SOON

The world is too much with us; late and soon,
Getting and spending, we lay waste our powers:
Little we see in Nature that is ours;
We have given our hearts away, a sordid boon!
The Sea that bares her bosom to the moon;
The winds that will be howling at all hours,
And are up-gathered now like sleeping flowers;
For this, for everything, we are out of tune;
It moves us not.—Great God! I'd rather be
A Pagan suckled in a creed outworn;

So might I, standing on this pleasant lea,
Have glimpses that would make me less forlorn;
Have sight of Proteus rising from the sea;
Or hear old Triton blow his wreathed horn.

—William Wordsworth

THE BOOK OF WISDOM

I met a seer,
He held a book in his hands,
The book of wisdom.
"Sir," I addressed him,
"Let me read."
"Child—" he began.
"Sir," I said,
"Think not that I am a child,
For already I know much
Of that which you hold;
Aye, much."

He smiled.
Then he opened the book
And held it before me.
Strange that I should have grown so suddenly blind.

—"The Book of Wisdom" from *Poems*
by Stephen Crane. Reprinted by
permission of Random House, Inc.

TO HIS COY MISTRESS

Had we but world enough, and time,
This coyness, Lady, were no crime.
We would sit down and think which way
To walk and pass our long love's day.
Thou by the Indian Ganges' side
Shouldst rubies find; I by the tide
Of Humber would complain. I would
Love you ten years before the Flood,
And you should, if you please, refuse
Till the conversion of the Jews.
My vegetable love should grow
Vaster than empires, and more slow;
An hundred years should go to praise

Thine eyes and on thy forehead gaze;
Two hundred to adore each breast,
But thirty thousand to the rest;
An age at least to every part,
And the last age should show your heart.
For, Lady, you deserve this state,
Nor would I love at lower rate.

   But at my back I always hear
Time's winged chariot hurrying near;
And yonder all before us lie
Deserts of vast eternity.
Thy beauty shall no more be found,
Nor, in thy marble vault, shall sound
My echoing song; then worms shall try
That long preserved virginity,
And into ashes all my lust:
The grave's a fine and private place,
But none, I think, do there embrace.

   Now therefore, while the youthful hue
Sits on thy skin like morning dew
And while thy willing soul transpires
At every pore with instant fires,
Now let us sport us while we may,
And now, like amorous birds of prey,
Rather at once our time devour
Than languish in his slow-chapt power.
Let us roll all our strength and all
Our sweetness up into one ball,
And tear our pleasures with rough strife
Through the iron gates of life:
Thus, though we cannot make our sun
Stand still, yet we will make him run.

—Andrew Marvell

SUMMER AND WINTER

It was a bright and cheerful afternoon,
Towards the end of the sunny month of June,
When the north wind congregates in crowds
The floating mountains of the silver clouds
From the horizon—and the stainless sky
Opens beyond them like eternity.
All things rejoice beneath the sun; the weeds,

The river, and the corn-fields, and the reeds;
The willow leaves that glance in the light breeze,
And the firm foliage of the larger trees.

It was a winter such as when birds die
In the deep forests; and the fishes lie
Stiffened in the translucent ice, which makes
Even the mud and slime of warm lakes
A wrinkled clod as hard as brick; and when,
Among their children, comfortable men
Gather about great fires, and yet feel cold:
Alas, then, for the homeless beggar old!

—Percy Bysshe Shelley

Literature of High Resolve

Literature of high resolve, though it may overlap with other types, can be considered individually here. Into this category we put public addresses, editorials, biblical selections, inspirational poems, serious essays, and patriotic and biographical selections that reflect a spirit of moral or ethical values.

LETTER TO MRS. BIXBY

Dear Madam:

I have been shown in the files of the War Department a statement of the Adjutant General of Massachusetts that you are the mother of five sons who have died gloriously on the field of battle. I feel how weak and fruitless must be any words of mine which should attempt to beguile you from the grief of a loss so overwhelming. But I cannot refrain from tendering to you the consolation that may be found in the thanks of the Republic they died to save. I pray that our Heavenly Father may assuage the anguish of your bereavement and leave you only the cherished memory of the loved and lost and the solemn pride that must be yours to have laid so costly a sacrifice upon the altar of freedom.

Yours very sincerely and respectfully,
Abraham Lincoln

SIMPLIFY, SIMPLIFY

I was seated by the shore of a small pond, about a mile and a half south of the village of Concord and somewhat higher than it, in the midst of an extensive wood between that town and Lincoln, and about two miles south of that our only field known to fame, Concord Battle Grounds; but I was so low in the woods that the opposite shore, half a mile off, like the rest, covered with wood, was my most distant horizon. For the first week, whenever I looked out on the pond it impressed me like a tarn high up on the side of a mountain, its bottom far above the surface of other lakes, and, as the sun arose, I saw it throwing off its nightly clothing of mist, and here and there, by degrees, its soft ripples or its smooth reflecting surface was revealed, while the mists, like ghosts, were stealthily, withdrawing in every direction into the woods, as at the breaking up of some nocturnal conventicle. The very dew seemed to hang upon the trees later into the day than usual, as on the sides of mountains.

.   .   .

I went to the woods because I wished to live deliberately, to front only the essential facts of life, and see if I could not learn what it had to teach, and not, when I came to die, discover that I had not lived. I did not wish to live what was not life, living is so dear; nor did I wish to practice resignation, unless it was quite necessary. I wanted to live deep and suck out all the marrow of life, to live so sturdily and Spartanlike as to put to rout all that was not life, to cut a broad swath and shave close, to drive life into a corner, and reduce it to its lowest terms, and, if it proved to be mean, why then to get the whole and genuine meanness of it, and publish its meanness to the world; or if it were sublime, to know it by experience, and be able to give a true account of it in my next excursion. For most men, it appears to me, are in a strange uncertainty about it, whether it is of the devil or of God, and have *somewhat hastily* concluded that it is the chief end of man here to "glorify God and enjoy him forever."

Still we live meanly, like ants; though the fable tells us that we were long ago changed into men; like pygmies we fight with cranes; it is error upon error, and clout upon clout, and our best virtue has for its occasion a superfluous and evitable wretchedness. Our life is frittered away by detail. An honest man has hardly need to count more than his ten fingers, or in extreme cases he may add his ten toes, and lump the rest. Simplicity, simplicity, simplicity! I say, let your affairs be as two or three, and not a hundred or a thousand; instead of a million count half a dozen, and keep your accounts on your thumb-nail. In the midst of this chopping sea of civilized life, such are the clouds and storms and quicksands and thousand-and-one items to be allowed for, that a man has to live, if he would not founder and go to the bottom and not make his port at all, by dead reckoning, and he must be a great calculator indeed who succeeds. Simplify, simplify.

—from Henry David Thoreau, *Walden*

THE SPIRIT OF LIBERTY

We have gathered here to affirm a faith, a faith in a common purpose, a common conviction, a common devotion. Some of us have chosen America as the land of our adoption; the rest have come from those who did the same. For this reason we have some right to consider ourselves a picked group, a group of those who had the courage to break from the past and brave the dangers and the loneliness of a strange land. What was the object that nerved us, or those who went before us, to this choice? We sought liberty: freedom from oppression, freedom from want, freedom to ourselves. This we then sought; this we now believe that we are by way of winning. What do we mean when we say that first of all we seek liberty? I often wonder whether we do not rest our hopes too much upon constitutions, upon laws and upon courts. These are false hopes, believe me, these are false hopes. Liberty lies in the hearts of men and women; when it dies there, no constitution, no law, no court can save it; no constitution, no law, no court can even do much to help it. While it lies there, it needs no constitution, no law, no court to save it. And what is this liberty which must lie in the hearts of men and women? It is not the ruthless, the unbridled will; it is not freedom to do as one likes. That is the denial of liberty, and leads straight to its overthrow. A society in which men recognize no check upon their freedom, soon becomes a society where freedom is the possession of only a savage few; as we have learned to our sorrow.

What then is the spirit of liberty? I cannot define it; I can only tell you my own faith. The spirit of liberty is the spirit which is not too sure that it is right; the spirit of liberty is the spirit which seeks to understand the minds of other men and women; the spirit of liberty is the spirit which weighs their interests alongside its own without bias; the spirit of liberty remembers that not even a sparrow falls to earth unheeded; the spirit of liberty is the spirit of Him who, near two thousand years ago, taught mankind that lesson it has never learned, but has never quite forgotten: that there may be a kingdom where the least shall be heard and considered side by side with the greatest. And now in that spirit, that spirit of an America which has never been, and which may never be; nay which never will be, except as the conscience and the courage of Americans create it; yet in the spirit of that America which lies hidden in some form in the aspirations of us all; in the spirit of that America for which our young men are at this moment fighting and dying; in the spirit of liberty and of America I ask you to rise and with me to pledge faith in the glorious destiny of our beloved country.

I pledge allegiance to the flag of the United States of America and to the Republic for which it stands, one nation indivisible, with liberty and justice for all.

—from *The Spirit of Liberty,* by Learned Hand and edited by Irving Dilliard, pp. 189–191. Published 1952 by Alfred A. Knopf, Inc. Reprinted by permission.

A COWBOY'S PRAYER

Oh Lord. I've never lived where churches grow.
   I love creation better as it stood
That day You finished it so long ago
   And looked upon Your work and called it good.
I know that others find You in the light
   That's sifted down through tinted window panes,
And yet I seem to feel You near tonight
   In this dim, quiet starlight on the plains.

I thank You, Lord, that I am placed so well,
   That You have made my freedom so complete;
That I'm no slave of whistle, clock or bell,
   Nor weak-eyed prisoner of wall and street.
Just let me live my life as I've begun
   And give me work that's open to the sky;
Make me a pardner of the wind and sun,
   And I won't ask a life that's soft or high.

Let me be easy on the man that's down;
   Let me be square and generous with all.
I'm careless sometimes, Lord, when I'm in town,
   But never let 'em say I'm mean or small!
Make me as big and open as the plains,
   As honest as the hawse between my knees,
Clean as the wind that blows behind the rains,
   Free as the hawk that circles down the breeze!

Forgive me, Lord, if sometimes I forget.
   You know the reasons that are hid.
You understand the things that gall and fret;
   You know me better than my mother did.
Just keep an eye on all that's done and said
   And right me, sometimes, when I turn aside,
And guide me on the long, dim trail ahead
   That stretches upward toward the Great Divide.

> —"A Cowboy's Prayer" by Badger Clark, from *Sun
> and Saddle Leather* (Boston, Chapman and Grimes,
> 1915), by permission of The Westerners Founda-
> tion, College of the Pacific.

STUDYING THE SELECTION

After choosing a piece of prose or poetry, you must become well
acquainted with it; you cannot interpret the material for your audience
unless you understand it thoroughly. First of all, it is necessary to dis-

cover the essential thoughts and feelings behind the author's words. Next, break the selection down and analyze its smaller components.

The analysis, then, is our present object of consideration. At another point in the chapter, under the heading "Practicing the Selection," we will discuss the selection's synthesis: the selection in its whole form with all parts functioning together as a unit.

Discovering its Thoughts and Feelings

1. *What is the central idea or theme?* Look for the author's main point by reading the selection silently. Do not despair if you are unable to grasp the central idea during the first reading. Go over it again, and do not be satisfied until you can state it in one or two sentences. Seeking the central idea may take you into a study of the background or setting related to the material. To understand the theme of Tom Paine's essay, *The Crisis,* for instance, it is necessary to know the chain of historical events that led to its publication.

2. *Can you express the content in your own words?* Paraphrase the selection. Write it out in *your* language. This is one of the surest ways to teach yourself the meaning of difficult prose or poetry.

3. *What is the author's purpose?* Does he wish to arouse and cause his "audience" to act? Is it his design to give information, to entertain, to point out the beauty or ugliness of life, to eulogize a person, or to poke fun? Did Jonathan Swift write *Gulliver's Travels* to entertain children? Parts may appear to be for young people, but, basically, the book is a satire on the stupidity of human behavior. To interpret an author's work faithfully, you need to know his aim.

4. *What are the author's attitudes?* What feelings does he express in his work? A reader who is not sensitive to the author's attitudes will present little more than an uninteresting pile of words. Oral interpretation entails communication of feeling as well as thought. Neither should be neglected. If you know when the author's mood suggests contentedness and when it displays bitterness, jealousy, fear, anger, contempt, or love, you will be able to suggest such emotions in your interpretative reading.

5. *What is the author's background?* Find out about the elements that have influenced his writing: where he has lived, his character and personality, his associates, his family. There is good reason for this investigation, for his writing will reflect his personality, philosophy of life, and general rearing. Is it not logical that a study of an author will help you to gain a better understanding of and appreciation for his works? When you read "The Raven," if you know that Edgar Allen Poe led a turbulent life filled with disappointment, grief, and illness, it is very likely that you will be able to communicate to your listeners

considerably more of the "Poe in Poe." The more you know of what lies behind the material, the better you will be able to convey its meaning.

6. *What moved him to write the selection?* Can you determine a specific motivating factor? Edwin Markham's "The Man With the Hoe" was inspired by Millet's classic painting of a French peasant "bowed by the weight of centuries." To understand Alfred Tennyson's "In Memoriam," one must know that this long series of lyrics was motivated by grief over the death of Arthur Hallam, Tennyson's closest friend.

Analyzing the Details

After discovering the essential thoughts and feelings latent in your selection, you will need to study certain relevant details.

1. *Do you know the meanings of all the words and phrases?* We become overconfident at times and occasionally choose to ignore details. The result can prove embarrassing. Take the case of Marilyn who was reading a short story about football to a class. It was quite evident that she had not prepared adequately. One thing was certain: she had not bothered to define questionable words. How did the class know? Well, whenever she read "offensive lineman" or "offensive halfback," she did so with an obvious indication of disgust. To her, she later confessed, *offensive* had but one meaning—*obnoxious.*

We color our expression of words, naturally, according to our knowledge of their meanings and our feelings about them. Words have at least two meanings in most cases, perhaps in all cases. There is the dictionary definition; then there is the meaning that an author implies, either by the way he uses the word or by the setting into which he puts it. That is, a word in each context carries a different *connotation* or signification. The reader must be alert to the author's intent, what he wants his words to say. "Love," for example, may connote *fondness* in one place and *rapture* in another. You should be able to interpret each faithfully. (Consult Chapter Seven for a full discussion of connotation and denotation.)

2. *Can you explain all figures of speech?* We also referred to figures of speech in Chapter Seven. They are the language symbols used by speakers and writers to beautify and strengthen their thoughts. What does William Hamilton Hayne mean to say with this metaphor in his "A Sea Lyric"?

> For the sea is a harp, and the winds of God
>   Play over his rhythmic breast,

Explain the meaning of this beautiful simile from Byron's "Childe Harold."

> Parting day
> Dies like a dolphin, whom each pang imbues
> With a new colour as it gasps away,

Literature is full of figures of speech, and the oral reader must be able to translate them if he is to be effective in communication.

3. *Can you pronounce all the words?* When in doubt, check the dictionary; do not guess. Our language can play tricks on us, especially when words are not pronounced as they are spelled. It is hard for many to understand how the people in Massachusetts can get something sounding like "wurster" out of "Worcester" or how "quay" is pronounced "key."

INTRODUCING THE SELECTION

To set the scene and put your audience in a receptive mood, you should prepare an introduction to your reading. Plan your remarks carefully, and present them extemporaneously. One or more of the following topics could be covered:

1. Reasons for reading the selection.
2. A biographical sketch of the author.
3. Background elements of the selection such as time, place, and setting.
4. Explanation of the theme.

PRACTICING THE SELECTION

When you are satisfied that you have discovered the essential thought and feeling in the selection, analyzed the smaller parts, and composed a fitting introduction, you are ready for the final phase of preparation. You will need to practice reading the material aloud to insure communication of what the author has put into it.

Find a place where you can practice without being disturbed. Practice purposefully, with your goal of transmitting the meaning firmly in mind. Expressiveness in oral interpretation comes primarily from a desire to share with others what you know and feel about a selection. Without the urge to communicate, without a willing and enthusiastic attitude, it is difficult to make printed words come alive on a page.

Knowledge of content and willingness to express it make conscious concern for such factors as pitch and rate variation unnecessary. Reading is not a mechanical activity. You do not succeed in communication by "pulling levers" or "pushing buttons" as you reach prescribed points on the page. It cannot be overemphasized that success in oral reading is achieved by responding fully to the facts and inward feelings that you have accumulated from a comprehensive study of the material.

Be conscious of the need for eye contact as you practice. During rehearsal sessions you will learn that you can let your eyes leave the page from time to time without losing your place and breaking the continuity. Hold the book or manuscript high enough for ease in reading and low enough to allow visual contact.

When practicing a selection of poetry, do not be hindered by its unique form. Be careful not to let rhyme or meter push thought into the background. Undue emphasis of these elements can result in a singsong kind of reading.

Do not stop at the end of each line of poetry. Let the meaning tell you when to pause or drop your voice. Punctuation marks will help you to understand the poem, and in most cases you should treat them as though they were being used in prose writing. If the punctuation and sense of the poem suggest that you should read on, then read on. Carry the thought along, naturally and expressively, and stop only when the meaning dictates a pause.

Read to convey the beauty and melody of a poem. Above and beyond thought content, poetry has emotion and music which must be communicated if the reader is to be faithful to the author. Release yourself. Do not be afraid to let yourself respond. You may find that for the first time in your life you are *truly* expressing yourself.

Always remember that audiences are made up of *real people* who can be moved by your interpretation of a selection of literature. By thinking of your reading as an opportunity to share a worthwhile piece of writing with them, you can make them forget that you are completing an assignment for class credit. Read to them. Read directly to them. Read sincerely, naturally, and willingly to them.

LET US SUMMARIZE

Again and again during your life, occasions for reading aloud will arise; now is the time to prepare for those eventualities. Such preparation will help you also in making original speeches, since many speeches include quoted material. Then, too, the expressiveness that one acquires from training in oral reading is carried over to other forms of speech communication.

Before beginning the first assignment, reconsider the suggestions we have made:

1.   Appreciate the reader's role.
2.   Find an appropriate selection.
3.   Study the selection.
4.   Introduce the selection.
5.   Practice the selection.

Clarence T. Simon, Professor Emeritus of speech at Northwestern University, has a bit of sound advice:

> If the student wishes to develop and deepen his appreciation, he must be willing to surrender himself to the reactions which are prompted. He must allow the responses to sweep through him. There must be no undue holding back.[3]

Suggested Exercise A

Find a two-minute selection of prose or poetry that you would *like* to read. (The purpose of this exercise is to help you to become accustomed to reading aloud before an audience.) Strive to do your best. Study the selection carefully and practice aloud conscientiously.

Suggested Exercise B

For future use, make a bibliography of ten library references that contain information about authors.

Suggested Exercise C

Complete a bibliography of ten anthologies of prose and poetry that are to be found in your library.

Suggested Exercise D

Choose a narrative poem of two to four minutes in length that you would like to read. Submit an analysis of the meaning to your instructor. Be sure to cover these points:

1. The central idea.
2. A short paraphrase of the selection.
3. The author's purpose.
4. The author's attitudes.
5. The author's background.
6. The author's reasons for writing the selection.

Prepare for an appropriate introduction and practice with a desire to communicate. (Repeat this exercise for the next three Suggested Exercises, making the indicated substitutions.)

Suggested Exercise E

Substitute a folklore, dialect, or children's selection of prose or poetry.

Suggested Exercise F

Substitute a lyric poem. Bring out the feeling and melody along with the meaning.

---

[3] Clarence T. Simon, "Appreciation in Reading," *Studies in the Art of Interpretation*, Gertrude E. Johnson, ed. (New York, 1940), p. 27.

Suggested Exercise G

Substitute a literary selection of high resolve (printed speech, biblical selection, essay, editorial, inspirational poem, or so forth). Convey to your audience the high principles and moral or ethical values contained in the selection.

Suggested Exercise H

Prepare a four- to seven-minute lecture-recital type of program, either alone or with other members of the class. This is an exercise in which you develop a certain theme with either two or more selections of prose, poetry, or both. Choose a theme of special interest to you. It may be concerned with characteristics of people, sports, the seasons, love, death, patriotism, places, children, adventure, or so forth. Introduce the selections and connect them with meaningful transitions.

Submit analyses of the selections to your instructor.

Suggested Exercise I

Prepare a speech in which you rely heavily on quotations as supporting material. Use lengthy quotations in the introduction, in developing each main head, and in the conclusion.

PART IV

APPENDIXES

Practical Methods Applied: Model Speeches

1   *Remarks On Jefferson Day*

BOWER ALY[1]

Dr. Aly, Professor of Speech at the University of Oregon and former president of the Speech Association of America, is not only a recognized scholar in the field but also a prominent speaker. His speeches consistently reveal significant thought that is logical and stimulating. His audiences find themselves compelled to listen for fear of missing something that they will never have a chance to hear again. As a listener reported on one occasion: "I had an appointment, but I just couldn't leave Aly's speech."

Such was the response to his speech at the University of Missouri on April 13, 1955.

Mr. Chairman: We have come this morning to do honor to Thomas Jefferson, author of the Declaration of American Independence, and of the Statute of Virginia for Religious Freedom, and the Father of the University of Virginia. We have come to honor him, even though we realize that his fame has long since passed beyond our power to praise. Indeed, this morning it behooves us to ask ourselves the searching question whether we are worthy to praise him.

Thomas Jefferson declared eternal warfare against every form of tyranny over the minds of men. In this generation we have

[1] Text from A. Craig Baird, ed., *Representative American Speeches: 1955–1956* (New York, H. W. Wilson, 1956), pp. 59–61. Reprinted by permission.

quietly witnessed an onslaught on our liberties by those whose plan of attack on Russian tyranny begins with the destruction of American liberty. Are we worthy to praise Thomas Jefferson?

Thomas Jefferson believed in the Constitution, under which he served, and in the Bill of Rights, in which were embodied his ideas of liberty under law. Today we sit complacently while those who would destroy our Bill of Rights slander the precious Fifth Amendment by attaching to it the epithet "Communist." Are we worthy to praise Thomas Jefferson?

Thomas Jefferson welcomed honest dissent boldly expressed as the surest evidence of liberty prevailing. Today we see timid men fleeing to conform; and we witness citizens as yet unconvicted of any crime harried by government informers and suborners of perjury who gain their fees, without our protest, from taxes we have paid. Are we worthy to praise Thomas Jefferson?

In an age which, like our own, knew grave danger, Thomas Jefferson and his contemporaries cast out fear and stood unafraid. Americans today, though rich and powerful, stand irresolute and fearful when they should be confident and strong. Are we worthy to praise Thomas Jefferson?

Mr. Chairman: We Americans of this generation did not earn our liberties. We merely inherited them. We inherited them with our Constitution, our Bill of Rights, and our government of free men established by Washington, Hamilton, and Jefferson. We stand in present danger of being disinherited. No less a person than the Chief Justice of the Supreme Court of the United States has recently warned us of the grave and growing dangers to our ancient liberties. We shall be disinherited unless we learn how to defend the values handed down to us by Jefferson and his compatriots.

Mr. Chairman: I submit that we Americans today have not kept faith with Thomas Jefferson. Since we have not kept true faith with him in our deeds we have no right to praise him with our words. I propose, therefore, that we offer as our tribute today a solemn and inward determination so to live in protest against every form of tyranny that our actions may earn for us the right to praise Jefferson in happier days to come.

2   *Making Lincoln Live*

HOWARD W. RUNKEL[2]

Dr. Runkel, Professor of Rhetoric and Public Address at Willamette University, has addressed nearly 700 audiences throughout the West.
[2] Reprinted by permission.

Usually, he speaks at conventions, commencements, service club meetings, and so forth.

On February 12, 1957, he spoke before the Oregon state legislature as it was convening in joint session to commemorate the birth of Abraham Lincoln. The text, as supplied by Professor Runkel, is a model of first-class speech composition.

A few years ago 55 outstanding authorities in American history were invited to Harvard University to rate the Presidents of the United States in five categories—great, near great, average, below average and failure. The only one to receive every vote for the top rank was Abraham Lincoln.

More than one writer has linked the American Civil War President with Jesus and Socrates as the three transcendently great figures of all time. Russia's Count Tolstoy, whose tremendous volume *War and Peace* immortalized its author, declared that "Lincoln aspired to be divine and he was."

Abraham Lincoln has become the most biographized human being in history; more than 5,000 books have been written about his life. His letters, state papers and speeches in print today total over 1,100,000 words, more than are contained either in the Bible or the sum of Shakespeare's works. At least two of Lincoln's speeches, the Address at Gettysburg and the Second Inaugural, have been translated into nearly every known language and are recorded on monuments and plaques the world over. The Lincoln Memorial in our nation's capital is year after year our most visited shrine. Countless thoughtful legislators admit having derived inspiration and guidance by standing in contemplation before that moving statue of the Great Emancipator.

Lincoln's likeness appears on millions of coins and adorns the walls of thousands of classrooms. The ethical quality of the name "Lincoln" has given priceless impetus to numerous political campaigns, sales programs and philanthropic drives. It is no secret that if one can quote Lincoln on behalf of his cause he is more nearly assured of success.

That this remarkable man should have been the product of our newly freed soil; that he should have been nurtured in the budding institutions of this infant nation has always been a matter of justifiable pride to us Americans. It is only natural, therefore, that the anniversary of the birth of Abraham Lincoln, sixteenth President of the United States, has traditionally become an occasion for redetermination on our part "that this nation, under God, shall have a new birth of freedom."

Today, February 12, 1957, is the 148th anniversary of Lincoln's birth. Any eulogist is tempted once again to dwell upon those uniquely appealing qualities of this extraordinary personality— his integrity, his patriotism, his gentleness, his humor, his tact, his insight, his vision. However, were Lincoln alive he would, characteristically, be more impressed by tributes in the form of action, rather than diction. To this end, let us briefly note only three of his qualities which every one of us, regardless of party, color, creed or tongue, might well exercise as he attempts to live worthily in these complex and perilous times.

I

Abraham Lincoln was, above all, humble of spirit. No tribute ought to omit reference to this, his most endearing quality. Few, if any, are the instances in which he succumbed to mankind's most fundamental failing—the inability to put self in proper perspective among people and issues.

Do you remember how Lincoln drove out of Washington after a wearying day behind the desk in the White House to confer with his subordinate, General McClellan? The arrogant McClellan, aware of his commander-in-chief's presence, loftily instructed his orderly to tell the President that no interview was possible any more that evening; that he had gone to bed and was not to be disturbed. A witness to the embarrassing scene indignantly besought Lincoln to "pull his rank." "Are you going to tolerate such insubordination?" he pleaded. The stooped and worn figure merely shrugged and answered: "I'd hold McClellan's horse if that would give us victories." History records that on that evening the immortal had waited upon the mortal.

Then there was the time that a high government official discovered Lincoln in the act of blacking his own boots. "Mr. President, gentlemen don't black their own boots," was the protest. Lincoln looked up and replied innocently: "No? Whose boots do they black?"

Almost touching was that priceless little autobiography Lincoln submitted upon request for a minor "Who's Who?" of his day. It is well worth reading again. Here is what this humble man wrote:

My parents were of "second families." I can read, write and cipher to the rule of three, but this is all. I was raised to farm work. I became postmaster at a very small post office. There is not much of this autobiography for the reason, I suppose, that there is not much of me.

Such a man must inevitably recognize the omniscience of his Creator. Hence, when a lady pushed through to him at a public gathering and cried: "Oh, Mr. President, do you think God is on our side in this terrible war?" Lincoln could only reply gravely: "Madame, I'm more concerned with whether or not we are on God's side."

The living memory of him whom we commemorate here this morning teaches us, every one, the truth of the Beatitude: "Blessed are the meek, for they shall inherit the earth."

II

Abraham Lincoln was a man of rare understanding. Historians marvel at the discernment of this rough, unschooled frontiersman. It showed in his interpretation of the war as a struggle for survival of the Union; it was evidenced by his saving of the border states for the North when one false move would have driven them into the Southern fold; it was seen in his timing of the Emancipation Proclamation which, by giving the war an anti-slavery twist, made all but impossible British intervention in behalf of the Confederacy. And it is clear in his familiar definition of democracy: "As I would not be a slave, so I would not be a master. This expresses my idea of democracy."

But more touchingly, Lincoln's understanding is manifest in his associations with individuals. In 1864 he wrote words of sympathy to a grieving mother in Boston. This is one of the most quoted personal letters in our language.

Dear Madam:

I have been shown in the files of the War Department a statement of the Adjutant General of Massachusetts that you are the mother of five sons who have died gloriously on the field of battle. I feel how weak and fruitless must be any words of mine which should attempt to beguile you from the grief of a loss so overwhelming. But I cannot refrain from tendering to you the consolation that may be found in the thanks of the Republic they died to save. I pray that our Heavenly Father may assuage the anguish of your bereavement, and leave you only the cherished memory of the loved and lost, and the solemn pride that must be yours to have laid so costly a sacrifice upon the altar of freedom.

Yours very sincerely and respectfully,
Abraham Lincoln

This letter, replete with humility and understanding, has become a part of the American bible. How it stands out as peculiarly symbolic of our democratic heritage is dramatically revealed in contrast to a letter written by Kaiser Wihelm to a German mother whose loss was not five but *nine*-fold! Written in the third person of royalty, the letter reads:

Madame:
    His Majesty the Kaiser hears that you have sacrificed nine sons in defense of the Fatherland in the present war. His Majesty is immensely gratified at the fact and in recognition is pleased to send you his photograph with silver frame and autograph signature.

Wilhelm II

Lincoln's understanding of human nature was expressed, too, in a letter written to General Joseph Hooker. Hooker had distinguished himself more as an imprudent critic of the President than as a winner of battles. Lincoln had every right to accuse him of remarks smacking of disloyalty. But note the letter with its tactfully worded rebuke:

General:
    I have placed you at the head of the Army of the Potomac. Of course I have done this upon what appear to me to be sufficient reasons, and yet I think it best for you to know that there are some things in regard to which I am not quite satisfied with you. I believe you to be a brave and skillful soldier, which of course I like. I also believe you do not mix politics with your profession, in which you are right. You have confidence in yourself, which is a valuable if not an indispensable quality. You are ambitious, which, within reasonable bounds, does good rather than harm; . . . .
    I have heard, in such a way as to believe it, of your recently saying that both the army and the government needed a dictator. Of course it was not for this, but in spite of it, that I have given you the command. Only those generals who gain successes can set up dictators. What I now ask of you is military success, and I will risk the dictatorship. . . .
    And now beware of rashness. Beware of rashness, but with energy and sleepless vigilance go forward and give us victories.

Note how Lincoln opens with a series of compliments, then administers his rebuke and concludes with a challenge. The General has been reprimanded but with that understanding that spares feelings.

Can any of us today say he needs not more of his rare quality of understanding—in the home, at the workplace, in the classroom, yes, even in legislative chambers. The life of Abraham Lincoln gives new vitality to the words of the Old Testament: "Wisdom is the principal thing; therefore get wisdom; and with all thy getting get understanding."

III

Abraham Lincoln was a man of generous spirit. He was the President who commuted scores of death sentences for condemned soldiers. To critics of this policy he answered: "Must I shoot a simple-minded soldier boy who deserts, while I must not touch a hair of a wily agitator who induces him to desert?"

Lincoln was the President who, smarting under harsh criticism of the imperious but capable Edwin M. Stanton, nevertheless appointed him Secretary of War. The snobbish Salmon Chase treated the President with condescension and caused humiliation on more than one occasion. The big man in the White House did not let this blind him to Chase's qualifications and he made him Chief Justice of the Supreme Court of the United States.

Of course Abraham Lincoln's most imperishable expression of bigness of spirit is contained in his Second Inaugural Address, considered by scholars here and abroad to be one of the glories and treasures of mankind. On this occasion he spoke amid the drama of the war's climax. The victory of the North was clearly in sight. Already meaner spirits were calling for a vengeful peace. But Lincoln counselled his huge audience in the words of the Sermon on the Mount: "Judge not that ye be not judged." Then he summed up his message:

With malice toward none; with charity for all; with firmness in the right, as God gives us to see the right, let us strive on to finish the work we are in; to bind up the nation's wounds; to care for him who shall have borne the battle and for his widow, and his orphan—to do all which may achieve and cherish a just and lasting peace among ourselves, and with all nations.

As a thoughtful boy in Indiana Abraham Lincoln had spoken for himself; as a prairie lawyer in Illinois he had spoken for clients; as a politician-debater he had spoken for a faction; as a campaigner for the Presidency he spoke for the North; as President he spoke for the Nation; now, at the Second Inaugural, he was speaking out for all humanity.

As Lincoln lay dying only six weeks later, one of his most severe critics who had come to appreciate the heroic qualities of this humble, discerning and generous man, pointed at the figure on the bed and said: "There lies the most perfect ruler of men this world has ever seen."

My fellow citizens: Each of us has inherited the legacy of this great American ruler as he faces the tremendous public problems and perils of our day. God grant on this 148th anniversary of

Abraham Lincoln's birth that we in his spirit may resolve to "take increased devotion to that cause for which he gave the last full measure of devotion." Then, and only then, will we have made Lincoln live in our time.

3   *The Waste of War*

ANN BLASDELL[3]

Miss Blasdell's speech won her a first place in a speech tournament sponsored by Occidental College in 1956. In shaping the speech for the contest, she drew upon methods and types of materials that she had become acquainted with in her speech classes at Compton College.

This is December Seventh. What does that date mean to you? What does it mean in the history of our country and the world? December 7th, 1941. Fifteen years ago today Pearl Harbor was bombed, and this meant war. This meant a war which was to reduce massive stone buildings to rubble; a war which would mean crawling over hot dirt; clipping barbed wire fences; marching gun-in-hand through city streets; a war which dictated the establishing of beach-heads and the occupying of towns like San Pablo. San Pablo, near Manila, offered to its occupants jagged buildings; electrical wires dangling from poles; glass, wood, and steel in careless heaps. This was a town where animals, trees, and other living things were strewn among the dead.

This World War II swept southward into Italy. One night, before the German retreat, Nazis marched into an Italian home where a young boy named Giuseppe lived. They ordered the boy's father outside. They forced him to dig his own grave, and they shot him into it. Giuseppe, having hidden some hand-grenades, threw them at the Germans; and they machine-gunned him, leaving him for dead. Soon after, a truck ran over his leg, forcing amputation—a tragedy seemingly at its limit, but there's more. When heavy bombings came, his family's meager shelter was hit, killing all but he, who was outside at the time: a boy of only nine, left without a family, a home, or a whole body—nothing unusual, just a result like the countless thousands of deaths, deformations and other results of war. Nothing unusual—unless it was your son, your daughter, or mine.

These incidents show a limited portion of the waste of war, and war is waste.

It is an economic waste. What about our uranium and atomic power? In 1955, 2,050 millions of dollars were spent for an atomic

[3] Reprinted by permission.

energy program. If atomic defense costs and the need for defense mechanisms could only be abolished, the hours and the energy spent by our scientists could be united for domestic progress instead of scientific massacre. Modern methods of medicine would lessen or wipe out the 794,000 lives taken in 1953 from heart disease; the 219,000 dead in 1952 from cancer. These keen minds would be working on the mystery of leukemia, not the formula for bigger and better bombs. What could a nation do with the over 40,000 million dollars spent a year for military defense? These expenditures could be converted to schools for the illiterate, hospitals for the sick, jets for a forward future.

The material waste of war damages a nation, but how does this war affect the individual: the fighting soldier? Don't the attitude and the atmosphere of war influence his moral beliefs? Of course they do. The morals he has been taught since a child have suddenly been reversed. The Commandment, "Thou shalt not kill," has been replaced with a warranted education in the ways of self-protection. Thomas Hardy wrote about the man he killed, in a poem of many verses. However, the last verse, to me, expresses the complete thought.

> Yes; quaint and curious war is!
> You shoot a fellow down
> You'd treat if met where any bar is,
> Or help to half-a-crown.[4]

A young man once told me that when you are in combat, it isn't as if you are killing human beings. They are an outlet for the tension felt on the fighting front. They are the fear for one's own life. They are the reason you're not home with your wife, or your girl. Are these sufficient reasons for any persons to have the right to take the life of one of God's children and to place this life to rest on some bloody, forgotten hill?

Though some die, there are those who live—those who return after the crisis to society. And who can judge the personal harm, the mental and the physical handicap that these veterans bring home with them? Certainly not I. Let us imagine a train is pulling into a depot. As the train hurries into the station, about ten veterans peer anxiously through the window, almost frantically searching for a familiar face—each one nursing his well-worn memory. Sitting three seats from the rear of the car, a young man,

---

[4] "The Man He Killed" by Thomas Hardy from *The Collected Poems of Thomas Hardy*. Copyright 1925. Reprinted by permission of The Macmillan Co.; also Macmillan & Co., Ltd., London.

about twenty-eight, seems to be blankly staring through the glass. He remains silent—engrossed in his own thoughts. He remembers a brown-eyed baby girl with hardly any hair. They'd named her Jeannie. She was still in her crib when he left, unaware that her daddy was leaving her. Hard to believe—that was almost two years ago. His wife Helen said the baby was walking now—could really get around—and that wispy fuzz on her head was blossoming into thick little ringlets. "She must look like an angel," he thought. The train roared into the depot, and he knew soon would come the moment he had pictured in his mind a thousand times over. He clenched his fingers around his cane; he rose, and he groped his way down the aisle—grateful for the assistance of a fellow-passenger. A tear fell from his unseeing eyes.

Can you understand how this war is waste? It is a waste economically; it is personally and morally an affliction. Yes, this is war: A river of sacrifice that flows through the heart of our country and its people; a river that rushes forward, eroding and corroding as it gathers momentum, strength, and depth, unless we can stop it—dam it up. Only with the grace of wisdom and tolerance can we stop this river, this eternal scourge.

Our United States is the most advanced in education, justice, and science. Therefore, we must be the leaders in an attempt for peace. We must try to open the eyes of our brother-countries that they might see—that they might see that peace is the only way. We must look back into the pages of our history and be constantly reminded of our debt to our boys who have fought and died—to the soldier beneath the tombstone which reads: "Here rests, in honored glory, an American soldier known but to God."

4   *Social Responsibility of Science*

HARRISON S. BROWN[5]

Dr. Brown, teacher of geochemistry at California Institute of Technology, is deeply concerned about the future of mankind. In addition to teaching and conducting research, he has made himself available to audiences throughout the country—and beyond. As speaker on such topics as the uses and functions of science, he commands world-wide respect.

He delivered the following address to a teen-age audience in New York in 1949. His pattern of organization is five-part, based on John Dewey's problem-solving formula that is discussed in Chapter Twelve. That a scientist should use this plan is not astonishing at all, considering its kinship to the scientific method.

[5] Text from A. Craig Baird, ed., *Representative American Speeches: 1948–1949* (New York, H. W. Wilson, 1949), pp. 140–144.

Whenever I am asked to speak before a group of young men and women, my thoughts drift back to the days when I was graduated from high school and a prominent business man in my home town spoke at our commencement. "The world is in a sorry plight," he told us, "it is up to you—the citizens of tomorrow—to mold the world into a globe fit for human habitation. It is up to you to abolish war and to see to it that the necessities of life are made available to all mankind."

Such graduation speeches were given that year throughout the United States and throughout the world, and for all I know they are still being given.

But what happens when the high school graduate goes out into the world and attempts to change things for the better? He suddenly finds himself called "naive," "rash," "inexperienced." He learns that the oldsters really don't want the youngsters to remake the world after all. The soreness of the tops of many young heads (resulting from much battering against stone walls) testifies amply to the resistance that confronts them.

Yet if we look back a few years we find that the majority of the soldiers who fought and died in the last war were in their early twenties and younger. The majority of the scientists who contributed actively toward the development of the atomic bomb were in their twenties. Youngsters, we are told, are old enough to fight and die; they are old enough to help figure out how to make atomic bombs—but they are too young to have anything to say about what to do about the frightening problems that face the modern world and threaten to destroy it.

In speaking today about the social responsibilities of science, I will speak of things which are relatively easy for young people, but difficult for older persons, to understand. This is because young people possess a quality that in general diminishes with years: the quality of imagination. Imagination is a quality which is an integral part of science, and naturally endowed to young people. It is a quality which sadly enough evaporates with advancing age, yet it is a quality which our unhappy world needs in abundance at the present time.

For the last three centuries the findings of science have had marked impact upon society, but people on the whole have not understood just how our world has been affected, nor have they cared. From the time of Newton men began to realize that through technology, which is based upon the findings of science, substantial comforts and profits could be gained. From the time of Pasteur men began to realize that through the application of science to medicine they might be able to live longer.

From the time of Leonardo da Vinci, men appreciated that science could materially aid in winning wars. As years went by a technological materialism was developed; demands for new technical knowledge became greater and greater; more and more men became scientists and technologists. The scientist came to be looked upon as the creator of a new and abundant life. To make substantial profits, to work less, to live longer, to win wars—what more could the people of a nation desire? In the valor of its ignorance humanity accepted science and technology as its benefactors seldom questioning, seldom asking where it was leading.

And where has it led? To a large part of the world it has brought unprecedented comfort. To an even larger part of the world it has brought unprecedented agony.

To the world of the future (the world in which you young people must live) technological expansion may bring total catastrophe, or it may aid in the moulding of a balanced world in which men may have the opportunity to live in reasonable harmony with their environment and with each other. The end result will depend upon the wisdom and imagination with which we plan for the future—upon the wisdom and imagination with which we integrate our scientific and technical knowledge from other fields of human endeavor, into a pattern for a peaceful and stable world.

Let's look at the record. It is not a happy one! Science and technology have placed in the hands of the rulers of nations tools of coercion and persuasion of unprecedented effectiveness. Modern implements of war make it possible for small groups of men to enforce their rule over large groups of people. In modern totalitarian states, the weapons in the hands of rulers make impossible successful popular revolts.

In the past, uprisings against despotism by masses of people armed only with crude weapons were possible. Today, applied science makes despotism invulnerable to internal overthrow by violent means.

Improvements in transportation and communication have increased the effectiveness of police action. Revolutionary methods of mass communication, rotary presses, radio and motion pictures provide powerful tools for persuasion. Today, when propaganda can be spread to millions of people, when the governed can be unknowingly fed with untruths and kept in ignorance of the truth by government control of communications outlets, the people become powerless.

It would be pleasant to believe that by creating new techniques in transportation and communication, thus making the world effectively smaller, some sort of a dent might have been made in minimizing the concept of intense nationalism. But the reverse has been true. The creation of vast industrial nations, competing with one another, and the creation of centralized national authorities of ever-increasing power have more than overbalanced the effect upon nationalism of increasing communication and education.

History has taught us that intense nationalism sooner or later results in wars between nations. Today wars are, more than ever before, wars of competing technologies. The first half of the twentieth century will go down in history as the period within which technological developments took place which converted destruction from a difficult operation into a fantastically easy one. But as yet, we have seen only the crude beginnings of what can be done, should circumstances dictate. Now that nations, each in the interest of its own military security, have mobilized science, we can expect developments in the technology of war to proceed at an accelerated pace.

Even our good intentions have brought trouble. The spread of sanitation measures and the control of disease to ever-increasing bodies of humanity has created the problem of overpopulation. With the population check of disease removed, we are now confronted with the gigantic task of finding ways to feed people and to keep populations in check.

Increased populations and wars have, in turn, placed tremendous drains upon our natural resources, upon our power reserve, upon our arable land.

Indeed, it is not a pretty picture that confronts us. It has caused many persons to say that perhaps, like the dinosaur, mankind is doomed to extinction.

But fortunately our position is somewhat different from that of the dinosaur, whose size, which once permitted him to survive, destroyed him when his environment changed. The dinosaur did not create the environment that destroyed him. Man, through his thoughtless misuse of science, has created his. The dinosaur had no control over his environment. Man, if he wishes and if he is willing to apply science and technology properly, may have control over his.

Science and technology offer man important tools that may enable him to control his destiny. Man must learn how to use those tools properly and he must apply his imagination to the task of devising the social and political institutions that will permit him to utilize the tools with maximum effectiveness.

As we have not thought sufficiently far into the future, the net result of our haphazard and unplanned use of science and technology has been disastrous to society. We should now, realizing the danger that confronts us, study the future, plan accordingly and utilize those aspects of science that can aid us in moulding a more hopeful destiny than that which now confronts us.

The first social responsibility of science is to shout from the housetops whenever it sees science and technology being used in the dangerous ways in which they have been used in the past.

The second responsibility is to develop wherever possible constructive solutions to the political problems that now confront mankind: the production of food, clothing and shelter.

A third, and in many respects an even more important responsibility exists, and that is to disseminate far and wide an attitude that I like to call the "scientific attitude."

The scientific attitude is at once a way of thought, a way of conduct and a way of life. It is an attitude that has been found essential for constructive scientific progress—an attitude which, if it were to be more widely disseminated, accepted, appreciated and used, would go a long way toward helping mankind resolve the many dilemmas that now confront it. A scientific attitude has many component parts, the most important of which are straightforward and easy to understand:

The scientist must avoid dogmatism. He must always insist upon valid argument. He must proceed cautiously, yet he must be ready for change. He must insist upon the truth. He cannot permit national fetishisms to influence his judgment. And above all, he must insist upon complete, undistorted and uncompromising freedom of speech.

The assimilation of a scientific attitude will enable all of you to build the kind of world you want to live in—a world free of fear, free of war and free of want.

5   *Habits and Customs of People*

NELLIE WILLIAMS[6]

Mrs. Williams admirably followed the standard practices of good speech composition in a speech that she gave to a speech class at Southern Oregon College in 1963. In the printed version the reader can easily perceive the clarity of organization, uses of transitions, use of developmental materials, and so forth, but he cannot really appreciate other aspects of the speaker's work. For example, her warmth, charm, and gentleness—showing in voice and manner—are reflected in the printed text, but not to the degree experienced by her willing and delighted listeners.

[6] Reprinted by permission.

We've had speeches on camping, traveling, creativity, and so forth. Today, my speech is somewhat different. Perhaps it could be considered a hobby, too, because I think I must collect the habits and customs of people. I'd like to talk to you about the differences in parts of the country and about the lasting friendships that I have made in these various areas.

Some of the habits and customs of the two areas in which I have lived might be of interest to you.

In 1942, when following a soldier-husband, I found myself in a little town, Toccoa, Georgia, about ninety miles north of Atlanta. I had difficulty in finding a home at first because it seems that all of the apartments were to have been rented to officer's wives, and I was an enlisted man's wife. Finally I found a home with a lovely couple, out in the country. This couple was Vera and Troy Meeks. They had two children: Jeannie and Charles. The custom of that family—the custom of politeness in that family—was just beautiful. They not only said "Yes, ma'am" and "No, ma'am" and "Yes, sir" and "No, sir" to each other; but they said it to their father and their mother—in fact, to whomever they spoke, as long as they were adult.

Their way of greeting people was interesting, too. One day Vera and I were downtown in Toccoa and I heard someone say, "Hey, there!"

And I called to Vera, "Someone's calling us."

And she turned around and saw her friend, and she said, "Hey!"

And after we went on I made a remark to Vera, "That's an odd way to speak to someone."

And she said, "Well, what would you have said?"

And I said, "Well, I think I would have said 'Hello' or 'Hi.' " And she remarked that if someone said "Hi" to her, she would be tempted to tell them how tall she was.

Another custom in the 1940s—in fact, I had never been acquainted with this custom—was the way the laundry was done. When it came time to do our laundry (I knew she didn't have a washing machine) I was curious as to how we would do it. We went down to the spring in the back of the house where she heated the water in a large iron kettle. She would dip her clothes into this soapy water, lay them on a big rock, and then beat them with a battering stick. I made the mistake once of calling it a battering ram.

Because they wanted to do something for the war effort (of course her husband worked in a war plant and his brothers were in the service—but she wanted to do something too) she wouldn't take any pay for our being there, and so for Christmas, we bought them a washing machine. Do you know, that even after buying that washing machine she still would batter her clothes before she put them in the machine, until one day, she discovered that my clothes were just about as clean as hers, and I didn't beat mine any more.

In 1953, following my husband again, I found myself in Dorena, Missouri. Now, Dorena, Missouri, is a rural community about twelve miles in area, just across the river from Hickman, Kentucky, about thirty miles from the juncture of the Ohio and Mississippi rivers. Dorena is on the Mississippi River, by the way. I had forgotten—my family came from Missouri; my husband is a Hoosier—but I had forgotten that on Saturday night everybody went to town. Saturday afternoon everybody gets out good clothing, takes a bath, drives to town to do the shopping or to go to a show or to have a date or to meet with friends. And really, many of them just sit in their cars, parked along the street, and visit with whoever comes by. It's quite interesting, because people are the most interesting, well, of "anything you can do."

Then there was the custom of the cotton vacation in school. I had forgotten that one too, but about six weeks after school started we were dismissed for a period of from two to six weeks so people could pick cotton. And it was during this time that many of the children picked the cotton and bought their clothing so they'd have all new clothes to come back to school in. Our children always looked so nice when they came back to school. They'd have new dresses and new jeans and new shoes to wear.

The politeness of these people was just as beautiful as the politeness of the people in Georgia. I remember one time I went to church, a very large lady, who was very beautifully dressed and had her white hair just done to perfection, looked especially attractive that Sunday morning; and I mentioned the fact that she looked very attractive and had on a pretty dress. And she said, "Thank you, I'll let you wear it some time." Well, knowing that I was much smaller than she, at that time anyway, I didn't know whether to protest, or feel embarrassed, or what to do, so I just smiled and walked away. But a few days afterward I told a little girl that she had on some pretty, new, patent leather shoes, and she, too, said, "Thank you, I'll let you wear them sometime." So I knew by then that that was just a habit or a way of telling people that—well, to thank them for a compliment.

Another interesting aspect of this area in which we lived was— that I, too, had forgotten—was the sitting up with the dead. The subject. He was an unlimited monarch. His power to punish for any offense or for no offense at all was as broad as that which the attorney general claims for himself and his brother officers under the United States. But he was more cautious how he used it. He had a dangerous rival, from whom he apprehended the most serious peril to the "life of his government." The necessity to get rid of him was plain enough, but he could not afford to shock the moral sense of the world by pleading political necessity for a murder. He must

Mask the business from the common eye.

Accordingly, he sent for two enterprising gentlemen, whom he took into his service upon liberal pay,—"made love to their assistance,"—and got them to deal with the accused party. He acted as his own judge advocate. He made a most elegant and stirring speech to persuade his agents that Banquo was their oppressor, and had "held them so under fortune" that he ought to die for that alone. When they agreed that he was their enemy, then said the king:

So is he mine, and though I could,
With barefaced power, sweep him from my sight,
And bid my will avouch it, yet I must not,
For certain friends, who are both his and mine,
Whose loves I may not drop.

For these, and "many weighty reasons" besides, he thought it best to commit the execution of his design to a subordinate agency. The commission thus organized in Banquo's case sat upon him that very night, at a convenient place beside the road where it was known he would be traveling; and they did precisely what the attorney general says the military officers may do in this country,—they took and killed him, because their employer at the head of the government wanted it done, and paid them for doing it out of the public treasury.

But of all the persons that ever wielded this kind of power, the one who went most directly to the purpose and object of it was Lola Montez. She reduced it to the elementary principle. In 1848, when she was minister and mistress to the King of Bavaria, she dictated all the measures of the government. The times were troublesome. All over Germany the spirit of rebellion was rising; everywhere the people wanted to see a first-class revolution, like that which had just exploded in France. Many persons in Bavaria disliked to be governed so absolutely by a lady of the character

mortuary did not close at ten o'clock as it does in places that I had been before. They sat up all night with the dead. The thing that made it most interesting was that on the death of one of my neighbors, another neighbor lady came along and asked me what I was going to cook to take to the mortuary. Well, I was astonished, because I didn't know that you took food to the mortuary, and the first thing I thought of was, "My, my, dead people don't eat." But anyway, she explained to me that they had a coffee room, and there they provided coffee and food for the people who sat up all night long. Well, I soon took my place with the rest of the people in the community because I wanted to be a part of it. And I, too, sat up with the dead; and I, too, ate a sandwich occasionally, and drank some coffee.

Of all these areas (of many areas in which I have lived) these are two of the most outstanding. It's interesting to learn of the customs that are peculiar to a locality. You find wonderful people; you create friendships that are so lasting and so worthwhile that you just never do forget them. And I found that the people in Oregon and the friendships already made in the year's stay in Oregon are just as lasting, just as good, and just as beautiful. People everywhere are very nice to know. And as my mother told me when I was only ten: In order to have a friend, you have to be a friend.

6   *Nominating Calvin Coolidge*

WILL ROGERS[7]

This "speech" was written in political jest as a newspaper report during the time of the drawn-out Democratic Nominating Convention of 1924. Although never given as a speech, it is included here to illustrate the use of gentle satire (Calvin Coolidge was a Republican) and the inductive organizational plan which calls for placing the proposition near the end.

Oh, my friends, I am too good a Democrat not to be appreciative of what the party has done for me, not to try and warn you while there is yet time.

We are not gathered here just to name a nominee of the next election, but we are here to name the next President of the grand and glorious United States, of which this party today is the sole refuge for the true patriot.

In naming a man for this high and lofty office there are certain

[7] Text from Donald Day, ed., *Sanity Is Where You Find It*, pp. 30–32. Copyright © 1955. Reprinted by permission of Houghton Mifflin Co.

traditions and specifications which we must hold in mind, if we want to reach a successful victory in November.

The man we name to carry us to victory must be geographically strong enough to carry a majority of New England. The man I am about to name knows these mysterious canny people.

The man we name must be able to go into the far Westland and reap a majority. The man I am about to name possesses the attributes to do that very deed.

The man we name must be able to remove any doubtful States into the realm of certainty. The man I am about to name can give you a majority that will look like a census report.

The man we name here must be a man who never earned outside of public life a fee of over $10. The man I am about to name has that honorable reputation.

The man we name here must have no taint of Morgan or Wall Street. The man I am about to name never saw Wall Street.

The man we name here must have absolutely no affiliation with the Klan. The man I am about to name is not a member of the Klan.

The man we name must be of no minority religious creed. The man I am about to name belongs to the creed whose voters are in the majority.

On account of the present length of the convention, the man we name must not be of too many score years of age. The man I am about to name has many useful and unworried years of public service ahead of him.

The man we name must have had no connection with oil. The man I am about to name never used oil, except at Government or State Expense.

Oh, gentlemen of the grand and glorious Democratic party, let us not make a mistake. We have our greatest chance this year to bring home victory. That great scandal in our opponents' party and their close affiliation with predatory wealth has given us an unbounded opportunity.

Don't let us disrupt the party when we can win. We will go to a sure Democratic defeat if we name the wrong man. Oh, my friends, let us be connected with a victory in this glorious year of 1924. Why court defeat?

The man I am about to name is the only man in these grand and glorious United States who, if we nominate, we can go home and have no worry as to the outcome. Don't, oh, my Democratic Colleagues, listen to my friend Bryan. He named ten candidates; ten men can't win! Only one man can win. Oh, my newly made

friends, have confidence in me. Trust me just this onc lead you out of this darkened wilderness into the g White House. Oh, my tired and worn friends, there man. That man I am about to name to you is Calvi

7   Model Use of Examples

Below are excerpts from two speeches—one of 100 year other of our time. Standing as models of graphic illustrati onstrate the skillful use of forceful examples to support i tivate listeners.

The first excerpt is from the speech that the great Jere master courtroom speaker, gave before the United States ! in 1866.[8] Black's eloquent plea resulted in the reversal o decision and the sparing of the life of his client, who had to death.

At this point in the appeal, Black's goal is to illustr: despotism.

Under the old French monarchy, the favorite fa: a *lettre de cachet,* signed by the king, and this wot party to a loathsome dungeon until he died, forg world. An imperial *ukase* will answer the same pi sia. The most faithful subject of that amiable au down in the evening to dream of his future prospe daybreak he will find himself between two dragoo the mines of Siberia. In Turkey, the verbal order any of his powerful favorites will cause a man to sack and cast into the Bosphorus. Nero accused F spreading a "pestilent superstition," which they (He heard their defense in person, and sent them t wards he tried the whole Christian church in one of setting fire to the city, and he convicted them, not only that they were innocent, but that he mitted the crime. The judgment was followed tion. He let loose the Praetorian guards upon children, to drown, butcher and burn them. good political reasons, closely affecting the ; reign in Judea, to punish certain possible trai by anticipation. This required the death of : that city under two years of age. He issued h and his provost marshal carried it out with so zeal that in one day the whole land was filled lamentation. Macbeth understood the whole

[8] Text from Black's Defense of Milligan.

which Lola Montez bore, and some of them were rash enough to say so. Of course that was treason, and she went about to punish it in the simplest of all possible ways. She bought herself a pack of English bulldogs, trained to tear the flesh, and mangle the limbs, and lap the life blood, and with these dogs at her heels, she marched up and down the streets of Munich with a most majestic tread, and with a sense of power which any judge advocate in America might envy. When she saw any person whom she chose to denounce for "thwarting the government" or "using disloyal language," her obedient followers needed but a sign to make them spring at the throat of their victim.

The second excerpt is from a speech given to the Harvard Business School Club of New York in 1965 by Jack I. Straus, top executive of Macy Stores.[9] Notice his effective use of compelling examples to support the point that customers ought to be treated with "courtesy, consideration, and caring."

Recently Mrs. Straus and I were in the market for a station wagon and we went to see one of the best automobile dealers in New York who was a friend of ours. He was out of town so we were turned over to his assistant, a thoroughly nice young man. We found the car we wanted except that we didn't exactly like the upholstery. I suggested that perhaps something might be done about it. I was told that we had no choice, that you took what the factory offered—period! I was advised that I might be able to find something more to my taste somewhere else.

This wasn't said with rancor. It just expressed a total lack of interest on the part of the salesman. This point of contact for a vast multi-billion dollar enterprise with huge factories, long assembly lines, massive advertising budgets, smart designers, and I can't remember how many employees, killed the sale.

I took the young man's advice and went elsewhere, despite my friendship for the dealer. I don't doubt I could have been sold that car—what I asked for was not a major change. I know the limitations of mass production to make exceptions. But he just didn't care. The second dealer did. He made a minor alteration and got the sale.

One day I walked into our Herald Square store just after the doors had opened in the morning and I saw a sales manager and two salesgirls deeply engaged in conversation while two customers stood waiting for attention. I walked over to the manager, who

[9] Text from "Wanted: Concern for the Customer," *Vital Speeches of the Day*, XXXII (December 1, 1965), 109–112. Reprinted by permission.

did not recognize me, and pointed out that he had two waiting customers. "Can't you see I'm busy!" he said.

Now the truth is that he actually *was* busy. He was doing some very necessary clerical chores. But the most important fact was that two prospective purchasers were standing there waiting. We might lose them. We might lose not only the sale but future business if they went away dissatisfied. After all, we do have competition. They might even talk to others about bad service and influence countless other purchasers. I think that I persuaded the young man that customers are entitled to a high priority of service so that he won't make the same mistake again. However, everything that high-salaried and skillful buyers had done to get choice and exclusive merchandise at attractive prices—all that the advertising staff had done to bring in customers—all that the store display had done to present the merchandise attractively was going down the drain because these vital members of the organization were doing clerical work and neglecting the main chance—to sell.

Not long ago I received a complaint from a college professor's wife in Athens, Georgia. Our Davison division has a store there. It seems that this customer and her husband had gotten their signals mixed and both had bought an item that they had wanted, so one was returned for credit. I remember the price very well— $5.09. Instead of getting the credit, she was billed for $10.18. She paid $5.09 expecting the credit for the other on her next bill. P. S. She never got the credit so she started a correspondence that I am sure must have cost us at least $150 in labor, overhead, postage, and executive time. Finally, six months later, she sent the correspondence to me—the whole big bundle of it.

You can be sure that by the time any complaint gets to me, the customer is really hot. This one was exasperated almost to tears.

The minute I read her letter I phoned our division headquarters and said: "Pay the lady her $5.09 and apologize to her. Don't bother about the facts of the case now. But when you have apologized, check all the facts and I'll bet you will find we made a mistake." They did as I suggested and sure enough we had made the mistake. We had not credited the item which had been returned.

Readings in Speech

This section contains a variety of selected writings (most of them excerpts) which refer to varying facets of the man-and-speech relationship. These excerpts demonstrate that relationship and are included here to provide a number of possible services. The following are a few suggested uses:

1. For oral reading
2. To motivate study and research activities
3. To suggest case-study projects
4. To stimulate group discussion
5. To stimulate selection of speech subjects
6. To stimulate reflection on our heritage and on our ethical responsibilities.

1 *Stolen Thunder*

CHARLES HEBER CLARK[1]

The chairman began with a short speech in which he went over almost precisely the ground covered by my introduction; and as that portion of my oration was . . . reduced to a fragment . . . I quietly resolved to begin, when my turn came, with point number two.

The chairman introduced to the crowd Mr. Keyser, who was received with cheers. He was a ready speaker, and he began, to my deep regret, by telling in capital style my story number three, after which he used up some of my number six arguments, and

---

[1] Text from *Out of the Hurly-Burly*, 1874.

concluded with the remark that it was not his purpose to occupy the attention of the meeting for any length of time, because the executive committee in Wilmington had sent an eloquent orator who was now upon the platform and would present the cause of the party in a manner which he could not hope to approach.

Mr. Keyser then sat down, and Mr. Schwartz was introduced. Mr. Schwartz observed that it was hardly worth while for him to attempt to make anything like a speech, because the gentleman from New Castle had come down on purpose to discuss the issues of the campaign, and the audience, of course, was anxious to hear him. Mr. Schwartz would only tell a little story which seemed to illustrate a point he wished to make, and he thereupon related my anecdote number seven. . . . The point illustrated I was shocked to find was almost precisely that which I had attached to my story number seven. The situation began to have a serious appearance. Here, at one fell swoop, two of my best stories and three of my sets of arguments were swept off into utter uselessness.

When Schwartz withdrew, a man named Krumbauer was brought forward. Krumbauer was a German, and the chairman announced that he would speak in that language for the benefit of those persons in the audience to whom the tongue was pleasantly familiar. Krumbauer went ahead, and the crowd received his remarks with roars of laughter. After one particularly exuberant outburst of merriment, I asked the man who sat next to me, and who seemed deeply interested in the story,

"What was that little joke of Krumbauer's? It must have been first rate."

"So it was," he said. "It was about a Dutchman up in Berks county, Penn., who got mixed up in his dates."

"What dates?" I gasped, in awful apprehension.

"Why, his Fourths of July, you know. Got seven or eight years in arrears and tried to make them all up at once. Good, wasn't it?"

"Good? I should think so; ha! ha! My very best story, as I'm a sinner!"

It was awfully bad. I could have strangled Krumbauer and then chopped him into bits. The ground seemed slipping away beneath me; there was the merest skeleton of a speech left. But I determined to take that and do my best, trusting to luck for a happy result.

But my turn had not yet come. Mr. Wilson was dragged out next, and I thought I perceived a demoniac smile steal over the countenance of the cymbal player as Wilson said he was too hoarse to say much; he would leave the heavy work for the brilliant young orator who was here from New Castle. He would skim rapidly over the ground and then retire. He did. Wilson rapidly skimmed all the cream off my arguments numbers two, five, and six, and wound up by offering the whole of my number four argument. My hair fairly stood on end when Wilson bowed and left the stand. What on earth was I to do now? Not an argument left to stand upon; all my anecdotes gone but two, and my mind in such a condition of frenzied bewilderment that it seemed as if there was not another available argument or suggestion or hint or anecdote remaining in the entire universe. In an agony of despair, I turned to the man next to me and asked him if I would have to follow Wilson.

He said it was his turn now.

"And what are you going to say?" I demanded suspiciously.

"Oh, nothing," he replied—"nothing at all. I want to leave room for you. I'll just tell a little story or so, to amuse them, and then sit down."

"What story for instance?" I asked.

"Oh, nothing, nothing; only a little yarn I happen to remember about a farmer who married a woman who said she could cut four cords of wood, when she couldn't."

My worst fears were realized. I turned to the man next to me, and said, with suppressed emotion.

"May I ask your name, my friend?"

He said his name was Gumbs.

"May I inquire what your Christian name is?"

He said it was William Henry.

"Well, William Henry Gumbs," I exclaimed, "gaze at me! Do I look like a man who would slay a human being in cold blood?"

"Hm-m-m, n-no; you don't," he replied, with an air of critical consideration.

"But I AM!" said I, fiercely—"I AM; and I tell you now that if you undertake to relate that anecdote about the farmer's wife I will blow you into eternity without a moment's warning; I will, by George!"

Mr. Gumbs instantly jumped up, placed his hand on the railing of the porch, and got over suddenly into the crowd. He stood there pointing me out to the bystanders, and doubtless advancing the theory that I was an original kind of lunatic, who might be expected to have at any moment a fit which would be interesting when studied from a distance.

The chairman looked around, intending to call upon my friend Mr. Gumbs; but not perceiving him, he came to me and said:

"Now is your chance, sir; splendid opportunity; crowd worked up to just the proper pitch. We have paved the way for you; go in and do your best."

"Oh yes; but hold on for a few moments, will you? I can't speak now; the fact is I am not quite ready. Run out some other man."

"Haven't got another man. Kept you for the last purposely, and the crowd is waiting. Come ahead and pitch in, and give it to 'em hot and heavy."

It was very easy for him to say "give it to them," but I had nothing to give. Beautifully they paved the way for me! Nicely they had worked up the crowd to the proper pitch! Here I was in a condition of frantic despair, with a crowd of one thousand people expecting a brilliant oration from me who had not a thing in my mind but a beggarly story about a fire extinguisher and a worse one about a farmer's wife. I groaned in spirit and wished I had been born far away in some distant clime among savages who knew not of mass meetings, and whose language contained such a small number of words that speechmaking was impossible.

But the chairman was determined. He seized me by the arm and fairly dragged me to the front. He introduced me to the crowd in flattering, and I may say outrageously ridiculous, terms, and then whispering in my ear, "Hit 'em hard, old fellow, hit 'em hard," he sat down.

The crowd received me with three hearty cheers. As I heard them I began to feel dizzy. The audience seemed to swim around and to increase tenfold in size. By a resolute effort I recovered my self-possession partially, and determined to begin. I could not think of anything but the two stories, and I resolved to tell them as well as I could. I said,

"Fellow-citizens: It is so late now that I will not attempt to make a speech to you." (Cries of "Yes!" "Go ahead!" "Never mind the time!" etc., etc.) Elevating my voice, I repeated: "I say it is so late now that I can't make a speech as I intended on account of its being so late that the speech which I intended to make would keep you here too late if I made it as I intended to. So I will tell you a story about a man who bought a patent fire-extinguisher which was warranted to split four cords of wood a day; so he set fire to his house to try her, and—No, it was his wife who was warranted to split four cords of wood—I got it wrong; and when the flames obtained full headway, he found she could only split two cords and a half, and it made him—What I mean is that the farmer, when he bought the exting—courted her, that is, she said she could set fire to the house, and when he tried her, she collapsed the first time—the extinguisher did, and he wanted a divorce because his house—Oh, hang it, fellow-citizens, you understand that this man, or farmer, rather, bought a—I should say courted a—that is, a fire-ex—" (Desperately.) "Fellow-citizens IF ANY MAN SHOOTS THE AMERICAN FLAG, PULL HIM DOWN UPON THE SPOT; BUT AS FOR ME, GIVE ME LIBERTY OR GIVE ME DEATH!"

As I shouted this out at the top of my voice, in an ecstasy of confusion, a wild, tumultuous yell of laughter came up from the crowd. I paused for a second beneath the spell of that cold eye in the band, and then, dashing through the throng at the back of the porch, I rushed down the street to the depot, with the shouts of the crowd and the uproarious music of the band ringing in my ears. I got upon a freight train, gave the engineer five dollars to take me along on the locomotive and spent the night riding to New Castle.

2   *How to Tell a Story*

MARK TWAIN[2]

I do not claim that I can tell a story as it ought to be told. I only claim to know how a story ought to be told, for I have been almost daily in the company of the most expert story-tellers for many years.

There are several kinds of stories, but only one difficult kind—the humorous. I will talk mainly about that one. The humorous story is American, the comic story is English, the witty story is French. The humorous story depends for its effect upon the *manner* of the telling; the comic story and the witty story upon the *matter*.

The humorous story may be spun out to great length, and may wander around as much as it pleases, and arrive nowhere in particular, but the comic and witty stories must be brief and end with a point. The humorous story bubbles gently along, the others burst.

The humorous story is strictly a work of art—high and delicate art—and only an artist can tell it; but no art is necessary in telling the comic and the witty story; anybody can do it. The art of tell-

[2] Text from *The Writings of Mark Twain*, Author's National Edition (New York, 1899) vol. XXII, 7–15.

ing a humorous story—understand, I mean by word of mouth, not print—was created in America, and has remained at home.

The humorous story is told gravely; the teller does his best to conceal the fact that he even dimly suspects that there is anything funny about it; but the teller of a comic story tells you before-hand that it is one of the funniest things he has ever heard, then tells it with eager delight, and is the first person to laugh when he gets through. And sometimes, if he has good success, he is so glad and happy that he will repeat the "nub" of it and glance around from face to face collecting applause, and then repeat it again. It is a pathetic thing to see.

Very often, of course, the rambling and disjointed humorous story finishes with a nub, point, snapper, or whatever you like to call it. Then the listener must be alert, for in many cases the teller will divert attention from that nub by dropping it in a care-fully casual and indifferent way, with the pretense that he does not know it is a nub.

Artemus Ward used that trick a good deal; then when the be-lated audience presently caught the joke he would look up with innocent surprise, as if wondering what they found to laugh at. Dan Setchell used it before him. Nye and Riley and others use it today.

But the teller of the comic story does not slur the nub, he shouts it at you—every time. And when he prints it, in England, France, Germany, and Italy, he italicizes it, puts some whooping exclama-tion-points after it, and sometimes explains it in a parenthesis. All of which is very depressing and makes one want to renounce joking and lead a better life.

3   *Figures of Speech*

HUGH BLAIR[3]

What is meant by figures of speech?

In general, they always imply some departure from simplicity of expression; the idea which we intend to convey, not only enun-ciated to others, but enunciated, in a particular manner, and with some circumstance added, which is designed to render the impres-sion more strong and vivid. When I say, for instance, 'That a good man enjoys comfort in the midst of adversity'; I just express my

[3] Text from *Lectures in Rhetoric and Belles Lettres* by Hugh Blair, ed. by H. F. Harding (Southern Ill., 1965).

thought in the simplest manner possible. But when I say, 'To the upright there ariseth light in darkness'; the same sentiment is expressed in a figurative style; a new circumstance is introduced; light is put in the place of comfort, and darkness is used to suggest the idea of adversity. In the same manner, to say, 'It is impossible, by any search we can make, to explore the divine nature fully,' is to make a simple proposition. But when we say, 'Canst thou, by searching, find out God? Canst thou find out the Almighty to perfection? It is high as heaven, what canst thou do? deeper than hell, what canst thou know?' This introduces a figure into style; the proposition being not only expressed, but admiration and astonishment being expressed together with it.

But, though figures imply a deviation from what may be reckoned the most simple form of speech, we are not thence to conclude, that they imply any thing uncommon, or unnatural. This is so far from being the case, that, on very many occasions, they are both the most natural, and the most common method of uttering our sentiments. It is impossible to compose any discourse without using them often; nay, there are a few sentences of any length, in which some expression or other, that may be termed a figure, does not occur. From what causes this happens, shall be afterwards explained. The fact, in the mean time, shows, that they are to be accounted part of that language which nature dictates to men. They are not the inventions of the schools, nor the mere product of study: on the contrary, the most illiterate speak in figures, as often as the most learned. Whenever the imaginations of the vulgar are much awakened, or their passions inflamed against one another, they will pour forth a torrent of figurative language as forcible as could be employed by the most artificial declaimer.

What then is it, which has drawn the attention of critics and rhetoricians so much to these forms of speech? It is this: They remarked, that in them consists much of the beauty and the force of language; and found them always to bear some characters, or distinguishing marks, by the help of which they could reduce them under separate classes and heads. To this, perhaps, they owe their name of figures. As the figure, or shape of one body, distinguishes it from another, so these forms of speech have, each of them, a cast or turn peculiar to itself, which both distinguishes it from the rest, and distinguishes it from simple expression. Simple expression just makes our idea known to others; but figurative language, over and above, bestows a particular dress upon that idea; a dress, which both makes it to be remarked, and adorns it.

Hence, this sort of language became early a capital object of attention to those who studied the powers of speech.

4   *Ridicule*

GEORGE CAMPBELL[4]

The intention of raising a laugh is either merely to divert by that grateful titillation which it excites, or to influence the opinions and purposes of the hearers. In this also, the risible faculty, when suitably directed, hath often proved a very potent engine. When this is the view of the speaker, there is always an air of reasoning conveyed under that species of imagery, narration or description, which stimulates laughter, these, thus blended, obtain the appellation of ridicule, the poignancy of which hath a similar effect in futile subjects to that produced by what is called the vehement in solemn and important matters.

Nor doth all the difference between these lie in the dignity of the subject. Ridicule is not only confined to questions of less moment, but is fitter for refuting error than for supporting truth, for restraining from wrong conduct, than for inciting to the practice of what is right. Nor are these the sole restrictions; it is not properly levelled at the false, but at the absurd in tenets; nor can the edge of ridicule strike with equal force every species of misconduct: it is not the criminal part which it attacks, but that which we denominate silly or foolish. With regard to doctrine, it is evident that it is not falsity or mistake, but palpable error or absurdity, (a thing hardly confutable by mere argument), which is the object of contempt; and consequently those dogmas are beyond the reach of cool reasoning which are within the rightful confines of ridicule. That they are generally conceived to be so, appears from the sense universally assigned to expressions like these, 'Such a position is ridiculous.—It doth not deserve a serious answer.' Every body knows that they import more than 'It is false,' being, in other words, 'This is such an extravagance as is not so much a subject of argument as of laughter.' . . . Those things which principally come under its lash are awkwardness, rusticity, ignorance, cowardice, levity, foppery, pedantry, and affectation of every kind. But against murder, cruelty, parricide, ingratitude, perfidy, to attempt to raise a laugh, would shew such an unnatural insensibility in the speaker, as would be excessively disgustful to any audience.

---

[4] Text from *Philosophy of Rhetoric* by George Campbell, ed. by Lloyd F. Bitzer (Southern Ill., 1963).

5   *Method in Persuasion*

CICERO[5]

But to return to my method. When, after hearing and understanding the nature of a cause, I proceed to examine the subject
matter of it, I settle nothing until I have ascertained to what point
my whole speech, bearing immediately on the question and case,
must be directed. I then very diligently consider two other points;
the one, how to recommend myself, or those for whom I plead;
the other, how to sway the minds of those before whom I speak
to that which I desire. Thus the whole business of speaking rests
upon three things for success in persuasion; that we prove what
we maintain to be true; that we conciliate those who hear; that
we produce in their minds whatever feeling our cause may require.
For the purpose of proof, two kinds of matter present themselves
to the orator; one, consisting of such things as are not invented by
him, but, as appertaining to the cause, are judiciously treated by
him, as deeds, testimonies, covenants, contracts, examinations,
laws, acts of the senate, precedents, decrees, opinions of lawyers,
and whatever else is not found out by the orator, but brought
under his notice by the cause and by his clients; the other, consisting entirely in the orator's own reasoning and arguments: so
that, as to the former head, he has only to handle the arguments
with which he is furnished; as to the latter, to invent arguments
likewise.

6   *Let There Be Unlicensed Expression*

JOHN MILTON[6]

And now the time in special is, by privilege to write and speak
what may help to further discussing of matters in agitation. The
temple of Janus with his two controversial faces might now not
unsignificantly be set open. And though all the winds of doctrine
were let loose to play upon the earth, so Truth be in the field,
we do injuriously, by licensing and prohibiting, to misdoubt her
strength. Let her and Falsehood grapple; who ever knew Truth
put to the worse, in a free and open encounter? Her confuting
is the best and surest suppressing. He who hears what praying
there is for light and clearer kowledge to be sent down among us,
would think of other matters to be constituted beyond the dis-

---

[5] Text from *De Oratore*, trans. by J. S. Watson (New York, 1875).
[6] Text from *Areopagitica*, first published in 1644.

cipline of Geneva, framed and fabricked already to our hands. Yet when the new light which we beg for shines in upon us, there be who envy and oppose, if it come not first in at their casements. What a collusion is this, whenas we are exhorted by the wise man to use diligence, to seek for wisdom as for hidden treasures early and late, that another order shall enjoin us to know nothing but by statute? When a man hath been laboring the hardest labour in the deep mines of knowledge; hath furnished out his findings in all their equipage; drawn forth his reasons as it were a battle ranged; scattered and defeated all objections in his way; calls out his adversary into the plain, offers him the advantage of wind and sun, if he please, only that he may try the matters by dint of argument; for his opponents then to skulk, to lay ambushments, to keep a narrow bridge of licensing where the challenger should pass, though it be valour enough in soldiership, is but weakness and cowardice in the wars of Truth.

For who knows not that Truth is strong, next to the Almighty? She needs no policies, no strategems, nor licensings to make her victorious; those are the shifts and the defences that error uses against her power.

7   *The Golden Mean*

ARISTOTLE[7]

We must premise that every excellence or virtue perfects that thing of which it is the virtue, and causes it to discharge its especial function well. The special excellence of the eye, for example, makes the eye good, and perfects its function; for it is only by the virtue of the eye that we can see well. So, too, the excellence of the horse makes it a good horse, swift, and strong to carry its rider, and bold to face his enemies. And if this be true, as it is in all cases, it follows that the virtue of man will be such a habit as will make him a good man, and enable him to discharge his especial function well. And how this is to be brought about we have already said: but we shall make the matter yet clearer if we consider wherein exactly it is that the nature of moral virtue consists. In everything that is continuous, and consequently capable of division, we can mark off an amount which will be either more than, or less than, or equal to the remainder; and can do so either objectively, that is to say with reference to the matter in question, or subjectively, that is to say

[7] Text from *Nichomachean Ethics,* trans. by Robert Williams (New York, 1879).

with reference to ourselves. Now that which is equal is a mean between excess and defect. And by the mean of the matter I understand that which, as is the point of bisection in a line, is equally distant from either extreme, and which is for all persons alike one and the same. But by the mean with reference to ourselves I understand that which is neither too much for us or too little, and which consequently is not any one fixed point which for all alike remains the same. If, for example, ten pounds be too much and two pounds be too little, we take as the mean reference to the matter six pounds, which itself exceed two pounds by as much as they are exceeded by ten. This is what is called a mean in arithmetical progression. But the mean with reference to ourselves must not be thus fixed. For it does not follow that, if ten pounds of meat be too much to eat, and two pounds be too little, our trainer will therefore order us six pounds. This may be either too little for him who is to eat it, or too much. For Milo, for example, it would be too little, while for one who is to begin training it would be too much. And in running, and in wrestling, the same rule holds good. And so, too, all skilled artists avoid the excess and the defect, while they seek and choose the mean, that is to say not the absolute but the relative mean. And since it is thus that all skilled knowledge perfects its results, by keeping the mean steadily in view, and by modeling its work upon any good work, that neither to it can anything be added, nor from it can anything be taken away; inasmuch as excess and defect destroy perfection, while moderation preserves it; since, then, all good artists, as we have said, always work with the mean in view, and since virtue is, as also is nature, more exact, and higher than is any art, it follows that virtue also will aim at the mean. And when I say virtue I mean moral virtue, for moral virtue is concerned with our emotions, that is to say with our actions; and in these excess and defect are to be found, and also moderation. Fear, for example, and confidence, and desire, and anger, and pity, and generally any pleasure or pain, we can feel both more and less than we ought, and in either case we feel them not well. But to feel them when we ought, and at what we ought, and towards whom we ought, and for the right motive, and as we ought—in all lies the mean, and, with the mean, perfection; and these are characteristics of virtue. And so, too, with reference to our actions, no less than our emotions, excess and defect are possible, and with them consequently moderation. Now virtue is concerned with our emotions and with our actions. It is in these that excess is an error, and that defect is blamed as a fault; while moderation meets with praise and with success, both of which things are marks of virtue. And hence it is that all virtue is a mean, in that it aims at which is the mean. Moreover the forms of wrong are manifold (for evil is of the infinite, as said the allegory of the Pythagoreans, and good of the finite), while of right the form is but one. Hence the one is easy, the other hard; easy is it to miss, hard to hit our aim. And from this again it follows that to vice belong excess and defect, and to virtue belongs moderation.

8   *The "All-Purpose" Speech*

ROBERT H. DAVIS[8]

Mr. Chairman, Ladies and Gentlemen: It is indeed a great and undeserved privilege to address such an audience as I see before me. At no previous time in the history of human civilization have greater problems confronted and challenged the ingenuity of man's intellect than now. Let us look around us. What do we see on the horizon? What forces are at work? Whither are we drifting? Under what mist of clouds does the future stand obscured? My friends, casting aside the raiment of all human speech, the crucial test for the solution of all these intricate problems to which I have just alluded is the sheer and forceful application of those immutable laws which down the corridor of Time have always guided the hand of man, groping, as it were, for some faint beacon light for his hopes and aspirations. Without these great vital principles we are but puppets responding to whim and fancy, failing entirely to grasp the hidden meaning of it all. We must readdress ourselves to these questions which press for answer and solution. The issue cannot be avoided. There they stand. It is upon you—and you—and yet even upon me that the yoke of responsibility falls.

What, then, is our duty? Shall we continue to drift? No! With all the emphasis of my being I hurl back the message No! Drifting must stop. We must press onward and upward toward the ultimate good to which all must aspire. But I cannot conclude my remarks, dear friends, without touching briefly upon a subject which I know is steeped in your very consciousness. I refer to that spirit which gleams from the eyes of a new-born babe; that animates the toiling masses; that sways all the hosts of humanity past and present. Without this energizing principle all commerce, trade and industry are hushed and will perish from

[8] Reprinted by permission of the estate of Robert H. Davis.

this earth as surely as the crimson sunset follows the golden sunshine. Mark you, I do not seek to unduly alarm or distress the mothers, fathers, sons and daughters gathered before me in this vast assemblage, but I would indeed be recreant to a high resolve which I made as a youth if I did not at this time and in this place and with the full realizing sense of responsibility which I assume publicly declare and affirm my dedication and my concentration to the eternal principles and receipts of simple, ordinary, commonplace JUSTICE.

For what, in the last analysis, is justice? Whence does it come? Where does it go? Is it tangible? It is not. Is it ponderable? It is not. It is all of these things combined. While I cannot tell you what justice is, this much I can tell you: That without the encircling arms of justice, without her shield, without her guardianship, the ship of state will sail through uncharted seas, narrowly avoiding rocks and shoals, headed inevitably to the harbor of calamity.

Justice! Justice! Justice! To thee we pay homage. To thee we dedicate our laurels of hope. Before thee we kneel in adoration, mindful of thy great power, mute before thy inscrutable destiny!

9 *The Good Man*

QUINTILIAN[9]

Let the orator, then, whom I propose to form, be such a one as is characterized by the definition of Marcus Cato, a good man skilled in speaking. . . .

My judgment carries me still further; for I not only say that he who would answer my idea of an orator must be a good man, but that no man, unless he be good, can ever be an orator. To an orator discernment and prudence are necessary; but we can certainly not allow discernment to those, who, when the ways of virtue and vice are set before them, prefer to follow that of vice; nor can we allow them prudence, since they subject themselves, by the unforeseen consequences of their actions, often to the heaviest penalty of the law, and always to that of an evil conscience. But if it be not only truly said by the wise, but always justly believed by the vulgar, that no man is vicious who is not also foolish, a fool, assuredly, will never become an orator. . . .

Since an orator, then, is a good man, and a good man cannot be conceived to exist without virtuous inclinations and virtue, though

[9] Text from *Institutes of Oratory,* trans. by J. S. Watson (London, 1856).

it receives certain impulses from nature, requires notwithstanding to be brought to maturity by instruction, the orator must above all things study morality, and must obtain a thorough knowledge of all that is just and honourable, without which no one can either be a good man or an able speaker.

| 10 | *The Modes of Persuasion* |

ARISTOTLE[10]

Of the modes of persuasion furnished by the spoken word there are three kinds. The first depends on the personal character of the speaker; the second on putting the audience into a certain frame of mind; the third on the proof, or apparent proof, provided by the words of the speech itself. Persuasion is achieved by the speaker's personal character when the speech is so spoken as to make us think him credible. We believe good men more fully and more readily than others: this is true generally whatever the question is, and absolutely true where exact certainty is impossible and opinions are divided. This kind of persuasion, like the others, should be achieved by what the speaker says, not by what people think of his character before he begins to speak. It is not true, as some writers assume in their treatises on rhetoric, that the personal goodness revealed by the speaker contributes nothing to his power of persuasion; on the contrary, his character may almost be called the most effective means of persuasion he possesses. Secondly, persuasion may come through the hearers, when the speech stirs their emotions. Our judgments when we are pleased and friendly are not the same as when we are pained and hostile. It is towards producing these effects, as we maintain, that present-day writers on rhetoric direct the whole of their efforts. This subject shall be treated in detail when we come to speak of the emotions. Thirdly, persuasion is effected through the speech itself when we have proved a truth or an apparent truth by means of the persuasive arguments suitable to the case in question.

There are, then, these three means of effecting persuasion. The man who is to be in command of them must, it is clear, be able (1) to reason logically, (2) to understand human character and goodness in their various forms, and (3) to understand the emotions—that is, to name them and describe them, to know their causes and the way in which they are excited.

[10] Text from Aristotle's *Rhetoric,* trans. by W. Rhys Roberts, in Vol. XI of *The Works of Aristotle,* translated into English under the editorship of W. D. Ross. By permission of the Clarendon Press, Oxford.

11   *Persuasion*

ABRAHAM LINCOLN

When the conduct of man is designed to be influenced, persuasion, kind, unassuming persuasion, should ever be adopted. It is an old and true maxim "that a drop of honey catches more flies than a gallon of gall." So with men. If you would win a man to your cause, first, convince him that you are his sincere friend.

Therein is a drop of honey that catches his heart, which, say what he will, is the great highroad to his reason, and which, when once gained, you will find but little trouble in convincing his judgment of the justice of your cause, if indeed that cause really be a just one.

On the contrary, assume to dictate to his judgment, or to command his action, or to mark him as one to be shunned and despised, and he will retreat within himself, close all the avenues of his head and his heart; and though your cause be naked truth itself, transformed to the heaviest lance, harder than steel, and sharper than steel can be made, and tho' you throw it with more than Herculean force and precision, you shall be no more able to pierce him than to penetrate the hard shell of a tortoise with a rye straw.

Such is man, and so must he be understood by those who would lead him, even to his own best interest.

12   *Conversational Delivery*

JAMES ALBERT WINANS[11]

Why is it that a small boy in school reads "See—the—horse—on—the—hill" without a trace of meaning in his tone, and yet five minutes later on the playgrounds shouts the same words to his playmates with perfect expression? And why is it that if the teacher insists that Johnnie read over his sentence and get its meaning before reading it aloud, he will read with far better expression? And why, if the teacher then asks him to stand facing his class and read or tell the story to them, does he read with really good expression? The reason for his first improvement is apparent: in his first reading all his mind is given to recognizing words as words. They are without content for him; they bring no meaning, no picture to his mind. His expressionless voice is a true index of his impressionless mind; or rather, to be strict, his

[11] Text from *Public Speaking*, 1916.

high strained tone expresses truly the anxious strain of his attention to the symbols before him. When he grasps the meaning, expression comes into his voice. He not only understands, but if he has a marked success, he has more than bare understanding: the objects and incidents of which he reads are present to his imagination. The horse is to him a real and significant object at the instant he speaks the words. He has approached the conditions of his playground conversation. He is "thinking on his feet"; *he creates, or re-creates, the thought at the moment of delivery.*

But our small boy is still more successful in his reading when he is made to feel that he is reading or telling his story to his classmates. To throw the statement into a phrase we shall make much use of, Johnnie succeeds when he reads or speaks with a *sense of communication*. On the playground he has the most perfect expression of all, when with no thought of how he says things, he uses perfect tone, emphasis, and inflection. Still the advice, "Forget your delivery," will be of little aid to the embarrassed beginner. We can forget only by turning our attention to something else. Forget embarrassment then by holding your mind to your subject-matter and your business with your audience. Hold firmly to the conception that you are there to interest them, not in your speaking, but in your ideas; to convince or persuade them. Look for their response. Stand behind your speech, and embarrassment will disappear. As soon as you can carry out these injunctions, whatever your faults, you will be a speaker.

What to do. To summarize, then, your delivery will have the desired conversational quality when you retain upon the platform these elements of the mental state of live conversation:

1. *Full realization of the content of your words as you utter them,* and
2. *A lively sense of communication.*

INDEX

Index

A

Acceptance, speeches of, 272

Adaptation of ideas, 154–155, 164
to the audience, 21
see also Common ground and
identification

Adler, Mortimer J., quoted, 189

Aids, audio, 93

Aids, in strengthening thought,
66–75
see also Transition, restatement,
repetition, definition, and explanation

Aids, visual, 89–100

à Kempis, Thomas, quoted, 259

Alliteration, 146

"All-Purpose" Speech, The, 340–
341

Aly, Bower, quoted, 307–308

Amiel, Henri Frédéric, quoted,
35

Analogy, 110
reasoning by, 206
reasoning by in persuasion, 237

use of in persuasion, 251
see also Comparison

Analysis, as an aid in listening,
183–184

Announcements, preparation of,
266

Appeals, in persuasion, 235–247
logical (logos), 235–238
personal (ethos), 244–247
psychological (pathos), 238–244

Aristotle, 6, 10, 39, 235, 236;
quoted, 338–340, 342

Arnold, Carroll C., quoted, 5

Articulation, 161, 163–166

Attention, holding in persuasion,
243–244

Audience
adaptation to, 21
analysis of for persuasion, 241–
243
as an influence on subject
choice, 20–23
dynamics of, 63–65
see also Common ground and
identification

B

Backing, of Toulmin system, 209–210

Bacon, Francis, quoted, 83, 109

Baird, A. Craig, quoted, 115–116

Ballad of the Oysterman, The, 281–282

Barkley, Alben, quoted, 247

Behavior, characteristics of human, 239–241

Bismarck, Otto von, quoted, 123

Black, Jeremiah S., quoted, 325–327

Blair, Hugh, 7; quoted, 26, 111, 334–336

Blasdell, Ann, quoted, 314–316

Body, in delivery, 156–158

Body, of the speech, 43–49
   see also Main heads

Book of Wisdom, The, 292

Breathing, and speech production, 158–159

Brigance, William Norwood, quoted, 31

Bright, John, 23

Brown, Charles T., quoted, 138

Brown, Harrison S., quoted, 316–320

Burke, Edmund, quoted, 75

Burke, Kenneth, 7

Byron, Lord, quoted, 25–26, 299–300

C

Caesar, Julius, 146

Campbell, George, 6; quoted, 26, 336

Card catalog, as research aid, 202, 204

Carroll, Lewis, quoted, 121

Cato, quoted, 74

Cellini, Benvenuto, 109

Children's literature, 288–291

Choices, faced by the speaker, 14–15

Churchill, Winston, 87–88; quoted, 41

Cicero, 6, 10, 111; quoted, 337

Clark, Badger, poem, 297

Clark, Charles Heber, quoted, 329–333

Clay, Henry, 4

Climax, 146

Cohen, Herman, quoted, 162

Colbert, R. C., quoted, 245

Common ground, 4–5, 10, 36, 39–41, 71–73
   in language usage, 140
   see also Identification and adaptation

Communication
   challenges to, 64–65, 71–73
   definition of, 4
   see also Confusion, forces of in communication

Comparison, examples to show, 110
   see also Analogy

Conclusion, functions of, 49–52

Conclusion, of Toulmin system, 209–210

Confusion, forces of in communication, 63
   see also Communication, challenges to

Connotation, 137–140
   in reading aloud, 299

Consonants, formation of, 163

Constitution and by-laws, model of, 229–230

Contrast, examples to show, 110–111

Conversational Delivery, 343–344

Conviction, distinguished from persuasion, 27

Coolidge, Calvin, quoted, 177

Corax, 6
Cowboy's Prayer, A., 297
Cowper, William, quoted, 145
Crane, Stephen, poem, 292
Criticism
  acceptance of, 12
  classroom modes of, 12–13
  definition of, 12
Crockett, David, quoted, 285–286
Crowell, Thomas Lee, Jr., 164

D

Daly, T. A., poem, 283–284
Dan'l, 284–285
Data, of Toulmin system, 209–210
Davis, Robert H., quoted, 340–341
Davy Crockett, Speechmaker, 285–286
Deduction, in organizing persuasive speeches, 247–249
Definition, use of, 71–74
de la Bruyere, Jean, quoted, 256
Delight in Disorder, 291
Delivery, 154–176
  as adapting ideas, 154–155
  body in, 156–158
  development of, 11
  effectiveness in, 32
  eye contact in, 157–158
  persuasion in, 235, 252–253
  personality in, 155–156
  preparing for, 167–168
  related to content, 154
  use of notes in, 157
  voice and articulation in, 158–166
Demosthenes, 111
de Musset, Alfred, quoted, 115
Denotation, 137–140
Description, 106–107
de Toqueville, Alexis, quoted, 253
Dewey, John, 194, 248

Dialect, 283–287
  see also Folklore
Diaphragm, 158
Discussion, *see* Group discussion
Donne, John, 9
Douglas-Home, Sir Alec, quoted, 274
Dryden, John, quoted, 35
Duration, of sound, 162

E

Eisenhower, Dwight D., 270–271
Elements of Rhetoric, 7
Elephant's Child, The, 288
Eliot, George, quoted, 76
Emerson, Ralph Waldo, quoted, 140
Empathy, in reading aloud, 278–279
Ends of speaking, general, 26–28
Enthymeme, 206–209
  persuasion in, 236–237
Environment, physical, 65
Esthetic distance, in reading aloud, 279
Ethics, of persuasion, 241
Euphemisms, 142
Evidence, in persuasion, 238, 243
  see also Developmental materials, Chapters Five and Six
Examples
  illustration, 106–109
  instance, 106, 108–109
  model use of, 325–328
  special characteristics of, 110–111
  use of, 106–111
Exhalation, and speech production, 159–160
Explanation, 74–75
Expression, forms of, 146–147
  improvement of, 166–167
Extemporaneous mode, 30–32

Eye contact, 157–158
  in reading aloud, 301

F

Facts and opinions, 117–119
  see also Opinions and facts
Fallacies, in reasoning, 211
Fear, in speaking, 7–8, 10
  as influencing subject choice, 20
  as listening problem, 180–181
Feedback, 5, 157–158
Ferris, Elmer E., quoted, 234
Field, Eugene, poem, 289–291
Figures of Speech, 334–336
Figures of speech, 144–145
  awareness of in reading aloud,
    299–300
Fleming, Alexander, 119
Folklore, 283–287
  see also Dialect
Formality, level of, 164
Forum, in group discussion, 201–
    202
Fosdick, Harry Emerson, quoted,
    8, 44
Foxworth, Jo, quoted, 108–109
Franklin, Benjamin, 109; quoted,
    35
Frost, Robert, quoted, 32

G

General education, and the speech
    class, 6–7
Generalization, as a form of in-
    duction, 205
Glenn, John H. Jr., quoted, 272
Goals, of the speech class, 10-11
Goethe, Johann Wolfgang von,
    109
Golden Mean, The, 338–340
Good Man, The, 341–342
Group discussion, 189–216

audience participation in, 201–
    202
checking materials for, 204–205
choosing subjects for, 191–192
forms of, 195–202
gathering materials for, 202–204
leadership of, 213–214
narrowing subjects for, 192
organization of, 194–195, 214
participating in, 211–213
process of, 190–191
reasoning in, 205–211
recording data for, 204
topics for, 215–216
types of questions for, 193
wording questions for, 192
  see also Forum
Guillotin, J. I., 73

H

Habits and Customs of People,
    320–323
Hall, Robert A., Jr., quoted, 140
Hand, Learned, quoted, 295–296
Harte, Bret, poem, 286–287
Hayne, William Hamilton,
    quoted, 299
Henry, Patrick, 141; quoted, 75,
    236–237, 240
Herrick, Robert, poem, 291
High resolve, literature of, 294–
    297
Hockett, Homer Carey, quoted,
    119
Holmes, Oliver Wendell, poem,
    281–282
Horn, Francis H., quoted, 42, 51–
    52
How to Tell a Story, 333–334
Hughes, Charles Evans, quoted, 23
Humor
  in after-dinner speeches, 268–
    270
  in persuasion, 244

Humphrey, Hubert H., quoted, 253–54

I

Identification
in persuasion, 233–235, 240, 244–247, 249–250, 252, 253–254
of speaker and audience, 71–73
see also Common ground and adaptation
Impromptu speech, requirements of, 264–266
Induction
as reasoning in persuasion, 237–238
in organizing persuasive speeches, 249
see also Reasoning
Ingersoll, Robert G., quoted, 157, 169
Inhalation, and speech production, 158–159
Insertion, as a fault of articulation, 165
Institutes of Oratory, 6
Introduction, for a speech, 39–42
Introduction, speech of, 266–267
Irony, 145

J

Jim Hawkins Finds Ben Gunn, 288–289
Johnson, Gertrude E., quoted, 283
Johnson, Lyndon B., quoted, 273
Joubert, Joseph, 5

K

Katz, Daniel, quoted, 233, 234
Keats, John, quoted, 115
Kennedy, John F., quoted, 70, 112, 114, 140–141, 143, 144, 146–147, 237, 271–272

Kipling, Rudyard, quoted, 288
Kirk, Grayson, quoted, 107–108

L

Language, 135–153
as a social agreement, 136–137
figurative, 144–145
formal and informal, 136, 147–148
improvement of, 10–11
in group discussion, 213
in persuasion, 235, 249–252
problems in use of, 135–136
rhetorical values of, 137
semantics of, 49
standard and substandard, 136, 148–149
suggestions for use of, 140–150
variety in use of, 69, 70
see also Denotation and connotation, expression, and common ground in language usage
Larynx, 159
Laughton, Charles, quoted, 276
Lecture-panel, as group discussion form, 200–201
Lectures on Rhetoric and Belles Lettres, 7
Leibman, Joshua Loth, quoted, 156
Letter to Mrs. Bixby, 294
Let there Be Unlicensed Expression, 337–338
Lewis, Thomas R., quoted, 179
Lincoln, Abraham, quoted, 70, 117, 172, 234, 250, 251, 252, 294, 343
Listening, 177–186
breakdown of, 179–181
contrasted with hearing, 178
guides to good, 182–184
importance of, 177
improvement of, 11, 181–184

Listening (*continued*)
  in group discussion, 213
  in persuasion, 233–235
  nature of, 178
  purposes of, 178–179
Literature
  children's, 288–291
  folklore and dialect, 283–287
  lyric poetry, 291–294
  narrative, 280–283
  of high resolve, 294–297
Locke, John, 109
Luce, Claire Booth, quoted, 237–238

M

McCall, Roy C., 8, 44; quoted, 162
McGovern, Charles, quoted, 114–115
MacArthur, General Douglas, 129–130
Macaulay, Thomas B., quoted, 214
Main heads, 43–49
  choosing for impromptu speeches, 265
  see also Body of the speech
Making Lincoln Live, 308–314
Markham, Edwin, 299
Marshall, T. R., quoted, 132
Marvell, Andrew, poem, 292–293
Materials
  selection and use of physical, 86–100, 105
  see also Aids, visual and audio aids
  selection and use of verbal, 86–87, 105–132, 265
  see also Examples, statistics, quotations, facts and opinions
Melville, Herman, quoted, 282–283

Metaphor, 144
Method in Persuasion, 337
Mia Carlotta, 283–284
Miller, Henry, 118
Miller, Jack, quoted, 118
Milton, John, quoted, 337–338
Minutes, of meetings, 226
Misarticulation, contrasted with mispronunciation, 163–164
Misplacement of accent, 166
Mizner, Wilson, 177
Mode, oral, 65–66
  see also Speaking contrasted with writing
Modes of Persuasion, The, 342
Motions, in parliamentary procedure, 220–226
  fundamental handling of, 220
  incidental, 223–224
  main, 221
  privileged, 224–225
  subsidiary, 221–223
  table of, 228
  to amend, 222–223
  unclassified, 225
  voting on, 220, 225–226
Moudy, James M., quoted, 71

N

Nakai, Raymond, quoted, 112
Narration, 107
Narrative literature, 280–283
Needs, characteristics of human, 239–241
Neibuhr, Reinhold, quoted, 253
Nichols, Ralph G., quoted, 179, 184
Nitze, Paul H., quoted, 245
"Noise," as a problem in communication, 137
Nominating Calvin Coolidge, 323–325

Nomination, speech of, 270–271
Notes, speaking
    model of, 57
    use of, 56

O

Occasion
    influencing subject choice, 23–24
    meeting demands of, 264–275
Omission, as fault in articulation, 165
"One-thing-at-a-time," as a method of instruction, 15
    see also "Stone-upon-stone"
Opinion and facts, 117–119
    see also Facts and opinion
Organization, of speeches, 31–52
    in persuasion, 235, 247–249
    orders in, 46–49
Organization, starting an, 226–227
Outline, use of an, 31–32
    for group discussion, 196, 213
Outlines, model; see Chapters Three to Six and Twelve
    for persuasion, 255–260
Outlining, 36–39

P

Paine, Tom, 298
Panel, as discussion form, 195–199
Parallelism, 146
Parliamentary procedure, 218–231
    chairman, 219–220
    order of business, 219
    participating under, 220
    recording business, 226
    see also Minutes, of meetings
    starting an organization, 226–227
    uses of, 218–219

voting under, 220, 225–226
    see also Motions
Payne, John Howard, quoted, 100
Personal life, improvement of, 7–8
Personality, in delivery, 155–156
Personification, 144–145
Persuasion, 232–263
    assumptions regarding, 232–235
    audience analysis for, 241–243
    common ground in, 233–235, 240, 244–247, 249-250, 252, 253–254
    see also Identification
    delivery in, 252–253
    distinguished from conviction, 27
    ethics of, 241
    holding attention in, 243–244
    human needs and behavior in, 239–241
    language in, 249–252
    model speech outlines for, 255–260
    modes of appeal in, 235–247
    see also Appeals, in persuasion
    organization in, 247–249
    probability in, 235–237
    themes for, 254–255
    use of evidence in, 238, 243
    see also Developmental materials, Chapters Five and Six
Persuasion, 343
Phaedrus, 39
Pharynx, 160
Phillips, Harold C., quoted, 107
Philosophy of Rhetoric, 6
Phonation, 159–160
Phonemes, 135, 169–171
Phonetic alphabet, 169–171
Pitch, as a vocal characteristic, 162
Plato, quoted, 39
Pliny, quoted, 100
Poe, Edgar Allen, 298–299

Poetry
  compared to prose, 280
  lyric, 291–294
  reading of, 301
Pope, Alexander, quoted, 77, 115
Practice, in speaking, 32
Presentation, speeches of, 271–272
Probability
  as a basis for reasoning, 207–209
  in persuasion, 235–237
Problem-solution, as pattern of ar-
    rangement, 48
Pronunciation
  appropriateness of, 300
  defined, 163
Proposition, of a speech, 28–30,
    41–43, 50, 265
Prose, compared to poetry, 280

Q

Qualifier, of Toulmin system, 209–
    210
Quality, as vocal characteristic,
    162–163
Quintilian, 6, 10; quoted, 15, 167,
    341–342
Quotations, use of, 114–117

R

Rankin, Paul, 177
Reade, Charles, quoted, 115
Reader's Guide to Periodical Lit-
    erature, 204
Reading aloud, 276–303
  act of, 277–278
  compared to original speech,
    277
  empathy in, 278–279
  esthetic distance in, 279
  finding selections for, 279–297
  introducing the selection for,
    300

practicing the selection for, 300–
    301
  reader's role in, 277–279
  studying the selection for, 297–
    300
  uses of, 276–277
Readings in Speech, 329–344
Reason, as pattern of arrange-
    ment, 47–48
Reasoning
  by analogy, 206, 211
  causal, 205–206, 211, 237–238
  deduction, 206-209, 211, 236–
    237
  fallacies in, 211
  induction, 205–206, 211
Rehearsal, steps in, 166–167
Remarks on Jefferson Day, 307–
    308
Repetition, 69–71
  see also Restatement
Reservation, of Toulmin system,
    210
Resonation, 160–161
Responsibilities, of a speaker
  to himself, 11–13
  to society, 14–15
  to the class, 13–14
Restatement, 69–71, 146–147
  see also Repetition
Rhetoric of Aristotle, The, 6, 21
Richard Cory, 280–281
Ridicule, 336
Robert, Henry M., quoted, 218
Robinson,   Edwin   Arlington,
    quoted, 280
  poem, 280–281
Roebling, Mary G., quoted, 75
Rogers, Will, 108; quoted, 14, 156,
    323–325
Roosevelt, Franklin D., quoted,
    173, 237
Roosevelt, Theodore, quoted, 116–
    117

Runkel, Howard W., quoted, 308–314

Rusk, Dean, quoted, 238, 244

S

Shakespeare, William, quoted, 100, 115

Shaw, George Bernard, quoted, 121–122

Shelley, Percy Bysshe, poem, 293–294

Sherman, W. T., quoted, 122

Simile, 144

Simon, Clarence T., quoted, 302

Simplify, Simplify, 294–295

Smith, Eugene, quoted, 31

Smith, Howard K., quoted, 74

Sociability, concept of in speaking, 164–165

    as a factor in persuasion, 235, 242

Social life, improvement of, 8–9

Social Responsibility of Science, 316–320

Society Upon the Stanislaus, The, 286–287

Socrates, quoted, 39, 130

Soper, Paul L., quoted, 163–164

Sophocles, quoted, 259

Space, as pattern of arrangement, 47

Speaking

    contrasted with performing, 5

    contrasted with writing, 65–66

Speciousness, guarding against, 265–266

Speech

    a class in, 5

    as a social act, 3

    benefits of instruction in, 6–10

    definition of, 10

    heritage of, 6–7

    production of, 158–161

    uses of, 3–4

Speeches

    after-dinner, 268–270

    model, 307–328

    to entertain, 27–28

    to inform, 26–27

    to persuade, 27

Spirit of Liberty, The, 295–296

Statistics, use of, 111–114

Steinbeck, John, quoted, 54

Stevenson, Adlai E., quoted, 70–71, 115–116

Stevenson, Robert Louis, quoted, 3, 288–289

Stolen Thunder, 329–333

"Stone-upon-stone," as method of instruction, 15

    see also "One-thing-at-a-time"

Straus, Jack I., quoted, 327–328

Subject

    choosing, 18–21, 31, 265

    narrowing of, 24–26

Substitution, as fault of articulation, 165

Summer and Winter, 293–294

Sutherland, George, quoted, 50

Swift, Jonathan, 298

Syllogism, 206–207, 208, 209

Symposium, as discussion form, 200

T

Taylor, Bayard, quoted, 115

Tennyson, Alfred, 299

There She Blows!, 282–283

Thoreau, Henry David, quoted, 294–295

Time, as pattern of arrangement, 46–47

Timing, in group discussion, 199–200, 201

Tisias, 6

To His Coy Mistress, 292–293

Topical, as pattern of arrangement, 48
Topics
  as distinguished from subjects, 24
  for persuasion, 254–255
Toulmin, Stephen, system of, 209–211
Townsend, Lynn A., quoted, 139
Trachea, 159
Transitions
  and the listener, 183
  value and use of, 66–69
Twain, Mark (Samuel Clemens), 269; quoted, 146, 284–285, 333–334

V

Van Loon, H. W., quoted, 74
Vocal folds, 159–160, 162
Vocation, speech preparation for, 9–10
Voice
  and articulation, in delivery, 158–166
  production of, 162–163
Volume, as vocal characteristic, 162
Vowels, formation of, 160–161

W

Warrant, of Toulmin system, 209–210
Washington, Booker T., quoted, 167–168
Washington, George, quoted, 172-173
Waste of War, The, 314–316
Watson, Thomas J. Jr., quoted, 73
Webster, Daniel, quoted, 246
Welcome
  response to speech of, 273–274
  speech of, 273
Wert, Robert J., quoted, 75
Whately, Richard, 7
Whyte-Melville, George John, quoted, 123, 125
Wiener, Norbert, quoted, 63
Williams, Nellie, quoted, 320–323
Wilson, Woodrow, quoted, 173
Winans, James Albert, 7; quoted, 33, 253, 343–344
Wordsworth, William, poem, 291–292
World is Too Much with Us; Late and Soon, The, 291–292
Wylie, Philip, quoted, 123
Wynken, Blynken, and Nod, 289–291